I0282616

THE HISTORY OF AL-ṬABARĪ

AN ANNOTATED TRANSLATION

VOLUME XXII

The Marwānid Restoration

THE CALIPHATE OF ʿABD AL-MALIK

A.D. 693–701/A.H. 74–81

The History of al-Ṭabarī

Editorial Board

Ihsan Abbas, University of Jordan, Amman

C. E. Bosworth, The University of Manchester

Jacob Lassner, Wayne State University, Detroit

Franz Rosenthal, Yale University

Ehsan Yar-Shater, Columbia University *(General Editor)*

SUNY

SERIES IN NEAR EASTERN STUDIES

Said Amir Arjomand, Editor

The general editor acknowledges with gratitude the support received for the execution of this project from the Division of Research Programs, Translations Division of the National Endowment for the Humanities, an independent federal agency.

Bibliotheca Persica
Edited by Ehsan Yar-Shater

The History of al-Ṭabarī
(Ta'rīkh al-rusul wa'l-mulūk)

VOLUME XXII

The Marwānid Restoration

translated and annotated
by

Everett K. Rowson

Harvard University

State University of New York Press

The preparation of this volume was made possible in part by a grant from the Division of Research Programs of the National Endowment for the Humanities, an independent federal agency.

Published by
State University of New York Press, Albany
© 1989 State University of New York
All rights reserved
Printed in the United States of America
No part of this book may be used or reproduced in any manner whatsoever without written permission except in the case of brief quotations embodied in critical articles and reviews.
For information, address State University of New York Press, State University Plaza, Albany, N.Y., 12246

Library of Congress Cataloging-in-Publication Data

[Ta'rīkh al-rusul wa-al-mulūk. English. Selections]
The Marwānid restoration / translated and annotated by Everett K. Rowson.
p.cm. — (The history of al-Ṭabarī = Ta'rīkh al-rusul wa'l -mulūk : v. 22) (SUNY series in Near Eastern studies) (Bibliotheca Persica)
Translation of extracts from: Ta'rīkh al-rusul wa-al-mulūk.
Bibliography: p. Includes indexes.
ISBN 0-88706-975-4. ISBN 0-88706-976-2 (pbk.)
1. Islamic Empire—History—661-750. 2. Iraq—History—634-1534.
I. Rowson, Everett K. II. Title. III. Series. IV. Series: Ṭabarī, 838?–923. Ta'rīkh al-rusul wa-al-mulūk. English; v. 22.
V. Series: Bibliotheca Persica (Albany, N.Y.)
DS38.2.T313 1985 vol. 22
[DS38.5]
909'.1 s—dc19
[909'.097671] 88-16086
CIP

10 9 8 7 6 5 4 3 2 1

Preface

The History of Prophets and Kings *(Ta'rīkh al-rusul wa'l-mulūk)* by Abū Ja'far Muḥammad b. Jarīr al-Ṭabarī (839–923), here rendered as the *History of al-Ṭabarī*, is by common consent the most important universal history produced in the world of Islam. It has been translated here in its entirety for the first time for the benefit of non-Arabists, with historical and philological notes for those interested in the particulars of the text.

Ṭabarī's monumental work explores the history of the ancient nations, with special emphasis on biblical peoples and prophets, the legendary and factual history of ancient Iran, and, in great detail, the rise of Islam, the life of the Prophet Muḥammad, and the history of the Islamic world down to the year 915. The first volume of this translation will contain a biography of al-Ṭabarī and a discussion of the method, scope, and value of his work. It will also provide information on some of the technical considerations that have guided the work of the translators.

The *History* has been divided here into 38 volumes, each of which covers about two hundred pages of the original Arabic text in the Leiden edition. An attempt has been made to draw the dividing lines between the individual volumes in such a way that each is to some degree independent and can be read as such. The page numbers of the original in the Leiden edition appear on the margins of the translated volumes.

Al-Ṭabarī very often quotes his sources verbatim and traces the chain of transmission (*isnād*) to an original source. The chains of transmitters are, for the sake of brevity, rendered by only a dash

(—) between the individual links in the chain. Thus, According to Ibn Ḥumayd—Salamah—Ibn Isḥāq means that al-Ṭabarī received the report from Ibn Ḥumayd who said that he was told by Salamah, who said that he was told by Ibn Isḥāq, and so on. The numerous subtle and important differences in the original Arabic wording have been disregarded.

The table of contents at the beginning of each volume gives a brief survey of the topics dealt with in that particular volume. It also includes the headings and subheadings as they appear in al-Ṭabarī's text, as well as those occasionally introduced by the translator.

Well-known place names, such as, for instance, Mecca, Baghdad, Jerusalem, Damascus, and the Yemen, are given in their English spellings. Less common place names, which are the vast majority, are transliterated. Biblical figures appear in the accepted English spelling. Iranian names are usually transcribed according to their Arabic forms, and the presumed Iranian forms are often discussed in the footnotes.

Technical terms have been translated wherever possible, but some, such as dirham and imām, have been retained in Arabic forms. Others that cannot be translated with sufficient precision have been retained and italicized as well as footnoted.

The annotation aims chiefly at clarifying difficult passages, identifying individuals and place names, and discussing textual difficulties. Much leeway has been left to the translators to include in the footnotes whatever they consider necessary and helpful.

The bibliographies list all the sources mentioned in the annotation.

The index in each volume contains all the names of persons and places referred to in the text, as well as those mentioned in the notes as far as they refer to the medieval period. It does not include the names of modern scholars. A general index, it is hoped, will appear after all the volumes have been published.

For further details concerning the series and acknowledgments, see Preface to Volume I.

Ehsan Yar-Shater

Contents

Preface / v

Abbreviations / ix

Translator's Foreword / xi

The Events of the Year 74 (693/694) / 1

The Important Events of This Year / 1
Al-Muhallab and the War against the Azraqites / 3
The Reason for the Dismissal of Bukayr and Appointment of Umayyah / 7

The Events of the Year 75 (694/695) / 12

The Events of This Year / 12
The Revolt of the Baṣran Troops against al-Ḥajjāj / 23
Al-Muhallab and the War against the Azraqites / 25
The Rebellious Activities of Ṣāliḥ during This Year / 31

The Events of the Year 76 (695/696) / 32

The Events of This Year / 32
The Rebellion of Ṣāliḥ b. Musarriḥ and the Reason for It / 32
Shabīb's Entry into al-Kūfah and His Dealings with al-Ḥajjāj There, and Why Shabīb Did This / 44
ʿAbd al-Malik Reforms the Coinage / 90

The Events of the Year 77 (696/697) / 93

Shabīb Kills ʿAttāb b. Warqāʾ and Zuhrah b. Ḥawiyyah / 93
Shabīb's Second Entry into al-Kūfah and His Battle with al-Ḥajjāj / 107
Account of Shabīb's End / 122
Account of Muṭarrif's Rebelling and Throwing Off His Allegiance to ʿAbd al-Malik b. Marwān / 128
Account of the Dissension among the Azraqites and the Reason for Its Breaking Out, until They Came to Ruin / 150
Destruction of the Azraqites / 162
Umayyah b. ʿAbdallāh Kills Bukayr b. Wishāḥ in Khurāsān / 165

The Events of the Year 78 (697/698) / 177

The Important Events Occurring in This Year / 177
The Officials Whom al-Ḥajjāj Appointed in Khurāsān and Sijistān, and Why He Appointed Whom He Did, with Further Details / 177

The Events of the Year 79 (698/699) / 182

The Important Events of This Year / 182
The Campaign by ʿUbaydallāh b. Abī Bakrah in Sijistān / 183

The Events of the Year 80 (699/700) / 187

The Important Events of This Year / 187
Al-Muhallab Attacks Kish / 188
ʿAbd al-Raḥmān b. al-Ashʿath Campaigns in Sijistān / 190

The Events of the Year 81 (700/701) / 196

The Events of This Year / 196
Account of Baḥīr b. Warqāʾ's Death in Khurāsān / 196

Bibliography of Cited Works / 201

Index / 207

Abbreviations

Aghānī[1]: Abū al-Faraj al-Iṣfahānī. *Kitāb al-Aghānī.* 20 vols. Būlāq, 1285 (1868).
BGA: Bibliotheca Geographorum Arabicorum
EI[1]: *Encyclopaedia of Islam,* 1st ed. Leiden, 1913–38.
EI[2]: *Encyclopaedia of Islam,* 2nd ed. Leiden, 1960–.
EI[2] *Suppl.*: *Encyclopaedia of Islam,* 2nd ed., *Supplement,* Leiden, 1982–.
GAL: C. Brockelmann. *Geschichte der arabischen Litteratur,* Leiden, 1937–49.
GAS: F. Sezgin, *Geschichte des arabischen Schrifttums.* Leiden, 1967–.
SEI: *Shorter Encyclopaedia of Islam.* Leiden, 1953.
WKAS: *Wörterbuch der klassischen arabischen Sprache.* Wiesbaden, 1970–.

Translator's Foreword

In this volume al-Ṭabarī chronicles the first nine years of the Marwānid restoration, the period following the final defeat and death of ʿAbdallāh b. al-Zubayr in Mecca and the reunification of the Islamic polity under his opponent, the caliph ʿAbd al-Malik. After twelve years of continuous civil war, this was a period of relative tranquillity, at least in the western provinces of the Hijaz, Syria, and Egypt. Concerning events in these areas al-Ṭabarī has little to say. Border warfare with the Byzantine Empire was resumed, but the annual summer campaigns produced few results, and we are given only the briefest mention of them. From other sources, we know of a series of fundamental administrative reforms implemented by the caliph at the capital in Damascus, but al-Ṭabarī reports only the most important of these: the institution of an official, aniconic, Islamic coinage. About such significant events as the building of the Dome of the Rock in Jerusalem he is totally silent. As in much of his *History*, al-Ṭabarī focuses his attention in this volume almost exclusively on Iraq and, to a lesser extent, the eastern provinces of Khurāsān and Sijistān; while this concentration can be explained in part by the nature of the source material available to him, it also reflects the continuing high level of conflict in these regions at this time, in contrast to the West.

In Iraq, despite the defeat of Ibn al-Zubayr's brother Muṣʿab, there remained widespread disaffection with the Marwānid regime from several quarters, and Iraqi troops were still occupied with a war against the Azraqite Khārijites in Khūzistān and Fārs. A forceful and effective governor was needed, and ʿAbd al-Malik found him in the redoubtable al-Ḥajjāj b. Yūsuf, whose appointment to Iraq immediately after his successful siege of Ibn al-Zubayr in Mecca marked the beginning of an era. From his inaugural harangue to the Kūfans immediately upon his arrival—perhaps the most celebrated speech in the history of Arabic literature—al-Hajjāj dominates this section of al-Ṭabarī's annals. After crushing a mutiny by the Baṣran forces, he prosecuted the Azraqite war with vigor, until dissension among the Azraqites themselves, perhaps between Arabs and non-Arabs, made possible their final and total defeat. Meanwhile, another group of Khārijites, small but pertinacious, harried Iraq itself, first under Ṣāliḥ b. Musarriḥ, then under Shabīb b. Yazīd. Al-Ṭabarī slows his narrative to give a full account of the saga of Shabīb, who, with only a few hundred men, roamed through Iraq with impunity, and even entered al-Kūfah twice. Every commander sent out against him was defeated or killed, as Shabīb pursued his guerrilla tactics, until al-Ḥajjāj finally turned the tide by himself taking the field and defeating him before al-Kūfah; as Shabīb's forces retreated, their leader was thrown by his horse from a bridge and drowned. Quoting participants from both sides of this conflict, al-Ṭabarī here offers, in reminiscence and anecdote, a vivid picture of life on campaign in Iraq at this time. Particularly interesting is his account of negotiations between Shabīb and the disaffected commander, Muṭarrif b. al-Mughīrah, who was induced to rebel against his governor and caliph but rejected Shabīb's own claim to legitimate rule; Muṭarrif's independent rebellion, a good indication of the degree of alienation from the central authority among the Iraqi forces, was quickly put down.

Farther east, in Khurāsān, the campaign of conquest had slowed and then stopped as tribal feuds and rivalries fractured the unity of the Arab troops and settlers. ʿAbd al-Malik's appointment of a neutral governor from his own tribe of Quraysh stopped the fighting, but the wounds were slow to heal, and this volume begins and ends with accounts of the fates of Baḥīr and Bukayr, the leaders of the two factions of the divided Tamīm, the largest tribal group in Khurāsān. Al-Ḥajjāj's successes in Iraq led ʿAbd al-Malik to add Khurāsān and Sijistān to his governorship, and al-Ḥajjāj sent out, as his sub-governor over Khurāsān, al-Muhallab b.

Abī Ṣufrah, the victorious general of the Azraqite war. Al-Muhallab was able to resume the Islamic campaigns, but without notable success.

Al-Ḥajjāj's sub-governor to Sijistān, ʿUbaydallāh b. Abī Bakrah, fared considerably worse. After penetrating far into enemy territory, his troops were surrounded and decimated. In response, al-Ḥajjāj raised and outfitted the "Peacock Army," on which he lavished great sums, and appointed ʿAbd al-Raḥmān b. al-Ashʿath to command it. This volume closes with the latter's modest successes in Sijistān—before his decision to rebel presented al-Ḥajjāj with the gravest challenge of his career.

In this section of his annals, al-Ṭabarī relies essentially on two authors. His account of events in Khurāsān is attributed throughout to al-Madā'inī (d. 225/839), while the much lengthier sections on Iraq depend almost exclusively on the monographs of Abū Mikhnaf (d. 157/774). Abū Mikhnaf is in fact al-Ṭabarī's sole acknowledged source for the Azraqite wars and the rebellion of Muṭarrif b. al-Mughīrah, as well as the disastrous expedition to Sijistān. Only in his account of Shabīb's attacks on al-Kūfah does al-Ṭabarī occasionally offer variant reports, from ʿUmar b. Shabbah (d. 264/877) and an anonymous source. For al-Ḥajjāj's simultaneous appointment of governors to Khurāsān and Sijistān, al-Ṭabarī presents parallel accounts from both Abū Mikhnaf and al-Madā'inī. Other authorities are mentioned only occasionally. Al-Wāqidī (d. 207/823) is the source for al-Ṭabarī's very exiguous report on the coinage reform; Aḥmad b. Thābit is cited annually for the identity of the leader of the pilgrimage.

My translation follows the text of the Leiden edition by I. Guidi throughout, with only a very few emendations, required or suggested by context, and specified in the notes. Guidi's five (in one section six) manuscripts provide, on the whole, a satisfactory text, except for a number of abrupt transitions where the natural sequence seems disturbed. The philological commentary on al-Ḥajjāj's oration, for example, is interrupted by a narrative that probably should succeed it (II, 868); and the additions to Abū Mikhnaf's account of Shabīb's attacks on al-Kūfah, derived from other sources, seem in part to have been inserted in the wrong places, resulting in dangling transition sentences and perhaps some omitted *isnāds* (II, 910–919, 962–969). These problems have been merely identified in the notes; their solution must await an eventual re-edition of the text.

I have provided relatively full citations of parallels to Al-Ṭabarī's information from available earlier sources, as well as from the *Kāmil* of Ibn al-Athīr, which is largely a summary of al-Ṭabarī and occasionally of textual importance. The most important of the early sources, specifically for the Khārijite wars, is the *Kitāb al-Futūḥ* of Ibn Aʿtham al-Kūfī, whose rather detailed account diverges considerably from that offered by al-Ṭabarī. Al-Mubarrad's *Kāmil* also includes a long digression on the Khārijites, which seems to share features with both al-Ṭabarī and Ibn Aʿtham. It is unfortunate that the section of al-Balādhurī's *Ansāb* on the reign of ʿAbd al-Malik, another independent early source, remains unpublished and has been unavailable to me; I have, however, cited parallels from al-Balādhurī's section on al-Ḥajjāj, which appears in the volume of the *Ansāb* published by Ahlwardt under the title *Anonyme arabische Chronik*.

Besides making reasonable efforts to identify individuals and places mentioned in the text, I have regularly supplied information on tribal affiliations, relying most heavily on Caskel's analytical edition of Ibn al-Kalbī's *Jamharat al-nasab*. Al-Ṭabarī presents the conflicts in Khurāsān in this period as essentially tribal in nature and makes it clear that tribal solidarities and rivalries played an important role in the Khārijite disturbances in Iraq as well; while not attempting an original analysis of these tribal factors, I have thought it best to provide the basic information al-Ṭabarī would have assumed as general knowledge among his original readership.

I would like to express my gratitude to Dr. Hans Hinrich Biesterfeldt and Professor Gerhard Endress of the Rühr-Universität Bochum for facilitating my stay there and use of the library of the Seminar für Orientalistik, where much of the annotation was completed. I am also grateful to Professor Jacob Lassner of Wayne State University for his careful editing of my manuscript.

Everett K. Rowson

The Events of the Year 74 [854]

(May 13, 693–May 1, 694)

The Important Events of This Year

Among the events of this year: ʿAbd al-Malik dismissed Ṭāriq b. ʿAmr[1] from Medina and appointed as its governor al-Ḥajjāj b. Yūsuf.[2] It is reported that the latter came to Medina, stayed there a month, and then left to perform the lesser pilgrimage (*ʿumrah*).[3]

In this year, it is reported, al-Ḥajjāj b. Yūsuf dismantled the structures of the Kaʿbah that Ibn al-Zubayr had put up. The latter had incorporated the Ḥijr inside the Kaʿbah and given the Kaʿbah two doors; al-Ḥajjāj restored it to its original form.[4] He then went

---

1. Governor since 72 (691–692) or 73 (692–693), after taking the city from the governor of the rival caliph Ibn al-Zubayr in Mecca; see text above, II, 834, 852.

2. See Ibn Khayyāṭ, *Taʾrīkh* (Najaf), 294, 298; Balādhurī, *Ansāb*, XI, 67f., 188f.; *EI²*, s.v. al-Ḥadjdjādj b. Yūsuf; J. Périer, *La vie d'al-Ḥadjdjādj ibn Yousof* (Paris, 1904), 54ff. As commander of the Umayyad forces, al-Ḥajjāj had, the previous year, with the assistance of Ṭāriq b. ʿAmr, successfully besieged Ibn al-Zubayr in Mecca, and been appointed governor there; he was now given the governorship of Medina as well. See text above, II, 844–52, 853–54.

3. The "lesser pilgrimage" to Mecca can be performed at any time of year; see *SEI*, s.v. ʿumra.

4. The Ḥijr is a semicircular area adjoining the Kaʿbah wall, whose special

back to Medina, in Ṣafar (June-July), and stayed there three months, treating the people of Medina harshly and arbitrarily. He built a mosque there, in the area of the Banū Salimah, which is still known by his name.[5] He treated the companions of the Messenger of God with contempt, forcing them to wear seals around their necks.[6]

According to Muḥammad b. 'Umar[7]—Ibn Abī Dhi'b: Someone saw Jābir b. 'Abdallāh[8] with a seal on his hand. According to Ibn
[855] Abī Dhi'b: Isḥāq b. Yazīd saw Anas b. Mālik[9] with a seal around his neck; al-Ḥajjāj did that to humiliate him.

According to Ibn 'Umar—Shuraḥbīl b. Abī 'Awn—his father: I was there when al-Ḥajjāj sent for Sahl b. Sa'd[10] and asked him, "What was it that prevented you from supporting the Commander of the Faithful 'Uthmān b. 'Affān?" He replied, "But I did!" Al-Ḥajjāj said, "You are lying!" Then he ordered a lead seal put on his neck.

In this year, according to al-Wāqidī, 'Abd al-Malik appointed Abū Idrīs al-Khawlānī as judge.[11]

---

sanctity is variously explained; most often it is identified as the burial place of Ishmael and Hagar. See *EI*², s.v. Ka'ba. On Ibn al-Zubayr's construction, see text above, II, 592. On al-Ḥajjāj's reconstruction, see also Azraqī, *Akhbār Makkah* (Leipzig), 145f.; Ibn Khayyāṭ, *Ta'rīkh*, 268; Balādhurī, *Futūḥ* (Leiden), 47; Dīnawarī, *al-Akhbār al-ṭiwāl* (Leiden), 321; Ya'qūbī, *Ta'rīkh* (Leiden), II, 325; Theophanes, *Chronographia*, A. M. 6183; Ibn al-Athīr, *Kāmil* (Leiden), IV, 365; Ibn Kathīr, *Bidāyah* (Cairo, 1932), IX, 2–3.

5. The Banū Salimah b. Sa'd were a clan of the Khazraj; see 'U. Kaḥḥālah, *Mu'jam qabā'il al-'arab* (Damascus, 1949), II, 537. Later geographical writers do not mention this mosque.

6. See Balādhurī, *Ansāb*, XI, 68: al-Ḥajjāj put seals on the hands of Jābir b. 'Abdallāh and others, "as is done with the *dhimmah*." On the use of seals to indicate payment of taxes among *dhimmīs*, and corresponding practices among Byzantines and Sasanians, see M. Morony, *Iraq after the Muslim Conquest* (Princeton, 1984), 112f.

7. Abū 'Abdallāh Muḥammad b. 'Umar al-Wāqidī, d. 207 (823); see *EI*¹, s.v. al-Wāḳidī.

8. D. 78 (697); see F. Sezgin, *GAS*, I, 85; Ibn Kathīr, *Bidāyah*, IX, 22.

9. D. c. 91 (708); see *EI*², s.v. Anas b. Mālik. In 65 (684) he had led the prayer in al-Baṣrah at the behest of Ibn al-Zubayr; see text above, II, 465. According to Ibn 'Abd Rabbih, *'Iqd* (Cairo, 1940), V, 36–41, al-Ḥajjāj's further abuse of Anas two years later, in al-Baṣrah, prompted the latter to write a letter of complaint to 'Abd al-Malik, who was furious with al-Ḥajjāj and forced him to apologize; a variant of this story appears also in Ibn al-Athīr, *Kāmil*, IV, 385–87.

10. D. 88 (706–707) or 91 (709–710); see Ibn Ḥajar, *Tahdhīb* (Hyderabad), IV, 252.

11. In Damascus; see *EI*², s.v. al-Khawlānī.

In this year, according to some reports, Bishr b. Marwān left al-Kūfah for al-Baṣrah, to become governor there.[12]

In this year, al-Muhallab was entrusted by ʿAbd al-Malik with the war against the Azraqites.[13]

Al-Muhallab and the War against the Azraqites

When Bishr had arrived in al-Baṣrah, ʿAbd al-Malik sent him the following letter, according to Hishām[14]—Abū Mikhnaf[15]—Yūnus b. Abī Isḥāq—his father:

> Send forth al-Muhallab against the Azraqites with the men of his garrison and have him select from among them the best horsemen and the most distinguished, capable and experienced among them, for he knows them best. Let him follow his own judgment in conducting the campaign, for I have total confidence in his experience and his concern for the welfare of the Muslims. Send out also a large force of Kūfans, and appoint as their leader a well-known and respected man, of pure and noble lineage, someone known for his strength, courage, and experience in battle. Mobilize the men of these two garrisons against the Azraqites and have them pursue them wherever they go, until God annihilates and exterminates them. Peace. [856]

Bishr summoned al-Muhallab, gave him the letter to read, and

---

12. Bishr was ʿAbd al-Malik's brother. He had been governor of al-Kūfah for three years. According to some reports, his move to al-Baṣrah, or at least his additional appointment as governor there, replacing Khālid b. ʿAbdallāh, occurred in 73 (692–693); see text above, II, 852–54. See also Ibn Aʿtham al-Kūfī, *Futūḥ* (Hyderabad), VI, 313f.; Ibn Khayyāṭ, *Taʾrīkh*, 268, 294; Balādhurī, *Ansāb*, V, 178, and XI, 26; *EI²*, s.v. Bishr b. Marwān.

13. The Azraqites were extremist Khārijites, originally followers of Nāfiʿ b. al-Azraq (d. 65 [685]); at this time they were led by Qaṭarī b. al-Fujāʾah. They had been defeated at al-Ahwāz and driven back to Fārs by Khālid b. ʿAbdallāh in 72 (691–692); earlier, al-Muhallab had fought against them for both Muṣʿab b. al-Zubayr and ʿAbd al-Malik. See text above, II, 583ff., 765, 822ff. See also Ibn Aʿtham al-Kūfī, *Futūḥ*, VI, 314–19; Mubarrad, *Kāmil* (Leipzig), 662ff.; Ibn al-Athīr, *Kāmil*, IV, 365–67; Ibn Kathīr, *Bidāyah*, IX, 3; *EI¹*, s.v. al-Muhallab b. Abī Ṣufra; *EI²*, s.v. Azāriḳa.

14. Hishām b. Muḥammad al-Kalbī, d. c. 204 (819); see *EI²*, s.v. al-Kalbī.

15. D. 157 (774); see *EI²*, s.v. Abū Mikhnaf; U. Sezgin, *Abū Miḫnaf* (Leiden, 1971).

ordered him to select whomever he wished. Al-Muhallab sent Juday' b. Sa'īd b. Qabīṣah b. Sarrāq al-Azdī, who was the maternal uncle of his son Yazīd, ordering him to go to the military roll (*dīwān*)[16] and select the men. Bishr was annoyed that the command had been given to al-Muhallab by 'Abd al-Malik, so that he was unable to send out someone else;[17] this caused him as much resentment against al-Muhallab as if the latter had done him a personal injury. Bishr b. Marwān then summoned 'Abd al-Raḥmān b. Mikhnaf[18] and sent him to the Kūfans, ordering him to select the best horsemen and the most distinguished, capable and courageous of the men.

According to Abū Mikhnaf—men of the tribe—'Abd al-Raḥmān b. Mikhnaf: Bishr b. Marwān summoned me and said: "You know the position you enjoy with me and the preferment I have shown you. Now I have decided to put you in charge of the army, basing my decision on what I know of your courage, capability, nobility, and boldness. I expect you to live up to my good opinion of you. See that such-and-such happens to al-Muhallab; take over his command completely, accepting neither his advice nor his opinion; belittle his abilities and make much of his shortcomings." He neglected to give me any counsel about the troops, fighting the enemy, or seeing to the welfare of the Muslims, but kept on trying to incite me against my clansman[19]—as if I were a dunce or someone who could be treated like a child or a fool! Never have I seen someone make an appeal to a respectable man of my appearance and position like the appeal this boy made to me! 'Amr has outgrown the neck-ring![20] When Bishr saw that I
[857] did not respond with alacrity, he said, "What is the matter?" I replied, "May God be good to you! Do I have any choice but to carry out your orders, whether willingly or reluctantly?" "Go,

16. See *EI*[2], s.v. dīwān.

17. Mubarrad, *Kāmil*, 663, names Bishr's preference as 'Umar b. 'Ubaydallāh b. Ma'mar, who had recently defeated the Khārijite Abū Fudayk; see text above, II, 852f.

18. Great-uncle of Abū Mikhnaf; see U. Sezgin, *Abū Miḫnaf*, 225, n. 128; Kh. Ziriklī, *al-A'lām* (Cairo, 1953–59), IV, 111.

19. Both men belonged to the tribe of Azd.

20. I.e., "How childish of him!" See Maydānī, *Majma' al-amthāl* (Cairo, 1342), II, 75; Tha'ālibī, *Thimār al-qulūb* (Cairo, 1908), 505.

then," he said, "and have a safe trip." I bade him farewell and withdrew.

Al-Muhallab then set out with the Baṣran forces and proceeded as far as Rāmhurmuz, where he found the Khārijites; he then entrenched himself there. ʿAbd al-Raḥmān b. Mikhnaf set out with the Kūfans, accompanied by the following commanders: Bishr b. Jarīr, in charge of the quarter of the Medinese; Muḥammad b. ʿAbd al-Raḥmān b. Saʿīd b. Qays, in charge of the quarter of the Tamīm and Hamdān; Isḥāq b. Muḥammad b. al-Ashʿath, in charge of the quarter of the Kindah and Rabīʿah; and Zaḥr b. Qays, in charge of the quarter of the Madhḥij and Asad.[21] ʿAbd al-Raḥmān marched out and encamped about a mile (*mīl*)[22] or a mile and a half from al-Muhallab, so that the two armies were within sight of each other at Rāmhurmuz. But then, only ten days later, word came to the men of the death of Bishr b. Marwān in al-Baṣrah, and many from the forces of both al-Baṣrah and al-Kūfah deserted.[23] Bishr was replaced by Khālid b. ʿAbdallāh b. Khālid b. Asīd,[24] whose deputy over al-Kūfah was ʿAmr b. Ḥurayyith.[25]

Among the Kūfan deserters were Zaḥr b. Qays, Isḥāq b. Muḥammad b. al-Ashʿath, and Muḥammad b. ʿAbd al-Raḥmān b. Saʿīd b. Qays. ʿAbd al-Raḥmān b. Mikhnaf sent his son Jaʿfar after them. Jaʿfar brought back Isḥāq and Muḥammad—Zaḥr b. Qays eluded him—and confined them for two days, then charged them not to part from him. But they stayed only one day before leaving again, taking a different route. They were pursued without success, and kept moving until they caught up with Zaḥr b. Qays in al-Ahwāz, where many of the men who were heading for al-

21. Mubarrad, *Kāmil*, 664, specifies a force of two thousand men from each quarter, but garbles the names of two of the commanders. For the division of the Kūfan army into quarters, see text above, II, 131, 644, 701; Morony, *Iraq after the Muslim Conquest*, 245.

22. A *mīl* is a third of a *farsakh*, or about two kilometers. See W. Hinz, *Islamische Masse und Gewichte* (Leiden, 1970), 63.

23. According to al-Wāqidī, Bishr died in 73 (692–693); see text above, II, 852.

24. An Umayyad (Ibn Ḥazm, *Jamharah* [1948], 104), he had already been governor of al-Baṣrah, until replaced by Bishr; see text above, II, 818, and notes 12, 13 above.

25. He retained this position, having already been deputized by Bishr when the latter transferred to al-Kūfah; see text above, II, 853. ʿAmr had earlier served as deputy in al-Kūfah for Ziyād b. Abīhi and his son ʿUbaydallāh as well; see text above, II, 115, 459ff.

[858] Baṣrah came together. When word of this reached Khālid b. ʿAbdallāh, he wrote a letter to the men and sent an emissary to bring them to their senses and make them return. One of his clients brought the letter and read it out to the men, who had been assembled to hear it:

> In the name of God, the Merciful, the Compassionate. From Khālid b. ʿAbdallāh to those Muslims and believers whom this letter of mine reaches. Greetings. To you I offer praise of God; there is no god but He. The matter: God has imposed the duty of jihād on His servants, and required obedience to those who govern them. He who participates in jihād does so only to his own benefit, but he who gives up jihād for God will be forsaken by God. Moreover, he who defies the governors and rightful authorities brings down God's wrath on himself, merits corporal punishment, and makes himself liable to confiscation of his property as spoil, cancellation of his stipend (*ʿaṭā'*),[26] and exile to the most remote and evil of lands. O Muslims! Know who it is whom you have so boldly defied! It is ʿAbd al-Malik b. Marwān, the Commander of the Faithful, a man with no weaknesses, from whom rebels can expect no indulgence! On the one who defies him falls his whip, and on the one who opposes him falls his sword! I spare no pains to warn you! Do not pave the way to your own destruction! Servants of God! Return to your assigned places[27] and to the obedience of your caliph, and persist no longer in your defiance and opposition, lest you be afflicted with what you would avoid. I swear by God that after this letter of mine any rebel that I find I will surely slay, God willing. Peace and God's mercy be upon you.

As Khālid's client read out this letter to them, every line or two Zaḥr interrupted to say, "Get to the point!" He replied, "By God, I hear the words of a man who does not want to understand what he hears! I bear witness that he has not the slightest interest in
[859] what is in this letter!"[28] Zaḥr then said to him, "Read, then, what

26. See *EI*², s.v. ʿaṭāʾ.
27. *Maktab*; see Dozy, *Supplément*, s.v.; *WKAS*, s.v. Some MSS read *amkinah*, "places."
28. *Lā yaʿīju bi-shay' mimmā fī hādhā al-kitāb*. Other MSS read *lā tahīju fitnah*

you were commanded to, you pale-faced slave, and then go back to your own people. You have no idea how we feel." The client finished reading the letter, but the men paid no attention to what was in it. Zaḥr, Isḥāq b. Muḥammad, and Muḥammad b. ʿAbd al-Raḥmān set off and camped at a village belonging to the Ashʿath clan, near al-Kūfah. They sent the following letter to ʿAmr b. Ḥurayyith:

> When the men heard of the death of the amīr—may God have mercy on him—they dispersed, not one remaining with us. We have come now to the amīr and to our garrison, but prefer not to enter al-Kūfah without informing the amīr and receiving his permission.

ʿAmr b. Ḥurayyith wrote back:

> You have abandoned your assigned places and come here in rebellion and disobedience. You have from us neither permission nor safe conduct.

When they received this reply, they waited until night, then entered their lodgings, and remained there until the arrival of al-Ḥajjāj b. Yūsuf.

In this year, ʿAbd al-Malik dismissed Bukayr b. Wishāḥ from Khurāsān and appointed as governor there Umayyah b. ʿAbdallāh b. Khālid b. Asīd.[29]

The Reason for the Dismissal of Bukayr and Appointment of Umayyah

According to Abū al-Ḥasan,[30] Bukayr b. Wishāḥ ruled as governor

---

illā kunta ra'sahā—"whenever there is internal strife, you are always at the head of it!"

29. See Ibn Aʿtham al-Kūfī, *Futūḥ*, VI, 288–90; Ibn Khayyāṭ, *Ta'rīkh*, 297 (year 73 [692–693]); Balādhurī, *Futūḥ*, 416, and *Ansāb*, IVB, 152–54, 164–66; Yaʿqūbī, *Ta'rīkh*, II, 324, and *Buldān*, (*BGA*, VII), 299; Gardīzī, *Zayn al-akhbār* (Tehran, 1374 solar), 108f. (year 72 [691–692], but very garbled); Ibn al-Athīr, *Kāmil*, IV, 367f.; Ibn Kathīr, *Bidāyah*, IX, 3; *EI²*, s.v. Bukayr b. Wishāḥ. C. E. Bosworth, *Sīstān under the Arabs* (Rome, 1968), 49, notes a dirham minted by Umayyah in Sijistān, dated 73 (692–693).

30. Abū al-Ḥasan ʿAlī b. Muḥammad al-Madā'inī, d. c. 228 (843); see *EI²*, s.v. al-Madā'inī.

of Khurāsān for two years until Umayyah arrived to take over the post; for Ibn Khāzim was killed in the year 72 (691–692), and Umayyah arrived in the year 74 (693–694). The reason Bukayr was dismissed from Khurāsān was as follows: ʿAlī[31]—al-Mufaḍ-
[860] ḍal:[32] Baḥīr was imprisoned by Bukayr b. Wishāḥ because of his role in the business I mentioned previously about Ibn Khāzim's head; that is, when the latter was killed,[33] Baḥīr remained Bukayr's prisoner until ʿAbd al-Malik appointed Umayyah b. ʿAbdallāh b. Khālid b. Asīd governor. When Bukayr heard of this, he sent to Baḥīr with an offer of reconciliation, but the latter refused, saying, "Bukayr thought that Khurāsān would remain his without opposition."[34] Messengers shuttled between them, but Baḥīr continued to refuse. Then Ḍirār b. Ḥuṣayn al-Ḍabbī came to see him, saying, "It seems to me that you are being very foolish. Here your clansman[35] sends you an apology, when you are his captive and the sword is in his hand, and if he killed you a goat wouldn't fart over you[36]—yet you will not accept it from him! This is hardly in your own interest! Accept this truce and regain your freedom!" Baḥīr yielded to his advice and made peace with Bukayr. Bukayr then sent him forty thousand dirhams, on the condition that he not take up arms against him.[37]

Now the Tamīm in Khurāsān were at odds: Muqāʿis and the Buṭūn sided with [Baḥīr, while ʿAwf and the Abnā' took Bukayr's side].[38] The forces of Khurāsān feared that war would resume and

31. Al-Madā'inī.

32. Al-Mufaḍḍal b. Muḥammad al-Ḍabbī (d. c. 170 [786]), the noted philologist and compiler of the *Mufaḍḍaliyyāt*; see *GAL* I, 116.

33. See text above, II, 833: Baḥīr had led the forces that defeated and killed the Zubayrid governor Ibn Khāzim. However, when Baḥīr refused to give up the latter's head to Bukayr, who was Ibn Khāzim's former deputy but had accepted ʿAbd al-Malik's appointment as governor, Bukayr struck him and took the head, and then imprisoned him. The remainder of this paragraph seems anticipatory, and the reason for Bukayr's dismissal follows in the next; Ibn al-Athīr in his summary (*Kāmil*, IV, 367) reverses them.

34. *Ẓanna Bukayr anna Khurāsān tabqā lahu fī al-jamāʿah*; see Balādhurī, *Futūḥ*, glossarium, s.v. *jamāʿah*.

35. Both men belonged to the tribe of Tamīm; see next paragraph.

36. For the proverb, see Maydānī, *Amthāl*, II, 157; Thaʿālibī, *Thimār*, 304.

37. Ibn Aʿtham al-Kūfī, *Futūḥ*, VI, 288–90, gives a fuller account of Ḍirār's intercession.

38. The addition is from Ibn al-Athīr, *Kāmil*, IV, 367. Baḥīr belonged to the clan of Ṣuraym b. Muqāʿis b. ʿAmr b. Kaʿb b. Saʿd, and Bukayr to the ʿAwf b. Kaʿb b. Saʿd.

that the region would be devastated, and that their enemies among the polytheists would then overpower them. So they wrote to ʿAbd al-Malik b. Marwān, saying that Khurāsān would only recover from its disarray under the direction of a man of Quraysh, one who would be the object of neither their envy nor their partisanship. ʿAbd al-Malik said, "Khurāsān is the frontier of the East. It has had its troubles under the governance of this Tamīmī, and the troops have broken into factions. Fearing that they will return to the factionalism of the past, and that the region and its people will then be destroyed, they have asked me to appoint as governor over them a man of Quraysh, whom they would heed and obey." To this Umayyah b. ʿAbdallāh replied, "O Commander of the Faithful, send out to them a man from your own family." ʿAbd al-Malik said, "Were it not for your retreat from Abū Fudayk, you would be that man!"[39] Umayyah pro- [861]
tested, "By God, O Commander of the Faithful, I retreated only when I could no longer fight, the men having deserted me. Then I thought it would be better for me to fall back to a rear echelon[40] than to expose a small remaining band of Muslims to annihilation. Marrār b. ʿAbd al-Raḥmān b. Abī Bakrah knows about this, and Khālid b. ʿAbdallāh also wrote to you that he had been informed of my excuse." Khālid had indeed written to him with Umayyah's excuse, informing him that the men had deserted him; and Marrār also confirmed Umayyah's statement, saying, "O Commander of the Faithful, he held out until he could no longer put up a fight, the men having deserted him." ʿAbd al-Malik then made Umayyah governor of Khurāsān.

ʿAbd al-Malik loved Umayyah and used to say, "He is from the same brood as I"—that is, they were born at the same time. The people said, "We have never seen anyone compensated for a de-

Kaʿb b. Saʿd and ʿAmr b. Saʿd constituted the Buṭūn, while the Abnāʾ were descendants of Saʿd's other sons; but the ʿAwf b. Kaʿb joined the Abnāʾ rather than the Buṭūn. See W. Caskel, *Ǧamharat an-nasab: Das Genealogische Werk des Hišām ibn Muḥammad al-Kalbī* (Leiden, 1966), I, 75, II, 135, 230; Ibn Ḥazm, *Jamharah,* 204–8; Kaḥḥālah, *Muʿjam qabāʾil al-ʿarab,* I, 3, II, 860, III, 1131.

39. Abū Fudayk was a Khārijite rebel; see *EI*², s. v. Abū Fudayk. For Umayyah's defeat at his hands, see text above, II, 829; Balādhurī, *Ansāb,* IVA, 459.

40. *Fiʾah;* see Lane, *Lexicon,* s. v.: "a company of soldiers who fight in the rear of an army, and to whom the latter has recourse in the case of fear or defeat."

feat the way Umayyah was compensated: he fled from Abū Fudayk and then was made governor of Khurāsān!"

A man from Bakr b. Wā'il, who was being held in prison by Bukayr b. Wishāḥ, recited these verses:[41]

The red-white camels, snorting through their nose-rings,
their saddlecloths pushed back from their shoulders,
With the places of their saddle-girths looking like
spotted doves perched in churches,
Brought you a noble man from Umayyah, impeccable, like a great white hawk,
with a countenance gleaming like a polished sword.

At this time Baḥīr was in al-Sinj.[42] He asked about Umayyah's progress, and when he heard that he was approaching Abarshahr,[43] he spoke with a man named Razīn, or Zarīr, from the
[862] Persians of Marw, saying, "Show me a shortcut, so that I may meet the amīr before he arrives, and I will give you such-and-such and reward you generously." This man did know the way, and he set out with him from al-Sinj, proceeding as far as the Sarakhs region in a single night. He then took him on to Nishapur, and Baḥīr reached Umayyah when he came to Abarshahr.[44] Meeting Umayyah there, he informed him about Khurāsān and what would be best as regards its people, so as to ensure their willing obedience and make them easier for the governor to deal with. Baḥīr also accused Bukayr of ill-gotten gains and warned Umayyah of his treachery.

Baḥīr then accompanied Umayyah to Marw. Umayyah was a man of noble and generous character and made no move against Bukayr or his functionaries. He proposed to Bukayr that the latter take charge of his security force (*shurṭah*),[45] but Bukayr refused

---

41. Vv. 1, 3 appear in *Aghānī*[1], XII, 72, in quite a different context, attributed to ʿAbd al-Raḥmān b. al-Ḥakam and addressed to Muʿāwiyah.

42. One day's march west of Marw; see Yāqūt, *Muʿjam* (Leipzig), II, 161; Le Strange, *Lands*, 400.

43. Official name of the city of Nishapur; see *EI*[2], s.v. Abarshahr.

44. It was normally six days from Marw to Sarakhs, and another six from Sarakhs to Nishapur; see Yaʿqūbī, *Buldān*, 279.

45. The troops responsible for internal order, or police. See *EI*[1], s.v. *shurṭa*; N. Fries, *Das Heereswesen der Araber zur Zeit der Omaijaden nach Ṭabarī* (Tübingen, 1921), 22.

this, so he gave to the post to Baḥīr b. Warqā'. Then some of Bukayr's men reproached him, saying, "You refused the post, so he gave it to Baḥīr—and you know what is between the two of you." But Bukayr replied, "Yesterday I was governor of Khurāsān, with javelins[46] carried before me. Shall I now become head of the security force and carry a javelin myself?"

Then Umayyah said to Bukayr, "Choose any district of Khurāsān you wish!" He replied, "Tukhāristān," whereupon Umayyah said, "It is yours." Bukayr spent a great deal of money preparing for his departure, but then Baḥīr said to Umayyah, "If Bukayr goes to Tukhāristān, he will rebel against you." He kept on warning Umayyah until the latter was convinced and ordered Bukayr to remain with him.

In this year the leader of the pilgrimage was al-Ḥajjāj b. Yūsuf.[47] He had put 'Abdallāh b. Qays b. Makhramah in charge of the judiciary in Medina before setting off there himself, according to the report of Muḥammad b. 'Umar.[48] Al-Ḥajjāj b. Yūsuf was governor of Medina and Mecca; Bishr b. Marwān of al-Kūfah and al-Baṣrah; and Umayyah b. 'Abdallāh b. Khālid b. Asīd of Khurāsān. Shurayḥ b. al-Ḥārith was in charge of the judiciary in al-Kūfah,[49] [863] and Hishām b. Hubayrah was in charge of the judiciary in al-Baṣrah.[50] According to some reports, 'Abd al-Malik b. Marwān performed the lesser pilgrimage in this year, but we are uncertain of the truth of this.

---

46. *Ḥarbah.* See Ṭabarī, glossarium, s.v.; Fries, *Heereswesen,* 51.

47. Ibn Khayyāṭ, *Ta'rīkh,* 268, 301; Ya'qūbī, *Ta'rīkh,* II, 336.

48. Ibn Khayyāṭ, *Ta'rīkh,* 294, 299; Balādhurī, *Ansāb,* XI, 68, 188f.

49. On Shurayḥ b. al-Ḥārith (d. at an advanced age in 78 [697]), see Ibn Sa'd, *Ṭabaqāt* (Leiden), VI, 90–100; Ibn Khallikān, *Wafayāt al-a'yān* (Beirut, 1968–72), II, 460–63; Ibn Kathīr, *Bidāyah,* IX, 22–26.

50. Ibn Khayyāṭ, *Ta'rīkh,* 298. On Hishām b. Hubayrah (d. 75 [694]), see Ibn Sa'd, *Ṭabaqāt,* VII, i, 109f.; Ziriklī, *A'lām,* IX, 88f.

The Events of the Year 75

(May 2, 694–April 20, 695)

The Events of This Year

Among the events of this year: Muḥammad b. Marwān's summer expedition when the Byzantines attacked near Marʿash.[51]

In this year, ʿAbd al-Malik appointed Yaḥyā b. al-Ḥakam b. Abī al-ʿĀṣ governor of Medina.[52]

In this year, ʿAbd al-Malik appointed al-Ḥajjāj b. Yūsuf governor of Iraq, excluding Khurāsān and Sijistān.[53] Al-Ḥajjāj proceeded to al-Kūfah.

---

51. According to Ibn Khayyāṭ, *Ta'rīkh*, 269f., the Byzantines advanced to al-ʿAmq or al-Aʿmāq in the environs of Marʿash in Jumādā I 75 (August–September 694), where they suffered a defeat; see also Balādhurī, *Ansāb*, V, 186; Yaʿqūbī, *Ta'rīkh*, II, 337; Ibn al-Athīr, *Kāmil*, IV, 374; Ibn Kathīr, *Bidāyah*, IX, 7. Muḥammad was ʿAbd al-Malik's brother.

52. Ibn Khayyāṭ, *Ta'rīkh*, 294ff., 299; Balādhurī, *Ansāb*, V, 160–63, and XI, 69, 188f.; Ibn Kathīr, *Bidāyah*, IX, 7. Yaḥyā b. al-Ḥakam was ʿAbd al-Malik's paternal uncle.

53. See Ibn Aʿtham al-Kūfī, *Futūḥ*, VII, 1–3; Ibn Khayyāṭ, *Ta'rīkh*, 295f.; Balādhurī, *Ansāb*, XI, 69, 266f., 269f.; Yaʿqūbī, *Ta'rīkh*, II, 326f.; Masʿūdī, *Murūj* (Paris, 1861–77), V, 291f.; Ibn al-Athīr, *Kāmil*, IV, 374–79; Ibn Kathīr, *Bidāyah*, IX, 7; Périer, *Vie d'al-Ḥadjdjādj*, 65ff. The dramatic accounts in Ibn Aʿtham al-Kūfī and

According to Abū Zayd[54]—Muḥammad b. Yaḥyā Abū Ghassān—ʿAbdallāh b. Abī ʿUbaydah b. Muḥammad b. ʿAmmār b. Yāsir: Al-Ḥajjāj b. Yūsuf left Medina when he received the letter from ʿAbd al-Malik appointing him governor of Iraq, after the death of Bishr b. Marwān. He left with a party of twelve riders on thoroughbred camels. They reached al-Kūfah, unannounced, at midday. Al-Muhallab had been sent off by Bishr against the Ḥarūriyyah.[55] Al-Ḥajjāj went directly to the mosque, entered it, and ascended the pulpit, his face covered by a red silk turban. He called out, "Summon the men!" They thought that he and his companions were Khārijites, and came ready to attack them. But when the men were assembled, he rose, uncovered his face, and [864]
said:[56]

I am the son of splendor, who scales the heights;
when I remove the turban, you will know me.[57]

By God! I take full accounting of wickedness, match it in return, and pay it back in kind! I see heads ripe and ready for harvest, and blood ready to flow between turbans and beards!

She has tucked up her skirts in readiness.[58]

The time for attack has come, so drive hard, war,
to whom night has brought a violent driver.

Masʿūdī place al-Ḥajjāj at ʿAbd al-Malik's court in Damascus at the time of his appointment.

54. Abū Zayd ʿUmar b. Shabbah, d. 264 (877); see Sezgin, *GAS*, I, 345.

55. The Ḥarūriyyah are the Khārijites, so called from their assembling against ʿAlī at Ḥarūrāʾ, near al-Kūfah; see text above, I, 3387–89; Mubarrad, *Kāmil*, 450; *EI*², s. v. Ḥarūrāʾ.

56. This most famous of all Umayyad orations is reproduced in a wide range of sources, with considerable variation in its order and structure; some authorities assign parts of it to a later parallel oration in al-Baṣrah. Relatively early versions include Ibn Aʿtham al-Kūfī, *Futūḥ*, VII, 5–10; Jāḥiẓ, *Bayān* (Cairo, 1956), II, 347–50; Ibn Qutaybah, *ʿUyūn al-akhbār* (Cairo, 1925), II, 243; Balādhurī, *Ansāb*, XI, 266ff.; Yaʿqūbī, *Taʾrīkh*, II, 326f.; Mubarrad, *Kāmil*, 215ff.; Ibn ʿAbd Rabbih, *ʿIqd*, V, 17–19; Masʿūdī, *Murūj*, V. 292–302; *Aghānī*¹, XI, 266ff. See also A. Ṣafwat, *Jamharat rasāʾil al-ʿarab* (Cairo, 1937), I, 274; Périer, *Vie d'al-Ḥadjdjādj*, 70ff.

57. Verse by Suḥaym b. Wathīl al-Riyāḥī, d. c. 40 (661); see Sezgin, *GAS*, II, 202f. Further verses in Aṣmaʿī, *Aṣmaʿiyyāt* (Cairo, 1964), 17–20, and *Aghānī*¹, XII, 13f. See also Ibn Aʿtham al-Kūfī, *Futūḥ*, VII, 5; Mubarrad, *Kāmil*, 215; Maydānī, *Amthāl*, I, 28.

58. A version of this proverb appears in Maydānī, *Amthāl*, II, 35, where "she" is glossed as "disaster" (*dāhiyah*).

No ordinary herder of sheep or camels he,
    nor a butcher working at his slaughter-board![59]

Night has brought them a harsh driver,
    mettlesome, well traveled in the desert,
    but a settled man, no bedouin he.[60]

It is not the time to despise the mixed herds
    that she has brought, or the young unbridled she-camels
    that scurry along like racing sand-grouse.[61]

By God, O people of Iraq, I cannot be squeezed like a fig, or abashed by rattling old waterskins at me.[62] I have been proven to be at the height of my vigor and have run the longest races. The Commander of the Faithful, ʿAbd al-Malik, has emptied out his quiver and tested the wood of his arrows;
[865] he found me the strongest and least likely to break, and thus aimed me at you. Long have you pursued a course of faction and followed the path of waywardness; but now, by God, I will bark you as one does a tree, hack you as one does a mimosa,[63] and beat you as one does a camel not of the herd at the watering-hole. By God, I do not make promises without fulfilling them, and I do not measure without cutting. I will see no more of these gatherings, with "it was said" and "he said" and "what does he say?"—what does all this have to do with you? By God, you will stay on the straight paths of the right, or else I will leave every man of you preoccupied with the state of his body. If I find any man from al-Muhallab's expedition still here after three days, I will spill his blood and seize his property.

---

59. Attributed variously to Ruwayshid b. Rumayḍ al-ʿAnazī, al-Ḥuṭam al-Qaysī, and Abū Zughbah al-Khazrajī. See Ibn Manẓūr, *Lisān al-ʿarab*, s.vv. ḥuṭam, waḍam; *Aghānī*[1], XIV, 44; Mubarrad, *Kāmil*, 215f. My translation conforms to the glosses given in the text below.

60. No attribution in the sources. Ibn Manẓūr, s.v. ʿaṣlab, glosses "them" as camels.

61. No attribution in the sources. For *sābiq*, "racing," some MSS read *sāʾiq*, "driver" (of a sand-grouse).

62. As is done to make camels run; see Maydānī, *Amthāl*, II, 191.

63. For the phrase, see Maydānī, *Amthāl*, II, 191.

Then he went into his residence, without saying anything more.

Another account: When al-Ḥajjāj stood a long time silently before speaking, Muḥammad b. ʿUmayr[64] took some pebbles and was going to pelt him with them, saying, "May God oppose him! Not only tongue-tied, but ugly, too; and I expect that what he has to say will match his appearance!" But when al-Ḥajjāj spoke, the pebbles began to spill from his hands without his even noticing. Al-Ḥajjāj said in his oration:

> Faces scowl because God has coined "a similitude: a village which was safe and secure, its sustenance coming to it in abundance from every side; but they were ungrateful for God's blessings, and God made them taste the garment of hunger and fear, because of what they had been doing."[65] You are like them, just the same! Obey your herdsman, and go straight, for, by God, I will make you taste abasement until you learn how, and hack you as one does a mimosa until you consent to be led. I swear by God, you shall embrace justice and leave off this seditious talk, with your "It was thus and thus," and "I was informed by So-and-so on the authority of So-and-so," and "The Cutting; what is the Cutting?"[66] I will give you a Cutting with the sword which will leave your [866] women widows and your children orphans—and that until you leave off these gossamer fantasies and give up all this "See here! See here!" Let me see no more of these gatherings. No man among you shall ride except alone. If rebels were allowed to get away with their insubordination, no spoil[67]

---

64. Presumably Muḥammad b. ʿUmayr b. ʿUṭārid al-Tamīmī, a former supporter of al-Mukhtār; see text above, II, 635. In the version of Mubarrad, *Kāmil*, 215, and others, however, the subject of this anecdote is ʿUmayr b. Ḍābiʾ al-Burjumī, who was subsequently al-Ḥajjāj's first victim in al-Kūfah, as related below, II, 869ff.

65. Qurʾān 16:112.

66. *Al-habr wa-mā al-habr*, perhaps imitating Qurʾānic phraseology (e.g., 101:1–2: *al-qāriʿah mā al-qāriʿah*), although *habr* does not occur in the Qurʾān. *Habr* refers to the cutting up of meat; Ṭabarī, glossarium, s.v., notes Ibn Manẓūr (*Lisān*, s.v.): *wa-fī ḥadīth al-shurāh fa-habarnāhum bi-l-suyūf* ("and in the *ḥadīth* [?] of the Khārijites, 'we sliced them up with swords.'").

67. *Fay'*, originally meaning "booty," but quickly shading off to "revenue." See *EI*², s.v. *fay'*; F. Løkkegaard, *Islamic Taxation in the Classic Period* (Copenhagen, 1950), 38ff.

would be collected and no enemy fought, and the frontiers would be unmanned; and were they not compelled by force to go out and fight, they would never do so voluntarily. I have heard how you defied al-Muhallab and came back to your garrison, mutinous rebels! I swear to you by God, if, after three days, I find any of you here, I will cut off his head!

Then he summoned the marshals (*'urafā'*)[68] and said to them, "Take the men to join al-Muhallab and bring me the vouchers of their arrival;[69] and let the gates of the bridge remain open night and day until this has been accomplished."

Commentary on the oration:[70] "Son of splendor" is the morning, because its splendor chases away the darkness. The "heights" are small promontories among the mountains. Fruit "ripens" when it reaches maturity. Where he says, "Drive, *ziyam*," *ziyam* is a word for war.[71] A "violent" person is one who destroys everything he encounters. A "slaughter-board" is what protects meat from touching the ground. A "harsh driver" is a severe one. The "desert" is a desolate land where one can hear the sound of the camels' steps. An "unbridled" camel is one without a head-rope, as in this line reported by Abū Zayd al-Aṣma'ī:[72]

Umm al-Fawāris rode the feisty, unbridled camel bareback,
spurring it on to a trot and a gallop.

"*Shinan*" is the plural of "*shannah*," meaning a worn-out, dried-up waterskin, as in this verse:[73]

You are like one of the camels of the Banū Uqaysh,

---

68. Sg. *'arīf*, officials responsible for pay and discipline of small units of men (originally ten). See *EI²*, s.v. 'arīf; Dozy, *Supplément*, s.v.; Fries, *Heereswesen*, 17f.

69. *Barā'āt*; see Ṭabarī, glossarium, s.v.; Dozy, *Supplément*, s.v.

70. This commentary is missing in some MSS, but appears, abridged, in Ibn al-Athīr, *Kāmil*, IV, 377. Mubarrad, *Kāmil*, 217ff., supplies rather different glosses.

71. Mubarrad glosses *ziyam* as (the name of) a horse or camel.

72. An error (?) for Abū Sa'īd al-Aṣma'ī, the famous philologist, d. 213 (828) (see *EI²*, s.v. al-Aṣma'ī), perhaps conflated here with his contemporary, Abū Zayd al-Anṣārī, d. 214–215 (830–831) (see *EI²*, s.v. Abū Zayd al-Anṣārī). The following verse is by Abū Du'ād al-Ru'āsī, fl. c. 81 (700); see Sezgin, *GAS*, II, 414; Ibn Manẓūr, *Lisān*, s.v. 'uluṭ.

73. Verse by al-Nābighah al-Dhubyānī, d. c. 602 A. D.; see Sezgin, *GAS*, II, 110f.; Mubarrad, *Kāmil*, 376; W. Ahlwardt, *The Divans of the Six Ancient Arabic Poets* (London, 1870), 30.

whom they frighten by rattling an old waterskin at its rump.

He "tested" (*'ajam*) the wood means he bit it; *'ajam* also means "grape-stone," as in this half-verse by al-A'shā:[74] [867]

Their new-cast young were like grape-stones scattered on the ground (?).

By the "strongest" wood he means the hardest; one says a rope is "strong" if it is tightly twisted. "I will hack you as one does a mimosa": "hacking" is cutting, and the mimosa is a kind of thorny tree. "I do not measure without cutting": "measuring" (*khalq*) is projecting, as in God's words, "From a sperm-drop, measured and not measured,"[75] that is, projected and not projected, meaning those which come to term and those which miscarry. Al-Kumayt[76] said, describing a waterskin:

Which no women measuring undertook to cut out,
and from whose interior no stream of water poured.

Here he is actually describing the gizzards of birds, saying they are not like such a waterskin. Also, a "measured" (*khalqā'*) stone is a smooth one, as in this verse:[77]

And a broad chest above swaying legs,
like a measured stone used as a sliding area for children to play on.

One says "I cut (*faraytu*) the hide" if he makes something of it; but if one uses the fourth form of the verb "cut" (*afraytu*), he means he spoils it. "Gossamer fantasies" means what is untrue. Abū 'Amr al-Shaybānī[78] said this word originally meant what the

74. Al-A'shā Maymūn, d. after 5 (625); see *EI²*, s. v. al-A'shā. Variants of this verse appear in Mubarrad, *Kāmil*, 219; Al-A'shā, *Dīwān* (ed. Geyer, GMS, n. s. VI), no. IV, line 25.

75. Qur'ān 22:5. "Projecting" is *taqdīr*.

76. D. 126–127 (743–744); see *EI²*, s. v. al-Kumayt. For the verse (with variant), see *Die Hāšimijjāt des Kumait*, ed. and trans. J. Horovitz (Leiden, 1904), no. III, line 123.

77. Verse by Imru' al-Qays, d. c. A.D. 550; see *EI²*, s. v. Imru' al-Qays b. Ḥudjr. The verse, with variants, is in Ahlwardt, *Divans*, 118.

78. D. c. 213 (828); see *EI¹*, s. v. al-Shaibānī.

common people call "Satan's snot," that is, the "sun's drool" or gossamer, which appears at midday. Abū al-Najm al'Ijlī[79] said:

The sun's drool flowed and covered things,
    and the balance of time stood in equilibrium.

"Gatherings" are groups of people. End of commentary.

[868] According to Abū Ja'far[80]—'Umar—Muḥammad b. Yaḥyā—'Abdallāh b. Abī 'Ubaydah: On the third day, al-Ḥajjāj heard "God is Great" (*takbīr*)[81] pronounced in the market, and went out and took his seat in the pulpit and said:

> O people of Iraq! O people of faction and hypocrisy, and of vicious morals! I have heard a *takbīr*—not a *takbīr* meant to inspire devotion to God, but rather a *takbīr* meant to inspire fear; and I know that this is a dust cloud with a violent wind behind it. Sons of slatterns! Slaves of the rod![82] Scions of husbandless women! Is there not a man among you who will take into account his lameness,[83] value his life, and watch his step? I swear by God, I am on the point of dealing you a blow that will serve as a punishment for those who come before and an example for those who come after!

When he says a "violent wind" he means a strong gale. A "slattern" is a foolish woman, that is, a brutish servant girl. "Lameness" is weakness and fatigue from too much walking.

In the line "Which scurry along like racing sand-grouse," *ghuṭāṭ*, with a *u*, is a kind of bird.[84] On the other hand, al-Aṣma'ī said that the *ghaṭāṭ*, with an *a*, is a kind of bird, citing this line by Ḥassān b. Thābit:[85]

---

79. D. after 105 (724); see *EI²*, s. v. Abū al-Nadjm al-'Idjlī.

80. Al-Ṭabarī.

81. The expression *Allāhu akbar* ("God is great!"), enunciated at the beginning of prayer, but also as a call to attack; see A. Noth, *Quellenkritische Studien zur Themen, Formen und Tendenzen frühislamischer Geschichtsüberlieferung* (Bonn, 1973), I, 128f.

82. For the story behind this proverbial expression of contempt, see Maydānī, *Amthāl*, I, 424.

83. That is, acknowledge his limitations; see Maydānī, *Amthāl*, I, 268.

84. The commentary reverts here to al-Ḥajjāj's previous speech.

85. D. c. 40 (659); see *EI²*, s. v. Ḥassān b. Thābit. The *Diwan of Ḥassān b. Thābit* (ed. 'Arafat, GMS, n. s. XXV), no. 13, line 12, reads *sawād*, "crowd," for *ghaṭāṭ*.

They are visited so often that their dogs do not whine;
they are undisturbed by a hubbub of approaching sand-grouse—

with *ghaṭāṭ* with an *a*. Then he said that *ghuṭāṭ* with a *u* is the mixture of light and darkness at the end of the night, as in this [869] *rajaz* verse:

He rose and went to a dusky lady at daybreak,
walking along with what looked like a tent-upright.

End of commentary.

Then ʿUmayr b. Ḍābiʾ al-Tamīmī al-Ḥanẓalī[86] came to al-Ḥajjāj and said, "May God be gracious to the amīr! I am a member of this expedition, but I am an old man, and sick. Here is my son; he has more vigor than I." Al-Ḥajjāj said, "And who are you?" He said, "I am ʿUmayr b. Ḍābiʾ al-Tamīmī." Al-Ḥajjāj said, "Did you hear what I said yesterday?" He said, "Yes." Al-Ḥajjāj said, "Was it not you who attacked the Commander of the Faithful ʿUthmān?" He said, "Yes, it was." Al-Ḥajjāj asked, "What impelled you to do that?" He said, "He had imprisoned my father, who was an old man." Al-Ḥajjāj said, "And wasn't it he who said this verse:

I meant to do it, but I didn't—I was about to—and would that I had!—
left ʿUthmān's wives weeping over him!

It seems to me that killing you would be a service to the two garrisons. Take him, guards, and strike off his head!" One of the men approached and struck off his head. His property was also seized.[87]

According to one account, ʿAnbasah b. Saʿīd[88] said to al-Ḥajjāj, "Do you know who this is?" He said, "No." ʿAnbasah said, "This

---

86. Ḥanẓalah is a clan of Tamīm. In the variant of this story given below, the man is called al-Burjumī; the Barājim were a subclan of Ḥanẓalah. See Ibn Ḥazm, *Jamharah*, 211f.

87. On this incident, see text above, I, 3033–36, 3048; Ibn Aʿtham al-Kūfī, *Futūḥ*, VII, 11–14; Balādhurī, *Ansāb*, IVA, 575–77, and XI, 272, 274f.; Mubarrad, *Kāmil*, 217, 219f., 665f.; Masʿūdī, *Murūj*, V, 298; *Aghānī*[1], XIII, 42; Ibn al-Athīr, *Kāmil*, IV, 377–79; Ibn Kathīr, *Bidāyah*, IX, 9.

88. An intimate of al-Ḥajjāj; see Balādhurī, *Ansāb*, IVA, 453, and XI, 274f.

is one of the murderers of the Commander of the Faithful 'Uthmān." Then al-Ḥajjāj said, "O enemy of God, you did not
[870] send a substitute on your expedition against the Commander of the Faithful, did you?" and ordered his head struck off. Then he ordered a herald to proclaim through the town, "Hear ye! 'Umayr b. Ḍābi', having heard the proclamation, has come after the third day, and we have ordered his execution. Hear ye! God's protection is withdrawn from any member of al-Muhallab's forces who spends this night in the town." At this, the men began to move out, and there was soon a crowd at the bridge. The marshals went to al-Muhallab, who was at Rāmhurmuz, and took from him letters vouching for their arrival. Al-Muhallab said, "Today a real man has come to Iraq, and from today the enemy will see what battle is."

According to the account of Ibn Abī 'Ubaydah, four thousand men of the tribe of Madhḥij crossed the bridge that night. Then al-Muhallab said, "Today a real man has come to Iraq."

According to 'Umar—Abū al-Ḥasan: When al-Ḥajjāj had 'Abd al-Malik's letter read out to the men, the reader began, "After a greeting of peace, I praise God to you." Al-Ḥajjāj said, "Stop! O slaves of the rod, when the Commander of the Faithful gives you a greeting of peace, does no one among you return the greeting? These are the manners of Ibn Nihyah![89] By God, I swear I will teach you better manners than these! Start the letter again!" This time, when he reached the words "After a greeting of peace," every one of them without exception responded, "And upon the Commander of the Faithful be peace and God's mercy!"

According to 'Umar—'Abd al-Malik b. Shaybān b. 'Abd al-Malik b. Misma'—'Amr b. Sa'īd: When al-Ḥajjāj arrived in al-Kūfah, he addressed the men and said, "You are deserters from al-Muhallab's army! Let not a single man from his forces remain here after three days!" After the three days had passed, a man came to him with blood dripping from his head. Al-Ḥajjāj asked him, "Who did this to you?" He said, "'Umayr b. Ḍābi' al-Bur-
[871] jumī. I ordered him to go out to his camp, but he was incensed and struck me."[90] Al-Ḥajjāj sent for 'Umayr b. Ḍābi', and he was

89. According to a gloss on Mubarrad's *Kāmil*, 216, Ibn Nihyah was a former head of the *shurṭah* in al-Baṣrah; see also Mas'ūdī, *Murūj*, V, 298.

90. *Fa-ḍarabanī wa-kadhaba 'alayhi.*

brought in, an old man. Al-Ḥajjāj asked him, "What kept you away from your camp?" He said, "I am an old man, without vigor; so I sent my son as a substitute, since he is both stronger and younger than me. Ask around to see if what I say is true; if it is not, then punish me." But ʿAnbasah b. Saʿīd said, "This is the man who went up to ʿUthmān's corpse and slapped his face, then jumped on it and broke two of his ribs." Al-Ḥajjāj then ordered him executed, and this was carried out.

ʿAmr b. Saʿīd said: By God, while I was on my way between al-Kūfah and al-Ḥīrah, I heard the chant of some Muḍarite camel-drivers.[91] I turned to meet them and asked, "What news?" They said, "A man came to us from the foulest of the tribes of the Arabs, that tribe descended from Thamūd.[92] He had spindly legs, and no flesh on his buttocks, and he was bleary-eyed.[93] He took the chief of the tribe, ʿUmayr b. Ḍābiʾ, and he struck off his head."

When al-Ḥajjāj executed ʿUmayr b. Ḍābiʾ, Ibrāhīm b. ʿĀmir, who was one of the Banū Ghāḍirah of the Banū Asad, met ʿAbdallāh b. al-Zabīr[94] in the market and asked him about the news. Ibn al-Zabīr said:

Meeting Ibrāhīm, I say to him,
'I see things have become difficult and complicated.
Get ready, get going, and catch up with the army! I see
no alternative to the army but perdition.
Take your choice! You must either visit Ibn Ḍābiʾ [872]
ʿUmayr, or else visit al-Muhallab.

91. *Samiʿtu rajazan Muḍariyyan;* see Ṭabarī, glossarium, s.v. rajaz. The Muḍar tribal grouping included Tamīm.

92. That is, the tribe of Thaqīf, frequently derided for their uncertain ancestry. For traditions linking Thaqīf to the semi-legendary Thamūd, whose destruction by God is described in the Qurʾān, see I. Goldziher, *Muhammedanische Studien* (Halle, 1888–90), I, 99f. Al-Ḥajjāj is reported to have responded to such accusations by appealing to Qurʾān 53:51, *wa-Thamūda fa-mā abqā,* misinterpreting this as "Thamūd, and what (of them) He preserved" and arguing that only the best of them would have been so preserved; al-Ḥasan al-Baṣrī, however, countered with the correct interpretation, "Thamūd, and He did not preserve (them)." See *Aghānī*[1], IV, 74; Mubarrad, *Kāmil,* 266; Périer, *Vie d'al-Ḥadjdjādj,* 2.

93. Compare the unflattering descriptions in Masʿūdī, *Murūj,* V, 289, 327f.

94. On this poet, see Sezgin, *GAS,* II, 329f.; the following verses, with numerous variants, appear also in Ibn Aʿtham al-Kūfī, *Futūḥ,* VII, 13f.; Balādhurī, *Ansāb,* XI, 272; Mubarrad, *Kāmil,* 217, 666; Masʿūdī, *Murūj,* V, 300f.; *Aghānī*[1], XIII, 42; Ibn al-Athīr, *Kāmil,* IV, 379.

Faced with these two disagreeable courses, your only salvation is
to ride off on a snowy-gray one-year-old.'
In such circumstances, were he required to ride to Khurāsān,
it would seem as near as the market, or yet nearer!
And how many a flabby man you see now, forced to ride,
who has become so intimate with the bend of the saddle that he is hunch-backed.

It is reported that al-Ḥajjāj's arrival in al-Kūfah was in the month of Ramaḍān of this year (December 694–January 695).[95] He sent out al-Ḥakam b. Ayyūb al-Thaqafī as amīr in charge of al-Baṣrah and ordered him to treat Khālid b. ʿAbdallāh harshly.[96] When word of this reached Khālid, he left al-Baṣrah before al-Ḥakam entered it, and went to al-Jalḥā'.[97] The men of al-Baṣrah turned out to see him off, and Khālid did not leave his place of prayer (*muṣallā*) until he had distributed a million dirhams among them.[98]

[873] According to Aḥmad b. Thābit—anonymous—Isḥāq b. ʿĪsā—Abū Maʿshar: The leader of the pilgrimage in this year was ʿAbd al-Malik b. Marwān.[99] In this year, Yaḥyā b. al-Ḥakam went to ʿAbd al-Malik b. Marwān, leaving Abān b. ʿUthmān as his deputy in charge of Medina; but ʿAbd al-Malik ordered Yaḥyā b. al-Ḥakam to continue in his position as governor of Medina.[100] Al-

95. This statement is contradicted by the text below, II, 874, 944, which implies that al-Ḥajjāj arrived in Rajab (October–November 694), as stated explicitly by Ibn Khayyāṭ, *Ta'rīkh*, 295f., and Balādhurī, *Ansāb*, XI, 269f.

96. Ibn Khayyāṭ, *Ta'rīkh*, 295; Balādhurī, *Ansāb*, V, 179; Ibn al-Athīr, *Kāmil*, IV, 379; Ibn Kathīr, *Bidāyah*, IX, 9. Balādhurī, *Ansāb*, XI, 275, however, puts al-Ḥakam's appointment after al-Ḥajjāj's own arrival in al-Baṣrah.

97. A place on the pilgrim road from al-Kūfah, some 140 miles south of the latter; see A. Musil, *Northern Neğd* (New York, 1928), 206f., 210, 235, and references there.

98. A *muṣallā* is a large open space reserved for collective prayers on certain formal occasions; see *EI*[1], s.v. muṣallā. On Khālid's *muṣallā*, see text above, II, 628, and below, II, 1704; L. Massignon, "Explication du plan de Kufa," *Mélanges Maspéro*, III (1935–40), 336, places it on the western edge of the town. Khālid apparently distributed the local treasury to the populace or resident troops, before it could fall into the hands of al-Ḥajjāj; perhaps the intention of this assertion is to justify al-Ḥajjāj's subsequent rescinsion of the troops' pay increase (see below). This anonymous report is not confirmed by other sources.

99. Ibn Khayyāṭ, *Ta'rīkh*, 301; Yaʿqūbī, *Ta'rīkh*, II, 327, 336; Ibn Kathīr, *Bidāyah*, IX, 9.

100. Ibn Khayyāṭ, *Ta'rīkh*, 294, 299. On Abān b. ʿUthmān, son of the third

Ḥajjāj b. Yūsuf was in charge of al-Kūfah and al-Baṣrah; Umayyah b. 'Abdallāh was in charge of Khurāsān; Shurayḥ was in charge of the judiciary of al-Kūfah; and Zurārah b. Awfā was in charge of the judiciary of al-Baṣrah.[101]

In this year, al-Ḥajjāj left al-Kūfah for al-Baṣrah, appointing Abū Ya'fūr 'Urwah b. al-Mughīrah b. Shu'bah as his deputy over al-Kūfah;[102] the latter remained in this position until al-Ḥajjāj returned to al-Kūfah after the battle of Rustaqubādh.

In this year, the men rebelled against al-Ḥajjāj in al-Baṣrah.

The Revolt of the Baṣran Troops against al-Ḥajjāj

According to Hishām—Abū Mikhnaf—Abū Zuhayr al-'Absī: Al-Ḥajjāj b. Yūsuf left al-Kūfah immediately after arriving and having Ibn Ḍābi' executed, and went on to al-Baṣrah. There he gave an oration like the one he had given to the Kūfans, threatening them in the same way. A man of the Banū Yashkur[103] was brought to him, accused of desertion. The man said, "I have a hernia, and Bishr saw it and exempted me; and you will find that my stipend has been returned to the treasury." But al-Ḥajjāj did not accept his excuse and had him killed. This alarmed the [874]
Baṣrans, and they began to pour out of the town, descending in throngs on the reviewer[104] at the bridge at Rāmhurmuz. Then al-Muhallab said, "A real man has come to the troops."

Al-Ḥajjāj went out to Rustaqubādh, where he arrived at the beginning of Sha'bān 75 (late November 694).[105] Led by 'Abdallāh b. al-Jārūd, the men rebelled against al-Ḥajjāj. Al-Ḥajjāj had

---

caliph, see Balādhurī, *Ansāb*, IVA, 617f.; *EI²*, s.v. Abān b. 'Uthmān. He was appointed governor the following year; see text below, II, 940.

101. Zurārah b. Awfā al-Ḥarashī, d. 93 (711–712); see Ibn Sa'd, *Ṭabaqāt*, VII, i, 109 (reading 93 for 73).

102. Other reports in Ibn Khayyāṭ, *Ta'rīkh*, 296, make the deputy Ḥawshab b. Ruwaym al-Shaybānī, who was head of the *shurṭah*, according to the text below, II, 918; see also Ibn al-Athīr, *Kāmil*, IV, 380.

103. His name was Sharīk b. 'Amr; see Balādhurī, *Ansāb*, XI, 275f.; Ibn al-Athīr, *Kāmil*, IV, 381. He is called Dhū al-Kursufah ("man with the eye-patch") by Mubarrad, *Kāmil*, 666.

104. *'Āriḍ*; see *EI²*, s.v. isti'rāḍ.

105. Rustaqubādh is the later 'Askar Mukram, some ninety miles northeast of al-Baṣrah and sixty-five miles northwest of Rāmhurmuz; see *EI²*, s.v. 'Askar Mukram; Le Strange, *Lands*, 237.

ʿAbdallāh b. al-Jārūd killed and sent eighteen heads to be set up before the men in Rāmhurmuz. This stiffened the backs of the Muslims, and the Khārijites, who had been hoping that there would be conflict and factionalism among the men, were disappointed. Then al-Ḥajjāj returned to al-Baṣrah.

The reason behind this affair with ʿAbdallāh b. al-Jārūd is as follows:[106] When al-Ḥajjāj ordered the troops in al-Baṣrah to join al-Muhallab, and they set off, al-Ḥajjāj himself went as far as Rustaqubādh, which is near Dastawā;[107] this was at the end of Shaʿbān (late December 694). He had with him the elite of the Baṣran forces. He and al-Muhallab were about eighteen *farsakhs*[108] apart. Then al-Ḥajjāj stood before the men and said, "The increase in your stipends that Ibn al-Zubayr granted you is the increase of a sinner and hypocrite,[109] and I will not sanction it." Then ʿAbdallāh b. al-Jārūd al-ʿAbdī[110] approached him and said, "It is not the increase of a sinner and hypocrite, but the increase of the Commander of the Faithful ʿAbd al-Malik, who confirmed that we should have it." When al-Ḥajjāj called him a liar and threatened him, Ibn al-Jārūd rebelled against him, followed by the elite of the forces. Severe fighting broke out, and al-Ḥajjāj killed Ibn al-Jārūd and a group of his companions. He sent Ibn al-Jārūd's head and those of ten of his companions to al-Muhallab, and himself went back to al-Baṣrah.[111] He then wrote

106. This is a different version of the rebellion from that just given, as is clear from variants in detail.

107. A town in the district of al-Ahwāz; see Yāqūt, *Muʿjam,* II, 574.

108. A *farsakh* is about six kilometers; see *EI*², s.v. farsakh.

109. *Fāsiq munāfiq.* These are specific theological terms, the status of the *fāsiq* being one of the primary points of contention among various groups at this time; to Khārijites a *fāsiq* was an unbeliever (*kāfir*), while the view that he was a hypocrite is attributed to al-Ḥasan al-Baṣrī. See *EI*², s.v. *fāsiḳ;* Watt, *Formative Period,* 17, 80.

110. ʿAbdallāh b. al-Jārūd (Bishr) belonged to the tribe of ʿAbd al-Qays of Rabīʿah; see Caskel, *Ǧamharat an-nasab,* I, 141, 169, and II, 109.

111. Much more detailed than these two brief accounts of Ibn al-Jārūd's rebellion is that of Balādhurī, *Ansāb,* XI, 277–94. According to the latter, when al-Ḥajjāj's first proposal to cancel Muṣʿab b. al-Zubayr's doubling of the men's stipends met resistance, he temporized for some months before attempting again to impose it. The rebellion broke out only in Rabīʿ II 76 (July–August 695), and al-Ḥajjāj was very hard pressed until dissension arose among the rebels and appreciable numbers returned to his side. Balādhurī agrees with Ṭabarī's first account that Ibn al-Jārūd and eighteen others were killed. See also Ibn Khayyāṭ, *Taʾrīkh,* 269;

to al-Muhallab and to ʿAbd al-Raḥmān b. Mikhnaf, saying: "When this letter reaches you, move against the Khārijites. Peace." [875]

In this year, al-Muhallab and Ibn Mikhnaf expelled the Azraqites from Rāmhurmuz.

Al-Muhallab and the War against the Azraqites

According to Hishām—Abū Mikhnaf—Abū Zuhayr al-ʿAbsī: Al-Muhallab and Ibn Mikhnaf moved against the Azraqites in Rāmhurmuz, in accordance with the letter of al-Ḥajjāj to them, on Monday, 19 Shaʿbān 75 (December 13, 694).[112] They ejected them from Rāmhurmuz without much fighting, advancing slowly against them and driving them off. The Azraqite forces retreated as if they were the rearguard of a defeated army, and moved to a region of Sābūr called Kāzarūn.[113] Al-Muhallab and ʿAbd al-Raḥmān b. Mikhnaf then set out after them and encamped opposite them on 1 Ramaḍān (December 25). Al-Muhallab had a defensive trench dug. According to the Baṣrans, al-Muhallab said to ʿAbd al-Raḥmān b. Mikhnaf, "If you think you should dig a defensive trench, then do so;" but ʿAbd al-Raḥmān's forces disdained to do so, saying, "Our trench is our swords." The Azraqites crept up on al-Muhallab by night, hoping to take him by surprise, only to find that he had taken precautions. They then turned instead to ʿAbd al-Raḥmān b. Mikhnaf, and, discovering that he had not dug a trench, attacked him. As his forces were driven back, he joined in the fray with a group of them, but was killed together with those around him. The Khārijite poet said:

Whose camp is this, adorned with fallen men,
    a mass of corpses?

Ibn Qutaybah, *Maʿārif* (Cairo, 1969), 338f.; Balādhurī, *Ansāb*, V, 271, 280 (Muṣʿab's decision to pay the stipends twice a year), and *Futūḥ*, 281; Masʿūdī, *Murūj*, V, 298–302; Ibn al-Athīr, *Kāmil*, IV, 380–86; Ibn Kathīr, *Bidāyah*, IX, 10; Périer, *Vie d'al-Ḥadjdjādj*, 81–86; A. A. Dixon, *The Umayyad Caliphate* (London, 1971), 143–47; R. Sayed, *Die Revolte des Ibn al-Ašʿaṯ und die Koranleser* (Freiburg, 1977), 129f.

112. Sunday.

113. In Fārs, some sixty miles west of Shīrāz. Kāzarūn town supplanted Sābūr town (Shāpūr, Bishāpūr), for which the district was named, in the fourth (tenth) century. See *EI²*, s.v. Kāzarūn; Le Strange, *Lands*, 262, 266f.

See how the wind scatters coarse sand over them,
they who had trailed their garments in their pride!

[876] The account of the Kūfans: Al-Ḥajjāj's letter came to al-Muhallab and ʿAbd al-Raḥmān b. Mikhnaf, saying: "Move against the Khārijites when my letter reaches you." They moved against them on Wednesday, 20 Ramaḍān 75 (January 12, 695),[114] and met them with fighting as intense as any between them previously. This was shortly after midday. The Khārijites threw all their strength against al-Muhallab b. Abī Ṣufrah and drove him back into his camp. He hurriedly sent off some of his trusted men to ʿAbd al-Raḥmān, and they came to him and said, "Al-Muhallab says to you: Our enemy is one, and you can see what the Muslims are up against; so send reinforcements to your brethren, God's mercy on you." ʿAbd al-Raḥmān began to send him reinforcements of both cavalry and infantry, a group at a time. By late afternoon, the Khārijites, seeing the cavalry and infantry coming from ʿAbd al-Raḥmān's camp to al-Muhallab's camp, and surmising that ʿAbd al-Raḥmān's forces would be depleted, put five or six detachments[115] opposite al-Muhallab's camp, while the rest went off all together to ʿAbd al-Raḥmān b. Mikhnaf. When the latter saw them drawn up against him, he went out to oppose them, having with him the Qur'ān-reciters,[116] led by Abū al-Aḥwaṣ,[117] the companion of ʿAbdallāh b. Masʿūd,[118] and Khuzaymah b. Naṣr,[119] the father of Naṣr b. Khuzaymah al-ʿAbsī, who was killed with Zayd b. ʿAlī and gibbeted with him in al-Kūfah.[120] Also with ʿAbd al-Raḥmān were seventy-one of his own picked men.

---

114. Tuesday.

115. Sg. *katībah.* See *WKAS,* s.v.; Fries, *Heereswesen,* 41.

116. *Qurrāʾ,* here translated according to the traditional interpretation. For the controversies over the identity of this political interest group, and M. A. Shaban's reinterpretation of the term as "villagers," see M. A. Shaban, *Islamic History* (Cambridge, 1971), I, 50ff., 67f., 103ff.; *EI²*, s.v. ḳurrāʾ; R. Sayed, *Die Revolte des Ibn al-Ašʿat̲,* ch. V (arguing for the traditional interpretation); and further literature cited in these discussions.

117. On him, see Ibn Saʿd, *Ṭabaqāt,* VI, 126.

118. The famous Companion and Qur'ān-reader, d. 32 (652–653); see *EI²*, s.v. Ibn Masʿūd.

119. A former supporter of al-Mukhtār; see text above, II, 625f. He belonged to the Banū ʿAbs of Ghaṭafān of Qays ʿAylān; see *EI²*, s.v. Ghaṭafān.

120. In 122 (740); see text below, II, 1703–11.

The Khārijites attacked them and engaged them in heavy fighting. But ʿAbd al-Raḥmān's forces fell back, leaving him with a [877] small band of stalwart men who held their ground with him. His son Jaʿfar b. ʿAbd al-Raḥmān, who had been among those he had sent to al-Muhallab, called on the forces to follow him to his father's aid, but only a few did; he approached his father, but the Khārijites kept him from reaching him, and he fought until the Khārijites wounded him and he was forced to withdraw from the battle. ʿAbd al-Raḥmān b. Mikhnaf and those with him fought on, on a commanding hill, through some two-thirds of the night, until he was killed amidst his companions.[121]

The next morning, al-Muhallab came and found him, and buried him and prayed over him. He wrote to inform al-Ḥajjāj of his death, and al-Ḥajjāj wrote to inform ʿAbd al-Malik b. Marwān, who received the news at Minā[122] and blamed the Kūfans. Al-Ḥajjāj then sent out ʿAttāb b. Warqāʾ[123] to take command of ʿAbd al-Raḥmān b. Mikhnaf's forces, and ordered him, if he joined with al-Muhallab in battle, to heed and obey him. ʿAttāb was unhappy about this but saw no alternative to obeying al-Ḥajjāj, being unable to get him to reconsider. He went to join the army and fought the Khārijites as al-Muhallab's subordinate, but proceeded to act virtually without consulting al-Muhallab on anything. Seeing this, al-Muhallab picked out some men from among the Kūfans, one of whom was Bisṭām b. Maṣqalah b. Hubayrah, and incited them against ʿAttāb.

According to Abū Mikhnaf—Yūsuf b. Yazīd: ʿAttāb came to al-

---

121. Other sources do not reflect the sharp conflict here between Baṣran and Kūfan accounts of this battle. Ibn Aʿtham al-Kūfī, *Futūḥ*, VII, 17, reports that al-Muhallab marched from Rāmhurmuz to Arrajān, where he spent three days, and then on to Sābūr, where he spent three years; and although he gives a far more detailed account of the fighting in Sābūr than does Ṭabarī (see text below, II, 1003ff.), he does not mention ʿAbd al-Raḥmān b. Mikhnaf. Mubarrad, *Kāmil*, 667–70, combines elements of both of Ṭabarī's accounts, mentioning first a day battle in which al-Muhallab received reinforcements from ʿAbd al-Raḥmān, and then a night attack on the latter, who had refused to entrench himself. Ibn al-Athīr, *Kāmil*, IV, 388f., essentially summarizes Ṭabarī.

122. Outside Mecca, site of pilgrimage rites; see *EI*², s.v. ḥadjdj. ʿAbd al-Malik performed the pilgrimage in this year; see text above, II, 873, and below, II, 881.

123. At this time governor of Iṣfahān, where he had already fought the Azraqites; see text above, II, 762–64. He belonged to the Banū Riyāḥ b. Yarbūʿ b. Ḥanẓalah of Tamīm; see Caskel, *Ǧamharat an-nasab*, I, 68, II, 205.

Muhallab to ask him to provision his men. Al-Muhallab seated ʿAttāb next to himself;[124] but when ʿAttāb asked him to provision
[878] his men, he did so in a brusque and frowning manner. Al-Muhallab retorted, "Remember where you are, you son of an uncircumcised woman!" The Banū Tamīm assert that ʿAttāb returned the insult, while Yūsuf b. Yazīd and others maintain that he said, "By God, she is a woman of noble lineage on both sides, and I rejoice that God has made a distinction between you and me." They exchanged words until al-Muhallab went to raise his staff against him; at this, his son al-Mughīrah jumped up and seized the staff, saying, "May God cause the amīr to prosper! This is one of the noble and eminent figures among the tribesmen. If you hear something from him that displeases you, put up with it from him, for indeed he merits that from you." Al-Muhallab heeded him.

ʿAttāb rose and left him, but was then confronted by Bisṭām b. Maṣqalah, who assailed him with insults and slander. In view of all this, ʿAttāb wrote to al-Ḥajjāj to complain of al-Muhallab, informing him that he had incited against him some insolent men from the garrison, and requesting that he recall him. This came at a time when al-Ḥajjāj was in need of him because of the troubles the notables of al-Kūfah were encountering with Shabīb; so he sent to him, saying, "Come, and leave the command of that army to al-Muhallab." Al-Muhallab then put Ḥabīb b. al-Muhallab in command of it.[125]

---

124. *Ajlasahu al-Muhallab maʿahu ʿalā majlisihi.*

125. The tribal rivalries behind this story are rather clearer in the somewhat divergent version in Mubarrad, *Kāmil*, 675–77. According to the latter, it was al-Ḥajjāj who sent ʿAttāb to al-Muhallab, stipulating that the supreme command should depend on whether the Kūfans or Baṣrans had originally conquered the area of operations; because Baṣrans had conquered Sābūr, al-Muhallab retained ultimate authority. When al-Ḥajjāj recalled ʿAttāb to face Shabīb (see text below, II, 940), he ordered al-Muhallab to provision the armies, but the latter refused provisions to the Kūfans. In the subsequent quarrel, the Tamīm of al-Baṣrah supported ʿAttāb, their tribesman, while the Azd of al-Kūfah supported the Azdī al-Muhallab, as did their allies the Bakr. Bisṭām b. Maṣqalah was a Shaybānī (see text above, II, 773—the Banū Shaybān were a tribe of Bakr); Yūsuf b. Yazīd and Abū Mikhnaf belonged to the Banū Azd. Mubarrad states explicitly that al-Muhallab relented and provisioned the Kūfans, after his son al-Mughīrah intervened. Mubarrad's account dates ʿAttāb's stay with al-Muhallab from one of the Jumādās 76 (August–October 695) into 77 (696–697), placing it after that of al-Barāʾ b. Qabīṣah

Verses by Ḥumayd b. Muslim,[126] elegizing ʿAbd al-Raḥmān b. Mikhnaf:

If they killed you early in the morning, Abū Ḥakīm,
many a valiant man had you attacked and killed in your time.
And if they have deprived us of a true chief chosen by his people,
a man of noble character, bountiful and generous,
A murder like this has crushed your people, all of them—
one who used to bear their burdens for them,
One who used to settle their obligations, and their fighting,
on a day when the fighting was close and fierce.
I swear, he received no mortal wound
until he had already donned a breastplate of blood.
Under his banner the heroes exchanged blows, [879]
their Mashrafī swords in their hands,
Through a long day, and on to the end of the night,
when they saw a crescent moon appear in the sky;
Then the lines of infantry and his cavalry were driven back from him,
And there the spears found him and he faltered.

Verses by Surāqah b. Mirdās al-Bāriqī:[127]

Be generous, my eyes, with your flowing tears,
like a torn old waterskin carried by a rider,
Over Azd, the best of whom have been struck down—
wail for a miserable existence after that!
We try to go on after losing them, but are hindered
by the obstacles of death and clashing detachments.
Before Ibn Mikhnaf was killed, our condition was good,
but every man one day must meet his fate some way.
He has brought tears to the eyes of the white-haired old men of his garrison,

(see text below, II, 1004) and al-Jarrāḥ b. ʿAbdallāh (not mentioned by Ṭabarī in this context). Ibn Aʿtham al-Kūfī does not mention ʿAttāb at all.

126. This man appears frequently in Ṭabarī as an authority for Abū Mikhnaf's authorities, but is otherwise unknown; see U. Sezgin, *Abū Mih̲naf*, 218.

127. D. c. 80 (699); see Sezgin, *GAS*, II, 327f. The poet was an Azdī.

and brought white to the locks of the young men before its time.
He fought on until he died the noblest of deaths,
and fell to the dust on a noble cheek and brow.
Fighting off the rebels around him was a band
of men of Azd, brandishing sharp swords.
May no woman ever give birth, and may no absent one return
to his people, so long as he cannot return.
[880] So weep, my eye, for Mikhnaf and Ibn Mikhnaf,
and for the horsemen of my people, my relatives near and distant.

Another elegy of ʿAbd al-Raḥmān b. Mikhnaf by Surāqah:

The chief of the two Azds, Azd Shanū'ah and Azd ʿUmān,
has found his last rest, the pledge of a grave in Kāzir.[128]
He fought on until he died the noblest of deaths,
with a keen, cutting sword, flashing like lightning.
And about that hill, under his banner, were felled
those of a noble company who nobly fought.
Ibn Mikhnaf lost his life on the day of that encounter,
when all the weak and uncaring abandoned him.
He sent support, but did not receive it; and he went to God
with his robe tucked up for battle, not dressed in the garb of a traitor.

Al-Muhallab remained at Sābūr, fighting the Khārijites, for about a year.[129]

In this year, Ṣāliḥ b. Musarriḥ, one of the Banū Imru' al-Qays,[130] revolted openly. He held the opinions of the Ṣufriyyah, and it is said that he was the first of the Ṣufriyyah to rebel.[131]

---

128. On the two Azds, who united in al-Baṣrah, see *EI*², s.v. Azd. Kāzir is poetic license for Kāzirūn (or Kāzarūn).

129. Three years in Ibn Aʿtham al-Kūfī (see note 121 above); eighteen months in Mubarrad, *Kāmil*, 677.

130. The Banū Imru' al-Qays were a subtribe of Tamīm.

131. The beginnings of the Ṣufriyyah, and the origin of their name, are unclear. Among Khārijite subsects they are considered moderates, in particular for their rejection of *istiʿrāḍ* (indiscriminate massacre of their enemies; see note 157 below) and of condemnation of the children of unbelievers, both in contrast to the Azraqites. Al-Ashʿarī, *Maqālāt al-islāmiyyīn* (Wiesbaden, 1963), 101, 118, makes them

The Rebellious Activities of Ṣāliḥ during This Year

Ṣāliḥ b. Musarriḥ, one of the Banū Imru' al-Qays, made the pilgrimage in the year 75 (March–April 695), accompanied by Shabīb [881] b. Yazīd, Suwayd, al-Baṭīn, and others like them. In this same year, 'Abd al-Malik b. Marwān made the pilgrimage,[132] and Shabīb determined to assassinate him. 'Abd al-Malik received some indication of their plans and wrote to al-Ḥajjāj after his departure, ordering him to hunt them down. Ṣāliḥ used to come to al-Kūfah for a month or so at a time, meeting his companions to put them in readiness;[133] but when al-Ḥajjāj began searching for him, al-Kūfah became uncongenial to Ṣāliḥ, and he avoided it.

---

the source of all doctrinal subbranches of the Khārijites except for the Azraqites, Najdites, and Ibāḍites. See also *EI*[1], s.v. al-Ṣufrīya; Watt, *Formative Period*, 25–34. Al-Ash'arī mentions Ṣāliḥ as a purported adherent of the Ṣufriyyah but remarks that he had no distinctive doctrines of his own. He otherwise refers to him only in the context of a schism not reflected in Ṭabarī's account (*Maqālāt*, 118, 120–22).

132. See text above, II, 873, 877.

133. I.e., for revolt: *li-yu'iddahum*; much less likely, *li-ya'idahum*, "to make promises to them." Some MSS read *li-yu'idda mā yaḥtāju ilayh*, "to prepare what he needed (for revolt)."

The Events of the Year 76

(April 21, 695–April 9, 696)

The Events of This Year

One of these was the rebellion of Ṣāliḥ b. Musarriḥ.[134]

The Rebellion of Ṣāliḥ b. Musarriḥ and the Reason for It

According to Hishām—Abū Mikhnaf—ʿAbdallāh b. ʿAlqa-

134. Ṣāliḥ's "rebellious activities" began at the end of the previous year with the abortive assassination plot against ʿAbd al-Malik, but his rebellion itself broke out only in this year. Three and a half months later Ṣāliḥ was killed, and the leadership of the movement taken over by Shabīb, who proved far more formidable. The next hundred pages of Ṭabarī's text are devoted almost exclusively to a detailed account of this revolt, based mainly on Abū Mikhnaf's *K. Shabīb al-Ḥarūrī wa-Ṣāliḥ b. Musarriḥ* (see U. Sezgin, *Abū Miḫnaf*, 82f., 109f.), with occasional supplementary information from other sources. Most of the other early sources available to us on Shabīb's rebellion ignore its beginning under Ṣāliḥ; for brief references to the latter, see Ibn Khayyāṭ, *Taʾrīkh*, 272; Ibn Qutaybah, *Maʿārif*, 410; Baghdādī, *Farq* (Cairo, 1910), 89 (two accounts, one dating the rebellion to the governorship of Bishr b. Marwān). Ibn al-Athīr, *Kāmil*, IV, 393–96, reproduces Ṭabarī. See also Périer, *Vie d'al-Ḥadjdjādj*, 109–15; Dixon, *Umayyad Caliphate*, 182ff.

mah[135]—Qabīṣah b. ʿAbd al-Raḥmān al-Khathʿamī: The reason for his rebellion is as follows: Ṣāliḥ b. Musarriḥ al-Tamīmī was an humble and pious man, sallow of mien,[136] and conscientious about his religious duties. He resided in Dārā[137] and the region of Mosul and the Jazīrah, where he had associates to whom he taught recitation of the Qur'ān and its interpretation[138] and delivered admonitory sermons.[139] Qabīṣah b. ʿAbd al-Raḥmān, who was one of those who subscribed to these people's opinions, told our companions[140] that he had possession of the sermon of Ṣāliḥ b. Musarriḥ; so they requested him to send them the text,[141] and [882]
he did so. This is his sermon:

> "Praise be to God, who created the heavens and the earth, and made the darkness and the light. Yet those who have disbelieved ascribe rivals to their Lord."[142] O God! We ascribe no rivals to You, we serve none but You, and none but You do we worship. Yours is the Creation and the Command, from You comes all benefit and harm, and to You is our destiny. We testify that Muḥammad is Your servant, whom You chose, and Your messenger, whom You selected and approved to convey Your messages and Your counsel for Your servants. We testify that he conveyed the message and counseled the community, summoned to the truth and acted equi-

---

135. D. 87 (706), the last of the Companions to die in al-Kūfah; see U. Sezgin, *Abū Mihnaf*, 191.

136. *Muṣfarr al-wajh*, perhaps rather "gaunt," in either case possibly because of an ascetic diet; see Ibn Manẓūr, *Lisān*, s.v. ṣafar, where one of the etymologies suggested for the Ṣufriyyah is the sallowness (*ṣufrah*) of their complexions.

137. Between Mardin and Nisibis; see *EI²*, s.v. Dārā; Le Strange, *Lands*, 96.

138. *Yufaqqihuhum*; see *EI²*, s.v. fiḳh.

139. *Yaquṣṣu ʿalayhim*; "sermon" below is *qaṣaṣ*. On the *qaṣaṣ* in medieval Islam see *EI²*, s.v. ḳāṣṣ, and J. Pedersen, "The Islamic Preacher: wāʿiẓ, mudhakkir, qāṣṣ," *Ignace Goldziher Memorial Volume* I (Budapest, 1948), 226–51, especially 239, where Ṣāliḥ's *qaṣaṣ* is partly translated. See also Périer, *Vie d'al-Ḥadjdjādj*, 110f., and, on the oratory for which the Khārijites were famed, C. E. Bosworth, *Sīstān under the Arabs*, 38ff.

140. *Aṣḥābanā*; the speaker is probably Abū Mikhnaf, referring to his own authorities, including ʿAbdallāh b. ʿAlqamah. Abū Mikhnaf's account of the following rebellion gains much from drawing on Khārijite authorities, such as Qabīṣah, as well as others from the government forces.

141. *Kitāb*.

142. Qur'ān 6:1.

tably, supported religion and strove against the polytheists, until God took him. I commend to you the fear of God, austerity in this world, desire for the afterlife, frequent recollection of death, avoidance of the sinners, and love for the believers. For austerity in this world encourages God's servant to desire what is with Him and frees his body for obedience to God; frequent recollection of death inspires the servant with fear of his Lord, so that he cries out for His succor and submits humbly to Him. Avoidance of the sinners is a duty for the believers, as God said in His book: "Do not pray over any of them who dies, ever, nor stand by his grave; they disbelieved in God and His messenger, and died as sinners."[143] Love for the believers is recommended because it is in this way that one obtains God's grace and mercy and His Paradise—may God cause us and you to be among the sincere and patient!

Indeed, it is a blessing from God on the believers that He
[883] sent to them a messenger from among themselves, who taught them the Book and the wisdom, purified and sanctified them, and led them aright in their religion; he was kind and merciful to the believers until God took him away, God's blessings be upon him! Then, after him, authority was taken by the God-fearing Veracious One,[144] with the approval of the Muslims. He followed the right guidance of the messenger and continued in his way[145] until he joined God, God's mercy be upon him. He designated ʿUmar as his successor, and God entrusted him with the authority over this flock. ʿUmar acted in accordance with the Book of God and kept to the way[146] of the messenger of God. He begrudged his flock none of their rights and feared the reproach of no one before God, until he joined Him, God's mercy be upon him. After him, the Muslims were ruled by ʿUthmān. He expropriated the spoils, failed to enforce the Qur'ānic punishments, rendered unjust judgments, and treated the believer with

143. Qur'ān 9:84.
144. *Al-Ṣiddīq*, epithet of the caliph Abū Bakr; see *EI²*, s.v. Abū Bakr.
145. *Sunnah.*
146. *Aḥyā sunnah.*

contempt and the evildoer with esteem.[147] The Muslims went to him and killed him, and God, His messenger and the upright among the believers were quit of him. After him, the people were governed by ʿAlī b. Abī Ṭālib. He did not hesitate to give men authority to judge in the affairs of God; he vacillated with regard to the people of error, and appeased and blandished them. We are quit of ʿAlī and his supporters.[148]

Prepare, then—God's mercy upon you—to strive against these fractious parties and unjust leaders of error, and to go out from the abode of transience to the abode of eternity and join our believing, convinced brethren, who sold the present world for the afterworld and expended their wealth in quest of God's good pleasure in the final reckoning.[149] Be not anxious about being killed for God's sake, for being killed is easier than dying naturally. Natural death comes upon you unexpectedly, separating you from your fathers, sons, wives, [884] and this world; if your anxiety and aversion to this is too strong, then, indeed, sell your souls to God obediently, and your wealth, and you will enter Paradise in security and embrace the black-eyed houris. May God make you and us among the grateful and mindful "who are guided by the truth and by it act justly."[150]

According to Abū Mikhnaf—ʿAbdallāh b. ʿAlqamah: During the

---

147. The first three of these accusations (*ista'thara bi-al-fay' wa-ʿaṭṭala al-ḥudūd wa-jāra fī al-ḥukm*) are repeated below (II, 984, and see II, 993); all are standard Khārijite complaints. See Bosworth, *Sīstān under the Arabs*, 40f.; Watt, *Formative Period*, 9–12; Morony, *Iraq after the Muslim Conquest*, 471, 477; G. R. Hawting, "The significance of the slogan *lā ḥukmᵃ illā lillāh* and the references to the *ḥudūd* in the traditions about the Fitna and the murder of ʿUthmān," *Bulletin of the School of Oriental and African Studies* 41 (1978), 453–63; and, for similar accusations against the deposed Khārijite leader Najdah b. ʿĀmir, Dixon, *Umayyad Caliphate*, 173. On the Qur'ānic punishments, see *EI²*, s.v. ḥadd.

148. The references here are to events at Ṣiffīn and afterward, when ʿAlī agreed to arbitration of his dispute with Muʿāwiyah; see Watt, *Formative Period*, 12–20.

149. The language here is Qur'ānic and quasi-technical: "strive" is *jihād*, "go out" is *khurūj*. "Selling" (*bāʿū*) this world for the other paraphrases Qur'ān 4:74: "Let those fight in the way of God who sell (*yashrūna*) the life of this world for the other"; echoed both here and below is also Qur'ān 2:207: "And of men there is he who sells (*yashrī*) his soul out of desire for God's good pleasure." It is from these passages that the Khārijites took their name Shurāh, "sellers"; see R. Brünnow, *Die Charidschiten unter den ersten Omayyaden* (Leiden, 1884), 28f.

150. Qur'ān 7:159; see also 9:111.

time when Ṣāliḥ's associates used to come frequently to see him, he said to them one day, "I know not what you are expecting or how long you will abide. You see how injustice has become the rule and justice has been effaced. These governors only increase in their excesses and arrogance toward the people, their remoteness from right, and their effrontery before the Lord. Ready yourselves, then, and send for your brethren who desire, as you do, to reject the wrong and summon to the right. Let them come to you, and then we will meet and consider what we are going to do, and, if we are going to revolt, when we should revolt."

Ṣāliḥ's associates sent out letters and met to discuss these plans. While they were engaged in this, al-Muḥallil b. Wā'il al-Yashkurī came to them with a letter from Shabīb[151] to Ṣāliḥ b. Musarriḥ, which read as follows:

> I have learned that you are wanting to set out; you have summoned me to that, and I am responding to you. If you are ready to do so now, you will be the shaykh of the Muslims, and we will hold no one among us as equal to you. But if you want to postpone that day, inform me of that; people die in the morning and the evening, and I cannot be sure that fate
> [885] will not cut me off before I can strive against the evildoers—what a cheat that would be, and what benefit lost! May God make you and us among those whose deeds are performed for the sake of God and His good pleasure, the blessing of gazing at His face, and the companionship of the righteous in the Abode of Peace. Peace be upon you.

When al-Muḥallil b. Wā'il came to Ṣāliḥ with this letter from Shabīb, Ṣāliḥ wrote back to him as follows:

> Your letter with your news was slow in reaching me, to the point that I had become concerned; for a man from among the Muslims had informed me that you had set out and were on your way. Now we praise God for the decree of our Lord, for your messenger has brought me your letter, and I have understood all that is in it. We are equipped and fully prepared to take the field; I have not done so until now only

151. For full references on Shabīb, see note 178 below.

because I was waiting for you. Come to us, then, and let us then begin the revolt whenever you please; for you are one of those whose opinion is indispensable and without whom things cannot be decided. Peace be upon you.

When this letter reached Shabīb, he sent to a number of his associates to come join him. These included his brother, Muṣād[152] b. Yazīd b. Nuʿaym, al-Muḥallil b. Wāʾil al-Yashkurī, al-Ṣaqr b. Ḥātim of the Banū Taym b. Shaybān, Ibrāhīm b. Ḥujr Abū al-Ṣuqayr of the Banū Muḥallim, and al-Faḍl b. ʿĀmir of the Banū Dhuhl b. Shaybān.[153] Then he set out and came to Ṣāliḥ b. Musarriḥ in Dārā. When he met him, he said, "Let us begin the revolt, may God have mercy on you, for, by God, the right path[154] only becomes more obliterated, and the evildoers only become more tyrannical." Ṣāliḥ sent his messengers abroad among his associates, setting the time of the revolt for the night of Wednesday, 1 Ṣafar 76 (May 21, 695).[155] They began to assemble, to equip and prepare themselves to raise the revolt on that night; and on that night they all assembled with him as appointed. [886]

According to Abū Mikhnaf—Farwah b. Laqīṭ al-Azdī: By God, I was with Shabīb in al-Madāʾin[156] when he told us that they were going to revolt. When we were ready to raise the revolt, we all assembled with Ṣāliḥ b. Musarriḥ on the night he set out. My opinion was that we should slaughter the people indiscriminately,[157] because of all the sin, oppression, and corruption in the earth that I saw. I went to Ṣāliḥ and said, "O Commander of the Faithful, how do you intend to proceed with these evildoers? Will

152. Or Maṣād; see Ibn Ḥajar, *Tabṣīr* (Cairo, 1964–67), 1293.

153. All of these men, with the exception of al-Muḥallil, belonged to clans of Shaybān b. Thaʿlabah; see Ibn Ḥazm, *Jamharah*, 302. Shabīb and his brother were of the Dhuhl b. Shaybān; see the genealogy in Ibn Khallikān, *Wafayāt*, II, 454. If al-Muḥallil belonged to the Yashkur b. Bakr (see Kaḥḥālah, *Muʿjam qabāʾil al-ʿarab*, 1265), then they were all members of the Bakr b. Wāʾil confederation, which included the Banū Shaybān.

154. *Sunnah.*

155. Friday.

156. The old Sasanian capital of Ctesiphon on the Tigris, about eighty miles northeast of al-Kūfah, still at this time an important administrative center. See *EI²*, s.v. al-Madāʾin.

157. *Istiʿrāḍ al-nās.* This term has clearly here its developed meaning of "massacre" rather than the earlier one of "interrogation"; see *EI²*, s.v. istiʿrāḍ, and note 131 above.

we kill them before summoning them to the faith, or will we summon them before fighting them? Let me give you my opinion about them before you give me yours. I think that we should kill everyone who disagrees with us, near and far; for we are taking up arms against people who wander in error, tyrants and oppressors who have abandoned the command of God and fallen completely under the control of Satan."

But he said, "No, on the contrary, we will summon them. By my life, it is only those who hold your opinions who will respond, while those who condemn you will surely fight you. Summoning them will silence their argument and strengthen ours against them." Then I asked him, "And what is your view on those we fight and overcome? What do you say about their lives and property?" He replied, "If we kill them and despoil them, that is our right; but if we forgo doing so and let them be, that is also our right and we will be rewarded." He spoke well and truly, God's mercy upon him and upon us!

According to Abū Mikhnaf—a man from the Banū Muḥallim: On the night they set out, Ṣāliḥ b. Musarriḥ said to his associates:

> Fear God, you servants of God, and be not overhasty to fight any one of the people, unless they be hostile people who intend you harm. You are rebelling only out of wrath for God, because His ordinances have been flouted, the earth filled
> [887] with disobedience, blood spilled unjustly, and property taken wrongfully. Do not reproach people for deeds and then do them yourselves; for you are yourselves responsible for all that you do. Now most of you are on foot, but there are riding beasts belonging to Muḥammad b. Marwān here in this district. Start here, then, and raid them, so that you may mount your footsoldiers and thereby strengthen yourselves against the enemy.

They set out, and in that same night seized the riding beasts and mounted their foot upon them, so that their footsoldiers became horsemen. They remained in the area of Dārā for thirteen nights, and the people of Dārā, Nisibis, and Sinjar fortified themselves against them. On the night Ṣāliḥ set out, he set out with 120 men, or, according to some, 110.

Word of this revolt came to Muḥammad b. Marwān, who was at

that time the amīr of the Jazīrah.[158] He minimized the problem, and sent against them ʿAdī b. ʿAdī b. ʿUmayrah of the Banū al-Ḥārith b. Muʿāwiyah b. Thawr,[159] with five hundred men. ʿAdī said to him, "May God cause the amīr to prosper! Would you send me against the man who has been at the head of the Khārijites for twenty years, and who is accompanied in his rebellion by men from the Rabīʿah[160] who came up against me[161] in the past and used to test their strength against us? Against such as these, one of whose footsoldiers is worth more than a hundred horsemen, would you send me with five hundred men?" Muḥammad replied, "Well, then, I will give you another five hundred, and you can go against them with a thousand."

ʿAdī set out from Ḥarrān with a thousand men. This was the first army that marched against Ṣāliḥ. ʿAdī marched toward him as if he were being driven to his death. ʿAdī was a pious man. He proceeded as far as Dawghān,[162] where he stopped the men, and sent ahead secretly to Ṣāliḥ b. Musarriḥ a man of the Banū Khālid of the Banū al-Wirthah named Ziyād b. ʿAbdallāh.[163] This man [888] said to Ṣāliḥ, "ʿAdī has sent me to you to ask you to leave this land and go to another land and fight the people there; for ʿAdī is reluctant to engage you." Ṣāliḥ replied, "Return to him and tell him: If you subscribe to our opinions, give us an indication of that which we will recognize, and we will set out this very night, leaving this land to you and going to another. But if you subscribe to the opinions of the tyrants and the evil imāms, we will see what we decide to do; if we wish, we will attack you, and if we wish, we will turn to someone else."

The messenger went to ʿAdī and reported this message to him. ʿAdī said, "Return to him and tell him: By God, I am not of your opinion, but I am reluctant to fight you or anyone else; so fight

158. See Balādhurī, *Ansāb*, V, 186.

159. Thawr is the Southern tribe of Kindah; see *EI²*, s.v. Kinda.

160. The Northern tribal confederation of which Bakr b. Wā'il was the leading component; see *EI²*, s.v. Bakr b. Wā'il.

161. Reading *samaw li-* for text *summū li-*, "were named to me"; see Lane, *Lexicon*, s.v. samā.

162. A market town between Ra's al-ʿAyn and Nisibis; see Yāqūt, *Muʿjam*, II, 621.

163. According to the Ibn Qutaybah, *Maʿārif*, 100, the Banū al-Wirthah were a subdivision of Dhuhl b. Shaybān; this man was thus a clansman of Ṣāliḥ's men.

someone other than me." Then Ṣāliḥ said to his associates, "Mount!" and they mounted; he held the man captive with him until they had set out, and then let him go. Ṣāliḥ proceeded with his associates until he came to ʿAdī b. ʿAdī b. ʿUmayrah in the market of Dawghān, while the latter was performing the forenoon prayer. Without warning, the Khārijite cavalry were bearing down on his men, and when they saw him coming, they began to shout to one another.

Ṣāliḥ put Shabīb with a detachment of his forces on his right and sent Suwayd b. Sulaym al-Hindī of the Banū Shaybān with a detachment to his left; he himself stood with a detachment in the center. As they approached ʿAdī's men, he saw that they were not formed in ranks, but running around in confusion, whereupon he ordered Shabīb to attack them. Then Suwayd attacked them as well, and this finished them; they would not fight. ʿAdī b. ʿAdī had his mount brought to him while he was praying, and he mounted
[889] it and rode off blindly. Ṣāliḥ b. Musarriḥ proceeded on to ʿAdī's camp and took possession of what was there.

The remnants of ʿAdī's men, and his leading commanders, went back to Muḥammad b. Marwān, who was furious. Muḥammad summoned Khālid b. Jaz' al-Sulamī and sent him off with fifteen hundred men, and summoned al-Ḥārith b. Jaʿwanah of the Banū Rabīʿah b. ʿĀmir b. Ṣaʿṣaʿah and sent him off with another fifteen hundred men.[164] To the two of them he said, "March against this foul little group of Khārijites, and do so quickly. Quicken the march, for whichever of you gets there first will have the command over the other."

They took their leave of him and marched out quickly. They made inquiries about Ṣāliḥ b. Musarriḥ and were told that he had set out toward Āmid.[165] They marched in pursuit and reached him at Āmid, where he was quartered with the people. They arrived at night and dug defensive trenches. When they arrived, they were still two separate forces, each commander by himself, with his men. Ṣāliḥ directed Shabīb against al-Ḥārith b. Jaʿwanah

164. The Banū Sulaym and Banū ʿĀmir b. Ṣaʿṣaʿah both belonged to Qays ʿAylān, one of the two major subgroups of Muḍar, which with Rabīʿah constituted the Northern tribes; see *EI²*, s.v. Ḳays ʿAylān.

165. Modern Diyarbakr; see *EI²*, s.v. Diyār Bakr.

al-ʿĀmirī with half his forces and rode himself against Khālid b. Jaz' al-Sulamī.

According to Abū Mikhnaf—al-Muḥallimī: They reached us at the beginning of the afternoon prayer time. Ṣāliḥ led us in performing the afternoon prayer, then set us in battle array against them. We fought as hard as any people have ever fought, and, by God, it began to look as if we would win. One of our men would attack ten of theirs and overcome them, or he would attack twenty, with the same result; and their cavalry began to lose ground to ours. Seeing this, their two commanders dismounted, ordering most of their men to dismount as well. Then we began to have trouble achieving our objectives with them. When we attacked them, their infantry met us with lances and their archers rained arrows upon us, their cavalry charging us all the while. We fought them until evening, when the darkness finally separated us. They had wounded many of us, and we of them; they had killed about thirty of our men, while we had killed more than seventy of theirs. By God, by the time evening arrived, we were sick of them, [890] as were they of us, and we maintained our positions before them, neither side advancing against the other; with evening, they withdrew to their camp, and we to ours. We prayed, rested, and ate some of our bread. Then Ṣāliḥ summoned Shabīb and his leading commanders, and said, "My dear friends, what do you think we should do?" Shabīb said, "My opinion is that we have encountered these men and fought them, and now that they have taken refuge behind their trench, I do not think we should continue with them." Ṣāliḥ said, "That is my opinion, also." Accordingly, they set out under cover of darkness, traveling across the land of the Jazīrah until they reached the Mosul region. They then crossed through it as well and continued on until they had come into al-Daskarah.[166]

When word of this reached al-Ḥajjāj, he sent against them al-Ḥārith b. ʿUmayrah b. Dhī al-Mishʿār al-Hamdānī[167] with three thousand Kūfans, one thousand from the regular forces and two thousand from the troops that al-Ḥajjāj had hired.[168] Al-Ḥārith

166. A district and town on the Diyālā River, northeast of al-Madā'in; see *EI*², s.v. Daskara; Le Strange, *Lands*, 62, 80.

167. Hamdān was a Southern tribe; see *EI*², s.v. Hamdān.

168. *Al-muqātilah al-ūlā* and *al-farḍ alladhī faraḍa lahum al-Ḥajjāj* respec-

set out, but when he drew near al-Daskarah, Ṣāliḥ b. Musarriḥ withdrew toward Jalūlā'[169] and Khāniqīn.[170] Al-Ḥārith b. ʿUmayrah pursued him as far as a village called al-Mudabbaj[171] in the Mosul region, on the border between it and the Jūkhā region.[172] Ṣāliḥ at this time had ninety men with him. Al-Ḥārith b. ʿUmayrah arranged his forces, putting Abū al-Rawwāgh al-Shākirī[173] on his right and al-Zubayr b. al-Arwaḥ al-Tamīmī on his left, and then, after the afternoon prayer, he attacked. Ṣāliḥ had arranged his forces in three squadrons,[174] one under his own command, one under Shabīb on his right, and one under Suwayd
[891] b. Sulaym on his left, each squadron consisting of thirty men.

When al-Ḥārith b. ʿUmayrah charged against them with all his men, Suwayd b. Sulaym was thrown back, but Ṣāliḥ b. Musarriḥ stood his ground and was killed. Shabīb fought until he was knocked from his horse and fell among some infantry. He charged them and they fell back, and he was able to reach Ṣāliḥ b. Musarriḥ's position, where he found him dead. He called, "To me, O company of Muslims!" and they rallied around him. Then he said to his men, "Stand all of you back to back and thrust at your enemies if they advance on you, and let us make our way into that fortress, where we can decide what to do." This they did, and Shabīb entered the fortress with seventy men.

Al-Ḥārith b. ʿUmayrah surrounded them. It was now evening, and he said to his men, "Burn down the gate until it is reduced to

---

tively. On *farḍ*, troops not on the muster roll and paid contractually, see Balādhurī, *Futūḥ*, glossarium, s.v. farḍ, and Fries, *Heereswesen*, 24; they tended to be younger men, as is clear from the incident below.

169. An important town about thirty miles northeast of al-Daskarah; see *EI²*, s.v. Djalūlā'.

170. A town about thirty miles again northeast of Jalūlā'; see *EI²*, s.v. Khāniḳīn.

171. Or al-Mudabbij. Yāqūt, *Muʿjam*, IV, 448, records it without vowels and apparently knows of it only from this incident.

172. East of the Tigris, stretching from Khāniqīn south to Khūzistān; see Yāqūt, *Muʿjam*, II, 143.

173. Or Abū al-Ruwāʿ (see Ibn Ḥajar, *Tabṣīr*, 612). See text above, II, 46–54, for the alternative spelling and for this man's previous experience combating the Khārijites. The Banū Shākir b. Rabīʿah were a branch of Hamdān; see Caskel, *Ǧamharat an-nasab*, II, 524.

174. Sg. *kurdūs*; see *WKAS*, s.v. According to the lexicographers, a *kurdūs* was smaller than a *katībah* (note 115 above), but see text below, II, 959, where the terms seem to be synonyms, and Fries, *Heereswesen*, 42.

burning embers, and then leave it; they will not be able to get out until we come to them in the morning and kill them." They burned the gate and then went off to their camp. Shabīb was looking down on them, with a group of his men, when one of the men from the hired troops said, "You sons of whores, has God not abased you?" They replied, "Indeed He has not, you sinners; you fight us back when we fight you because God has blinded you to the truth that we possess. What then is your excuse to God for slandering our mothers?" But to this the more temperate among them said, "This is just talk by some foolish youth among us, by God, and we neither like it nor consider it acceptable."

Then Shabīb said to his men, "What are you all waiting for here? By God, if these men come back to you early in the morning, it will be the end of you." They said, "Give us your orders." He said, "Night veils calamities.[175] Render the oath of allegiance to me or to whomever you wish among yourselves; then let us go out and attack them in their camp, since they are feeling secure [892] against any such thing from you. I pray that God may give you victory over them." They said, "Extend your hand, so that we may render you the oath of allegiance," and they did so.[176]

When they were about to go out, they found that their gate had been reduced to burning embers; but they managed to get across them by taking felt saddle-blankets, soaking them in water, and then throwing them over the embers. Al-Ḥārith b. ʿUmayrah and the troops in his camp were taken completely by surprise to find Shabīb and his men laying about them with their swords in the heart of their camp. Al-Ḥārith fought until he fell and was carried by his men as they retreated, leaving the camp and everything in it to the Khārijites. Then they returned to al-Madā'in. This army was the first one to be defeated by Shabīb.

Ṣāliḥ b. Musarriḥ fell on Tuesday, 17 Jumādā I of this year (September 2, 695).[177]

---

175. For the proverb, see Maydānī, *Amthāl*, II, 127.

176. According to Ibn Khayyāṭ, *Ta'rīkh*, 272, Ibn Qutaybah, *Maʿārif*, 410, and Baghdādī, *Farq*, 89, Ṣāliḥ appointed Shabīb his successor before his death.

177. Thursday. According to Ibn Khayyāṭ, *Ta'rīkh*, 272, 17 Jumādā II (October 2, a Saturday). Ibn Qutaybah, *Maʿārif*, 410, reports that later Khārijites used to shave their heads at his tomb.

In this year, Shabīb entered al-Kūfah, accompanied by his wife Ghazālah.[178]

Shabīb's Entry into al-Kūfah and His Dealings with al-Ḥajjāj There, and Why Shabīb Did This

According to Hishām—Abū Mikhnaf—'Abdallāh b. 'Alqamah—Qabīṣah b. 'Abd al-Raḥmān al-Khath'amī: The reason for this was as follows: When Ṣāliḥ b. Musarriḥ was killed at al-Mudabbaj and Ṣāliḥ's associates rendered the oath of allegiance to Shabīb, the
[893] latter went up to the Mosul region, where he met Salāmah b. Sayyār b. al-Maḍā' al-Taymī of the Taym Shaybān and summoned him to rebel along with him. He was already acquainted with Salāmah, as the latter had been registered on the military roll and participated in the expeditions.[179] Salāmah agreed to support him on the condition that he be allowed to pick out thirty of his horsemen, with whom he would then be gone for not more than precisely three nights. Shabīb agreed, and Salāmah selected the thirty horsemen and led them off toward the 'Anazah.[180] His object was to wreak his vengeance on them for murdering his brother Faḍālah.

The story behind this is that Faḍālah had rebelled with eighteen

---

178. Ṭabarī's account of Shabīb's rebellion is by far the most detailed known; it is summarized by Ibn al-Athīr, *Kāmil,* IV, 396–416, 419–33, and serves as the basis for accounts in Périer, *Vie d'al-Ḥadjdjādj,* 115–48, and Dixon, *Umayyad Caliphate,* 184–91. A quite different account appears in Ibn A'tham al-Kūfī, *Futūḥ,* VII, 84–92, omitting any reference to Ṣāliḥ b. Musarriḥ and identifying the first two commanders sent out (by al-Ḥajjāj) as 'Ubaydah b. Mikhrāq al-Qaynī and Yazīd b. Hubayrah al-Muḥāribī, neither of whom is mentioned by Ṭabarī. Brief accounts in Ibn Khayyāṭ, *Ta'rīkh,* 272–75, and Ya'qūbī, *Ta'rīkh,* II, 328, combine elements of both versions, as does the biography in Ibn Khallikān, *Wafayāt,* II, 454–58, which draws on other sources as well. See also Ibn Qutaybah, *Ma'ārif,* 410f.; Baghdādī, *Farq,* 89–92 (garbled); *EI*[1], s.v. Shabīb. Shabīb's genealogy back to the clan of Dhuhl b. Shaybān is given by Ibn al-Sikkīt, *Iṣlāḥ al-manṭiq* (Cairo, 1956), 324f., and his *kunyah* by Baghdādī, *Farq,* 89, as Abū al-Ṣaḥārā (or al-Ṣaḥārī) (confirmed by text below, II, 1633f.). Ibn A'tham al-Kūfī (followed by Baghdādī) precedes his account with a report that Shabīb had gone earlier to Damascus and attempted to get a *farḍ* from 'Abd al-Malik through the intercession of Rawḥ b. Zinbā'; when 'Abd al-Malik refused, saying he did not know him, Shabīb replied, "I hope, God willing, he *will* know me in the future!"

179. *Maghāzī,* against non-Muslim territory. Why this implied prior acquaintance is not clear.

180. A Rabī'ah tribe; see *EI*[2], s.v. 'Anaza.

men and stopped at a well called al-Shajarah in the region of al-Jāl.[181] There was a great tamarisk tree there, and there were ʿAnazah. When the ʿAnazah saw him, they said to one another, "Let us kill them, and in the morning take them to the amīr; we will receive a generous reward." They agreed on this, but the Banū Naṣr, who were Faḍālah's mother's clan, said, "By God's life, we will not aid you in killing our son!" Nevertheless, the ʿAnazah rode out against Faḍālah's men, fought them and killed them, and brought their heads to ʿAbd al-Malik b. Marwān. As a reward, ʿAbd al-Malik let them move into Bāniqiyā[182] and assigned them stipends, something they had rarely had before.[183]

Salāmah b. Sayyār recited these verses on the murder of his brother Faḍālah and the failure of his maternal kin to defend him:

I would not have imagined that a young man's maternal kin
  would deliver him over
  to the fall of a blade, until Naṣr did what it did.

The rebellion of Salāmah's brother Faḍālah preceded that of Ṣāliḥ b. Musarriḥ and Shabīb; therefore, when Salāmah rendered the oath of allegiance to Shabīb, he imposed on him this condition. He rode out with the thirty horsemen until he reached the ʿAnazah and began killing them in one settlement after another [894] until he came to a party of them that included his maternal aunt. She was bent over a son of hers, a boy in his adolescence; and she bared her breast to Salāmah and said, "I adjure you by the blood ties of this, Salāmah!" He replied, "No, by God! I have not seen Faḍālah since he halted at the great tree of al-Shajarah"—meaning his brother—"Now stand away from him, or I will take my lance to your withered dug." At that, she stood aside from her son, and Salāmah killed him.

181. Yāqūt, *Muʿjam*, II, 10, mentions two places with this name, one in Ādharbayjān and the other, pronounced al-Jāl or al-Gēl, about four *farsakh*s south of al-Madā'in. The latter, if either, seems the more likely to be meant here; but if the al-Jāl mentioned directly below is the same place, one would expect it to be rather somewhere north of the Diyālā River.

182. *Anzalahum Bāniqiyā*. This was at that time a fertile area on the western branch of the Euphrates below al-Kūfah and al-Ḥīrah; see A. Musil, *The Middle Euphrates* (New York, 1927), 288f.

183. *Faraḍa lahum wa-lam takun lahum farā'iḍ qabla dhālika illā qalīlah*; see note 168 above.

According to Abū Mikhnaf—al-Mufaḍḍal b. Bakr of the Banū Taym b. Shaybān: Shabīb and his companions then turned toward Rādhān.[184] When a group of the Banū Taym b. Shaybān heard of his approach, they withdrew in flight before him, along with a small number of other people, going as far as the monastery of Khurrazād,[185] near Ḥawlāyā,[186] where they stopped. There were about three thousand of them, while Shabīb had only some seventy men or a few more, but when he came among them, they feared him and fortified themselves against him. Then Shabīb set out by night, accompanied by twelve horsemen from among his companions, to go to his mother, who was camped in the foothills of Sātīdamā,[187] staying in one of the large hair-tents of the bedouin. Shabīb said, "I am going to bring my mother and put her in my camp so she will never be parted from me until one of us dies." Meanwhile, two men of the Banū Taym b. Shaybān, fearing for their lives, left the monastery and went out to join a group of their people who were camped at al-Jāl, about an hour's journey from them by day.[188] When Shabīb led out that party of his—there
[895] were twelve of them[189]—to meet his mother in the foothills, he unexpectedly ran into a group of the Banū Taym b. Shaybān heedlessly encamped with their herds, not imagining that Shabīb would pass their way, because of where they were, or be aware of them. But Shabīb attacked them with these horsemen of his and killed thirty of their shaykhs, including Ḥawtharah b. Asad and

184. Apparently at this time a district north of the Diyālā and east of the Tigris, although the sources are difficult to harmonize. See J. Markwart, *Südarmenien und die Tigrisquellen* (Wien, 1930), 277, and J. M. Fiey, *Assyrie chrétienne* (Beirut, 1965–68), III, 16 (map), 76–81, 257–60.

185. Yāqūt, *Mu'jam,* II, 422, mentions a town of Khurrazād Ardashīr (unvocalized) in the region of Mosul. Some MSS read Kh.r.dāb.

186. Yāqūt, *Mu'jam,* II, 366, mentions a village of this name in the Nahrawān (canal) region. At II, 932 below, the Ḥawlāyā is a river (or canal) in Upper Rādhān, in Jūkhā.

187. The modern Jabal Ḥamrīn, which is cut by the Tigris north of Takrīt and extends northwest and southeast from there. See Markwart, *Südarmenien,* 274–78; *EI²,* s.v. Ḥamrīn; Fiey, *Assyrie chrétienne,* III, 16 (map).

188. *Fa-laḥiqā bi-jamā'ah min qawmihimā wa-hum nuzūl bi-al-Jāl minhum 'alā masīrat sā'ah min al-nahār.*

189. *Wa-kharaja Shabīb fī ulā'ika al-rahṭ fī awwalihim wa-hum ithnā 'ashar.* Ibn al-Athīr, *Kāmil,* IV, 394, omits in his paraphrase any reference to the two men, and says simply *fa-sāra bihim sā'ah,* "and (Shabīb) had traveled with (his twelve men) for an hour, (when . . .)"

Wabarah b. ʿĀṣim, who had left the monastery and joined those at al-Jāl. Shabīb then went on to fetch his mother from the foothills and brought her back with him.[190]

Meanwhile, one of the men in the monastery, who was of the Bakr b. Wā'il, came out to speak to Shabīb's men from above. Shabīb had left his brother, Muṣād b. Yazīd, in charge of his men; the man who came out to them was named Sallām b. Ḥayyān. He said to them, "You people, the Qur'ān stands between us. Have you not heard God's words, 'And if any one of the unbelievers seeks your protection, then grant it him, so that he may hear the word of God, then convey him to his place of security'?"[191] They said, "Indeed we have." He said to them, "Then leave us alone until morning. We will come out to you then, with a safe-conduct from you so that we may not be subject to any treatment from you to which we object; and you can present this position of yours to us. If we accept it, then you have no rights to our lives and possessions, and we will be your brethren; if we do not accept it, you will return us to our place of security, and then proceed as you please with regard to what is between you and us." They replied, "We will grant you this."

The next morning, they went out to the Khārijites, and Shabīb's men stated their views to them and described their position. They accepted it in its entirety and joined up with them, becoming a full part of their group. When Shabīb came back, his men ex- [896] plained to him how this reconciliation had taken place, and he said, "You have acted well and correctly, and been granted a successful outcome."

Then Shabīb took to the road again, accompanied by one group, while another group remained where they were.[192] Among those who accompanied him on that day was Ibrāhīm b. Ḥujr al-Muḥallimī Abū al-Ṣuqayr, who had been staying with the Banū

---

190. On Shabīb's mother Jahīzah, see Ibn Khallikān, *Wafayāt*, II, 487, and text below, II, 976. Ṭabarī says nothing more about her accompanying Shabīb on his campaigns, but Ibn Aʿtham al-Kūfī, *Futūḥ*, VII, 87, and others attest to her presence at the occupation of al-Kūfah; see note 439 below.

191. Qur'ān 9:6. In a similar anecdote in Mubarrad, *Kāmil*, 528, Wāṣil b. ʿAṭā' appeals to the same verse; he, however, unlike the people here, does not join up in the end.

192. *Wa-aqāmat ṭā'ifah jāniḥah;* Ṭabarī, glossarium, s.v. janaḥa, suggests "inclined (toward peace)," but perhaps the meaning is rather "on the sidelines."

Taym b. Shaybān. Shabīb passed through the nearer parts of the Mosul region and the borderlands of Jūkhā, then went up toward Ādharbayjān. At this point, Sufyān b. Abī al-ʿĀliyah al-Khathʿamī appeared with some cavalry. He had been ordered to lead them into Ṭabaristān but then ordered to return, and was on his way back with some thousand horsemen, having made a truce with the ruler of Ṭabaristān.[193]

According to Abū Mikhnaf—ʿAbdallāh b. ʿAlqamah—Sufyān b. Abī al-ʿĀliyah al-Khathʿamī: I received this letter from al-Ḥajjāj:

> Proceed to al-Daskarah with the men you have with you and wait there until you are joined by the force of al-Ḥārith b. ʿUmayrah al-Hamdānī Ibn Dhī al-Mishʿār, the man who killed Ṣāliḥ b. Musarriḥ, as well as the cavalry scouts.[194] Then go and find Shabīb, and attack him.

Upon receipt of this letter, Sufyān proceeded to al-Daskarah and halted there, while proclamation was made to the army of al-Ḥārith b. ʿUmayrah in al-Kūfah and al-Madāʾin that no contractual obligation would protect any man belonging to the army of al-Ḥārith b. ʿUmayrah who did not go join Sufyān b. Abī al-ʿĀliyah in al-Daskarah.

They went out to join him. The cavalry scouts also arrived, five hundred strong under the command of Sawrah b. Abjar al-Tamīmī of the Banū Abān b. Dārim. Altogether, only about fifty men failed to show up. Sawrah sent ahead to Sufyān b. Abī al-ʿĀliyah, saying, "Do not set out with the army until I come to
[897] you." But Sufyān hurried off in pursuit of Shabīb and caught up with him at Khāniqīn, at the foot of a mountain. He put Khāzim b. Sufyān al-Khathʿamī of the Banū ʿAmr b. Shahrān[195] in charge of his right flank and ʿAdī b. ʿUmayrah al-Shaybānī[196] in charge of his left. Shabīb showed himself before them but then withdrew

---

193. The *iṣbahbadh,* first mentioned in a definite historical context two years later, by Yaʿqūbī, *Taʾrīkh,* II, 329; see *EI*², s.v. ispahbadh, and note 596 below.

194. *Khayl al-manāẓir;* see Lane, *Lexicon,* s.v. manẓarah: "a place on the top of a mountain, where a person observes and watches the enemy."

195. On the Khathʿam, associated with southern tribes but sometimes given a northern genealogy, and the Shahrān clan, see *EI*², s.v. Khathʿam.

196. On the basis of the name ʿAdī b. ʿAdī b. ʿUmayrah al-Kindī *thumma* al-Shaybānī in the text below, II, 921, one may assume that this is the ʿAdī b. ʿAdī already mentioned, although a clan of the Kindah named Shaybān is unknown.

from them as if avoiding an engagement. He had put his brother Muṣād with fifty men in an ambush party in a depressed area of the terrain, and when Sufyān's men had seen him, he assembled his forces and set off across the foothills heading east. They said, "The enemy of God has fled! After him!" ʿAdī b. ʿUmayrah al-Shaybānī warned them, "Do not hurry after them, men, before we can travel through the area and explore it. If they have set an ambush for us, our precautions will have been well taken; if not, we will still be able to pursue them." But the men would not listen, and hurried after them. When Shabīb saw that they had passed the place of ambush, he turned around against them; and when the men in the ambush saw that they had passed them, they sprang out against them as well. Thus Shabīb was attacking them from in front, and the ambush clamoring behind them, and they were defeated before anyone lifted a sword against them. But Ibn Abī al-ʿĀliyah stood his ground with some two hundred men and offered them a good, stiff fight until he thought that he had extracted his due from[197] Shabīb and his companions.

At this point, Suwayd b. Sulaym asked his companions, "Does any among you know the commander of these men, Ibn Abī al-ʿĀliyah? By God, if I find out which one he is, I will make every effort to kill him!" Shabīb replied, "Few people know him as well as I. Do you see the man on the horse with the blaze, there beyond the bowmen? That is he. But if it is him you are after, do not go [898]
just yet." Then he said, "Qaʿnab, you take twenty men and go take them from behind." Qaʿnab took twenty men and went up around them, and when they saw that he was intending to come at them from behind, they began to break ranks and slip away. Then Suwayd b. Sulaym attacked Sufyān b. Abī al-ʿĀliyah. First he thrust at him with his lance, but neither man's weapon found its target. Then they fought with their swords. Then they seized hold of each other and fell wrestling to the ground. Then Sufyān's men held back, and Shabīb attacked them and they were thrown back. A servant boy of Sufyān's named Ghazwān came to him, dismounted from his horse, and said, "Mount, master." Sufyān mounted and was surrounded by Shabīb's men. Ghazwān, who

197. *Intaṣafa min*; other MSS read *sayaẓharu ʿalā* or *sayaẓfaru bi-*, "he would defeat."

had been carrying his standard, fought to defend him and was killed. Sufyān b. Abī al-ʿĀliyah rode off to Bābil Mahrūdh,[198] where he halted and wrote to al-Ḥajjāj as follows:

> I hereby inform the amīr—may God cause him to prosper!—that I pursued these heretics and caught up with them at Khāniqīn. I engaged them in battle, and God smote their faces and granted us the victory over them. Then, while we were still enjoying our victory, there came to us men who had not been with them before, and attacked our men and routed them. I, however, with some men of religious conviction and fortitude, dismounted and fought them until I fell among the dead and was carried wounded off the field. I was brought to Bābil Mahrūdh, and am there now. The troops which the amīr sent me arrived, except for Sawrah b. Abjar. He did not come to me and was not present there with me; but when I arrived in Bābil Mahrūdh, he came to me saying I know not what, excusing himself with no excuse at all. Peace.

[899] When al-Ḥajjāj read this letter, he said, "Who has done as this man has, or shown such valor? He has done well!" Then he wrote him as follows:

> You have done well when tested and carried out your duty. When you are able to do so without pain, come to your people to receive your reward. Peace.

To Sawrah b. Abjar, al-Ḥajjāj wrote as follows:

> O son of the mother of Sawrah! It was unworthy of you to disregard my order and fail to join my troops. When this letter comes to you, send one of your stalwart men to the cavalry that is in al-Madā'in to choose five hundred men from it and bring them to you. Then lead them out to meet these heretics. Be resolute and use strategy against your enemy, for the best part of war is good strategy. Peace.

---

198. Mahrūdh was a subdistrict (*ṭassūj*) east of al-Madā'in, in the same district (*kūrah, astān*) as al-Daskarah and Jalūlā'; see Le Strange, *Lands*, 80. Bābil was presumably a town there, distinguished from Bābil al-Kūfah (Babylon); its *dihqān*, or resident lord, is mentioned below, II, 916, 942.

When Sawrah received the letter of al-Ḥajjāj, he sent ʿAdī b. ʿUmayrah to al-Madāʾin. There were a thousand horsemen there, and he chose five hundred of them. Then he went to see ʿAbdallāh b. Abī ʿUṣayfīr, who was then amīr of al-Madāʾin for his first time. The latter greeted him and gave him a thousand dirhams, a riding mount, and garments. Departing from him, ʿAdī set out with his companions and brought them to Sawrah b. Abjar in Bābil Mahrūdh. Sawrah then went out in search of Shabīb. Shabīb was moving about in Jūkhā, while Sawrah tried to track him down. But then Shabīb came to al-Madāʾin. The people of al-Madāʾin fortified themselves against him and took precautions against the frailty of the ancient buildings in al-Madāʾin.[199] Shabīb entered al-Madāʾin and seized many of the riding beasts of the troops there; and he killed anyone who appeared and did not stay indoors.

Then word was brought to him that Sawrah b. Abjar was on his way to him, so he and his companions departed and went to al-Nahrawān,[200] where they halted, performed their ablutions, and prayed. Then they visited the places where their brethren had been killed by ʿAlī b. Abī Ṭālib. They asked their brethren for forgiveness and declared themselves quit of ʿAlī and his associates; and they wept for a long time. Then they went out and cut the bridge at al-Nahrawān and took up positions on its eastern end. Sawrah, meanwhile, advanced as far as Qaṭrāthā,[201] where his spies came and informed him of Shabīb's position at al-Nahrawān. He summoned his chief officers and said to them: [900]

> Hardly ever have these men been encountered directly or in the open without extracting their due from you and getting the better of you. Now, being informed that they are only a few more than a hundred, I have decided to make a selection among you and march out with three hundred of the strong-

199. Reading *taḥadhdharū wahy abniyat al-Madāʾin al-ūlā* for *taḥarrazū wahy* (emended by the editors to *wa-wahiya*) etc.; see Freytag, *Lexicon Arabico-Latinum* (Halle, 1830–37), s.v. taḥadhdhara.

200. The town of al-Nahrawān was at the bridge over the al-Nahrawān canal, one stage east of the Tigris on the great Khurāsān road; see Le Strange, *Lands*, 61. On the battle of al-Nahrawān in 38 (658), in which ʿAlī inflicted a bloody defeat on the Khārijites, see text above, I, 3367ff.

201. Spelling and location uncertain.

est and bravest of you, and to come upon them now, when they are secure in their assumption that you are spending the night here. By God, I pray that God may strike them down on the spot where their brethren were struck down at al-Nahrawān before.

They replied, "Proceed as you wish!" Leaving Ḥāzim b. Qudāmah al-Khath'amī in charge of his army, he selected from his forces three hundred men noted for their strength, endurance, and courage, and set out with them for al-Nahrawān. But Shabīb, before retiring, had put the guard on alert; and when Sawrah's forces drew near them, they sent warning of them, and the men mounted their horses and arranged their ranks. By the time Sawrah and his forces arrived, they found them alerted and ready.

Sawrah and his forces charged them, but they withstood the attack and fought until Sawrah and his forces gave way. Then
[901] Shabīb raised the cry to his men and charged them until they left him the field; and his men charged with him. As he fought, Shabīb recited:

He who fucks a donkey fucks an expert fucker!
Two stones colliding with each other![202]

Sawrah returned to his army, his horsemen and men of strength defeated, and had them break camp and set off toward al-Madā'in; he reached them after having packed up and gained a lead on Shabīb.[203] Shabīb came in pursuit, hoping to catch up with him and attack and defeat his army as he had already defeated him, and he pressed with all speed after them. But Sawra's men reached al-Madā'in and entered it, and when Shabīb reached the houses of al-Madā'in and caught up with them, the men had gone inside. Then Ibn Abī 'Uṣayfīr came out with the people of al-Madā'in, and the people shot at Shabīb's men with arrows and threw stones down on them from the roofs of the houses.

Shabīb then turned away from al-Madā'in with his men and passed through Kalwādhā,[204] where he found many riding beasts

202. That is, you have more than met your match. Both lines are proverbial and do not normally appear together; see Maydānī, *Amthāl*, I, 160, and II, 232f.

203. *Fa-dafa'a ilayhim wa-qad taḥammala wa-ta'addā al-ṭarīq alladhī fīhi Shabīb.*

204. Some fifteen miles north of al-Madā'in, just south of Baghdad; see *EI*[2], s.v. Kalwādhā.

of al-Ḥajjāj's and took them. Leaving Kalwādhā, he traveled through the region of Jūkhā and then went on toward Takrīt.[205] In al-Madā'in, meanwhile, the people threw those troops into a panic, saying to them, "See how Shabīb has drawn near! He is intending to attack the people of al-Madā'in tonight!" When they heard this, most of the troops left and returned to al-Kūfah.

According to Abū Mikhnaf—'Abdallāh b. 'Alqamah al-Khath'amī: By God, they fled from al-Madā'in, saying, "We will [902] be attacked tonight!" when all the while Shabīb was in Takrīt! Then, when these defeated troops came to al-Ḥajjāj, he sent out al-Jazl b. Sa'īd b. Shuraḥbīl b. 'Amr al-Kindī.[206]

According to Abū Mikhnaf—al-Naḍr b. Ṣāliḥ al-'Absī[207] and Fuḍayl b. Khadīj al-Kindī: When the defeated troops came to al-Ḥajjāj, he said, "May God withhold his blessings from Sawrah! The man has wasted the army and the troops[208] and gone out to attack the Khārijites at night. By God, I shall give him a harsh requital for this!" He did have him imprisoned later, although he was eventually pardoned.[209]

According to Abū Mikhnaf—Fuḍayl b. Khadīj: Al-Ḥajjāj summoned al-Jazl, whose real name was 'Uthmān b. Sa'īd, and said to him, "Prepare to take the field against these heretics. When you encounter them, do not be overhasty, like those who act rashly, nor hold back, like the weak and timorous. Do you understand? What a man you are, you brother of the Banū 'Amr b. Mu'āwiyah!"[210] Al-Jazl said, "Yes, may God cause the amīr to prosper, I understand." Then al-Ḥajjāj said, "Go, then, and camp at Dayr 'Abd al-Raḥmān[211] until the men come to you." Al-Jazl said, "May God cause the amīr to prosper, please do not send with me

---

205. Another hundred miles up the Tigris, on the borders of the province of Mosul; see Le Strange, *Lands*, 57.

206. *Al-Jazl* means "having sound judgment," or "generous." This man's real name was 'Uthmān, as noted below.

207. This is the same man as Abū al-Zuhayr al-'Absī, above, II, 873, 875; see U. Sezgin, *Abū Mihnaf*, 214.

208. *Al-'askar wa-al-jund.* The distinction between the two here is not clear.

209. Ibn Khayyāṭ, *Ta'rīkh*, 272, mentions Sawrah as Shabīb's first opponent after the death of Ṣāliḥ, but provides no details, and then names the next commander as "Sa'īd b. 'Amr al-Kindī," apparently a distortion of al-Jazl's name. Other early authors mention neither name.

210. On this clan of Kindah, see Kaḥḥālah, *Mu'jam qabā'il al-'arab*, 836.

211. Placed just north of al-Kūfah by Ṣ. al-'Alī, "Minṭaqat al-Kūfah," *Sumer* 21 (1965), 240; see also *EI²*, s.v. Dayr 'Abd al-Raḥmān.

any men from those broken and defeated troops; fear has entered their hearts, and I am afraid that none of them will be of any use to you and the Muslims." Al-Ḥajjāj replied, "You are granted this; it seems to me that you have considered well and been rightly led."

Then al-Ḥajjāj summoned the officials in charge of the military rolls and said, "Select an expeditionary force from among the troops[212] and call up four thousand of them, a thousand men from each quarter; and be quick about it!" The marshals were assembled, and the officials in charge of the military rolls sat and
[903] selected the expeditionary force, calling up four thousand. Then al-Ḥajjāj ordered them to muster. They mustered, the call for departure was proclaimed, and they marched out. Al-Ḥajjāj's crier proclaimed that "No contractual obligation will protect any man we find shirking this expedition."

Al-Jazl b. Sa'īd set out, having placed before him 'Iyāḍ b. Abī Līnah al-Kindī over the vanguard, and he proceeded as far as al-Madā'in, where he halted for three nights. Ibn Abī 'Uṣayfīr sent him a riding horse, a nag, two mules, and two thousand dirhams, and he provided the men with meat and fodder sufficient for three days, until their departure; the men were able to take as much of this meat and fodder provided by Ibn Abī 'Uṣayfīr as they wished.

Then al-Jazl b. Sa'īd led the men out after Shabīb. He pursued him in the Jūkhā region, but Shabīb persisted in fighting shy of him, moving from *rustāq* to *rustāq* and from *ṭassūj* to *ṭassūj*[213] without making a stand. He was hoping thereby that al-Jazl would divide his forces and hasten to engage him with a small force not in formation; but al-Jazl persisted in marching only in formation and digging a defensive trench for himself whenever he halted. Shabīb finally became impatient, and one night ordered his forces to launch a night attack.

According to Abū Mikhnaf—Farwah b. Laqīṭ: Shabīb summoned us when we were in Dayr Bayrimmā,[214] 160 men al-

---

212. *Iḍrabū 'alā al-nās al-ba'th.*

213. These terms, inherited from Sasanian administration, signify, respectively, rural divisions of a district and districts of a province. See E. Yarshater, ed., *The Cambridge History of Iran,* III (Cambridge, 1983), 676, 727, 732f.

214. A station on the Khurāsān highway, four *farsakhs* east of al-Nahrawān and eight *farsakhs* west of al-Daskarah, according to Ibn Rustah, *A'lāq* (*BGA,* VII),

together. He appointed a man over each group of forty of his forces: he took forty himself, gave his brother Muṣād forty, sent out Suwayd b. Sulaym with forty, and sent out al-Muḥallil b. Wā'il with forty. His spies had come and informed him that al-Jazl b. Sa'īd was camped at Dayr Yazdajird,[215] and when he heard this, he summoned us and mustered us according to this arrangement. At his order, we gave the riding beasts their nosebags. He said to us, "Make your preparations, and once your beasts have had their grain, mount them. Every one of you is to go with the commander whom we have appointed over him; and every one of you is to heed the orders of his commander and obey him." [904]

Then he summoned our commanders and said to them, "I want to attack this camp tonight." To his brother Muṣād he said, "When you approach them, go around above them so that you approach them from their rear, from the direction of Ḥulwān.[216] I will approach them frontally, from the direction of al-Kūfah. You, Suwayd, approach them from the east; and you, Muḥallil, from the west. Every one of you must come in from the side with which he has been charged; and you are to give them no respite, charging and charging again, and raising the battle cry against them, until you receive orders from me."

We remained in this muster—I was among the forty with Shabīb—until the beasts had eaten. We set out at the beginning of the night, just when eyes begin to relax, and came to Dayr al-Kharārah,[217] where we encountered an advance party[218] under the command of 'Iyāḍ b. Abī Līnah. No sooner had we come upon them than Shabīb's brother Muṣād attacked them with his forty men. He was ahead of Shabīb, having intended to precede Shabīb and go up behind them and attack from the rear, as he had been ordered; but when he encountered these men, he fought them, and they tenaciously fought back for a time. Then we all came up

163—text: Dayr Tayrimah; see also Ibn Khurradādhbih, *Masālik* (*BGA*, VI), 18, 197, and al-Muqaddasī, *Aḥsan al-taqāsīm* (*BGA*, III), 135.

215. Unidentified in other sources, but apparently further up the Khurāsān highway.

216. The border town between the provinces of Iraq and al-Jibāl on the Khurāsān highway, some seventy-five miles east of al-Daskarah; see *EI*², s.v. Ḥulwān.

217. Spelling and location uncertain. Other MSS have al-Jarārah, al-Jarādah, al-Ḥarārah.

218. *Maslaḥah.*

on them and attacked them and drove them back. They took to
[905] the main road; it was only about a mile back to their camp at Dayr Yazdajird.

Shabīb said to us, "Stay hard on their heels, companies of Muslims, and try to enter the camp with them, if you can!" We pursued them, by God, sticking close to them and pressing them without respite, while they were fleeing with no goal but their camp. When they reached their camp, though, their comrades would not let them enter it, and they rained arrows upon us. They had spies who had come and informed them of our position. Al-Jazl had entrenched himself and been on his guard; and he had sent out the advance party that we encountered at Dayr al-Kharārah, as well as another advance party on the road toward Ḥulwān. When we reached the advance party at Dayr al-Kharārah and pushed them back to their main camp, the other advance parties came back and all joined together. But the men in the camp would not let them enter the camp, saying, "Fight, and defend yourselves with your arrows!"

According to Abū Mikhnaf—Jarīr b. al-Ḥusayn al-Kindī: Of the other two advance parties, ʿĀṣim b. Ḥujr was in charge of the one in the direction of Ḥulwān, and Wāṣil b. al-Ḥārith al-Sakūnī[219] was in charge of the other. When the advance parties came together, Shabīb kept attacking them until he forced them back to the trench; but the men in the camp rained down arrows on Shabīb's men until they drove them back from the men of the advance parties.

When Shabīb saw that he would be unable to get to them, he said to his men, "Come, now, and leave them," and set off on the road to Ḥulwān. When he drew near to the site of the tents of Ḥusayn b. Zafar of the Banū Badr b. Fazārah[220]—but the tents of
[906] Ḥusayn b. Zafar were there only after that—he said to his men, "Dismount here, eat, repair your arrows, rest, and pray two prostrations; then remount." They dismounted and did as he said. Then he led them back again to the camp of the Kūfans. He said, "March in the formation in which I mustered you in Dayr Bay-

219. The Banū Sakūn were a clan of Kindah; see Kaḥḥālah, *Muʿjam qabāʾil al-ʿarab*, 528.

220. The Banū Badr b. ʿAmr were the leading family of the Fazārah tribe of Qays ʿAylān; see Kaḥḥālah, *Muʿjam qabāʾil al-ʿarab*, 68.

rimmā at the beginning of the night; then encircle their camp, as I ordered before, and advance."

We advanced with him. The men of the camp had brought their advance parties inside with them and felt secure from us; they were completely unaware of our approach until they heard the hoofbeats of our horses close by. We reached them shortly before morning and surrounded their camp. We raised the war cry against them from every side, and they began to do battle with us from every side and attack us with arrows. Then Shabīb sent to his brother Muṣād, who was fighting them on the al-Kūfah side, saying, "Come to us and leave the way to al-Kūfah open to them." Muṣād came to him, leaving that side open, while we kept fighting them on the other three sides until morning. Morning came without our having broken through at all, so we rode away and left them. They called after us, "Where are you going, dogs of hell? Where, band of heretics? Give us a fight in the morning, and we will come out to you!" We withdrew from them about a mile and a half, dismounted, and performed the morning prayer. Then we set out on the road to Barāz al-Rūz[221] and went on to Jarjarāyā[222] and the surrounding region; and they set out after us.

According to Abū Mikhnaf—a client of ours[223] named Ghāḍirah or Qayṣar: I was working as a merchant with the troops when [907] they were in pursuit of the Ḥarūriyyah. Our commander was al-Jazl b. Saʿīd. As he pursued them, he always marched in formation and never camped without digging a trench. Shabīb was avoiding him and moving around in the region of Jūkhā and elsewhere, cutting off the land revenues.[224] Al-Ḥajjāj wearied of that and wrote to al-Jazl the following letter, which was read out to the men:

> I sent you out with the horsemen of the garrison and the elite troops and ordered you to go after these misguided and misguiding heretics until you find them, and then not to leave off until you have killed them all and exterminated

221. Southeast of the Khurāsān highway, between al-Nahrawān and al-Daskarah; see Le Strange, *Lands*, 61, 80.

222. A town on the east bank of the Tigris, some fifty miles south of al-Madā'in; see Le Strange, *Lands*, 37.

223. That is, the Azd.

224. *Yaksiru al-kharāj*; see *WKAS*, s.v. *kasara*, and *EI*², s.v. kharādj.

> them. But I see that you find spending your nights in villages and tenting behind trenches easier than carrying out my orders to confront and fight them. Peace.

This letter was read to us when we were in Qaṭrāthā and Dayr Abī Maryam.[225] Al-Jazl was much distressed; he ordered the troops to march, and they set out in serious pursuit of the Khārijites. Disquieting rumors began to circulate among us about our commander, saying, "He is going to be dismissed."

According to Abū Mikhnaf—Ismā'īl b. Nu'aym al-Hamdānī al-Namirī:[226] Al-Ḥajjāj sent out Sa'īd b. Mujālid[227] to take command of that army, charging him, "If you encounter the heretics, take the field against them, neither negotiating nor temporizing with them. Confront them, asking God's help against them; do
[908] not follow the example of al-Jazl. Pursue them like a lion and turn away from them like a hyena."[228]

Al-Jazl went in pursuit of Shabīb as far as al-Nahrawān, where he caught up with him. He kept to his camp, digging a defensive trench. Then Sa'īd b. Mujālid came to him and entered the camp of the Kūfans as their commander. He stood before them to address them, and after praising and glorifying God, he said:

> Men of al-Kūfah! You have shown yourselves to be weak and ineffectual and have brought on yourselves the anger of your amīr. You have been in pursuit of these scrawny bedouin for two months while they have laid waste your land and cut off your land revenues. Yet you remain cautiously behind these trenches, never leaving them unless word comes to you that they have departed and moved on to some land other than yours. Go out, in God's name, against them!

---

225. Unidentified, but apparently near Baraz al-Rūz; see text below, II, 910.

226. Text: al-Bursumī. He appears as al-Namirī in the text above, II, 117. Another possible reading in both places is al-Burmī. Both Namirah b. Aslam and Burmah b. Mālik were clans of Hamdān; see Caskel, *Ǧamharat an-nasab*, II, 230, 445.

227. Text here and twice below: al-Mujālid, but otherwise, and in other sources, without the article. He was either the father of the important *muḥaddith* and *akhbārī* Mujālid b. Sa'īd, or at least his fellow clansman. See Caskel, *Ǧamharat an-nasab*, I, 227, II, 418, 500, and note 237 below.

228. Apparently a reference to the hyena's ferocity once it has captured its prey; see *EI²*, *Suppl.*, s.v. ḍabu'.

Then he went out, leading the troops out with him. He mustered the cavalry of the army; when al-Jazl asked him what he intended to do, he replied, "I intend to advance against Shabīb with this cavalry." Al-Jazl said, "You stay with the body of the army, both cavalry and infantry, and I will go show myself to him. By God, he will assuredly advance against you. Do not divide your forces; that way it will be the worse for them and the better for you." But Sa'īd said, "You stay with the ranks!" Al-Jazl replied, "O Sa'īd b. Mujālid, what you do is no decision of mine. I take no responsibility for this decision of yours, in the hearing of God and those Muslims here present!" Sa'īd said, "It is my own decision. If I have decided rightly, it is because God has led me to do so; if I have not decided rightly, you are all quit of any responsibility for it."

Al-Jazl stayed in the ranks of the Kūfans, having brought them out beyond the trench. He put 'Iyāḍ b. Abī Līnah al-Kindī over his right flank, and 'Abd al-Raḥmān b. 'Awf Abū Ḥāmid al-Ru'āsī over his left flank.[229] Al-Jazl stayed with the main force while Sa'īd b. Mujālid advanced to the front and set out, leading the troops. [909]
Shabīb, meanwhile, had taken the road to Baraz al-Rūz and stopped at Qaṭīṭiyā;[230] he ordered its *dihqān*[231] to purchase for them the things they needed and to provide them with a midday meal, which he did. Shabīb entered the enclosure[232] of Qaṭīṭiyā and ordered the gate shut. He had not yet eaten his meal when Sa'īd b. Mujālid arrived with the forces of that army. The *dihqān* ascended the wall and saw the troops approaching and drawing near his fortress. When he came down, he was pale, and Shabīb asked him why he was so ashen. The *dihqān* replied, "The troops have come at you from every side." Shabīb said, "Never mind! Is our food ready?" He said, "Yes." Shabīb said, "Then bring it. The gate has been shut." The food was brought and he ate. Then he performed the ablutions and prayed two prostrations. Then he

229. The Banū Ru'ās b. al-Ḥārith were a clan of 'Āmir b. Ṣa'ṣa'ah; see Kaḥḥālah, *Mu'jam qabā'il al-'arab*, 450.

230. Spelling and location uncertain.

231. The *dihqāns* were the Sasanian landed gentry, who controlled the rural districts and collected taxes and often continued to do so under the Islamic regime; see *EI*², s.v. dihḳān.

232. *Madīnah*.

called for a mule of his and mounted it. His men assembled at the gate of the enclosure. He ordered the gate opened, and he rode out on his mule and charged the government forces, crying "Judgment belongs only to the Wise Arbiter![233] I am Abū Mudallah![234] Stand if you will!"

Sa'īd collected his troops and cavalry and began to advance them slowly after him,[235] saying, "What are these? Diners on a single head of cattle!"[236] But when Shabīb saw that they had become dispersed and scattered, he turned all his horsemen around, mustered them, and cried, "Slaughter them! And keep an eye on their commander, for, by God, either I will kill him or he will kill me!" Then he attacked them, slaughtering indis-
[910] criminately, and routed them. Sa'īd b. Mujālid stood his ground and called to his forces, "To me! To me! I am Ibn Dhī Murrān!"[237] He took off his skullcap and put it on the pommel of his saddle; but then Shabīb attacked him and crowned him with his sword, cutting through to the brain, and he fell dead.

The army continued to fall back, men falling on every side, until they reached al-Jazl. Al-Jazl dismounted and called out, "To me, men!" 'Iyāḍ b. Abī Līnah called out to them, "Men, if your new commander has perished, your fortunate and blessed commander is still alive and has not died!" Al-Jazl fought hard, until he had to be carried off from amidst the dead and taken to al-Madā'in, wounded. The remnants of that army went back to al-Kūfah. Among the men most severely tested in battle that day were Khālid b. Nahīk of the Banū Dhuhl b. Mu'āwiyah[238] and 'Iyāḍ b. Abī Līnah, who came together to al-Jazl's rescue when he was wounded.

---

233. *Lā ḥukm illā lil-ḥakam al-ḥakīm*, a paraphrase of the Qur'ānic phrase *in al-ḥukm illā lillāh* (6:57; 12:40, 67), and the rallying cry of the Khārijites from the beginning; see text above, I, 3339, 3360ff., and Watt, *Formative Period*, 13ff.

234. This *kunyah* of Shabīb's seems to be not otherwise attested; see note 178 above.

235. *Wa-ja'ala Sa'īd yajma'u qawmahu wa-khaylahu thumma yudlifuhā fī atharihi*. The sense of *yudlifu* here, if that is the correct reading, is unclear; neither the variant *yuzliqu*, "he causes to slip," nor the proposed emendation *yuzlifu*, "he brings near," seems more satisfactory.

236. That is, few in number; see Maydānī, *Amthāl*, I, 44.

237. Dhū Murrān was his grandfather or great-grandfather, of the tribe of Hamdān. See note 227 above.

238. A clan of Kindah; see Caskel, *Ǧamharat an-nasab*, I, 233, II, 239, 342.

This is the account of one group of men. According to the other account, the battle was between Dayr Abī Maryam and Barāz al-Rūz. Then al-Jazl wrote to al-Ḥajjāj.[239]

Shabīb advanced and crossed the Tigris at al-Karkh.[240] He sent word to the market of Baghdad, assuring those there of their safety. That day was their market day, and having heard that they were afraid of him he wanted to reassure them, because his companions were wanting to buy some animals, clothing, and other essential items from the market. Then he led them on toward al-Kūfah. They continued until nightfall and halted at ʿAqr al-Malik, near Qaṣr Ibn Hubayrah.[241] The next day he hurried on and spent that night between Ḥammām ʿUmar b. Saʿd[242] and Qubbīn.[243]

When al-Ḥajjāj was informed of Shabīb's position, he sent to Suwayd b. ʿAbd al-Raḥmān al-Saʿdī[244] and dispatched him with two thousand elite cavalry, saying, "Go out and meet Shabīb. Form right and left wings, then dismount and advance against him with your men.[245] If he falls back in a feint, let him go and do not pursue him." Suwayd went out and camped at al-Sabakhah.[246] He was informed that Shabīb was advancing on him, so [911]

---

239. This is the first of several dislocations in the text. The alternate version of the battle, on the authority of Hishām al-Kalbī, is given below, after an account of Shabīb's advance to al-Kūfah; this is followed in turn by the text of al-Jazl's letter, on the authority of Abū Mikhnaf.

240. Just north of Kalwādhā, on the west side of the Tigris, later a suburb of Baghdad; see *EI*², s.v. al-Karkh.

241. Qaṣr Ibn Hubayrah, whose name postdates these events, was the first of three stages from Baghdad to al-Kūfah and not far from the ruins of Babylon; see Le Strange, *Lands*, 70f.; Musil, *Middle Euphrates*, 43, 274ff. ʿAqr al-Malik, meaning "the king's palace," is presumably the same as "al-ʿAqr in the region of Bābil" mentioned by Masʿūdī, *Tanbīh* (*BGA*, VIII), 321f., but cannot be more precisely identified.

242. That is, the Bath of ʿUmar b. Saʿd b. Abī Waqqāṣ, the son of the founder of al-Kūfah; see Balādhurī, *Futūḥ*, 28. Musil, *Middle Euphrates*, 245f., 276 (there, as sometimes elsewhere, Ḥammām Ibn ʿUmar), locates it a short distance southwest of al-Ḥillah. On the founding of this and other baths, see Morony, *Iraq after the Muslim Conquest*, 268–70.

243. Mentioned and vocalized by Yāqūt, *Muʿjam*, IV, 35, but not precisely located.

244. The Banū Saʿd were a clan of Tamīm; for the genealogy, see Caskel, *Ǧamharat an-nasab*, I, 76, II, 519. This man had earlier fought against al-Mukhtār; see text above, II, 616, 618.

245. *Thumma inzil ilayh fī al-rijāl.* See note 249 below.

246. Literally, the salt marsh, just outside the city. See the map in Massignon,

he advanced as well, but as if his men were being driven toward death.

Al-Ḥajjāj then ordered ʿUthmān b. Qaṭan[247] to muster the troops at al-Sabakhah. He issued a proclamation, saying, "Hear ye! No contractual obligation will protect any man from these troops who spends this night in al-Kūfah and does not go out to join ʿUthmān b. Qaṭan at al-Sabakhah." Then he ordered Suwayd b. ʿAbd al-Raḥmān to take the two thousand men he had with him and meet Shabīb. Suwayd crossed over with his forces to Zurārah,[248] putting them in battle array and rousing their fighting spirits, because he was told that Shabīb was upon him. He then dismounted, along with most of his forces,[249] put his standard before him, and advanced to the far side of Zurārah. But then he was told that Shabīb had learned of his position and turned away from him; he had found a ford and crossed the Euphrates and was now on his way to al-Kūfah by a route that avoided Suwayd. Then he was asked, "Aren't you going to go after them?" Suwayd called out to his forces, and they rode after them. Shabīb, meanwhile, came to the provision depot[250] and halted. There he was told that the Kūfans were mustering en masse at al-Sabakhah. When they learned of Shabīb's position, they ran around shouting at one another and would have gone back into al-Kūfah, had they not been told that Suwayd b. ʿAbd al-Raḥmān had gone after him and his men and caught up with them, and was fighting them with the cavalry.

[912] According to Hishām—ʿUmar b. Bashīr:[251] When Shabīb halted at al-Dayr,[252] he ordered sheep to be slaughtered and prepared for him. The *dihqān* went up to the top of the wall, and when he came back down again he was pale. Shabīb asked him what was

"Explication du plan de Kufa," 336, placing it to the northeast, between the city and the Euphrates bridge.

247. On him, see note 288 below.

248. Across from the city on the east side of the Euphrates. See Balādhurī, *Futūḥ*, 282; Yāqūt, *Muʿjam*, II, 921.

249. *Fa-nazala wa-nazala maʿahu jull aṣḥābihi.* See note 245 above.

250. *Dār al-rizq.* Massignon, "Explication du plan de Kufa," 336, places it next to al-Sabakhah, between the city and the bridge.

251. Here begins the alternate version of the battle with Saʿīd b. Mujālid and al-Jazl.

252. Literally, "the monastery," probably Dayr Abī Maryam.

wrong, and he said, "By God, a large force has come against you!" Shabīb asked, "Is the roast done yet?" He said, "No." Shabīb said, "Never mind then." Then the *dihqān* went up to take another look and said, "By God, they have surrounded the fortress!" But Shabīb said, "Bring on the roast!" and began to eat, showing no concern about the troops outside. When he had finished, performed his ablutions, and prayed with his closest associates, he put on two swords over his coat of mail, grasped an iron mace, and ordered his mule saddled. His brother Muṣād asked him, "Is this a day to saddle a mule?" He replied, "Yes! Saddle it, men!" and mounted it. Then he said, "You, So-and-so, take the right wing, and you, So-and-so, the left." To Muṣād he said, "You take the center." Then he ordered the *dihqān* to have the gate opened before them.

Thus he set out against the troops, calling out that "Judgment is to God alone." Saʿīd and his forces kept falling back, until there was about a mile between them and al-Dayr. Saʿīd began calling out, "O company of Hamdān! I am Ibn Dhī Murrān! To me! To me!" Then he sent out some small parties with his son, having sensed that they would soon be upon him.[253] Shabīb looked at Muṣād and said, "May God bereave you of me if I do not bereave his son of him!" Then he assailed him with his mace, and he fell dead. His forces retreated, and Shabīb's men suffered only one casualty that day.

Saʿīd b. Mujālid's forces were driven back until they came to al-Jazl. Al-Jazl called out to them, "Men! To me! To me!" ʿIyāḍ b. Abī Līnah called out to them, saying, "Men, if this new commander of yours has perished, here is your other, fortunate commander! Rally to him and fight with him!" Some did rally to him, [913] while others rode off in a rout. Al-Jazl fought very hard until he fell wounded; then Khālid b. Nahīk and ʿIyāḍ b. Abī Līnah fought in his defense until they were able to rescue him. The defeated troops hurried back and entered al-Kūfah. Al-Jazl was brought to al-Madā'in, and from there wrote to al-Ḥajjāj b. Yūsuf.

According to Abū Mikhnaf—Thābit, the client of Zuhayr: This is the text of the letter:

I hereby inform the amīr—may God cause him to pros-

253. *Wa-wajjaha siraban maʿa ibnihi wa-qad aḥassa annahā takūnu ʿalayhi.*

per!—that I marched out with those troops I had with me, which the amir ordered me to lead against his enemy, following his orders to me and his decision with regard to them. My strategy was to go out against the enemy when I saw an opportunity, but to hold the troops back from them when I feared an awkward entanglement. I adhered to this strategy, and despite all the enemy's efforts to entice me into combat, he found me no fool. Then Sa'īd b. Mujālid—may God have mercy on his soul!—came to me. I ordered him to be circumspect and forbade him to do anything rash, and commanded him to fight them only when he had the entire force assembled together. But he disobeyed me and hurried off against them with the cavalry. I appeal to the men of both garrisons as witnesses against him that I took no responsibility for the decision he made and did not approve of his action. He went out and was struck down, may God grant him forgiveness; the men had to fall back on me, so I took the field, called them to me, and raised my standard for them. I fought until I was struck down, and my companions carried me off from amidst the dead. When I recovered consciousness, I found that they had already carried me a full mile from the battlefield. Today I am in al-Madā'in with a wound worse than some men die from but no worse than some men re-
[914] cover from. Let the amīr—may God cause him to prosper!—inquire about the advice I gave for him and his troops, about my strategems with his enemy,[254] and about my stand on the day of battle, and it will be clear to him that I have been true to him and offered sincere advice in his interest. Peace.

Al-Ḥajjāj's reply:

I have received your letter, read it, and understood everything you report in it. I believe all you have to say about yourself, including your sincere advice in your amīr's interest, your prudent concern for the men of your garrison, and your fierceness against the enemy. I also have understood what you have to say about Sa'īd and his rashness against the

254. *Mukāyadatī 'aduwwahu.* One MS has *m.kāb.tī,* a corruption from *Mukābadatī,* "my tenacity against," which may be the better reading.

enemy. I have approved both his rashness and your circumspection; his rashness has taken him to Paradise, and your circumspection has passed up no realistic opportunities for attack, whereas passing up unrealistic opportunities is a form of resolution. You have acted correctly, then, and done well when tested, and earned your reward; I consider you one of my trusted servants and counselors. I have sent Ḥayyān b. Abjar to you to nurse you and treat your wounds; and I have also sent you two thousand dirhams to spend on your needs and daily requirements. Peace.

Ḥayyān b. Abjar al-Kinānī of the Banū Firās,[255] who practiced cauterization and other forms of medical treatment, came to him and nursed him. ʿAbdallāh b. Abī ʿUṣayfīr also sent him a thousand dirhams, and visited him often and kept him company, bringing him gifts and presents.

Shabīb, meanwhile, advanced to al-Madāʾin, but realized that he had no way of gaining access to its people, within the city,[256] and went on to al-Karkh, crossing the Tigris to reach it. He sent word from al-Karkh to the people of the market of Baghdad, telling them to go ahead with their market without fear; it was their market [915]
day, and he had heard that they were afraid of him.[257]

Suwayd went out, putting the residences of Muzaynah and the Banū Sulaym[258] at his back and the backs of his forces. Shabīb launched a fearsome attack against them, in the evening, but was

---

255. For the Banū Firās b. Ghanm of Kinānah, see Kaḥḥālah, *Muʿjam qabāʾil al-ʿarab*, 911f. This physician is mentioned by Ibn Juljul, *Ṭabaqāt al-aṭibbāʾ wa-al-ḥukamāʾ* (Cairo, 1955), 59, and his family as one of physicians in al-Kūfah by Ibn Qutaybah, *Maʿārif*, 66; Ibn Ḥajar, *Iṣābah* (Cairo, 1328), I, 364, makes him out to have been a Companion of the Prophet. A highly confused report in Ibn Abī Uṣaybiʿah, *ʿUyūn al-anbāʾ* (Königsberg, 1884), I, 116, on an "ʿAbd al-Malik b. Abjar" at the time of ʿUmar b. ʿAbd al-ʿAzīz has misled modern scholars; see Sezgin, *GAS*, III, 205f., and the literature there. ʿAbd al-Malik b. Saʿīd b. Ḥayyān b. Abjar, noted there from Ibn Ḥajar, *Tahdhīb*, VI, 394f., is perhaps to be equated with the *ʿAbdallāh* b. Saʿīd b. Ḥayyān b. Abjar in the same author's *Iṣābah*, I, 364.

256. *Lā sabīla lahu ilā ahlihā maʿa al-madīnah.*

257. This ends the alternate version of the battle with Saʿīd and al-Jazl, and Ṭabarī reverts to the account of Suwayd's pursuit of Shabīb outside al-Kūfah.

258. On these two Northern tribes, see Kaḥḥālah, *Muʿjam qabāʾil al-ʿarab*, 543ff., 1083f. According to the text above, I, 2489f., the Sulaym were assigned an area in al-Kūfah north of the center, and Muzaynah east of it. See also the map in Massignon, "Explication du plan de Kufa," 336.

unable to achieve anything against them. He then took off through the residential area of al-Kūfah toward al-Ḥīrah,[259] and Suwayd pursued him, keeping to him all the way across the entire residential area of al-Kūfah and on to al-Ḥīrah. There, Suwayd found that Shabīb had cut the bridge at al-Ḥīrah as he passed, so he let him go and halted there until morning.

Al-Ḥajjāj sent orders to Suwayd to pursue Shabīb, and he did.[260] Shabīb continued on down into the Euphrates lowlands, where he found some of his clansmen, then went back up into the desert beyond Khaffān,[261] into a region called al-Ghilẓah.[262] There he encountered men of the Banū al-Wirthah and attacked them, forcing them back to a hard plain in the vicinity. They took stones from the outcroppings around them and threw them at Shabīb and his men until they ran out; then Shabīb was able to get to them and killed thirteen of them, including Ḥanẓalah b. Mālik, Mālik b. Ḥanẓalah, and Ḥumrān b. Mālik, all of the Banū al-Wirthah. This is according to Abū Mikhnaf—ʿAṭāʾ b. ʿArfajah b. Ziyād b. ʿAbdallāh al-Wirthī.

Shabīb then continued on until he came to his father's sons at al-Laṣaf,[263] a watering hole of his kin. This watering hole was under the control of al-Fizr b. al-Aswad, one of the Banū al-Ṣulb;[264] he had forbidden Shabīb to promulgate his opinions and
[916] corrupt his cousins and other kin, to which Shabīb responded, "By God, if I get hold of seven bridles, I will attack al-Fizr!" When Shabīb came with his horsemen to his kin, he asked about al-Fizr; but al-Fizr paid him off with an unbeatably swift horse, on which he rode out beyond the tents and out across the land, as men fled from him.[265] Having given the desert bedouin a good scare, he

---

259. About three miles south; see *EI²*, s.v. al-Ḥīra; Le Strange, *Lands*, 75.

260. But how far is unclear, as nothing more is said about this pursuit.

261. On the edge of the desert, but near the marshes, about thirty miles southeast of al-Kūfah; see Musil, *Middle Euphrates*, 357–60; Massignon, "Explication du plan de Kufa," 356.

262. Spelling and location uncertain. Some MSS have al-ʿUlṭah.

263. West of the pilgrimage road from al-Kūfah, some hundred miles southwest of there. See Yāqūt, *Muʿjam*, IV, 357; Musil, *Northern Neǧd*, 14, 195.

264. Text: Banū al-Ṣalt. See Caskel, *Ǧamharat an-nasab*, I, 146, II, 247. Shabīb was al-Fizr's second cousin once removed.

265. *Fa-ittaqāhu al-Fizr fa-kharaja ʿalā faras lā tujārā min warāʾ al-buyūt fa-dhahaba ʿalayhā fī al-arḍ.* For *ittaqā* in the sense of "to pay off," see Dozy, *Supplément*, s.v. Ibn al-Athīr, *Kāmil*, IV, 405, has al-Fizr riding the horse, but it is

came back and went on to al-Quṭquṭānah[266] and Qaṣr Muqātil,[267] then followed the bank of the Euphrates past al-Ḥaṣṣāṣah[268] and al-Anbār.[269] He proceeded to Daqūqā'[270] and then went off to the nearer parts of Ādharbayjān.

Al-Ḥajjāj let him be and moved to al-Baṣrah, leaving ʿUrwah b. al-Mughīrah b. Shuʿbah as his deputy over al-Kūfah. But the people had hardly caught their breath when ʿUrwah b. al-Mughīrah b. Shuʿbah received a letter from Mādharwāsb, the *dihqān* and lord of Bābil Mahrūdh, saying, "One of the merchants of al-Anbār, a fellow countryman of mine, came to me and said that Shabīb is planning to enter al-Kūfah at the beginning of the coming month. I wanted to inform you of this so you could make your plans. Then, only shortly later, two of my tax collectors came to tell me that Shabīb had arrived in Khānījār."[271]

ʿUrwah took this letter, rolled it up, and rushed it off to al-Ḥajjāj in al-Baṣrah. When al-Ḥajjāj read it, he went racing back to al-Kūfah. Shabīb continued his advance until he reached a village called Ḥarbā,[272] on the bank of the Tigris, where he crossed the river. He asked what the name of the village was and was told "Ḥarbā." He said, "War (*ḥarb*)—may your enemy roast with it—and lamentation (*ḥarab*)—may you bring it into their houses! Bad [917]
omens are only a matter for mantics and augurs."[273] Then he raised his standard and said to his companions, "March!" They

---

not clear with which of the following verbs the subject returns to Shabīb. Musil, *Northern Neğd,* 14, takes al-Fizr as the subject of *all* the following verbs, which seems highly improbable.

266. Probably modern al-Ṭuqṭuqānah, thirty miles due west of al-Kūfah. See Musil, *Northern Neğd,* 14, 199, 212; Ṣ. al-ʿAlī, "Minṭaqat al-Kūfah," 246f.

267. Identified by Caskel, "al-Ukhaiḍir," *Der Islam* 39 (1964), 28–37, with the ruins of al-Ukhayḍir, about thirty-five miles north-northwest of al-Ṭuqṭuqānah.

268. Near Qaṣr Ibn Hubayrah, according to Yāqūt, *Muʿjam,* II, 274; but presumably somewhat north of there, as it also lay on the route from Karbalā' to al-Anbār. See text above, II, 545, and Musil, *Middle Euphrates,* 41, 351.

269. A major town on the Euphrates, forty miles west of Baghdad; see *EI²,* s.v. al-Anbār.

270. Some 120 miles north of Baghdad; see *EI²,* s.v. Daḳūḳā'; Fiey, *Assyrie chrétienne,* III, 41ff.

271. Twenty miles south of Daqūqā'. See Yāqūt, *Muʿjam,* II, 394; Fiey, *Assyrie chrétienne,* III, 60ff.

272. Thirty miles north of Baghdad; see *EI²,* s.v. Ḥarbā'.

273. *Man yaqūfu wa-yaʿīfu.* On *qiyāfah* (physiognomy or the reading of traces on the ground) and *ʿiyāfah* (ornithomancy), see *EI²,* s.vv. ḳiyāfa, ʿiyāfa.

went on, halting at ʿAqarqūf.[274] Suwayd b. Sulaym said to Shabīb, "Commander of the Faithful, would you not have us move away from this village with such an ill-omened name?"[275] Shabīb replied, "Yet again you see bad omens! By God, I will not move from this village until I march from here against my enemy! Its ill omens, God willing, will apply rather to your enemy; here you will attack them, and the wounds (*ʿaqr*) will be theirs." Then he said to his companions, "Men, al-Ḥajjāj is not in al-Kūfah, and, God willing, nothing stands in the way between us and there. Let us march, then!" So he set out to get to al-Kūfah before al-Ḥajjāj.

ʿUrwah wrote to al-Ḥajjāj, saying, "Shabīb has set out and is rapidly approaching al-Kūfah! Hurry!" Al-Ḥajjāj swept past the halting places, racing with Shabīb for the city. Al-Ḥajjāj arrived there at the time of the noon prayer, and Shabīb reached al-Sabakhah at the time of the sunset prayer. After performing the sunset and evening prayers, he and his companions had a little to eat, mounted their horses, and rode into al-Kūfah. Shabīb reached the market, then drove on to the palace and struck its gate with his mace.[276]

According to Abū al-Mundhir: I saw where Shabīb struck the gate of the palace; it left a huge mark.

Then Shabīb came and stood at the platform (*maṣṭabah*),[277] and said:

Her hoof, whenever she crosses a thicket, is like
the measure with which a stingy miser measures out—
A slave with a spurious genealogy, who is really from Thamūd;
or, rather, it is said their father's father was Yaqdum.[278]

---

274. Text: ʿAqraqūfā. This site was four *farsakhs* from Baghdad, near the Dujayl canal (which extended to Ḥarbā), according to Yāqūt, *Muʿjam*, III, 697f. It has been identified as the Kassite city Dur Kurigalzu; see *EI*², s. v. ʿAḳarḳūf.

275. *ʿAqrā* is a form of imprecation, variously explained; see Lane, s.v. *Qūf* was presumably associated with *qiyāfah*; see note 273 above.

276. Of published early parallel accounts, only Yaʿqūbī, *Taʾrīkh*, II, 328, mentions this incident (without the accompanying verses).

277. A bench or raised platform, against a wall; see Lane, *Lexicon*, s.v.

278. These anti-Thaqīf verses are attributed (with variants) to Ḥassān b. Thābit; see his *Dīwān*, 438, and *Aghānī*¹, IV, 11 and XIV, 141. Yaqdum was a descendant of Iyād b. Nizār, through whom one of the respectable genealogies claimed for Thaqīf was made. See Yaʿqūbī, *Taʾrīkh*, I, 258; Goldziher, *Muhammedanische Studien*, I, 99f.

Then they stormed the great mosque, which was still full of people praying. Shabīb killed ʿUqayl b. Muṣʿab al-Wādiʿī, ʿAdī b. ʿAmr [918] al-Thaqafī, and Abū Layth b. Abī Sulaym, the client of ʿAnbasah b. Abī Sufyān. His men also killed Azhar b. ʿAbdallāh al-ʿĀmirī. Then they proceeded to the house of Ḥawshab,[279] who was head of the security forces (*shuraṭ*),[280] and stopped at his door, saying, "The amīr has summoned Ḥawshab." The latter's servant, Maymūn,[281] brought out Ḥawshab's horse for him to ride but seemed to look askance at them; they thought he had become suspicious, and when he began to go back in they said to him, "Stay where you are until your master comes out." Ḥawshab heard this and was incensed at these people, and came out to see them. When he saw the entire group of them, it was clear to him that they were up to no good, and he turned to leave them. They surged toward him, but he went inside and bolted the door. They then killed his servant Maymūn and took his horse, and went on to see al-Jaḥḥāf b. Nubayṭ al-Shaybānī, who was a kinsman of Ḥawshab's. Suwayd said to him, "Come down to us." Al-Jaḥḥāf replied, "What will you do if I do?" Suwayd said, "I will pay you the price of the young she-camel that I bought from you in the desert." Al-Jaḥḥāf said, "What a terrible time and place this is to pay off a debt! Could you not remember your obligation except when the night is dark and you are mounted on your horse? God's plague, O Suwayd, on a debt that cannot be settled and paid up except with the killing of relatives and spilling the blood of this community!"

Then they went on to the mosque of the Banū Dhuhl,[282] where they found Dhuhl b. al-Ḥārith; he had been praying in the mosque of his people, and taken a long time about it, and they caught him just as he was leaving to go home. They pounced on him to kill

---

279. Ḥawshab b. Yazīd b. al-Ḥārith b. Ruwaym al-Shaybānī; see text above, II, 775, and note 102.

280. Pl. of *shurṭah*, police; see note 45 above.

281. According to Yaʿqūbī, *Taʾrīkh*, II, 328, he was known as al-ʿAdhāb ("the chastisement"), or perhaps al-ʿAdhdhāb (otherwise known only as the name of a famous horse; see Zabīdī, *Tāj al-ʿarūs*, s.v.).

282. This mosque has been mentioned previously by Ṭabarī (II, 532), in a context suggesting that these are the Banū Dhuhl b. Muʿāwiyah, a clan of Kindah (so assumed by Caskel, *Ǧamharat an-nasab*, II, 239), rather than Shabīb's own Banū Dhuhl b. Shaybān or the Banū Dhuhl b. Thaʿlabah of Bakr (as implied by Ṭabarī, index, 183).

him, and he cried, "O God, I protest to You against these men and their wickedness and ignorance! O God, I am too weak to protect myself from them; come to my aid against them!" But they
[919] struck him down and killed him. Then they went on until they left al-Kūfah and headed toward al-Mardamah.[283]

According to Hishām—Abū Bakr b. ʿAyyāsh: He was encountered by al-Naḍr b. al-Qaʿqāʿ b. Shawr al-Dhuhlī,[284] whose mother was Nājiyah bint Hāni' b. Qabīṣah b. Hāni' al-Shaybānī,[285] and discomfited him when he looked at him—by "discomfited" he means he frightened him. Al-Naḍr said, "Peace be upon you, O amīr, and God's mercy." But Suwayd interrupted him, saying, "That's 'Commander (*amīr*) of the Faithful,' damn you!" He said, "Commander of the Faithful"—until they left al-Kūfah and headed toward al-Mardamah.[286]

Al-Ḥajjāj ordered the crier to proclaim, "O cavalry of God! Mount and rejoice!"[287] from above the gate of the palace. There was a lamp placed there, with a servant of his waiting. The first of

---

283. Location unknown. Ṭabarī's distinction between this first entry by Shabīb into al-Kūfah and a second attack much later (text below, II, 956–68) is not reflected in other early sources, which combine elements of both incidents into one account. Most of them stress the drama of Shabīb's mother and/or wife praying in the Friday mosque, which is mentioned by Ṭabarī only in passing, at the time of the second attack (see note 439 below). Yaʿqūbī, *Ta'rīkh*, II, 328, is closest to Tabarī in detail, but omits the second attack entirely; Ibn Khayyāṭ, *Ta'rīkh*, 272f., follows Ṭabarī's chronology more closely, but differs in detail; Ibn Aʿtham al-Kūfī, *Futūḥ*, VII, 87–91, knows only the second attack and diverges considerably. See also Ibn Qutaybah, *Ma'ārif*, 410f.; Masʿūdī, *Murūj*, V, 321; Baghdādī, *Farq*, 89ff.; Périer, *Vie d'al-Ḥadjdjādj*, 124–26; Dixon, *Umayyad Caliphate*, 185f.

284. Reading al-Qaʿqāʿ for text Qaʿqāʿ. Al-Qaʿqāʿ b. Shawr of the Banū Dhuhl b. Thaʿlabah of Bakr b. Wā'il was famed in al-Kūfah for his amicability and generosity; see Ziriklī, *Aʿlām*, VI, 48.

285. Hāni' b. Qabīṣah of the Banū Dhuhl b. Shaybān (Shabīb's clan) had led the Bakr b. Wā'il on the day of Dhū Qār; see Ziriklī, *Aʿlām*, IX, 52f. His grandson al-Naḍr was clearly a very respectable man, as well as a kinsman to Shabīb.

286. *Fa-qāla amīr al-mu'minīn ḥattā kharajū min al-Kūfah mutawajjihīn naḥwa al-Mardamah.* The text seems suspect here, as this rather awkwardly tacked-on phrase duplicates the end of the previous paragraph; furthermore, the more coherent variant of this anecdote presented below sets it outside al-Kūfah, at or beyond al-Mardamah. Ibn al-Athīr in his paraphrase (*Kāmil*, IV, 407) gives only the second version of the story, but at this point in the narrative.

287. *Yā khayl Allāh irkabī wa-abshirī*, a standard call to arms; see Fries, *Heereswesen*, 43. Except for the last word, this phrase was considered a prophetic *ḥadīth*; see Jāḥiẓ, *Bayān*, II, 16, and Ibn Manẓūr, *Lisān*, s. v. khayl.

the men to come to him was ʿUthmān b. Qaṭan b. ʿAbdallāh b. al-Ḥuṣayn Dhī al-Ghuṣṣah,[288] accompanied by his clients and some of his kinsmen. He said, "I am ʿUthmān b. Qaṭan. Inform the amir of where I am and let him issue his orders." The servant replied, "Stay where you are until the amīr's orders come to you." Then the men began to come from every direction, and ʿUthmān spent the night there with the men who had assembled with him.

In the morning, al-Ḥajjāj sent out Bishr b. Ghālib al-Asadī of the Banū Wālibah[289] with two thousand men, Zā'idah b. Qudāmah al-Thaqafī with two thousand men, Abū al-Ḍurays, the client of the Banū Tamīm, with a thousand clients, and Aʿyan, the Aʿyan of the Ḥammām Aʿyan and a client of Bishr b. Marwān,[290] with a thousand men.

ʿAbd al-Malik b. Marwān had sent out Muḥammad b. Mūsā b. Ṭalḥah[291] to take charge in Sijistān, writing him up a formal appointment as governor over it, and writing to al-Ḥajjāj, saying, "When Muḥammad b. Mūsā comes to you, supply him with two thousand men to take to Sijistān and hurry him on his way." ʿAbd al-Malik also ordered Muḥammad b. Mūsā to write to al-Ḥajjāj himself. When Muḥammad b. Mūsā arrived, he lingered over his preparations. His advisers urged him, "Hurry, O amīr, to your province, for you do not know what al-Ḥajjāj may be up to or what he may decide to do"; but he remained where he was, and the crisis with Shabīb developed. Then al-Ḥajjāj said to Muḥammad b. Mūsā b. Ṭalḥah b. ʿUbaydallāh, "Please go engage Shabīb and these Khārijites and fight them; then you may go on to your province." [920]

288. His great-grandfather al-Ḥuṣayn b. Yazīd, known as Dhū al-Ghuṣṣah, was a celebrated horseman, leader of the Banū al-Ḥārith of Madhḥij; and his father Qaṭan was a prominent Umayyad supporter in al-Kūfah and, according to one account, briefly governor there in 71 (690–691), before Bishr b. Marwān. See text above, II, 804, 816, and Caskel, *Ǧamharat an-nasab*, I, 261, II, 337, 468.

289. For the Banū Wālibah of Asad, of Muḍar, see Caskel, *Ǧamharat an-nasab*, I, 52, II, 227.

290. Aʿyan was a *mawlā* of Bishr b. Marwān (as reported here), or of the Bakr b. Wa'il (see text below, II, 966f.), or of Saʿd b. Abī Waqqāṣ (Balādhurī, *Futūḥ*, 281). His bath was across the Euphrates from al-Kūfah; according to Balādhurī he had bought it from the heirs of an ʿIbādī in al-Ḥīrah. See Morony, *Iraq after the Muslim Conquest*, 269f.; al-ʿAlī, "Minṭaqat al-Kūfah," 239.

291. Grandson of the famous Ṭalḥah b. ʿUbaydallāh, from the Banū Taym of Quraysh. See Ibn Qutaybah, *Maʿārif*, 233; Ibn Ḥazm, *Jamharah*, 130.

Al-Ḥajjāj also sent out with these commanders ʿAbd al-Aʿlā b. ʿAbdallāh b. ʿĀmir b. Kurayz al-Qurashī and Ziyād b. ʿAmr al-ʿAtakī.[292]

Shabīb, as we have said, left al-Kūfah and went to al-Mardamah. There was a man from Ḥaḍramawt there in charge of the tithes[293] named Nājiyah b. Marthad[294] al-Ḥaḍramī. When this man entered the bath, Shabīb went in after him, brought him out, and struck off his head. Shabīb also encountered al-Naḍr b. al-Qaʿqāʿ b. Shawr; the latter had been with al-Ḥajjāj when he set out from al-Baṣrah, but al-Ḥajjāj had left him behind when he went racing on to al-Kūfah. When Shabīb, who was with his companions, saw him, he recognized him and said, "O Naḍr b. al-Qaʿqāʿ! Judgment is to God alone!" His intention in saying this was to prompt him,[295] but al-Naḍr did not understand and simply replied, "We are God's, and to him we return."[296] Then Shabīb's
[921] companions said, "Commander of the Faithful, it is as if you meant by your words to prompt him!" They set upon al-Naḍr and killed him.

The above-mentioned commanders assembled in the Euphrates lowlands. But then Shabīb turned away from the direction in which these leaders were assembled and set off toward al-Qādisiyyah.[297] Al-Ḥajjāj sent out Zaḥr b. Qays with a company[298] of elite cavalry, eighteen hundred horsemen, saying, "Pursue Shabīb, and wherever you catch up with him, attack him, unless he is on the move elsewhere; if he is, then leave him

---

292. Veteran leader of the Azd in al-Baṣrah; see Caskel, *Ǧamharat an-nasab,* I, 203, II, 606. Al-ʿAtīk was a clan of Azd.

293. *ʿUshūr.* On the ambiguities of this term and its frequent application in the early period (as perhaps here) to illegal imposts, see P. G. Forand, "Notes on *ʿUshr* and *Maks,*" *Arabica* 8 (1961), 137–41.

294. Pointing uncertain. Some MSS have Mazyad, Murayd, etc.

295. *Talqīnah. Laqqana* means generally to dictate words for someone to repeat, but also, technically, to whisper *lā ilāha illā allāh* ("there is no god but God") in the ear of the deceased for him to repeat when interrogated by the two angels in the tomb; see Dozy, *Supplément,* s. v. Shabīb is here giving al-Naḍr a chance to save himself by repeating a phrase (*lā ḥukma illā lillāh*) that is in itself Qur'ānic and therefore unexceptionable; see the variant of this story given below, 968, and note 454.

296. Qur'ān 2:156. The verse begins, "(Believers) who, when they are struck by calamity, say . . ."

297. Nineteen miles southwest of al-Kūfah; see *EI*², s. v. al-Ḳadisiyya.

298. *Jarīdah;* see Lane, *Lexicon,* s. v.

alone, so long as he does not turn on you or halt and make a stand. If he does that, do not leave him without engaging him."

Zaḥr set out and went as far as al-Saylaḥīn.[299] Shabīb was informed of his progress toward him and set out to meet him. When they met, Zaḥr put ʿAbdallāh b. Kannāz al-Nahdī,[300] a very brave man, in charge of his right wing, and ʿAdī b. ʿAdī b. ʿUmayrah al-Kindī al-Shaybānī in charge of his left wing. Shabīb put all his horsemen together in a single compact formation[301] and threw them against the line. The line reeled and broke up, falling back to Zaḥr b. Qays. Zaḥr b. Qays dismounted and fought until he was felled, and his forces fell back. Shabīb's men thought they had killed him, but just before daybreak the cold revived him, and he got up and walked until he came to a village. He spent the night there, and then was conveyed to al-Kūfah. On his face and head were something between ten and twenty wounds, from sword and spear.

A few days later, Zaḥr went to see al-Ḥajjāj, with his face and wounds swathed in cotton. Al-Ḥajjāj sat him next to him on his [922] couch and said to those around him, "Anyone who would like to see a man from the people of Paradise, a martyr walking among men, let him look upon this man!"

Meanwhile, Shabīb's companions, thinking that they had killed Zaḥr, said to Shabīb, "We have defeated a force of theirs and killed one of their great commanders; let us depart, then, satisfied!" But he said, "Our killing this man and defeating this army will have panicked those other commanders and forces that have been sent out in pursuit of us; so let us rather, then, march against them! For, by God, if we kill them, then there will be nothing, God willing, between us and al-Ḥajjāj and the taking of al-Kūfah!" They said, "We hear and follow your decision and are obedient under your hands."

---

299. A town about halfway between al-Ḥīrah and al-Qādisiyyah; see Yāqūt, *Muʿjam*, III, 218f. (Saylaḥūn), and Musil, *Middle Euphrates*, 105. Al-Saylaḥīn was also the name of a canal, and of a *ṭassūj* of Bihqubādh al-Asfal (see note 304 below), which included the palace of al-Khawarnaq; see Ibn Khurradādhbih, *Masālik*, 8, 11; Massignon, "Explication du plan de Kufa," 336, 339, 356; al-ʿAlī, "Minṭaqat al-Kūfah," 248f.

300. Kannāz is a conjectural reading; variants in the MSS include K.thār, K.nān, K.nār, K.bār. The Banū Nahd b. Zayd belonged to Quḍāʿah, a tribal group of uncertain genealogy; see Caskel, *Ǧamharat an-nasab*, II, 443, and *EI*², s. v. Ḳuḍāʿa.

301. *Kabkabah*; see *WKAS*, s. v.

He came swooping down with them as far as Najrān[302]—this is the Najrān of al-Kūfah, in the area of ʿAyn al-Tamr.[303] There he inquired about the main body of enemy forces and was informed that they were assembled at Rūdhbār in the Euphrates lowlands, in Lower Bihqubādh,[304] at a distance of twenty-four *farsakh*s from al-Kūfah. Word came to al-Ḥajjāj of Shabīb's advance toward them, and he sent out to them ʿAbd al-Raḥmān b. al-Ghariq, the client of Ibn Abī ʿAqīl,[305] a man highly esteemed by al-Ḥajjāj, and said to him, "Go catch up with their assembled forces—that is, the assembled forces of the commanders—inform them that the heretics are marching against them and tell them that if they join in combat, the commander of the forces is to be Zā'idah b. Qudāmah." Ibn al-Ghariq went to them, informed them of this, and then departed from them.

[923] According to Abū Mikhnaf—ʿAbd al-Raḥmān b. Jundab: When Shabīb came to us, we had seven commanders with us, all under the supreme command of Zā'idah b. Qudāmah. Each commander had mustered his forces by themselves—Ziyād b. ʿAmr al-ʿAtakī was on our right and Bishr b. Ghālib al-Asadī on our left—and every commander was standing with his own forces. Then Shabīb came and stopped on a hill from which he could look out over the men; he was on a bay horse with a blaze. He looked at the way the troops were mustered, went back to his companions, and then advanced at a gallop with three detachments. As he drew near the troops, one detachment, led by Suwayd b. Sulaym, went and took up its position opposite our right; another detachment, led by Shabīb's brother Muṣād, went and took up its position opposite our left; and Shabīb came with a detachment and took up his position opposite our center.

---

302. On this Christian town, tied historically to the Najrān of Yemen, see Fiey, *Assyrie chrétienne*, III, 226ff.; J. S. Trimingham, *Christianity among the Arabs in Pre-Islamic Times* (London, 1979), 176ff., 195, 307; Massignon, "Explication du plan de Kufa," 336 and note 1.

303. About sixty miles northwest of al-Kūfah; see *EI*², s. v. ʿAyn al-Tamr.

304. The *astān* of Bihqubādh al-Asfal was the Euphrates area south of al-Ḥīrah. The location of Rūdhbār within it seems to be unattested, unless it is connected with the *ṭassūj* of Rūdhmastān; see Ibn Khurradādhbih, *Masālik*, 8, 11; al-ʿAlī, "Minṭaqat al-Kūfah," 251f. Twenty-four *farsakh*s from al-Kūfah would put Rūdhbār almost halfway to al-Baṣrah.

305. The text below, II, 945, has Abū ʿAqīl.

Zā'idah b. Qudāmah went out and passed among the troops, from the right wing to the left, encouraging the men and saying, "O servants of God, you are the virtuous many, afflicted by a wicked few. Hold steadfast—may I be your ransom—for two or three charges against them; then there will be no barrier or obstacle to victory. Take a look at them, by God! They are not even two hundred—diners on a single head of cattle! They are nothing but bandits and renegades, and they have come to you only to spill your blood and take your spoil. Do not let them show themselves more able to take it than you are to defend it! They are few, and you are many; they belong to a sect, while you belong to a community. Lower your eyes and meet them with your spear [924] points; but do not charge them until I order you to." Then he went back to his own position.

Suwayd b. Sulaym charged against Ziyād b. ʿAmr, and their line was thrown back; but Ziyād held his position with about half his forces. Suwayd withdrew from them for a bit, then charged them again, and they fought with spears for some time.

According to Abū Mikhnaf—Farwah b. Laqīṭ: By God, I was one of them that day.[306] We fought with spears for some time, and they held up against us to the point that I thought they would never give up. Ziyād b. ʿAmr fought fiercely, calling out "My horsemen!," lunging with his sword, and really fighting very fiercely. I also saw Suwayd b. Sulaym that day; he was the bravest and fiercest of the bedouin, and no one could stand up to him.

Then, finally, we withdrew from them. They thereupon broke formation, and Shabīb's men said to him, "Do you not see how they are breaking formation? Attack them!" But Shabīb replied, "Leave them be until they thin out a bit." They left them be for a little, and then he led a third attack against them, and they fell back. I saw Ziyād b. ʿAmr take repeated sword blows, but every one of them glanced off; he was wearing mail. I saw more than twenty swords in turn strike him, and he came through it all unhurt. When he finally fell back, he had one small wound; this was in the evening.

Then we charged against ʿAbd al-Aʿlā b. ʿAbdallāh b. ʿĀmir and drove him back; he did not put up much of a fight, having been

---

306. On Shabīb's side; see text above, II, 886, 903.

fighting with his sword for some time already, and, as I heard, having been wounded. Then he caught up with Ziyād b. ʿAmr, and the two kept falling back until we came to Muḥammad b. Mūsā b.
[925] Ṭalḥah, at sunset, who gave us a good fight and stood up to us.

According to Hishām—Abū Mikhnaf—ʿAbd al-Raḥmān b. Jundab and Farwah b. Laqīṭ: Shabīb's brother Muṣād attacked Bishr b. Ghālib, who was on the left wing. Bishr fought bravely and well, by God, and steadfastly. He dismounted, and other steadfast men dismounted with him, some fifty of them, and they fought with their swords until they were killed to a man. One of them was ʿUrwah b. Zuhayr b. Nājidh al-Azdī; his mother was Zārah, a woman who had children among the Azd and whose descendants are known as the Banū Zārah.[307]

When they had killed Bishr and his forces had been driven back, they turned and attacked Abū al-Ḍurays, the client of the Banū Tamīm, who was positioned next to Bishr b. Ghālib. They drove him back as well, as far as the position of Aʿyan. Then they attacked him and Aʿyan together and drove them back as far as Zā'idah b. Qudāmah. When they got to him, he dismounted and called out, "O people of Islam! Dismount! Dismount! To me! To me! Let not them be more steadfast in their unbelief than you in your faith!" He fought them through the night, until daybreak. Then Shabīb charged against him with a concentrated group of his forces and killed him and his companions, leaving those dedicated men a heap of bodies around him.

According to Abū Mikhnaf—ʿAbd al-Raḥmān b. Jundab: I heard Zā'idah b. Qudāmah raising his voice that night and saying, "Men, 'be steadfast and persevering!' 'You who believe, fight for God, and He will fight for you and plant your feet firmly!' "[308] Then, by God, he did not leave off fighting them, pushing for-
[926] ward, and never falling back, until he was killed, God have mercy on him.

According to Abū Mikhnaf—Farwah b. Laqīṭ: Abū al-Ṣuqayr al-Shaybānī claimed that it was he who actually killed Zā'idah b. Qudāmah, but his claim was disputed by another man named al-Faḍl b. ʿĀmir.

---

307. Text: Zurārah, but see Caskel, *Ǧamharat an-nasab*, II, 605 (Banū Zārah), 610 (Zuhayr b. Rabīʿah b. Nājid b. al-Akram), and Ibn Durayd, *K. al-Ishtiqāq* (Cairo, 1958), 491. The details of the genealogy are unclear.

308. Qur'ān 3:200 and 47:7.

When Shabīb killed Zā'idah b. Qudāmah, Abū al-Ḍurays and A'yan retreated into a large fortress. Shabīb said to his forces, "Hold back your swords from the men and summon them to render the oath of allegiance." They did this at dawn.

According to 'Abd al-Raḥmān b. Jundab: I was among those who came to him and rendered him the oath of allegiance, as he sat on his horse with his mounted cavalry before him. As each man came to render the oath of allegiance, his sword was taken from his shoulder and his other weapons taken from him; then he was led before Shabīb. He greeted Shabīb as Commander of the Faithful and was left free to go his way.

This was my situation when dawn broke. At this time, Muḥammad b. Mūsā b. Ṭalḥah b. 'Ubaydallāh was at the far end of the army, with a group of his comrades, and they were still holding out. When dawn broke, he ordered his muezzin to give the call to prayer. Shabīb, hearing the call to prayer, asked, "What is that?" and was told, "That is Muḥammad b. Mūsā b. Ṭalḥah b. 'Ubaydallāh; he is still making a stand." Shabīb said, "Indeed I thought his foolishness and vanity would make him do that. Now set these men apart from us, and let us dismount and pray."

He dismounted and gave the call to prayer himself, then stood before his companions and led them in prayer. He recited the Qur'ānic *sūrah*s "Woe to every slanderer and backbiter" and "Have you seen him who cries lies to religion?"[309] Then he gave the *taslīm*,[310] and they mounted their horses and attacked. One group of Muḥammad b. Mūsā's men were driven back, but another group held their ground.

According to Farwah: I will never forget what Muḥammad b. Mūsā was saying as we came up on him; he was fighting with his sword and saying, "*Alif. Lām. Mīm.* Do men think that they will [927]
be left at ease because they say 'We believe,' and will not be tested? We have tested those who were before them, and indeed God knows those who are sincere, and knows those who lie."[311] He fought until he was killed. I heard my companions say that it was Shabīb who killed him. Then we dismounted and took what-

309. Qur'ān 104 and 107, identified here by their first verses.

310. The formula *al-salāmu 'alaykum,* which concludes the prayer; see *SEI,* s. v. *ṣalāt.*

311. Qur'ān 29:1–3.

ever we could find in the camp. Those who had rendered the oath of allegiance to Shabīb fled, and not one of them remained.

Someone other than Abū Mikhnaf has reported something different with regard to Muḥammad b. Mūsā b. Ṭalḥah from what I have reported from Abū Mikhnaf, as follows: ʿAbd al-Malik b. Marwān had appointed Muḥammad b. Mūsā b. Ṭalḥah governor of Sijistān. Al-Ḥajjāj then wrote to him saying, "You have responsibility for every land you pass through. Now here is Shabīb in your path." So Muḥammad turned to confront Shabīb. Shabīb sent to him, saying, "You have been taken in! Al-Ḥajjāj has used you to protect himself, while you have a claim to protection as my neighbor![312] Go, then, to the place to which you were ordered, and godspeed! I will not harm you." But Muḥammad insisted on fighting him. Shabīb came out to meet him and sent the messenger to him again, but still he insisted on fighting him. He called for single combat, and al-Baṭīn came forward to challenge him, then Qaʿnab, then Suwayd; but he refused to fight anyone but Shabīb. They told Shabīb, "He refuses us and insists on you." Shabīb said, "What else would you expect of these notables?" Then he came forward to challenge Muḥammad, but said, "I adjure you by God, spare your life, for you have a claim to my protection!" Still he insisted on fighting him. Shabīb then charged him and struck him with an iron mace weighing twelve Syrian *raṭls*,[313] smashing his helmet and head, and he fell. Shabīb had him dressed in a shroud and buried, and he bought up the spoils that had been taken from his camp and sent them to his
[928] family. He justified himself to his companions, saying, "He was my neighbor in al-Kūfah, and I have the right to bestow the spoil I have taken on the people of apostasy[314] if I so wish."

---

312. *Wa-anta jār laka ḥaqq,* as also below, *laka jiwār* ("you are under protection"). For this principle of assuming responsibility for the security of a guest or neighbor, see *EI*², s. v. djiwār; W. Schmucker, *Untersuchungen zu einigen wichtigen bodensrechtlichen Konsequenzen der islamischen Eroberungsbewegung* (Bonn, 1972), 13ff.

313. If we calculate from the preserved Umayyad *raṭl*-weight from Syria, dated 744 A. D., which weighs 337.55 grams, this mace weighed a little over four kilograms. The *raṭl* varied considerably from city to city; for later periods, we know that the standard Damascus *raṭl* was 1.85 kg, the Aleppo *raṭl* 2.28 kg, etc. See Hinz, *Islamische Masse und Gewichte,* 3, 30f.

314. *Ahl al-riddah,* conventionally applied to the Arab tribes that renounced

According to ʿUmar b. Shabbah—Abū ʿUbaydah:[315] Muḥammad b. Mūsā had been with ʿUmar b. ʿUbaydallāh b. Maʿmar[316] in Fārs. He fought with him in the battle against Abū Fudayk, as commander of his right wing, and distinguished himself for bravery and valor.[317] ʿUmar b. ʿUbaydallāh b. Maʿmar gave him his daughter Umm ʿUthmān in marriage; his sister[318] had married ʿAbd al-Malik b. Marwān. ʿAbd al-Malik then appointed Muḥammad governor of Sijistān. On his way there he passed through al-Kūfah, when al-Ḥajjāj b. Yūsuf was there. It was suggested to al-Ḥajjāj that "if this man, with his bravery and his marriage ties to ʿAbd al-Malik, reaches Sijistān, and anyone you are pursuing takes refuge with him, he will not give him up to you." Al-Ḥajjāj asked what could be done and was told, "You should go to him, greet him, mention his bravery and valor, and how Shabīb is in his path, and has frustrated all your efforts, and that you hope God may relieve you of him through Muḥammad's hand, the fame and glory thereof accruing to Muḥammad himself."

So it happened. Muḥammad b. Mūsā b. Ṭalḥah b. ʿUbaydallāh turned aside to confront Shabīb, who came out to meet him.[319] Shabīb said to him, "I know all about al-Ḥajjāj's wiles. He has tricked you and managed to use you to protect himself. It seems to me that if the two rings of the saddle-girth should meet,[320] your companions would abandon you and you would be cut down like your comrades. Do as I say, then, and go off to your own business, for I value you too highly to see you die." But Muḥam-

---

their Islam after the death of the Prophet. According to Mubarrad, *Kāmil*, 573, the Khārijites used *riddī* to mean "someone who knows the truth of what they say, but suppresses it"; but here *ahl al-riddah* probably means only "non-Khārijite Muslims."

315. Abū ʿUbaydah Maʿmar b. al-Muthannā, the famous philologist, d. 209 (824–825); see *EI*², s. v. Abū ʿUbayda.

316. On him see Ziriklī, *Aʿlām*, V, 214. Like Muḥammad b. Mūsā, he belonged to the Banū Taym of Quraysh. For his governorship in Fārs and battles against the Azraqites there (for Muṣʿab b. al-Zubayr), see text above, II, 753ff. According to Ibn Khallikān, *Wafayāt*, V, 240, Abū ʿUbaydah was a *mawlā* of his family.

317. See text above, II, 852f.

318. ʿĀʾishah. See Ibn Ḥazm, *Jamharah*, 130.

319. Reading *fa-wāqafah* (as in the previous account) for text *fa-wāqaʿah*.

320. That is, if push came to shove; for the proverb, see Maydānī, *Amthāl*, II, 121.

mad b. Mūsā refused, and Shabīb engaged him in single combat and killed him.[321]

Returning to the account of Abū Mikhnaf—ʿAbd al-Raḥmān: Among the men who rendered him the oath of allegiance that night was Abū Burdah b. Abī Mūsā al-Ashʿarī.[322] When he rendered the oath, Shabīb asked him, "Are you not Abū Burdah?" He
[929] said, "Yes." Shabīb said to his companions, "My friends! This man's father was one of the two arbiters!"[323] They replied, "Let us kill him then!" But Shabīb said, "This man bears no blame for what his father did." They said, "Truly."

The next morning Shabīb set out for the fortress in which Abū al-Ḍurays and Aʿyan had taken refuge, but they attacked him with arrows and fortified themselves against him. He remained confronting them for that day, and then left them.

Then his companions said to him, "There is no one stopping us from going right on to al-Kūfah." But when he saw how many wounds they had sustained, he said, "I will not require of you more than what you have already done." He then led them to Niffar,[324] al-Ṣarāt,[325] and Baghdad, and proceeded on to Khānījār, where he halted.

---

321. Quite divergent from the three versions of Muḥammad b. Mūsā's fate given here is the notice in Ibn Khayyāṭ, *Ta'rīkh,* 273f., 297, which places his defeat and death at al-Ahwāz, the following year, after Shabīb had entered al-Kūfah the second time and was on his way to Kirmān (see text below, II, 972). Otherwise, Ibn Khayyāṭ follows Ṭabarī's chronology here, if summarily. Ibn Aʿtham al-Kūfī, *Futūḥ,* VII, 85f., on the other hand, in his list of commanders defeated or killed by Shabīb, puts Zaḥr b. Qays fourth, after ʿAbd al-Raḥmān b. al-Ashʿath (see text below, II, 930, and, for the first two, note 178 above), is silent on Zā'idah b. Qudāmah and his companions, and mentions Muḥammad b. Mūsā ninth, just before Shabīb's (only) entry into al-Kūfah. Ibn Qutaybah, *Maʿārif,* 410, names Muḥammad b. Mūsā as one of five commanders killed by Shabīb before attacking al-Kūfah, which agrees with Ibn Aʿtham al-Kūfī. See also Ibn al-Athīr, *Kāmil,* IV, 408–11; Périer, *Vie d'al-Ḥadjdjādj,* 127–29; Dixon, *Umayyad Caliphate,* 185f.

322. Later in charge of the judiciary in al-Kūfah. See *EI*², s.v. al-Ashʿarī, Abū Burda.

323. Abū Mūsā al-Ashʿarī was chosen as the arbiter (*ḥakam*) to represent ʿAlī in the conflict with Muʿāwiyah at Ṣiffīn; since the decision to arbitrate led to the secession of the Khārijites from ʿAlī's side, he would be held in particular opprobrium by them. See *EI*², s.v. al-Ashʿarī, Abū Mūsā.

324. The ancient Nippur, about fifty-five miles east of al-Kūfah; see *EI*¹, s.v. Niffar.

325. The Ṣarāt canal, extending east-west between the Euphrates and the Tigris, would be crossed some thirty miles north of Niffar on the route to al-Madā'in or

When al-Ḥajjāj heard that Shabīb was headed toward Niffar, he thought that his objective was al-Madā'in, which is the gateway to al-Kūfah; for he who takes al-Madā'in controls most of the region of al-Kūfah. This panicked al-Ḥajjāj, and he sent for ʿUthmān b. Qaṭan, and summoned him to hurry off to al-Madā'in; he put him in charge of its pulpit and prayer, of the security force (*maʿūnah*)[326] of all of Jūkhā, and of the land revenue of the district.[327] ʿUthmān went straight off to al-Madā'in, and al-Ḥajjāj dismissed ʿAbdallāh b. Abī ʿUṣayfir.

At this time, al-Jazl had been staying in al-Madā'in for some months, treating his wounds, and Ibn Abī ʿUṣayfir used to come visit him and treat him generously. But when ʿUthmān b. Qaṭan came to al-Madā'in, he did not come to visit him, frequent his company, or send him any gifts. Al-Jazl's comment was "O God, increase Ibn Abī ʿUṣayfir in generosity, liberality, and excellence, [930] and increase ʿUthmān b. Qaṭan in tightness and miserliness!"

Then al-Ḥajjāj summoned ʿAbd al-Raḥmān b. Muḥammad b. al-Ashʿath[328] and ordered him to select a force and go out in pursuit of this enemy; he stipulated a force of six thousand. ʿAbd al-Raḥmān made his selection from the horsemen and most prominent fighters, and also led out six hundred of his own men from Kindah and Ḥaḍramawt. Al-Ḥajjāj urged him to hurry with the muster, which he made at Dayr ʿAbd al-Raḥmān. When al-Ḥajjāj was ready to send them out, he wrote to them as follows:

> You have made humiliation into a habit, and turned and retreated on the day of advance. This is the behavior of unbelievers. I have forgiven you time after time after time after

Baghdad; see Le Strange, *Lands*, 72. In Ṭabarī al-Ṣarāt often refers to an area, or perhaps to an otherwise unidentified town; see, for example, text above, II, 37, 40.

326. A synonym for *shurṭah*, the police or internal security forces. See Ṭabarī, glossarium, s.v., and note 45 above.

327. *Kharāj al-astān*. It is unclear whether this refers to Jūkhā, or to one of the fiscal *astāns* listed by the geographers (and if so, which one; see Le Strange, *Lands*, 79ff.). Some MSS read al-Anbār, as does the paraphrase by Ibn al-Athīr, *Kāmil*, IV, 411 (*amīran ʿalā al-Madā'in wa-Jūkhā wa-al-Anbār*).

328. ʿAbd al-Raḥmān b. Muḥammad b. Maʿdīkarib (al-Ashʿath), grandson of the famous general and chief of the Kindah of Ḥaḍramawt, al-Ashʿath b. Qays; see *EI*², s.v. Ibn al-Ashʿath. He had earlier fought for Muṣʿab b. al-Zubayr against al-Mukhtār and for Bishr b. Marwān against the Azraqites; see text above, II, 733, 826f.

time. But now, I swear to you a solemn oath by God, if you act this way again, I will deal you a blow far worse than facing this enemy, from whom you flee through lowland valleys and mountain passes and from whom you hide in river bends and mountain clefts. He who has any sense will fear for himself and not put his life in jeopardy! The warner is excused,[329] and "If you had addressed a living being, you would have been heard"[330]—but those you address have no life! Peace be upon you.

Then al-Ḥajjāj dispatched Ibn al-Aṣamm, his muezzin, to ʿAbd al-Raḥmān b. Muḥammad b. al-Ashʿath. He came to Ibn al-Ashʿath at sunrise and said, "Set out immediately, and proclaim to the men that 'No contractual obligation will protect any member of this expedition whom we find malingering.'" ʿAbd al-Raḥmān b. Muḥammad b. al-Ashʿath marched out with the men as far as al-Madā'in and halted there for a day and a night while his forces bought what they needed. Then he gave the call for the
[931] men to saddle their mounts, and they did so and began to move out. ʿAbd al-Raḥmān stopped to see ʿUthmān b. Qaṭan and then went to see al-Jazl, asking him about his wounds and sitting to talk with him for a while. Al-Jazl then said to him, "Kinsman,[331] you are marching against the horsemen of the bedouin, sons of war, men never out of the saddle, by God, as if they had been created from their horses' ribs and raised on their backs. They are lions in the thickets, one horseman of theirs worth a hundred: if you do not attack him, he will attack you, and if you yell at him to chase him off[332] he will come at you. I have fought them and seen how they fight. When I showed myself to them in the open, they took their due from me and bested me; but when I put trenches around myself and fought them in narrow places, I got something of what I was after from them and achieved victory. If possible, then, do not encounter them when you are not either in formation or protected by a trench." When ʿAbd al-Raḥmān bade

329. *Aʿdhara man andhara*; see Maydānī, *Amthāl*, I, 435.

330. That is, "your words go unheeded," referring to himself; for the proverb, see Maydānī, *Amthāl*, II, 48.

331. Both men belonged to the tribe of Kindah.

332. *In hujhija*, a word applied specifically to lions (and camels); see Lane, *Lexicon*, s.v.

him farewell, al-Jazl said, "Here is my horse al-Fusayfisā'. Take her; she can outrun all others."

'Abd al-Raḥmān took the horse and led the men out against Shabīb; but when he drew near him, Shabīb withdrew from him to Daqūqā' and Shahrazūr.[333] 'Abd al-Raḥmān pursued him as far as the borders but then halted and said, "He is now in the Mosul region, so let them fight to defend their land, or let him be, as they please." But al-Ḥajjāj b. Yūsuf wrote to him, saying, "Pursue Shabīb and go after him wherever he goes, until you catch him and kill him or expel him. The authority is that of the Commander of the Faithful, and the troops are his troops. Peace."

When he read al-Ḥajjāj's letter, 'Abd al-Raḥmān set out again in pursuit of Shabīb. Shabīb's strategy had been to let 'Abd al-Raḥmān draw near him and then attempt a night attack; but [932]
when he found that 'Abd al-Raḥmān had taken precautions and dug a defensive trench, he would withdraw and again let him be, and 'Abd al-Raḥmān would pursue him. When Shabīb heard that he had started up and was on the march, he would advance on him with his cavalry; but when he reached him he would find that he had put the cavalry and infantry in battle array and brought up the archers, never catching him in a moment of negligence or weakness. Then he would again withdraw and let him be.

When Shabīb saw that he could not catch 'Abd al-Raḥmān unawares or find a way to get at him, he began to take his cavalry out when 'Abd al-Raḥmān drew near and would then dismount at a distance of twenty *farsakh*s, halting in a rough and barren area. 'Abd al-Raḥmān would come up, and when he drew near Shabīb, Shabīb would remount and go another fifteen or twenty *farsakh*s and dismount again, in a rough and rugged area. There he would halt until 'Abd al-Raḥmān again drew near.

According to Abū Mikhnaf—'Abd al-Raḥmān b. Jundab: Shabīb subjected that army to torments and agonies, wore down the hooves of their beasts, and put them through every sort of trial; but 'Abd al-Raḥmān kept pursuing him, passing by Khāniqīn, then Jalūlā', then Tāmarrā.[334] Then Shabīb went on and dis-

---

333. A district, and city, east of Daqūqā' and north of Ḥulwān; see Fiey, *Assyrie chrétienne*, III, 67ff.

334. A *ṭassūj* of the *astān* of Ḥulwān, in the area where the Diyālā River and the

mounted at al-Batt,[335] one of the villages of Mosul, just on the borders of that region, separated from the Sawād[336] of al-Kūfah only by a river called Ḥawlāyā.[337]

ʿAbd al-Raḥmān b. Muḥammad b. al-Ashʿath came and dismounted at the Ḥawlāyā River, in Upper Rādhān,[338] in the region of Jūkhā. He halted at some steep bends in the river; ʿAbd al-Raḥmān halted there where he did, because these bends im-
[933] pressed him as being like a natural trench and fortress.

Then Shabīb sent to ʿAbd al-Raḥmān, saying, "These days are feast days[339] for both us and you. If you would care to observe a truce for their duration, by all means do so." ʿAbd al-Raḥmān agreed—there was nothing dearer to ʿAbd al-Raḥmān than truces and delays.

But ʿUthmān b. Qaṭan wrote to al-Ḥajjāj, saying, "I hereby inform the amīr—may God cause him to prosper!—that ʿAbd al-Raḥmān b. Muḥammad has dug up Jūkhā in its entirety into one great trench while leaving Shabīb to cut off its land revenue and plunder its people. Peace."

Al-Ḥajjāj replied, "I have understood what you have told me about ʿAbd al-Raḥmān, and, by my life, he has indeed done as you say. Go, then, to the men, for you are to be their commander, and hurry out to confront the heretics. God will give you victory over them, God willing. Peace."

Nahrawān Canal (both also sometimes known as Tāmarrā) met. See Ibn Khurradādhbih, *Masālik,* 6; Le Strange, *Lands,* 59f., 80; Fiey, *Assyrie Chrétienne,* III, 13.

335. Yāqūt, *Muʿjam,* I, 488, mentions two towns with this name, one in the district of Baghdad, "near Rādhān," the other near Baʿqūbā. The first of these may be the place intended here, and was perhaps just north of the al-ʿUdhaym River (see note 337).

336. The Sawād ("blackness") is the alluvial plain of Mesopotamia; at this time, the Sawād of al-Kūfah was the entire province between the Sawād of al-Baṣrah to the south and the district of Mosul to the north, constituting with the former the Sawād of Iraq.

337. If Fiey's identification of Rādhān is accepted (see notes 184, 186), this may be the al-ʿUdhaym River, although that would imply administration from Mosul farther down the Tigris than was the case later, when the capital of the Iraq had been moved north from al-Kūfah to Baghdad.

338. *Rādhān al-Aʿlā.* Wherever Rādhān was, it was administratively divided into two parts, upper and lower; see Ibn Khurradādhbih, *Masālik,* 6, and note 184 above.

339. Presumably, the season of the ʿĪd al-Aḍḥā, or Greater Feast, celebrated on the tenth of Dhū al-Ḥijjah; see *EI*[2], s.v. ʿĪd al-Aḍḥā, and next note.

Al-Ḥajjāj sent Muṭarrif b. al-Mughīrah b. Shuʿbah to al-Madā'in, while ʿUthmān set out and came to ʿAbd al-Raḥmān b. Muḥammad and the Kūfans with him where they were camped on the River Ḥawlāyā, near al-Batt. This was the evening of Tuesday, the "Day of Watering" (8 Dhū al-Ḥijjah 76 [March 18, 696]).[340] ʿUthmān called to the men, as he sat on a mule, "Men, go out against your enemy!" The men came running to him, saying, "We adjure you by God! Night has fallen, and the men have not put themselves in the proper frame of mind for combat. First pass the night, then take the men out in formation." But he kept saying, "I will go out and engage them, and the lot will fall to my favor or theirs." Then ʿAbd al-Raḥmān came to them and seized the bridle of ʿUthmān's mount, pleading with him in God's name [934]
until he dismounted. ʿAqīl b. Shaddād al-Salūlī[341] said to ʿUthmān, "The engagement you want right now you can have tomorrow, and tomorrow will be better for both you and the men. There is wind and dust at this hour, and evening has come. Dismount, then, and we will all set out against them early in the morning." He dismounted then. The wind and the dust it raised irritated him, so the revenue collector[342] summoned the local inhabitants[343] to build him a large tent[344] to spend the night in.

The next morning, Wednesday, the people of al-Batt came to Shabīb, who was staying in their church, and said, "May God cause you to prosper! You are merciful to the weak and the people of the *jizyah;*[345] those you govern can speak to you and complain of their afflictions, and you concern yourself with them and pro-

---

340. The "day of watering" (*yawm al-tarwiyah*) is the first day of the pilgrimage rites in Mecca; there are various explanations for the name. See Lane, *Lexicon*, s.v. *tarwiyah*, and *EI*², s.v. ḥadjdj. March 18, 696, was a Saturday.

341. Called also "al-Ḥubshī" below; he was a descendant of the Companion Ḥubshī b. Junādah of the Banū Salūl of Hawāzin (of Qays ʿAylān), named after Salūl bint Dhuhl b. Shaybān, wife of Murrah b. Ṣaʿṣaʿah. See Caskel, *Ǧamharat an-nasab*, I, 92, 114, II, 327, 509.

342. *Ṣāḥib al-kharāj;* apparently the person locally responsible, who knew the inhabitants. See also note 375 below.

343. *ʿUlūj:* according to the lexicographers "brutes" or "infidels," but in this period essentially "peasants" or "non-Arabs"; see Løkkegaard, *Islamic Taxation*, 172.

344. *Qubbah;* see Dozy, *Supplément*, s.v.

345. The poll tax, levied on the non-Muslim population; see *EI*², s.v. djizya. The Khārijites were consistently as tolerant of non-Muslims as they were intolerant of non-Khārijite Muslims; see *EI*², s.v. Khāridjites.

tect them. But these people are oppressors; they will not be talked to, and they will accept no excuses. By God, if they hear that you are staying in our church, they will surely kill us once you go, if you are fated to do so. If you would, then, come stay next to the village, so they will have nothing to hold against us." Shabīb agreed to do so, and went out and encamped beside the village.

'Uthmān spent the entire night encouraging the troops. When Wednesday morning came, he led the men out, but they were met by a strong wind and dust, and cried to him, saying, "We adjure you by God, do not take us out today; for the wind is against us." He agreed to wait out that day. Shabīb was planning to fight them, and his forces went out, but when he saw that his opponents did not come out to him, he also waited out the day.

On Thursday eve, 'Uthmān went out and mustered the men by their quarters. He put each quarter on one side of the camp and told them to march out in that formation. He asked them who
[935] had been in command of their right wing, and they said Khālid b. Nahīk b. Qays al-Kindī, with 'Aqīl b. Shaddād al-Salūlī in command of their left wing. 'Uthmān summoned the two men and said to them, "Keep the same positions that you have had; I am putting you in command of the two wings. Stand fast and do not flee, for, by God, I shall abide as long as the palms of Rādhān abide on their trunks!" They replied, "And we, by God, other than Whom there is no god, will not flee, but stand until we achieve either victory or death." 'Uthmān said, "May God reward you richly."

'Uthmān waited until he had led the men in the morning prayer, and then set out.[346] He put the quarters of the Medinese and of Tamīm and Hamdān[347] on the left, toward the River Ḥawlāyā, and the quarters[348] of Kindah and Rabī'ah and of Madhḥij and Asad on the right. He himself dismounted and marched with the infantry. Shabīb also went forth, having 181 men with him that day, and crossed the river to meet his opponents. He was in the right wing of his forces, having put Suwayd

---

346. The day was 10 Dhū al-Ḥijjah, the 'Īd al-Aḍḥā.

347. Reading *rub'ay ahl al-Madīnah wa-Tamīm wa-Hamdān* for text *rub' ahl al-Madīnah Tamīm wa-Hamdān*.

348. Reading *rub'ay* for text *rub'*.

b. Sulaym over his left wing and his brother Muṣād b. Yazīd in the center. The two armies advanced and bore down on each other.

According to Abū Mikhnaf—al-Naḍr b. Ṣāliḥ al-ʿAbsī: ʿUthmān kept repeating, "'Flight will not avail you if you flee from death or killing; afterward you will not dwell in comfort but a little while.'[349] Where are those who uphold their religion and defend their spoil[350]?" ʿAqīl b. Shaddād b. Ḥubshī al-Salūlī said, "Perhaps I may be one of them—those others were killed on the day of Rūdhbār!"[351]

Then Shabīb said to his men, "I am going to attack their left wing, next to the river. If I defeat them, then the commander of [936]
my left should attack their right. But the commander of my center must not move until he receives my order." Then he charged with his right wing, next to the river, against ʿUthmān b. Qaṭan's left, and it was driven back. ʿAqīl b. Shaddād dismounted and fought until he was killed. Also killed that day was Mālik b. ʿAbdallāh al-Hamdānī al-Murhibī, the paternal uncle of ʿAbdallāh b. ʿAyyāsh al-Mantūf.[352] ʿAqīl b. Shaddād recited that day as he fought:

Indeed I strike with my keen sword
like a true stalwart scion of Salūl.

While Shabīb plunged into the midst of his opponents' forces, Suwayd b. Sulaym charged with Shabīb's left against ʿUthmān b. Qaṭan's right, commanded by Khālid b. Nahīk b. Qays al-Kindī, and drove them back. Khālid, who was in command of the quarter of Kindah and Rabīʿah that day, as well as being commander of the right wing, dismounted and fought fiercely, but Shabīb attacked him from the rear. Shabīb headed straight for him and came down on him with his sword, killing him. ʿUthmān b. Qaṭan, accompanied by the marshals and the tribal notables and horsemen

---

349. Qur'ān 33:16.

350. *Fay'*; see note 67 above.

351. *Laʿallī an akūna aḥadahum qutila ulā'ika yawm Rūdhbār.* Other MSS read *Laʿallī an akūna minhum aw aḥadahum wa-in kānū qad qutilū yawm Rūdhbār.*

352. Reading ʿAbdallāh b. ʿAyyāsh for text ʿAyyāsh b. ʿAbdallāh b. ʿAyyāsh, which is genealogically impossible. ʿAbdallāh b. ʿAyyāsh al-Mantūf of the Banū Murhibah b. Duʿām of Hamdān is cited frequently by Ṭabarī. See Caskel, *Ǧamharat an-nasab*, I, 231, II, 106, 432.

among his forces, who had dismounted with him, moved against the enemy center, where Shabīb's brother was positioned with some sixty men on foot. 'Uthmān b. Qaṭan drew up to them and charged them with his notables and stalwart men, and these pounded at them until they broke their ranks; but then Shabīb attacked them from behind with the cavalry, and before they knew it they were speared in the back and pitched forward on their faces. Now Suwayd b. Sulaym turned against them as well, with his cavalry, and Muṣād and his forces came back to the fray, after Shabīb had them dismount. There was a general melee for a
[937] time, and 'Uthmān b. Qaṭan fought and fought well; but then the enemy forces pressed his men and surrounded him, and Shabīb's brother Muṣād charged him and delivered a sword blow that spun him around. 'Uthmān said, "'And God's command was fulfilled,'"[353] and the enemy troops killed him. Also killed that day was al-Abrad b. Rabī'ah al-Kindī; he was on a hillock, when he tossed his spear[354] to his weapon bearer (*ghulām*) and gave him his horse; he then fought until he was killed.

'Abd al-Raḥmān had fallen, but Ibn Abī Sabrah al-Ju'fī,[355] who was mounted on a mule, saw him and recognized him. He dismounted, handed him his spear, and said, "Mount!" 'Abd al-Raḥmān b. Muḥammad asked, "Which of us is to ride behind?" Ibn Abī Sabrah replied, "Glory to God! You are the commander and should be in front!" 'Abd al-Raḥmān mounted and said to Ibn Abī Sabrah, "Call to the men that they are to come to Dayr Abī Maryam." He did so, and the two of them set off themselves. Meanwhile, Wāṣil b. al-Ḥārith al-Sakūnī saw 'Abd al-Raḥmān's horse, the one al-Jazl had given him, wandering about the battlefield; then one of Shabīb's men took it. Wāṣil assumed that 'Abd al-Raḥmān had been killed, and he looked for him among the dead but did not find him. He asked around about him, and was told, "We saw a man dismount from his beast and put him on it; it was probably him, in any case, as he had come this way only shortly before." Wāṣil b. al-Ḥārith set out after him on his nag,

353. Qur'ān 4:47, 33:37.

354. *Silāḥ*, meaning weapon in general, but perhaps here the spear with which one fights on horseback as opposed to the sword wielded on foot.

355. Muḥammad b. 'Abd al-Raḥmān b. Yazīd Abī Sabrah of the Banū Ju'fī b. Sa'd al-'Ashīrah of Madhḥij; see Caskel, *Ǧamharat an-nasab*, I, 268, II, 422.

taking his weapon bearer with him on a mule. As they drew near, Muḥammad b. Abī Sabrah said to ʿAbd al-Raḥmān, "By God, two horsemen are coming up on us!" ʿAbd al-Raḥmān asked, "Are there more than just the two?" Muḥammad said, "No." ʿAbd al-Raḥmān said, "Well, two can handle two."

ʿAbd al-Raḥmān continued talking with Ibn Abī Sabrah as if he were paying the two men no mind, until they caught up with them. Then Ibn Abī Sabrah said, "God's mercy on you, the two men have caught up with us." ʿAbd al-Raḥmān said, "Let us dismount, then." They dismounted and drew their swords, and then [938] went to meet them. When Wāṣil saw them, he recognized them and said, "You did not dismount when it was called for, so do not dismount now!" Then he drew his turban away from his face, and they recognized him and welcomed him. Wāṣil said to Ibn al-Ashʿath, "When I saw your horse wandering about the battlefield, I assumed you were on foot, so I brought you this nag of mine to ride." Ibn al-Ashʿath then left Ibn Abī Sabrah his mule and mounted the nag. ʿAbd al-Raḥmān b. al-Ashʿath then went off to Dayr al-Yaʿār.[356]

Shabīb ordered his men to hold back their swords from the troops, and he summoned the latter to render him the oath of allegiance. Those surviving from the infantry came and rendered the oath to him. Abū al-Ṣuqayr al-Muḥallimī said to him, "I killed seven Kūfans in the middle of the river; the last of them was a man who clung to my robe and screamed and almost succeeded in scaring me off. But then I went for him and killed him." On that day 120 from the Kindah were killed, and either a thousand or six hundred from the rest of the men. Most of the marshals were killed that day.

According to Abū Mikhnaf—Qudāmah b. Ḥāzim b. Sufyān al-Khathʿamī: I killed quite a number of them that day.

ʿAbd al-Raḥmān b. Muḥammad spent that night at Dayr al-Yaʿār. Two horsemen came to him and went up to see him on the roof, while another stood nearby. One of them closeted himself with ʿAbd al-Raḥmān for a long private conversation; then he and

---

356. Spelling and location uncertain. Other MSS read al-N.ʿār; Ibn al-Athīr, *Kāmil*, IV, 416, has al-B.qār.

his companions came back down. The men were saying to one another that that was Shabīb and that he had written to him.

At the end of the night, ʿAbd al-Raḥmān came out and rode to
[939] Dayr Abī Maryam. There he found that Muḥammad b. ʿAbd al-Raḥmān b. Abī Sabrah had provided the mounted troops with barley and clover heaped up like castles and slaughtered for them all the meat they could wish for; on that day they ate and fed their beasts. Then the men met with ʿAbd al-Raḥmān b. Muḥammad b. al-Ashʿath and said to him, "If Shabīb hears where you are, he will come to you and you will be easy pickings for him; the men are dispersed and gone, and the best of them have been killed. Get back to al-Kūfah, man!" ʿAbd al-Raḥmān set out for al-Kūfah, and the men returned, also. When he arrived, ʿAbd al-Raḥmān went into hiding from al-Ḥajjāj, until he was subsequently given safe conduct.[357]

ʿAbd al-Malik Reforms the Coinage

In this year, ʿAbd al-Malik b. Marwān ordered dīnārs and dirhams inscribed,[358] according to al-Wāqidī—Saʿd b. Rāshid—Ṣāliḥ b. Kaysān.

---

357. The campaigns of Ibn al-Ashʿath and ʿUthmān b. Qaṭan (in that order) are mentioned after that of Zāʾidah b. Qudāmah by Ibn Khayyāṭ, *Taʾrīkh*, 273, who dates ʿUthmān's defeat, like Ṭabarī, to Dhū al-Ḥijjah 76. Ibn Aʿtham al-Kūfī, *Futūḥ*, VII, 85, makes Ibn al-Ashʿath the third commander defeated by Shabīb, and does not mention ʿUthmān; Baghdādī, *Farq*, 90, gives a report parallel to Ibn Aʿtham's, but even briefer. See also Ibn al-Athīr, *Kāmil*, IV, 413–16; Périer, *Vie d'al-Ḥadjdjādj*, 129–32; Dixon, *Umayyad Caliphate*, 186.

358. *Naqsh*. This apparently refers to ʿAbd al-Malik's general monetary reform, in which purely aniconic dīnārs and dirhams, of standard (and redefined) weight, replaced the Byzantine gold and Sasanian silver coinage in circulation, as well as various previous Islamic adaptations of both. The earliest known aniconic dīnārs are in fact dated 77; aniconic dirhams appeared only in 79. The numismatic evidence suggests, however, that ʿAbd al-Malik may have first initiated an offical Islamic coinage, with "adapted" iconic issues in both gold and silver, as early as 72, in which case this statement would represent a conflation of this first attempt with his later aniconic reform. ("*Naqsh*" does not necessarily imply aniconic Arabic inscription as opposed to pictorial representation on earlier issues.) On this thorny question, which is far from resolved, see, most recently, M. Bates, "History, Geography and Numismatics in the First Century of Islamic Coinage," *Schweizerische Numismatische Rundschau* 65 (1986), 231–63, as well as G. C. Miles in *EI²*, s.vv. dīnār, dirham; H. Gaube, "Numismatik," in *Grundriss der arabischen Philologie*, I (Wiesbaden, 1982), 226–50; and the classic study by P.

According to Ibn Abī al-Zinād—his father:[359] ʿAbd al-Malik struck dirhams and dīnārs that year; he was the first to initiate the striking of them.[360]

According to Khālid b. Abī Rabīʿah—Ibn Hilāl—his father: The pre-Islamic units of weight (*mithqāl*s) by which ʿAbd al-Malik struck his coins were twenty-two *qīrāṭ*s, minus a *ḥabbah*; ten weighed seven.[361]

According to ʿAbd al-Raḥmān b. Jarīr al-Laythī—Hilāl b. Usāmah: I asked Saʿīd b. al-Musayyab[362] how much the *zakāt*[363] should be on dīnārs, and he said, "For every twenty *mithqāl*s in

---

Grierson, "The Monetary Reform of ʿAbd al-Malik," *Journal of the Economic and Social History of the Orient* 3 (1960), 241–64. See also the much fuller (if even more problematical) report in Balādhurī, *Futūḥ*, 465–70.

359. On Abū al-Zinād ʿAbdallāh b. Dhakhwān al-Qurashī, d. 131 (748), and his son ʿAbd al-Raḥmān, see Sezgin, *GAS*, I, 396, 405.

360. Balādhurī, *Futūḥ*, 467, 469, cites two versions of this report from Ibn Abī al-Zinād: one from al-Wāqidī stating that ʿAbd al-Malik was the first to strike gold and silver coins, after the "year of reconciliation" (*ʿām al-jamāʿah*), usually considered to be 73; and the other from Ibn Saʿd, referring only to gold coins, struck *in* the year of reconciliation, specified as 74. In either case the statement must refer to experiments with the existing iconic coinage, prior to ʿAbd al-Malik's general reform. A further report, in Balādhurī, *Futūḥ*, 240, and other authors, ostensibly referring to the aniconic coinage, attributes ʿAbd al-Malik's initiative to a quarrel with the Byzantine emperor over the Islamicization of the previously Christian superscription on papyrus imported by the Byzantines from Egypt; the emperor is said to have threatened to retaliate by putting an anti-Islamic inscription on his dīnārs, and ʿAbd al-Malik to have responded by freeing himself from Byzantine coinage altogether. For a full discussion of this story, about which Ṭabarī is completely silent, see A. Fahmī, *Fajr al-sikkah al-ʿarabiyyah* (Cairo, 1965), 38–53.

361. For various interpretations of this statement, and others like it in Balādhurī, see the articles by Grierson and Miles cited in note 358, and Hinz, *Islamische Masse und Gewichte*, 1f., 12f. The *mithqāl* was a unit of weight that varied with both geography and commodity; the same is true of the *qīrāṭ* and the *ḥabbah*. For monetary purposes, *mithqāl* was virtually synonymous with *dīnār*. According to Miles, ʿAbd al-Malik's reform dinars and dirhams were both considerably lighter than their respective prototypes, the Byzantine solidus and Sasanian dirham; so if, as seems likely, the *mithqāl Jāhilī* mentioned here is the weight of the solidus, ʿAbd al-Malik cannot have simply struck dinars *equal in weight* to this *mithqāl*. From reports in Balādhurī and elsewhere, we know that the *mithqāl* was subsequently set equal to twenty *qīrāṭ*s; what may be intended here, then, is that ʿAbd al-Malik recognized the old *mithqāl as equal to* 22- *qīrāṭ*s, and, defining a *qīrāṭ* on this basis, issued new dinars at 20 *qīrāṭ*s. The expression "ten weighed seven" refers to the weight ratio of dirhams to dinars, and, according to Miles, accords well with the reality of early post-reform coins and glass weights.

362. D. 94 (713); see Sezgin, *GAS*, I, 276.

363. The alms tax on Muslims, assessed on gold (and silver) at 2.5 percent; see *SEI*, s.v. zakāt.

[940] Syrian weights, a half *mithqāl.*" I said, "Why Syrian rather than Egyptian?" He replied, "It is by the Syrian that dīnārs are struck, and that was the weight of the (old?) dīnārs before the dīnārs were struck; they were twenty-two *qīrāṭs* minus a *ḥabbah.*"[364] Sa'īd said, "I know that, because I had sent some dīnārs to Damascus, and they were struck at that weight."[365]

In this year, Yaḥyā b. al-Ḥakam went to 'Abd al-Malik b. Marwān, and Abān b. 'Uthmān took charge of Medina; this was in Rajab (October–November 695).[366]

In this year, Nawfal b. Musāḥiq b. 'Amr b. Khudāsh of the Banū 'Āmir b. Lu'ayy was appointed to the judiciary.[367]

In this year, Marwān b. Muḥammad b. Marwān was born.[368]

The pilgrimage was led in this year by Abān b. 'Uthmān, who was amīr over Medina, according to Aḥmad b. Thābit—anonymous—Isḥāq b. 'Īsā—Abū Ma'shar; and also according to al-Wāqidī.[369] The governor of al-Kūfah and al-Baṣrah was al-Ḥajjāj b. Yūsuf, and the governor of Khurāsān was Umayyah b. 'Abdallāh b. Khālid. Shurayḥ was in charge of the judiciary in al-Kūfah, and Zurārah b. Awfā was in charge of the judiciary in al-Baṣrah.

---

364. Perhaps this statement can be given some point if we assume that the first *mithqāl* refers to weighing gold, while the second refers to currency of a half dinar, whatever the weight of a *mithqāl* may have been in Egypt.

365. A variant of this statement by Sa'īd appears in Balādhurī, *Futūḥ*, 467 (with a different *isnād*), with "uncoined gold" (*tibr*) instead of "dīnārs."

366. See text above, II, 873; apparently this time 'Abd al-Malik consented to the change of governors. Ibn Sa'd, *Ṭabaqāt*, V, 112f., records only one incident, with 'Abd al-Malik protesting but confirming Abān as Yaḥyā's successor.

367. In Medina. For Nawfal the text has Abān b. Nawfal, a slip; see text below, II, 1085, and Ibn Sa'd, *Ṭabaqāt*, V, 113. The Banū 'Āmir b. Lu'ayy were a clan of Quraysh; see Caskel, *Ǧamharat an-nasab*, I, 4, 27.

368. The later caliph Marwān II; see *EI*[1], s.v. Marwān II.

369. Ibn Khayyāṭ, *Ta'rīkh*, 301; Ya'qūbī, *Ta'rīkh*, II, 336.

The Events of the Year 77

(April 10, 696–March 29, 697)

In this year Shabīb killed ʿAttāb b. Warqāʾ al-Riyāḥī and Zuhrah b. Ḥawiyyah.

Shabīb Kills ʿAttāb b. Warqāʾ and Zuhrah b. Ḥawiyyah [941]

The reason for that, according to Hishām—Abū Mikhnaf—ʿAbd al-Raḥmān b. Jundab and Farwah b. Laqīṭ: When Shabīb defeated the army that al-Ḥajjāj had sent out against him with ʿAbd al-Raḥmān b. Muḥammad b. al-Ashʿath, and killed ʿUthmān b. Qaṭan, it was summer and very hot.[370] Because of the heat, he and his companions went to Māh Bihzādhān[371] for the summer, spending three months there. Many people looking for material gain came and joined him, as well as some people whom al-Ḥajjāj was pursuing for money or other penalties. Among the latter was

370. According to the text above, II, 933f., the battle was in March.

371. See Yāqūt, *Muʿjam*, IV, 406, and P. Schwarz, *Iran im Mittelalter* (Leipzig, 1896–1936), 666f. Yāqūt's suggestion that this place was near Bandanījān, that is, in the mountains east of al-Madāʾin, would fit the present context well.

a man from the tribe[372] named al-Ḥurr b. ʿAbdallāh b. ʿAwf. Two *dihqāns* among the inhabitants of the Durqīṭ Canal region[373] had mistreated and wronged him, and he had attacked them and killed them. He then joined Shabīb, was with him in Māh, and participated in his various battles, until Shabīb was killed. Then, when al-Ḥajjāj extended amnesty to all those who owed money or other penalties and had gone out to join Shabīb—that was after the day at al-Sabakhah[374]—al-Ḥurr came back to him with the others. The families of the two *dihqāns* came to demand that al-Ḥajjāj arrest him, and he was fetched and brought in; he had made his testament, despairing of his life. Al-Ḥajjāj said to him, "Enemy of God, you have killed two of the revenue collectors."[375] Al-Ḥurr replied, "The whole story, may God cause you to prosper, is worse than that." Al-Ḥajjāj asked, "How so?" He replied, "I forsook my obedience and separated myself from the community. But then you issued the amnesty for all who would come back to you. Here is my amnesty document, which you wrote for me." Al-Ḥajjāj said,
[942] "Curse you! I have indeed, by my life, done so." And he let him go.

After the heat had broken, Shabīb left Māh with some eight hundred men and headed for al-Madā'in, which was being governed by Muṭarrif b. al-Mughīrah b. Shuʿbah; he halted at the bridges of Ḥudhayfah b. al-Yamān.[376] Then Mādharwāsb, the lord of Bābil Mahrūdh, wrote to al-Ḥajjāj, saying: "I hereby inform the amīr—may God cause him to prosper!—that Shabīb has come and halted at the bridges of Ḥudhayfah. I do not know where he is headed."

---

372. That is, Azd, to which ʿAbd al-Raḥmān and Farwah (and Abū Mikhnaf) belonged.

373. Somewhere near the Kūthā Canal, south and probably west of al-Madā'in. See Ibn Khurradādhbih, *Masālik*, 7, 9; Yāqūt, *Muʿjam*, II, 568 (pointed as Darqīṭ, but without explicit specification of vocalization); Le Strange, *Lands*, 80; al-ʿAlī, "Al-Madā'in and Its Surrounding Area in Arabic Literary Sources," *Mesopotamia* 3–4 (1968–69), 438.

374. See text below, II, 958ff.

375. *Rajulayn min ahl al-kharāj.* This is presumably a plural of *ṣāḥib al-kharāj*, as used above (see note 342). A *dihqān* would collect the revenues from his peasants and then pay the central treasury; see Løkkegaard, *Islamic Taxation*, 95f.

376. Ḥudhayfah b. al-Yamān, d. 36 (656), was an important commander in the conquest of Iraq and an early governor of al-Madā'in; see Ziriklī, *Aʿlām*, II, 180. The location of his *qanāṭir* (stone bridges, arches) seems to be nowhere described more specifically than as "near al-Madā'in." See Balādhurī, *Futūḥ*, 272; Yāqūt, *Muʿjam*, IV, 180.

When al-Ḥajjāj read this letter, he stood before the men, praised and glorified God, and said, "By God, men, either you will fight to defend your land and your spoil,[377] or I will send for a force more compliant and obedient, and more steadfast in the rage and terror of battle than you, and they will fight your enemy and appropriate your spoil." At this, the men came to him from every side, saying, "We will fight them, and we will satisfy the amīr; let the amīr send us out against them, and we will go wherever pleases him." Among those who came to him was Zuhrah b. Ḥawiyyah,[378] an old man who was unable to stand up by himself without a helping hand; he said, "May God cause the amīr to prosper! You are sending out the men against them in bits and pieces. Better you should mobilize the men altogether and let them go to meet the enemy in a body. Then send forth as their commander a stalwart, courageous man, experienced in battle, a man who looks on flight as a crime and a disgrace and on steadfastness as glory and honor." Al-Ḥajjāj replied, "Such a man are you; you lead them, then!" Zuhrah said, "May God cause the amīr to prosper, what [943]
the troops need now is a man who carries a spear, wears a coat of mail, brandishes a sword, and sits firmly on horseback. But I can do none of these things; I have lost my strength and much of my eyesight. But do send me out among the forces with their commander. I can stay on a saddled riding-camel well enough and be with the commander in his camp to advise him with my opinions." Al-Ḥajjāj replied, "May God reward you handsomely for Islam and its people at the beginning of Islam, and may God reward you handsomely for Islam at the end of Islam, for you have given good and sincere advice! I will send out the forces altogether: Marching orders, men!"

The men set out marching without knowing who their commander would be, while al-Ḥajjāj wrote to ʿAbd al-Malik b. Marwān as follows:

> I hereby inform the Commander of the Faithful, may God be generous to him, that Shabīb has advanced to near al-

---

377. *Fay'*; see note 67 above.

378. D. 77 (696), of the Banū al-Ḥārith (al-Aʿraj) b. Kaʿb b. Saʿd b. Zayd Manāt of Tamīm, a renowned veteran of the conquest of Iraq, who distinguished himself particularly at the battle of al-Qādisiyyah. See text above, I, 2231ff., 2338ff., 2355ff., etc.; Caskel, *Ǧamharat an-nasab*, I, 75, II, 611; Ziriklī, *Aʿlām*, III, 85.

Madā'in and is threatening al-Kūfah. The Kūfans have fought him unsuccessfully in many battles; everywhere he kills their commanders and routs their forces. Perhaps the Commander of the Faithful will see best to send me the Syrians to fight their enemy for them and appropriate their land.[379] Peace.

When this letter reached ʿAbd al-Malik, he sent him Sufyān b. al-Abrad[380] with four thousand men and Ḥabīb b. ʿAbd al-
[944] Raḥmān al-Ḥakamī[381] of Madhḥij with two thousand; these he dispatched quickly to al-Ḥajjāj, as soon as he received the letter.

Meanwhile, the Kūfans were preparing to fight Shabīb, still without knowing who their commander would be; some said he would send out one, some another. Al-Ḥajjāj had in fact sent for ʿAttāb b. Warqā' to come to him. ʿAttāb was in command of the Kūfan cavalry with al-Muhallab; this was the army of Kūfans over which Bishr b. Marwān had sent out ʿAbd al-Raḥmān b. Mikhnaf as commander in the campaign against Qaṭarī.[382] ʿAbd al-Raḥmān b. Mikhnaf had held this position for only about two months before al-Ḥajjāj came out as governor of Iraq; after al-Ḥajjāj's arrival, ʿAbd al-Raḥmān b. Mikhnaf remained their commander only through Rajab and Shaʿbān (October–December 694). Qaṭarī killed ʿAbd al-Raḥmān at the end of Ramaḍān (late January 695),[383] and al-Ḥajjāj then sent out ʿAttāb b. Warqā' to command that army of Kūfans which had lost ʿAbd al-Raḥmān b. Mikhnaf. Al-Ḥajjāj ordered ʿAttāb to obey al-Muhallab, which ʿAttāb found vexing, and things became so bad between him and al-Muhallab that ʿAttāb wrote to al-Ḥajjāj asking to be relieved of his command of that army and recalled. When, therefore, he received al-Ḥajjāj's letter ordering him to come to him, he was very pleased.

---

379. *Ya'kulū bilādahum,* literally, "eat their land," as above they will "eat their *fay'*," that is, enjoy the revenues which are the conquerors' spoil.

380. Of the Banū Kalb; see Caskel, *Ǧamharat an-nasab,* II, 515.

381. Of the Banū al-Ḥakam b. Saʿd al-ʿAshīrah; see Caskel, *Ǧamharat an-nasab,* II, 294f.

382. Qaṭarī was the current leader of the Azraqites; see note 13 above and text below, II, 1003ff. This paragraph summarizes the account above, II, 855–59, 875–78.

383. See text above, II, 875f., where the date was, according to the Baṣrans, 1 Ramaḍān, and, according to the Kūfans, 20 Ramaḍān.

Al-Ḥajjāj summoned the notables of the Kūfans, among them Zuhrah b. Ḥawiyyah al-Saʿdī of the Banū al-Aʿraj and Qabīṣah b. Wāliq al-Taghlibī, and he asked them their opinions on whom he should send out to command that army. They replied, "Your opinion is best, O amīr." He said, "I have sent for ʿAttāb b. Warqāʾ, and he will be coming to you tonight or tomorrow night; it [945] will be he who marches out with the men." Zuhrah b. Ḥawiyyah said, "May God cause the amīr to prosper, you have hit them with the right stone.[384] No, by God, he will not come back to you until he has either achieved victory or been killed." Then Qabīṣah b. Wāliq said, "I will give you my opinion. If it is wrong, it is nevertheless the result of my sincere efforts to advise the Commander of the Faithful, the amīr, and all the Muslims; if it is right, it is God Who has led me to it. There is talk among us, and among the men, that an army has been sent out to you from Syria, the Kūfans having been defeated and routed, and shown themselves short on endurance and indifferent to the shame of flight, as if their hearts were not in themselves but in some other people. Perhaps you may decide to send to this army of yours that has been provided you from the Syrians, cautioning them to be on their guard and never to camp for the night without assuming that there will be a night attack on them. You are fighting a shrewd, crafty man, ever on the move. You have mobilized against him the Kūfans, in whom you are not entirely confident; and their brethren are these troops that have been sent to you from Syria. When Shabīb is in one area, suddenly he pops up in another; and I feel no assurance that he will not come on them unawares. But if they perish, we perish, and Iraq perishes." Al-Ḥajjāj said, "You impress me! This shows excellent judgment and is excellent advice."

Al-Ḥajjāj sent ʿAbd al-Raḥmān b. al-Ghariq, the client of Abū ʿAqīl,[385] to meet the advancing Syrians. He found them halted at Hīt[386] and brought them a letter from al-Ḥajjāj, saying: "When you reach Hīt, leave the Euphrates route to al-Anbār and follow [946] the ʿAyn al-Tamr route to al-Kūfah, God willing. Be on your guard

384. *Ramaytahum bi-ḥajarihim*; for the proverb, see Maydānī, *Amthāl*, I, 263.
385. The text above, II, 922, has Ibn Abī ʿAqīl.
386. On the west bank of the Euphrates, about fifty miles above al-Anbār; see *EI*², s.v. Hīt.

and speed the march. Peace." The men then came on quickly. Meanwhile, ʿAttāb b. Warqāʾ arrived on the night that al-Ḥajjāj had said he would. Al-Ḥajjāj ordered him to lead the troops out, and he camped with them at Ḥammām Aʿyan.

Shabīb[387] advanced as far as Kalwādhā, where he crossed the Tigris; then he came on and halted at the lower town of Bahurasīr,[388] so that only the bridge of boats spanning the Tigris separated him and Muṭarrif b. al-Mughīrah b. Shuʿbah. When Shabīb halted at the town of Bahurasīr, Muṭarrif cut the bridge. Then he sent to Shabīb, saying, "Send to me some of your leading commanders, together with whom I can study the Qur'ān and consider the stance that you advocate." Shabīb sent to him some of his leading commanders, including Qaʿnab, Suwayd, and al-Muḥallil; but when they were about to board the boat, Shabīb sent word to them not to do so until his messenger had returned from Muṭarrif. When the messenger returned,[389] he sent to Muṭarrif, saying, "Send to me the same number of your companions as I am sending of mine to you, for me to hold as hostages until you send my companions back to me." But Muṭarrif said to the messenger, "Go to him and say: Why should I trust you with my companions if I send them to you now, when you do not trust me with your companions?" The messenger returned to Shabīb and delivered this message. Shabīb then sent his reply, saying, "You
[947] know that we do not consider treachery permissible in our religion, whereas you not only do it but also consider it permissible." Muṭarrif then sent to him al-Rabīʿ b. Yazīd al-Asadī, Sulaymān b. Ḥudhayfah b. Hilāl b. Mālik al-Muzanī, and Yazīd b. Abī Ziyād, his client[390] and the captain of his guard. Once they were in Shabīb's custody, he sent off his companions and they went to Muṭarrif. They spent four days exchanging messages, but in the

387. The following paragraph is duplicated, with only minor differences in wording, at II, 982f. below; both accounts come from Abū Mikhnaf, but with different earlier authorities.

388. The city of Veh-Ardashir, on the west bank of the Tigris, opposite Ctesiphon, in the complex of al-Madā'in; see *EI*², s.v. al-Madā'in.

389. The parallel version below, and some MSS here, omit this phrase. If it is original, we must assume that Shabīb sent the messenger twice, once to agree, and then again to set conditions.

390. His father's client in the parallel version below.

end agreed on nothing.[391] When it became clear to Shabīb that Muṭarrif was not going to follow him or join in with him, he prepared to set off to meet ʿAttāb b. Warqāʾ and the Syrians.

According to Abū Mikhnaf—Farwah b. Laqīṭ: Shabīb summoned his chief companions and said to them, "The only one who ever frustrates my plans is this Thaqafī. Four days ago I told myself I should go out with a detachment of cavalry and meet this army coming from Syria, hoping to catch them off guard—or even on it, it doesn't matter. In any case I would be meeting troops cut off from the garrison, with no amīr like al-Ḥajjāj to have recourse to and no garrison like al-Kūfah to take refuge in. Then my spies came to me today and informed me that the first of these troops have reached ʿAyn al-Tamr and are thus now almost to al-Kūfah, while other spies came to me from the direction of ʿAttāb b. Warqāʾ, telling me that he is camped with the main body of Kūfan troops at al-Ṣarāt. He is thus exceedingly close, so let us prepare to set out against him."

Muṭarrif was afraid that word would reach al-Ḥajjāj about what he had done, treating with Shabīb, and he withdrew toward al-Jibāl,[392] intending to wait and see what would happen between Shabīb and ʿAttāb. Then Shabīb sent to him, saying, "Since you [948]
declined to render allegiance to me, I have correspondingly repudiated any obligations between us."[393] Muṭarrif said to his companions, "Let us declare open revolt. Al-Ḥajjāj will fight us in any case, so let him fight us with our strength at its greatest." He set out, abandoning[394] al-Madāʾin. Shabīb then restored the bridge and sent his brother Muṣād to al-Madāʾin.

ʿAttāb advanced toward him, halting at the market of Ḥakamah.[395] Al-Ḥajjāj had sent out the Kūfan forces en masse,

---

391. See the detailed account of the negotiations below, II, 983–88.

392. Media, the province centered on Hamadhān; see *EI²*, s.v. Djibāl; Le Strange, *Lands*, 185ff.

393. *Fa-qad nabadhtu ilayka ʿalā sawāʾ*: Qurʾānic phraseology, from Qurʾān 8:58: "If you fear treachery from a people, then repudiate (any agreement) with them correspondingly (*fa-nbidh ilayhim ʿalā sawāʾ*)."

394. Reading *taraka* for *nazala.* Ibn al-Athīr's paraphrase (*Kāmil,* IV, 422) omits the word. From the parallels below, II, 956, 988, it is clear that Muṭarrif set out for al-Daskarah.

395. Brief notices in Balādhurī, *Futūḥ,* 275, and Yāqūt, *Muʿjam,* III, 194, do not specify more closely the location of this place.

both the regular forces and the young men who were eager to fight; not counting these young men, the regular forces were 40,000. Those who arrived with ʿAttāb at the market of Ḥakamah that day were then 40,000 of the regular forces and 10,000 of the young men—or 50,000 altogether. Al-Ḥajjāj left behind no man of Quraysh nor any member of any noble Arab house.

According to Abū Mikhnaf—ʿAbd al-Raḥmān b. Jundab: I heard al-Ḥajjāj speak from the pulpit when he sent ʿAttāb with the men against Shabīb, saying, "Men of al-Kūfah! Go out with ʿAttāb b. Warqāʾ, all of you! No man is permitted to remain here except those I have appointed to administrative posts. Hear me! He who is steadfast and strives will earn honor and preferment. Hear me! He who shrinks and flees will earn disgrace and disdain. By Him than Whom there is no other god! If you perform in this battle as you have in previous battles, you will surely feel my rough side, and I will come down with my full weight on you!" Then he came down; and the men assembled with ʿAttāb at the market of Ḥakamah.

[949] According to Abū Mikhnaf—Farwah b. Laqīṭ: Shabīb reviewed us at al-Madāʾin; we were a thousand men. He stood before us, praised and glorified God, and said, "Company of Muslims! God has given you victory over them when you were a hundred or two hundred, and a few more than that, or a few less; but today you are hundreds and hundreds. I will perform the noon prayer and then lead you out." He performed the noon prayer, and proclamation was made to the men: "Cavalry of God! Mount and rejoice!" Shabīb then went out with his forces; but some of them began to straggle and fall behind. When he had crossed Sābāṭ[396] and we had halted with him, he delivered a sermon to us, reminding us of the battle-days of God and encouraging us to turn away from the world and fix our desire on the afterlife. He spoke for a long time, then ordered his muezzin to give the call to prayer. He did so, and Shabīb came forward and led us in the afternoon prayer. Then he set out and brought us up close to ʿAttāb b. Warqāʾ and his forces. As soon as he saw them, he dismounted and ordered his muezzin to give the call to prayer. He did so, and Shabīb came forward and

396. One *farsakh* south of Bahurasīr, at the bridge over the Malik canal. See *EI*², s.v. al-Madāʾin; Yaʿqūbī, *Buldān*, 321; Fiey, "The Topography of al-Madāʾin," *Sumer* 23 (1967), 12.

led us in the sunset prayer. His muezzin was Sallām b. Sayyār al-Shaybānī.

ʿAttāb b. Warqāʾ's spies had come to him and informed him that Shabīb had advanced on him, and he led out all the forces and put them in battle array. From the first day he camped there he had dug a trench, but every day had acted as if he intended to march on Shabīb in al-Madāʾin; informed of this, Shabīb said, "I would rather march against him than have him march against me," and went out to him. When ʿAttāb lined up his troops, he appointed Muḥammad b. ʿAbd al-Raḥmān b. Saʿīd b. Qays over his right [950] wing, saying to him, "O son of my brother,[397] you are a noble man, so be steadfast and vie in steadfastness!"[398] He replied, "As for me, by God, I will fight so long as one man stands with me!" ʿAttāb said to Qabīṣah b. Wāliq, who was at that time over a third of the Banū Taghlib, "Take care of the left wing for me." But Qabīṣah replied, "I am an old man, and it is a great effort for me just to stand beneath my standard. My strength is gone, and I cannot stand on my own without support. But here are ʿUbaydallāh b. al-Ḥulays and Nuʿaym b. ʿUlaym, both Taghlibīs"—each of these was over a third of the Taghlib; Qabīṣah said, "Appoint whichever of them you prefer, and whichever you appoint, you will be appointing a resolute and determined and capable man." ʿAttāb appointed Nuʿaym b. ʿUlaym, then, over the left wing. He appointed Ḥanẓalah b. al-Ḥārith al-Yarbūʿī, ʿAttāb's own paternal cousin and the shaykh of his clan, over the infantry and arrayed them in three ranks: a rank of men with swords, a rank of spear-bearers, and a rank of archers. ʿAttāb then went along the entire line, from the right wing to the left, passing by the men of each standard successively and urging them to fear God, charging them to be steadfast, and giving them sermons.

According to Abū Mikhnaf—Ḥaṣīrah b. ʿAbdallāh—Tamīm b. al-Ḥārith al-Azdī: He stood before us and gave us a lengthy sermon. I can remember these few words from what he said: "O people of Islam! Those who have the best lot in Paradise are the

397. Muḥammad b. ʿAbd al-Raḥmān was last mentioned (II, 857) as commander of the quarter of Tamīm and Hamdān at Rāmhurmuz. He was a Hamdānī (see Caskel, *Ǧamharat an-nasab*, II, 130, on his father), and ʿAttāb a Tamīmī (see note 123 above).

398. *Fa-ṣbir wa-ṣābir*, from Qurʾān 3:200: *iṣbarū wa-ṣābirū*.

[951] martyrs. God praises none of His creatures more than the steadfast; hear how He says, 'Be ye steadfast; God is with the steadfast.'[399] He whose deeds God praises, how great is his status! But God despises no one more than those who commit outrages. See how this enemy of yours slaughters the Muslims with his sword, and they insist that they thereby win God's favor. They are the most wicked people on earth, the dogs of the people of Hell! Where are the sermonizers?" When he asked that, not one of us, by God, answered him. Seeing this, he asked, "Where are those who recite the poetry of ʿAntarah?"[400] And no, by God, not a single man breathed a word of reply to this. He said, "We are God's! It seems to me I can see you fleeing from ʿAttāb b. Warqāʾ and leaving him with the wind whistling up his ass!"

ʿAttāb then went and sat in the center,[401] having with him Zuhrah b. Ḥawiyyah, who also was sitting, ʿAbd al-Raḥmān b. Muḥammad b. al-Ashʿath, and Abū Bakr b. Muḥammad b. Abī Jahm al-ʿAdawī.[402] Shabīb advanced with six hundred men, four hundred having stayed behind; he said, "Those who have stayed behind are those I would not care to have seen among us." He put Suwayd b. Sulaym with two hundred men on the left wing, put al-Muḥallil b. Wāʾil with two hundred in the center, and himself took the right wing with two hundred. It was between sunset prayer and the final, evening prayer, and the moon had come out. Shabīb called to the other side, "Whose are these standards?" They replied, "The standards of the Rabīʿah!"[403] Shabīb said,

---

399. Qurʾān 8:46.

400. ʿAntarah b. Shaddād, famous sixth-century poet and hero; see *EI*², s.v. ʿAntara, and Sezgin, *GAS*, II, 113ff. Perhaps the point here is to challenge both the men's religious fervor and their martial spirit.

401. Commanders seem often to have sat in battle. Below we are told that ʿAttāb was sitting on a *ṭinfisah*, a carpet, until the enemy got too close (when he stood up and fought);.it is not clear whether this carpet was on a platform or a sort of chair, but it was presumably not on a horse. At the later battle of al-Sabakhah, al-Ḥajjāj sat on a chair (*kursī*); see text below, II, 959, and note 427. See also Fries, *Heereswesen*, 76.

402. Of the Banū ʿAdī b. Kaʿb of Quraysh; see Caskel, *Ǧamharat an-nasab*, I, 26, and II, 423 (on his father).

403. These are the Taghlibīs speaking, from ʿAttāb's left wing. Taghlib and Bakr were the two branches of Wāʾil, the most important component of Rabīʿah; Shabīb's clan was the Banū Dhuhl b. Shaybān of Bakr b. Wāʾil, and thus he himself belonged to Rabīʿah (see text above, II, 887, and note 160). Unlike Bakr, whose role in both Islam and Khārijism was very mixed, the Taghlib remained mostly Chris-

"Standards that have often been on the side of the truth, but have also often been on the side of the false—they have had a share of [952] both! By God, I will strive against you and earn my reward for doing so! You are Rabīʿah, but I am Shabīb! I am Abū Mudallah! Judgment is to God alone! Stand if you will!"

Then he charged at them from a dike in front of the trench[404] and broke their line. The standard-bearers of Qabīṣah b. Wāliq, ʿUbayd[405] b. al-Ḥulays, and Nuʿaym b. ʿUlaym stood their ground, and they were killed, and the entire left wing was driven back. Men from the Banū Taghlib called to one another, "Qabīṣah b. Wāliq has been killed!" Shabīb said, "You have killed Qabīṣah b. Wāliq al-Taghlibī, O company of Muslims! God has said, 'And recite to them the account of him to whom We gave our signs, but he sloughed them off, so Satan pursued him and he became one of those who go astray.'[406] The same would describe your kinsman Qabīṣah b. Wāliq: he went to the Prophet and submitted,[407] then came with the unbelievers to fight you!" Then Shabīb came upon his body, and said, "Alas for you! If you had held fast to your first submission (*islām*), you would have had a happier destiny."

Then he attacked ʿAttāb b. Warqāʾ from the left, while Suwayd b. Sulaym attacked the right, which was under the command of Muḥammad b. ʿAbd al-Raḥmān. The latter fought on the right with men of the Banū Tamīm and Hamdān; they all fought very well and persevered until word came to them that ʿAttāb b. Warqāʾ had been killed, and then they dispersed. ʿAttāb, meanwhile, was still sitting on a carpet in the center, with Zuhrah b. Ḥawiyyah, when Shabīb suddenly descended on the troops of the center. ʿAttāb said, "O Zuhrah b. Ḥawiyyah, this is a day of large numbers but small profit! Alas! to have five hundred horsemen of

---

tian. See *EI²*, s.v. Bakr b. Wāʾil, and Kaḥḥālah, *Muʿjam qabāʾil al-ʿarab*, 120ff. (Taghlib).

404. *Wa-huwa ʿalā musannāh amāma al-khandaq.* It is not clear what trench is meant here, unless this is the village of Khandaq, mentioned earlier by Ṭabarī (without the article, I, 1041) as being in the *ṭassūj* of Bahurasīr; see al-ʿAlī, "Al-Madāʾin and Its Surrounding Area," 436.

405. His name is given as ʿUbaydallāh above.

406. Qurʾān 7:175.

407. *Aslama.* Qabīṣah does not appear in Ibn Saʿd; Ibn Ḥajar, *Iṣābah*, III, 223, includes him as a Companion on the basis of this passage in Ṭabarī, which he quotes.

the like of the men of Tamīm with me, rather than this entire army! Is there none who will be steadfast before the enemy? Is
[953] there none who will look beyond himself?"—for they dispersed and abandoned him. Zuhrah said to him, "Well spoken, ʿAttāb! You have done as one would expect of you! By God, by God! If you had turned from them and fled, you would not have lasted long! Rejoice, for I hope that God may have destined us for martyrdom at the end of our lives." ʿAttāb replied, "May God grant you the greatest reward He grants for good action." Thus did they spur each other on to religious fervor until Shabīb drew closer. Then ʿAttāb sprang forward with a small band who had held out with him, most of the troops having scattered left and right. ʿAmmār b. Yazīd al-Kalbī, a Medinese, said to him, "May God cause you to prosper! ʿAbd al-Raḥmān b. Muḥammad has deserted you, and many of the men have joined him!" ʿAttāb replied, "He has fled before, as well, and the young man did not seem to me then to be much bothered by what he did."[408]

Then he fought them for a time, saying, "Never have I seen a day of battle like this one! Never have I been so tried! Never have I seen fewer men fighting or more giving up and fleeing!" He was noticed by a man from the Banū Taghlib, one of Shabīb's companions, from the Banū Zayd b. ʿAmr, named ʿĀmir b. ʿAmr b. ʿAbd ʿAmr,[409] who had had one of his kin killed by ʿAttāb. He was one of the horsemen, and he went to Shabīb and said to him, "By God, I think that man speaking is ʿAttāb b. Warqāʾ!" He attacked him with his spear, and he fell; it was he who had been assigned the task of killing him. The horses trampled Zuhrah b. Ḥawiyyah; although he tried to protect himself with his sword, he was an old man and unable to get up, and al-Faḍl b. ʿĀmir al-Shaybānī came up to him and killed him.[410] Shabīb then reached him and found him dead; he recognized him and asked, "Who killed this man?"
[954] Al-Faḍl answered, "I killed him." Shabīb said, "This is Zuhrah b. Ḥawiyyah! By God, Zuhrah, if you were killed while in a state of

---

408. This statement should be seen in the context of ʿAbd al-Raḥmān b. al-Ashʿath's later rebellion, text below, II, 1052ff.

409. For the Zayd Allāh (or Zayd Allāt!) b. ʿAmr of Taghlib, see Caskel, *Ǧamharat an-nasab*, I, 163, II, 604.

410. This man had earlier claimed responsibility for killing Zāʾidah b. Qudāmah; see text above, II, 926.

error, nevertheless, on many a battle day of the Muslims did you show your mettle and render great service, and many a cavalry force of the polytheists did you defeat, many a detachment did you attack, many of their populous villages did you conquer! Yet God alone knew that you would be killed lending support to the oppressors."

According to Abū Mikhnaf—Farwah b. Laqīṭ: By God, we saw Shabīb grieving for this man, and one of the young men of Bakr b. Wā'il said, "By God, the Commander of the Faithful tonight grieves for a man of the unbelievers!" Shabīb said, "You know their error no better than I, but I also know of their past what you do not know; if they had held to it, they would have been brethren."

ʿAmmār b. Yazīd al-Kalbī was also killed in the battle, and Abū Khaythamah b. ʿAbdallāh was killed that day as well. When Shabīb had overcome the government troops and their leaders, he said, "Hold back your swords from them," and summoned them to render the oath of allegiance. The men promptly did so, but later escaped under cover of darkness; even as Shabīb received their oaths, he had said, "They will flee shortly." Shabīb then took possession of what was left in the camp and sent for his brother to come to him from al-Madā'in. When the latter reached him at the camp, he set out against al-Kūfah, having spent two days at his camp at Bayt Qurrah;[411] he now intended a direct confrontation with the Kūfan forces.

Meanwhile, Sufyān b. al-Abrad al-Kalbī and Ḥabīb b. ʿAbd al-Raḥmān al-Ḥakamī of Madhḥij had entered al-Kūfah with their Syrian troops. These stiffened al-Ḥajjāj's back, and he was thereby able to do without the Kūfan forces. Al-Ḥajjāj ascended the pulpit [955]
of al-Kūfah and said, after praising and glorifying God: "Men of al-Kūfah! May God give no glory to him who seeks glory through you, and may He give no victory to him who seeks victory with you! Leave us, and come not with us to fight our enemy! Go settle in al-Ḥīrah, with the Jews and Christians,[412] and fight not with

411. Location unknown. It is not the same as Dayr Qurrah (see text above, I, 2357–58 and II, 1072), which was on the other (western) side of the Euphrates; see *EI*², s.v. Dayr Ḳurra.

412. On the concentration of Jews and Christians in al-Ḥīrah, see Morony, *Iraq after the Muslim Conquest*, 309, 375f.

us, except for those of you who were working as our administrators or otherwise did not participate in the battle under ʿAttāb b. Warqāʾ."

According to Abū Mikhnaf—Farwah b. Laqīṭ: By God, we set out in pursuit of the government forces. I myself caught up with ʿAbd al-Raḥmān b. Muḥammad b. al-Ashʿath and Muḥammad b. ʿAbd al-Raḥmān b. Saʿīd b. Qays al-Hamdānī as they walked along, and ʿAbd al-Raḥmān's head looked to me as if it were completely covered with mud. I turned away from them, not wanting to alarm them. If I had alerted Shabīb's men to them, they would have been killed on the spot; but I said to myself, "If I bring about the death of two such men of my people as these, I am not thinking aright."[413]

Shabīb continued as far as the Ṣarāt Canal and halted there.

According to Abū Mikhnaf—Mūsā b. Suwār: Shabīb set out for al-Kūfah. When he reached Sūrā,[414] he called on the men, saying, "Which of you will bring me the head of the governor of Sūrā?" Al-Baṭīn, Qaʿnab, Suwayd, and two others among his companions volunteered. They hurried off to the revenue office, where the officials were busy with one of the tax levies.[415] They got into the building through a ruse, saying to the men, "Answer the summons of the amīr!" When asked which amīr, they said, "An amīr sent out from al-Ḥajjāj in pursuit of that sinner[416] Shabīb!" With these men out of the way, it was possible to come on the governor unawares; when they reached him, they drew their swords, raised the cry of "Judgment is to God alone!" and struck off his head.
[956] They seized what money was there and rejoined Shabīb. When they came to him, he asked, "What is this that you have brought me?" They replied, "We have brought you the head of the sinner and what money we found there"—the money was in its bags on a beast. But Shabīb said, "What you have brought me is factionalism for the Muslims! Give me your javelin, boy!" With this he ripped open the bags, then ordered the beast goaded, so that the

413. The three men all belonged to South Arab (Qaḥṭānī) tribes: Azd, Kindah, and Hamdān. See Caskel, *Ǧamharat an-nasab*, I, 176.

414. On the Upper Sūrā canal, the east (and in Sasanian times principal) branch of the Euphrates, north of Bābil. See Le Strange, *Lands*, 70–72; Musil, *Middle Euphrates*, 274–77.

415. *Samarajjah*; see Lane, *Lexicon*, s.v.

416. *Fāsiq*; see note 109 above.

money scattered from the bags in all directions, until it reached the Ṣarāt Canal. He added, "If there is any left then, throw it in the water!"

Then Sufyān b. al-Abrad went out against him with al-Ḥajjāj. He had earlier gone to al-Ḥajjāj and said, "Send me to confront him before he comes to you." But al-Ḥajjāj had said, "I would prefer that we stay together until I meet him as I stand among you, with al-Kūfah behind us and the citadel in our hands."

In this year Shabīb entered al-Kūfah for the second time.

Shabīb's Second Entry into al-Kūfah and His Battle with al-Ḥajjāj

According to Hishām—Abū Mikhnaf—Mūsā b. Suwār: Sabrah b. ʿAbd al-Raḥmān b. Mikhnaf came from al-Daskarah to al-Kūfah after the Syrian army had arrived there. Muṭarrif b. al-Mughīrah had written to al-Ḥajjāj saying, "Shabīb is upon me; send an expeditionary force to al-Madā'in!" and al-Ḥajjāj had sent him Sabrah b. ʿAbd al-Raḥmān b. Mikhnaf with two hundred horsemen. When Muṭarrif set out for al-Jabal, he took his men with him, having informed them of his intentions;[417] but he did not tell Sabrah. When he reached Daskarat al-Malik, he summoned Sabrah, informed him of his intentions, and invited him to join [957] him. Sabrah said, "Yes, I am with you"; but when he left his presence, he sent for his men, assembled them, and set off with them. Hearing that ʿAttāb b. Warqā' had been killed and Shabīb had gone on toward al-Kūfah, he advanced as far as a village called Bayṭarā.[418] Shabīb had halted at Ḥammām ʿUmar, and Sabrah went on to the Euphrates crossing at the village of Shāhī,[419] crossed the river, and doubled back until he reached al-Ḥajjāj. There he learned that the Kūfans were in disgrace. He went to see Sufyān b. al-Abrad and told him his whole story, informing him of his own obedience and his split with Muṭarrif, and pointing out

417. I.e., that he intended to rebel against al-Ḥajjāj and ʿAbd al-Malik; see text above, II, 946–48, and, on al-Jabal or al-Jibāl, note 392.

418. Location unknown.

419. An important ford and boat bridge, about fifteen miles north of al-Kūfah and about ten miles southwest of Ḥammām ʿUmar; see Musil, *Middle Euphrates*, 243; al-ʿAlī, "Minṭaqat al-Kūfah," 240.

that he had neither been with ʿAttāb nor participated in a defeat in any of the battles of the Kūfans—"And I am still working as an administrator for the amīr and have with me two hundred men who have never experienced defeat with me and who have maintained their obedience and never participated in factionalism." Sufyān then went to see al-Ḥajjāj and informed him of all that Sabrah b. ʿAbd al-Raḥmān had told him. Al-Ḥajjāj said, "He has spoken sincerely and truly. Tell him, then, that he is to join with us in encountering our enemy." Sufyān conveyed this message to Sabrah.

Shabīb continued his advance, halting at the location of Ḥammām Aʿyan.[420] Al-Ḥajjāj summoned al-Ḥārith b. Muʿāwiyah b. Abī Zurʿah b. Masʿūd al-Thaqafī and sent him out with some men from the security forces who had not participated in the battle with ʿAttāb and some men who had been working as administrators, as well as about two hundred men from the Syrians. Altogether, he set out with about a thousand and halted at Zurārah. When Shabīb learned of this, he came up to him quickly with his men, and when he reached him he attacked, killed him, and defeated his forces. The defeated men came back to al-Kūfah. Shabīb also came on, crossing the bridge and camping on the
[958] Kūfah side. Shabīb stayed in his camp three days. On the first day the only action was the killing of al-Ḥārith b. Muʿāwiyah. On the second day, al-Ḥajjāj sent out his clients and personal retainers,[421] armed, to occupy the approaches of the roads outside al-Kūfah. The Kūfan forces also went out and occupied the approaches of their roads, fearing the wrath of al-Ḥajjāj and ʿAbd al-Malik b. Marwān if they did not. Shabīb proceeded to have a mosque built on the edge of al-Sabakhah, next to where the fodder sellers are located, at the *īwān*;[422] this mosque is still standing today.

---

420. Across the Euphrates from al-Kūfah; see note 290 above.

421. *Ghilmān*, sg. *ghulām*. See *EI²*, s.v. ghulām; Morony, *Iraq after the Muslim Conquest*, 211f.

422. It is unclear to what structure this refers. *Īwān* may refer to either a palace or a specific type of audience hall; see *EI²*, s.v. Ṭabarī elsewhere refers only to the *īwān Kisrā*, the Sasanian palace at Ctesiphon/al-Madā'in (see text above, II, 776, and below, II, 1056). The *īwān* of al-Kūfah was presumably not the *dār al-imārah*, which was at the center of town and apparently far from al-Sabakhah; see Massignon, "Explication du plan de Kufa," 336.

On the third day, al-Ḥajjāj sent out Abū al-Ward, a client of his,[423] cuirassed, along with many men in cuirasses and some of his personal retainers. They said, "This is al-Ḥajjāj!" and Shabīb charged him and killed him, saying, "If this was al-Ḥajjāj, I have relieved you of him." Then al-Ḥajjāj sent out his retainer Ṭahmān,[424] similarly attired and accompanied, and again Shabīb attacked and killed him, saying, "If this was al-Ḥajjāj, I have relieved you of him." Then, in late morning, al-Ḥajjāj came out of the palace and said, "Bring me a mule to ride from here to al-Sabakhah." A mule with white ankles was brought, but he was told, "The local people, may God cause you to prosper, find ill omen in your riding a mule like this on a day like this." Al-Ḥajjāj said, "Bring it here, for this is a day with both white ankles and a white blaze."[425] He mounted the mule and set out with the Syrians, taking the post road[426] and coming out at the top of al-Sabakhah.

When al-Ḥajjāj saw Shabīb and his forces, he halted. Shabīb, who was with six hundred horsemen, saw that al-Ḥajjāj had come out against him, and he advanced with his forces. Sabrah b. ʿAbd al-Raḥmān came to al-Ḥajjāj and asked, "Where does the amīr [959]
order me to stand?" He replied, "Stand at the approaches of the roads, and if they come to you and fighting breaks out, then fight them." Sabrah went and took up his position with the assembled forces. Al-Ḥajjāj then had a chair brought to him, sat on it,[427] and

423. So also Ibn Aʿtham al-Kūfī, *Futūḥ*, VII, 85f.; but Ibn Khayyāṭ, *Ta'rīkh*, 274, calls him a client of the Banū Naṣr.

424. In Ibn Khayyāṭ, *Ta'rīkh*, 274, he is called a client of ʿUthmān, and in Ibn Aʿtham al-Kūfī, *Futūḥ*, VII, 85, where his death precedes that of Abū al-Ward, he is said to be a client of the Āl Banī Muʿayṭ. One of the two alternative versions of this incident given below (II, 963) identifies one of these two men as Aʿyan (of Ḥammām Aʿyan, see note 290 above) but does not identify the other, while the other version (966f.) identifies the two as Abū al-Ward and Aʿyan.

425. According to Jāḥiẓ, *K. al-Qawl fī al-bighāl* (Cairo, 1955), 136, mules were ridden into battle by leaders in order to show their men that they were prepared to stand or fall, being unable to flee on such a slow beast. Jāḥiẓ also mentions (*ibid.*, 96) that mules with white anklets were considered unlucky.

426. *Sikkat al-barīd*, here presumably the road leading east out of town, across the bridge, and on to al-Madā'in, although the term may also mean "post house," as in Balādhurī, *Futūḥ*, 286. See *ibid.*, glossarium, s. v. sikkah; Ibn al-Faqīh, *Buldān* (*BGA*, V), 183.

427. According to Ibn Rustah, *Aʿlāq*, 198, al-Ḥajjāj was the first Muslim commander to sit on a chair in battle; see Morony, *Iraq after the Muslim Conquest*, 61 and n. 111.

proclaimed, "Men of Syria! You are men who hear and obey, men of steadfastness and conviction. Let not this vermin's falseness overcome your truth. Lower your eyes, get down on your knees, and meet the enemy with the points of your spears." The men got down on their knees and pointed their spears at the enemy, looking like a field of black stones.

Shabīb advanced against them, and when he drew near he arrayed his forces in three squadrons: one with him, one with Suwayd b. Sulaym, and one with al-Muḥallil b. Wā'il. Shabīb told Suwayd to attack with his cavalry; but when he did, the government troops held their position until the Khārijites reached the points of their spears, then jumped up and rushed straight at Shabīb and his forces, thrusting their spears and advancing until he was driven off. Al-Ḥajjāj cried, "Men who hear and obey! That is the way to do it! Boy! Move my chair forward!" Then Shabīb ordered al-Muḥallil to attack them; but they treated him just as they had treated Suwayd, and al-Ḥajjāj again cried, "Men who hear and obey! That is the way to do it! Boy! Move my chair forward!" Then Shabīb himself attacked them with his squadron. They held their position until he reached the points of their spears, then jumped up and rushed straight at him. He fought long with them, but then the Syrians thrust their spears and advanced until they drove him back to the rest of his forces. Seeing their steadfastness, he called to Suwayd, saying, "Take your cavalry and
[960] attack the men on this road"—meaning the Laḥḥām Jarīr Road[428] —"and if you can drive the men from the road, you can come at al-Ḥajjāj from the rear, while we attack him from in front." Suwayd b. Sulaym accordingly separated off and attacked the men on this road; but he was assailed with arrows from the housetops and the approaches to the roads and forced to retreat. Al-Ḥajjāj had placed 'Urwah b. al-Mughīrah b. Shu'bah with some three hundred men from the Syrian forces as a rearguard for him and his troops so they would not be vulnerable to attack from that direction.

According to Abū Mikhnaf—Farwah b. Laqīṭ: On that day Shabīb said to us, "O people of Islam! We have sold ourselves to

---

428. Both Laḥḥām Jarīr (Jarīr's Butcher?) and its road are mentioned elsewhere by Ṭabarī (see text above, II, 624, 775), but without further identifying detail.

God; and he who has sold himself to God cares little for any harm or pain that may come to him for God's sake. Hold fast, and charge as you charged in your other noble battles!" He gathered his forces, and al-Ḥajjāj, seeing the coming attack, said to his men, "Men who hear and obey! Stand firm against this one charge, and, by the Lord of Heaven, nothing will remain in the way of victory!" The men got down on their knees, and Shabīb attacked them with his collected forces. When he reached them, al-Ḥajjāj called out to all his men to jump up and rush straight at him. They thrust with their spears and hacked with their swords, advancing and pushing back Shabīb and his forces as he fought them, as far as Bustān Zā'idah.[429] When they reached that place, Shabīb called to his men, "O friends of God! Dismount! Dismount!" He himself dismounted and ordered half his forces to dismount, leaving the other half with Suwayd b. Sulaym. Al-Ḥajjāj came to the mosque of Shabath,[430] and said, "Men of Syria! Men who hear and obey! This is the beginning of victory, by the One Who holds al-Ḥajjāj's soul in His hand!" Some twenty men went up to the mosque with him, armed with arrows, and he told them, "If they approach us, shoot at them." The fighting on the ground was extremely fierce and went on through the entire day, [961]
until the two parties had fought each other to a standstill. Then Khālid b. ʿAttāb said to al-Ḥajjāj, "Let me fight them, for I have a case of personal vengeance to settle, and I am a man whose counsel is above suspicion." Al-Ḥajjāj granted his permission, and Khālid said, "I will come at them from behind and raid their camp." Al-Ḥajjāj said, "Do as seems best to you."

Khālid went off with a band of Kūfans and entered their camp from the rear. He killed Shabīb's brother Muṣād, and Shabīb's wife, Ghazālah—she was actually killed by Farwah b. al-Daffān[431] al-Kalbī—and set fire to the camp. News of this came to both al-Ḥajjāj and Shabīb; al-Ḥajjāj and his men raised a single "God is great!" while Shabīb and every man on foot with him jumped on their horses. Al-Ḥajjāj said to the Syrians, "Charge them! This has

429. Zā'idah's Orchard (probably of palm trees), in al-Sabakhah; see text above, II, 619.

430. *Masjid Shabath,* according to the editor, comparing text above, II, 632; but the MSS have *masjid Shabīb,* which is supported by Ibn al-Athīr, *Kāmil,* IV, 427.

431. Reading uncertain. Some manuscripts have al-D.qān or al-D.fār.

broken their courage!" They charged them and defeated them, Shabīb remaining with the rear guard as it retreated.

According to Hishām—Aṣghar the Khārijite—one of the men who was with Shabīb: When the men were defeated and Shabīb retreated by the bridge of boats, al-Ḥajjāj's cavalry pursued him. Shabīb was nodding as if dozing off, and I said, "Commander of the Faithful, turn around and look behind you!" He turned around with an air of indifference,then bowed his head and began to nod off again. They drew nearer, and we said, "Commander of the Faithful, they are getting near!" By God, he turned around again, with the same air of indifference, and then began to nod off again. Then al-Ḥajjāj sent to his cavalry saying, "Leave him to burn in the fire of God." They left him and went back.

[962] According to Hishām—Abū Mikhnaf—Abū ʿAmr al-ʿUdhrī: Shabīb cut the bridge of boats after he crossed it. According to Farwah: I was with him when we were defeated, and he did nothing to the bridge; they did not pursue us as far as the bridge so that we should cut it.

Al-Ḥajjāj went back into al-Kūfah, ascended the pulpit, praised God, and said, "By God, Shabīb has not seen real battle before this! By God, he turned and fled, leaving his wife with a broken reed up her ass!"[432]

Another account of al-Ḥajjāj's battle with Shabīb in al-Kūfah is that of ʿUmar b. Shabbah—ʿAbdallāh b. al-Mughīrah b. ʿAṭiyyah—his father—Muzāḥim b. Zufar b. Jassās al-Taymī: When Shabīb broke through al-Ḥajjāj's detachments, al-Ḥajjāj permitted us to come see him in the apartment in which he slept. He was in bed, with a blanket over him. He said, "I have summoned you with regard to a matter in which sincere differences of opinion can be frankly expressed, and I want your advice. This man has pene-

432. This first account of Shabīb's second entry into al-Kūfah is now followed by a second, from ʿUmar b. Shabbah (in two versions), which emphasizes the role of Qutaybah b. Muslim, previously unmentioned. A third account, unattributed, beginning at 965 below, parallels the first, but with numerous differences in detail. The summary in Ibn Khayyāṭ, *Ta'rīkh*, 271, is closest to the first account. Ibn Aʿtham al-Kūfī, *Futūḥ*, VII, 85–91, lists the defeats of Ṭahmān and Abū al-Ward after that of ʿAttāb b. Warqā' but places all three among the commanders defeated well before the entry into al-Kūfah; in his account of the latter, Ibn Aʿtham al-Kūfī attributes the victory to al-Ḥajjāj and four thousand Syrians, mentioning no one else. See also Périer, *Vie d'al-Ḥadjdjâdj*, 139–44; Dixon, *Umayyad Caliphate*, 187f.

trated into the heart of your land, violated your territory, and killed your fighters. Advise me!" The men were silent, except for one, who moved his chair out of the line and said, "With the amīr's permission, I will speak." He said, "Speak!" The man said, "The amīr, by God, has neither feared God nor defended the Commander of the Faithful nor shown any commitment toward his subjects." Then he sat down on his chair, in line. This man was, in fact, Qutaybah.[433] Al-Ḥajjāj was enraged, threw aside the blanket, and let his legs dangle from the bed—I can see it even now—and asked, "Who said that?" Qutaybah then moved his chair out of the line again and repeated his words. Al-Ḥajjāj asked, "What do you suggest, then?" He said, "That you go out to him yourself and call him to account." Al-Ḥajjāj said, "Go find me a good place to muster the troops; then come back to me."

We went out cursing ʿAnbasah b. Saʿīd, for it was he who had recommended to al-Ḥajjāj that he make Qutaybah one of his associates. The next morning, having all made our last testaments, we [963] armed ourselves. Al-Ḥajjāj performed the morning prayer but then withdrew. His messenger kept coming out, hour after hour, to ask, "Has he come yet? Has he come yet?" but we did not know whom he meant, the *maqṣūrah* being already jammed with people.[434] Finally, the messenger came out and asked, "Has he come yet?" and there was Qutaybah walking into the mosque, wearing a yellow robe from Herat[435] and a red silk turban, with a broad sword on a short suspensory, so it looked as if it was tucked under his arm; he had tucked the tail of his robe into his belt, and his cuirass struck against his shanks. The door was opened for

433. Qutaybah b. Muslim, later famed as the conqueror of Transoxania, after being appointed governor of Khurāsān by al-Ḥajjāj in 86 (705); see text below, II, 1178, and *EI*², s.v. Ḳutayba b. Muslim.

434. Al-Ḥajjāj apparently withdrew from the mosque through a private entrance communicating directly with the governor's palace, which abutted the southern, *qiblah* side of the mosque; see K. A. C. Creswell, *Early Muslim Architecture* (Oxford, 1969), I, i, 42–58. This private entrance would be inside the *maqṣūrah*, a part of the mosque partitioned off for the governor's personal use (see *SEI*, s.v.). The following account suggests that the commanders and nobles awaited the governor in the *maqṣūrah* while the rest of the forces were assembled inside and around the mosque proper.

435. *Qabāʾ harawī aṣfar*; a sleeved garment, probably of silk. See Dozy, *Dictionnaire détaillé des noms des vêtements chez les Arabes* (Amsterdam, 1845), 352–62; B. Spuler, *Iran in früh-islamischer Zeit* (Wiesbaden, 1952), 350f., 394f., 405f.

him and he was admitted without delay, remained a long while, then came out again, bearing an unfurled standard. Al-Ḥajjāj prayed, making two prostrations, then rose and gave the word, and the standard was brought out the Elephant Door,[436] al-Ḥajjāj coming out behind it. There at the door was a reddish mule with blazes on its head and ankles, and al-Ḥajjāj mounted it. His personal servants offered to switch mounts with him, but he refused to ride any other. The men mounted their beasts, and Qutaybah mounted a bay horse with blazes on head and ankles, with a saddle so large that Qutaybah looked like a pomegranate in it. He set out along the Dār al-Siqāyah Road[437] until he came out at al-Sabakhah, where Shabīb had his camp. It was a Wednesday. They held back that day, then offered battle on Thursday morning. They resumed the attack early Friday morning, and, by the time of the prayer, the Khārijites were defeated.

According to Abū Zayd[438]—Khallād b. Yazīd—al-Ḥajjāj b. Qutaybah: Shabīb advanced after al-Ḥajjāj had sent out one commander against him and he had killed him, and another and he had killed him as well; one of the two was Aʿyan, the owner of the Ḥammām Aʿyan. Shabīb advanced and entered al-Kūfah. He was
[964] accompanied by Ghazālah, who had sworn an oath that she would pray two prostrations in the mosque of al-Kūfah, reciting in them the Qur'ānic *sūrah*s "The Cow" and "The Family of ʿImrān." And so she did.[439] Shabīb also had huts built in his camp.

At this point, al-Ḥajjāj stood and said, "It seems to me, men of Iraq, that you are not showing much commitment in fighting these people; and I have written to the Commander of the Faithful, asking him to send me reinforcements from the Syrians." Then Qutaybah stood up and said, "You have shown com-

436. *Bāb al-Fīl.* Various accounts of the naming of this mosque door are given by Ṭabarī (text above, II, 27) and Balādhurī (*Futūḥ*, 288).

437. The *dār al-siqāyah* was the public water supply, also mentioned above, II, 735.

438. ʿUmar b. Shabbah.

439. The rites of prayer require recitation of the Qur'ān with each prostration (see *SEI*, s.v. ṣalāh); short *sūrah*s are generally used, but *al-Baqarah* and *Āl ʿImrān*, the second and third, are by far the longest. For Ghazālah's vow see also Masʿūdī, *Murūj*, V, 320–21. Ibn Aʿtham al-Kūfī, *Futūḥ*, VII, 87ff., says nothing of a vow but has Shabīb himself recite the two *sūrah*s and place both Ghazālah and his mother al-Jahīzah on the pulpit; see also Baghdādī, *Farq*, 89–92.

mitment neither to God nor to the Commander of the Faithful in fighting them!"

According to ʿUmar b. Shabbah—Khallād—Muḥammad b. Ḥafṣ b. Mūsā b. ʿUbaydallāh b. Maʿmar b. ʿUthmān al-Taymī: Al-Ḥajjāj throttled him with his turban.

Returning to the account of al-Ḥajjāj b. Qutaybah:[440] Al-Ḥajjāj asked, "How is that?" Qutaybah replied, "You send out a noble man and then send out with him men from the riffraff; they deliver him a defeat, and he, ashamed, fights until he is killed." Al-Ḥajjāj asked, "What do you suggest?" He replied, "That you go out yourself, accompanied by men your equal, who will defend you as they do themselves." Those who were present cursed him for this; and al-Ḥajjāj said, "By God, I will go out to confront him tomorrow." The next day, the men assembled, and Qutaybah said, "Remember your oath, may God cause the amīr to prosper!" The men cursed him again, and al-Ḥajjāj said, "Go find me a good place to muster the troops!" He and his men went and made their preparations, then set out. He came to a place that was rather dirty, a dump site, and said, "Muster for me here." When they protested that the place was dirty, he said, "What you are summoning me to is dirtier! Here the earth below and the sky above are wholesome."

He dismounted and arrayed the men. Khālid b. ʿAttāb b. Warqāʾ was in disgrace and thus not among the forces. Shabīb and his companions came up, left their beasts in readiness nearby,[441] and marched out on foot. Shabīb said to them, "Do not shoot! Creep [965]
forward beneath your shields until the enemy's spears are above them, then shove them upward and go in under them so you can stand up and halt their advance. God permitting, this will defeat them." The men advanced, creeping toward them. But Khālid b. ʿAttāb took his personal forces,[442] circled around behind their camp, and set fire to their huts. When Shabīb's men saw the light of the fire and heard its crackle, they turned and saw that it was in their quarters, and hurried back to their horses. The troops then pursued them and inflicted a defeat on them. Al-Ḥajjāj was

440. Reading *bn Qutaybah* for *wa-Qutaybah*.

441. *Qarrabū dawābbahum*; see the parallel passage above (II, 629: *qarribū khuyūlakum baʿḍahā ilā baʿḍ*) and compare Lane, *Lexicon*, s.v. muqrab.

442. *Shākiriyyah*; see Fries, *Heereswesen*, 24f.

pleased with Khālid and entrusted him with the campaign against them.

When[443] Shabīb killed ʿAttāb, he aimed to enter al-Kūfah a second time and advanced to within a short distance of it. Al-Ḥajjāj sent out Sayf b. Hāni' and another man together to bring him information about Shabīb. When they came to his camp, he caught them and killed the other man, but Sayf got away. One of the Khārijites pursued him, but Sayf jumped with his horse over a stream and then asked the man for safe-conduct in exchange for telling him the truth. The man granted the safe-conduct, and he told him that al-Ḥajjāj had sent him and his companion to bring him information about Shabīb. The man said, "Tell him, then, that we are coming to him on Monday." Sayf returned to al-Ḥajjāj and informed him of this; al-Ḥajjāj said, "He is a liar and a fool."

[966] When Monday came, the Khārijites set out, heading for al-Kūfah, and al-Ḥajjāj sent out against them al-Ḥārith b. Muʿāwiyah al-Thaqafī. Shabīb encountered him at Zurārah and killed him and defeated his forces, then came on toward al-Kūfah. He sent al-Baṭīn with ten horsemen to find quarters for him on the bank of the Euphrates at the provision depot. Al-Baṭīn set out, but al-Ḥajjāj had sent Ḥawshab b. Yazīd with a group of Kūfans to occupy the approaches of the roads; al-Baṭīn fought them but was unable to overcome them. He sent to Shabīb for reinforcements and was sent some horsemen who managed to wound Ḥawshab's horse and defeat him, although he escaped with his life. Al-Baṭīn went on to the provision depot and set up camp on the bank of the Euphrates. Then Shabīb advanced, halting just past the bridge; when al-Ḥajjāj sent out no one against him, he advanced again, to al-Sabakhah, between al-Kūfah and the Euphrates. There he remained for three days, al-Ḥajjāj still sending out no one against him. Al-Ḥajjāj was advised to go out himself and sent out Qutaybah b. Muslim to prepare a place to muster for him. When Qutaybah returned, he said, "I have found the approach to them easy; go forth, then, with good omens." The call was issued to the men of al-Kūfah, and they marched forth, the notables marching out with al-Ḥajjāj, and took up positions at that place. The two sides now faced each other. Shabīb had, on his right, al-Baṭīn, and,

443. Here begins the third version of these events, introduced simply by *qāla.*

on his left, Qaʿnab, the client of the Banū Abī Rabīʿah b. Dhuhl;[444] he had some two hundred men. Al-Ḥajjāj put Maṭar b. Nājiyah al-Riyāḥī on his right and Khālid b. ʿAttāb b. Warqāʾ al-Riyāḥī on his left, with about four thousand men. Al-Ḥajjāj was told not to let Shabīb know where he stood, so he disguised himself and camouflaged his position and dressed his client Abū al-Ward to resemble him. When Shabīb saw Abū al-Ward, he attacked him and struck him with a rod weighing fifteen *raṭl*s,[445] killing him. Then al-Ḥajjāj dressed up Aʿyan, the owner of the Ḥammām Aʿyan in al-Kūfah, who was a client of Bakr b. Wāʾil;[446] Shabīb also killed him. Then al-Ḥajjāj mounted a mule with a white blaze and anklets, saying, "Religion has both a blaze and anklets!" and said to Abū Kaʿb, "Lead with the standard! I am Ibn Abī ʿAqīl!"[447] [967]

Shabīb attacked Khālid b. ʿAttāb and his forces, pushing them back to the great open space (*raḥabah*),[448] and attacked and defeated Maṭar b. Nājiyah. At this point, al-Ḥajjāj dismounted and ordered his men to dismount. He sat down on an *ʿabāʾah*[449] with ʿAnbasah b. Saʿīd. While they were thus situated, Maṣqalah b. Muhalhil al-Ḍabbī seized the bridle of Shabīb's horse and said to him, "What do you say about Ṣāliḥ b. Musarriḥ and how do you testify concerning him?" Shabīb said, "Here and now, in the midst of this situation, with al-Ḥajjāj looking on?" Shabīb declared himself quit of Ṣāliḥ, and Maṣqalah said, "May God be quit of you!" His men then left him, except for forty horsemen who were his closest companions; the rest withdrew to the provision depot.[450] Al-Ḥajjāj said, "They have had a dispute!" He sent for Khālid b. ʿAttāb, and he came and fought them. Ghazālah was killed, and a horseman was taking her head to al-Ḥajjāj when

444. A clan of the Banū Shaybān; see Ibn Ḥazm, *Jamharah*, 304, and note 153 above.

445. About five kilograms; see note 313 above.

446. See note 290 above.

447. His great-grandfather was Abū ʿAqīl; see Caskel, *Ǧamharat an-nasab*, I, 118, II, 291.

448. Or *raḥbah*, an open area, especially one for prayer either inside or outside the mosque; here apparently the square in which the mosque of al-Kūfah stood. See Lane, *Lexicon*, s.v.; Ibn Manẓūr, *Lisān*, s.v.

449. A coarse woolen sleeveless cloak, but also, as perhaps here, a saddle-cloth of the same material. See Dozy, *Supplément*, s.v.

450. This dispute over Shabīb's predecessor is not further elaborated here and not paralleled in other sources.

Shabīb recognized it and ordered ʿAlwān to attack the horseman, which he did, and killed him. He brought Shabīb the head, and he ordered it washed and buried, saying, "She is closer to you all in mercy"[451]—meaning Ghazālah. Shabīb's men then moved back to a defensive position. Khālid returned to al-Ḥajjāj and informed him that they had withdrawn, and al-Ḥajjāj ordered him to attack Shabīb. He attacked them and was drawn off by eight of them, including Qaʿnab, al-Baṭīn, ʿAlwān, ʿĪsā, al-Muhadhdhab, Ibn ʿUwaymir, and Sinān, as far as the great open space. Meanwhile, Ḥawṭ b. ʿUmayr al-Sadūsī[452] was brought to Shabīb where he
[968] stood, and Shabīb said to him, "Ḥawṭ, judgment is to God alone!" He replied, "Judgment is to God alone!" Shabīb said, "Ḥawṭ is really one of your companions but he was afraid"; and he let him go. Then he was brought ʿUmayr b. al-Qaʿqāʿ and said to him, "Judgment is to God alone, ʿUmayr!" But he did not understand, and said, "God be with my lost youth!"[453] Shabīb repeated to him, "Judgment is to God alone!" in order to let him off; but he would not understand, and Shabīb ordered him killed.[454]

Then Muṣād b. Yazīd, Shabīb's brother, was killed. Shabīb kept waiting for the party who had taken on Khālid, but they were slow to return, and Shabīb dozed off, until awakened by Ḥabīb b. Khidrah.[455] Al-Ḥajjāj's forces, meanwhile, would not advance on him, being in awesome fear of him. He went to the provision depot and began collecting the effects of those of his men who had been killed. Then his eight companions came to the place where he had been standing and, not finding him, thought that the enemy had killed him. Maṭar and Khālid returned to al-Ḥajjāj, who

---

451. A paraphrase of Qurʾān 18:81. The implication is that Ghazālah was a mother to them all; see Zamakhsharī, *Asās al-balāghah* (Beirut, 1979), s.v. ruḥm.

452. Reading Ḥawṭ with the Petersburg MS, against edited text Khūṭ. This man probably belonged to the Banū Sadūs b. Shaybān of the Dhuhl b. Thaʿlabah; see Caskel, *Ǧamharat an-nasab*, I, 152, and note 153 above.

453. *Fī sabīl Allāh shabābī*: a quotation? See Maydānī, *Amthāl*, II, 21, for a similar proverbial phrase.

454. This account is clearly a variant of the story told above (II, 920f.) of the well-known al-Naḍr b. al-Qaʿqāʿ, after Shabīb's first entry into al-Kūfah.

455. A client of the Banū Hilāl b. ʿĀmir b. Ṣaʿṣaʿah, one of the celebrated Khārijite poets and orators. His father's name appears in various sources as Khidrah, Khudrah, Jadarah, and Judrah; see Jāḥiẓ, *Bayān*, I, 346, III, 264; Mubarrad, *Kāmil*, 709; I. ʿAbbās, *Shiʿr al-Khawārij* (Beirut, 1963), 78–82, 144. Ṭabarī cites verses by him below, II, 1002.

ordered them to pursue the band of eight. They did so, while the band pursued Shabīb, all continuing until they crossed the bridge at al-Madā'in.[456] The Khārijites went into a monastery there with Khālid on their heels. He surrounded them in the monastery, but they came out against him and drove him back some two *farsakh*s, until his men pitched themselves into the Tigris on their horses; Khālid also pitched himself in on his horse but got across on it with his standard in his hand. Shabīb said, "God oppose such a man and such a horse! This man is the most valiant fighter, and his horse is the most powerful horse on earth!" He was informed that this was Khālid, son of ʿAttāb, and he said, "He has inherited his courage then. By God, if I had known, I would have plunged after him, even if he had plunged into Hell!"

Returning to the account of Abū Mikhnaf—Abū ʿAmr al- [969]
ʿUdhrī: When Shabīb was defeated, al-Ḥajjāj entered al-Kūfah, ascended the pulpit, and said, "By God, Shabīb has never been fought this way before! He turned and fled, by God, leaving his wife with a broken reed up her ass!" Then he summoned Ḥabīb b. ʿAbd al-Raḥmān al-Ḥakamī and sent him in pursuit of Shabīb with three thousand Syrian troops.[457] Al-Ḥajjāj said to him, "Be on your guard against night attacks from Shabīb and, wherever you encounter him, engage him immediately, for God has notched his blade and broken his fangs." Ḥabīb b. ʿAbd al-Raḥmān then went out and pursued Shabīb as far as al-Anbār, halting there. Al-Ḥajjāj also sent to the administrators, ordering them to spread word secretly among Shabīb's men that any of them who came over to them would be given safe-conduct. All those who lacked true zeal and had been worn down by the fighting began to come over and were granted safe-conduct. Al-Ḥajjāj had also,[458] before this, on the day of their defeat, proclaimed to them that any of them who came to him would be granted safe-conduct, and now many men separated themselves from Shabīb's forces. Shabīb was then informed that Ḥabīb b. ʿAbd al-Raḥmān was positioned at al-Anbār, and he advanced with his forces; when he

---

456. A distance of some seventy-five miles.

457. Ibn Khayyāṭ, *Ta'rīkh*, 274. The summaries in Ibn Aʿtham al-Kūfī, *Futūḥ*, VII, 91, and Yaʿqūbī, *Ta'rīkh*, II, 328, identify the commander as ʿAlqamah b. ʿAbd al-Raḥmān al-Ḥakamī. See also Périer, *Vie d'al-Ḥadjdjâdj*, 144.

458. Or *not: wa-qabla dhālika mā nādā fīhim . . . anna man jā'anā . . .*

was near their camp, he halted and led his men in the sunset prayer.

According to Abū Mikhnaf—Abū Yazīd al-Saksakī:[459] By God, I was among the Syrian forces the night Shabīb came and made a surprise attack on us. When we stopped for the night, Ḥabīb b. ʿAbd al-Raḥmān had assembled us and divided us into quarters, saying to each quarter, "For each quarter of you its own area should suffice; if one quarter is engaged in fighting, another
[970] quarter should not come to their aid. Word has reached me that these Khārijites are nearby; prepare yourselves, then, for a night attack and fighting." We remained in this muster until Shabīb came and attacked us. He charged the quarter commanded by ʿUthmān b. Saʿīd al-ʿUdhrī and fought long with them with swords, but not a single man's foot retreated a step. Then he left them and went up against another quarter, which had been given in charge to Saʿd b. Bajal al-ʿĀmirī, and fought them; but again not a single man's foot retreated a step. Then he left them and went up against the next quarter, commanded by al-Nuʿmān b. Saʿd al-Ḥimyarī, but he achieved nothing more against them. Finally, he came to the last quarter, commanded by Ibn Uqayṣir al-Khathʿamī, and fought them a long time without accomplishing anything. He kept circling around us and attacking us until three quarters of the night had passed. He stuck to us until we thought that he would never let us go. Then he dismounted and forced us to fight them on foot for a long time. By God, between us, hands were hacked off and eyes put out and the dead piled up. We killed about thirty of them, and they killed about a hundred of us. By God, it seemed to us that if they had been more than the hundred men they were, they would have destroyed us. I will swear to God on that! They did not withdraw from us until they were as sick and tired of us as we were of them. I would see one of our men strike one of their men with his sword and not hurt him at all because he was so weak and worn out; or I would see another of our men fighting sitting down, making feeble thrusts with his
[971] sword—too exhausted to stand. When finally they despaired of besting us, Shabīb mounted his horse and told those of his com-

459. On the Sakāsik of Kindah, who supported the Umayyads in Syria, see Caskel, *Ǧamharat an-nasab*, II, 503; al-Samʿānī, *Ansāb*, s. v. Saksakī.

panions who had dismounted to remount. Once they were all firmly on horseback, he led them away from us.

According to Abū Mikhnaf—Farwah b. Laqīṭ, referring to Shabīb: When we left them, in very low spirits and with many wounded, he said to us, "What a heavy blow for us—if we were pursuing only worldly goals; but what a light one in view of God's reward!" His companions replied, "Truly spoken, Commander of the Faithful!"

I will never forget how he rushed up to Suwayd b. Sulaym and told him the following story: "I killed two of their men yesterday, one of them the bravest of men and the other the most cowardly. I went out at dusk last night to scout for you and met three of them who had come into a village to buy what they needed there. One of them made his purchases and came out in advance of his fellows, and I went out with him. He said, 'It seems that you have not bought fodder.' I replied, 'I have some comrades who have taken care of that for me.' Then I asked him, 'Where do you think this enemy of ours is camped?' He said, 'I hear that he is camped nearby us here. I swear to God, I wish I could have met this Shabīb of theirs!' I said, 'Would you like to?' He said, 'Yes!' I said, 'Watch out, then, for, by God, I am Shabīb!' and I drew my sword. By God, the man dropped dead! I said to him, 'Get up, damn you!' and then went to see, and he really was dead! I left him and was starting back, when I met this other one coming out of the village. He said, 'Where are you going now? The men are all going back to their camp.' I said nothing to him and went on, spurring my horse
to a gallop. He came after me and caught up with me, and I pulled [972]
up and asked him, 'What is the matter?' He said, 'You, by God, are one of our enemy!' I said, 'Yes, I am, by God!' He said, 'By God, you will not leave here until either you have killed me or I have killed you!' I charged at him and he charged at me, and we fought with our swords for a time. By God, I was his superior in neither tenacity nor boldness; but my sword was sharper than his, and I killed him."

Then we traveled on, crossed the Tigris, and went through the Jūkhā region; we crossed the Tigris again in the area of Wāsiṭ,[460]

460. A town about 120 miles southeast of al-Madā'in, but only built (by al-Ḥajjāj for his Syrian troops) six years later, in 83 (702). See text below, II, 1125, and *EI*², s.v. Wāsiṭ.

went on toward al-Ahwāz, then toward Fārs, and then on to Kirmān.

In this year, Shabīb perished, according to the account of Hishām b. Muḥammad; according to another account, he perished in the year 78 (697–698).[461]

Account of Shabīb's End

According to Hishām—Abū Mikhnaf—Abū Yazīd al-Saksakī: It was al-Ḥajjāj himself who had sent us out against him[462]—that is, Shabīb—and now he distributed a great deal of money among us, giving a share to every man who had been wounded or shown particular valor. Then he ordered Sufyān b. al-Abrad to march out against Shabīb, and Sufyān prepared to do so. This distressed Ḥabīb b. 'Abd al-Raḥmān al-Ḥakamī, who said, "You send Sufyān against a man whom I routed and whose best horsemen I killed!" Two months later, however, Sufyān carried out his orders. Shabīb, meanwhile, had remained in Kirmān while he and his forces recuperated and restored themselves; he then set out on his way back and was met by Sufyān at the Ahwāz Dujayl Bridge.[463] Al-
[973] Ḥajjāj had written to al-Ḥakam b. Ayyūb b. al-Ḥakam b. Abī 'Aqīl, who was his son-in-law and his governor over al-Baṣrah, as follows: "Send out a noble, courageous man from among the Baṣrans with four thousand troops against Shabīb. Order him to join Sufyān b. al-Abrad and to heed and obey him." Al-Ḥakam sent out Ziyād b. 'Amr al-'Atakī with four thousand troops, and they had no sooner reached Sufyān than he encountered Shabīb. When they met, at the Dujayl Bridge, Shabīb crossed over to Sufyān. He found that Sufyān had dismounted and was among the infantry, having put Muhāṣir b. Ṣayfī al-'Udhrī over the cavalry; over his right wing he had put Bashīr b. Ḥassān al-Nahdī and over his left wing 'Umar b. Hubayrah al-Fazārī.[464] Shabīb advanced with his

461. What follow are two versions of Shabīb's death, both from Abū Mikhnaf. A third version, dated 78 (697–698) appears in Ya'qūbī, *Ta'rīkh,* I, 328, as well as, undated, in Ibn A'tham al-Kūfī, *Futūḥ,* VII, 92. See note 470 below.

462. *Aqfalanā al-Ḥajjāj ilayhi.*

463. A bridge of boats crossing the Dujayl River (now the Karun) at al-Ahwāz; the Dujayl of al-Ahwāz is distinguished from the Dujayl Canal north of Baghdad. See Le Strange, *Lands,* 232–36.

464. Later governor of Iraq and leader of the Qaysī tribal faction; see text below, II, 1433ff., and *EI²*, s.v. Ibn Hubayra.

forces in three squadrons, one under his own command, one under Suwayd, and one under Qaʿnab al-Muḥallimī. He left al-Muḥallil b. Wā'il behind in his camp.

While Suwayd, on Shabīb's right, attacked Sufyān's left, and Qaʿnab, on Shabīb's left, attacked Sufyān's right, Shabīb himself attacked Sufyān. We fought with swords much of the day, until they withdrew and returned to their original positions. Then Shabīb and his forces made more than thirty charges at us, but through it all we did not budge from our line. Sufyān said to us, "Do not disperse, but let the infantry advance on them as a body." By God, we kept at them with our swords and spears until we drove them back to the bridge. When Shabīb reached the bridge, he dismounted, along with about a hundred men. We fought them until evening, as fiercely as any army has ever [974] fought—as soon as they dismounted they fell on us with sword and spear in a way we had never seen an army fight before. When Sufyān saw that he would not be able to overcome them and could not even be sure that they would not overcome him, he summoned the archers and ordered them to attack them with arrows. This was in the evening, and the battle had begun at midday. The archers attacked them with arrows in the evening; Sufyān b. al-Abrad had set them in a line by themselves and put a man in charge of the bowmen.[465] They kept up the attack with arrows for a time; then the enemy charged them, but as they charged our archers, we charged them and diverted them.

As they continued to be attacked by the arrows, Shabīb and his companions mounted their horses and led another charge against the archers, which felled more than thirty of them. Then Shabīb turned with his mounted troops against us. He bore down directly on us, and we fought him with our spears until it became too dark. He withdrew from us then, and Sufyān said to his men, "Men, leave them be and do not pursue them! We will resume with them in the morning." We desisted from fighting them, with nothing dearer to us than that they should withdraw from us.

According to Abū Mikhnaf—Farwah b. Laqīṭ: Soon we got to the bridge, and Shabīb said, "Cross over, companies of Muslims, and we will take them on again in the morning, God willing." We

---

465. *Murāmiyah,* apparently synonymous with *aṣḥāb al-nabl,* "archers," above, and *rumāh,* "archers," below.

crossed over before him, while he stayed behind at our rear. Then he started across on his horse; but there was a Median mare[466] in front of him, and his horse lunged to mount her in the middle of the bridge. The Median became agitated, and Shabīb's horse's hoof went over the side of the boat and he fell in the water. As he fell, he said, "That God might determine a matter that was done."[467] He
[975] sank beneath the water, then came up again and said, "That is the ordaining of the Almighty, the All-Knowing."[468]

According to Abū Mikhnaf: These are the accounts of Abū Yazīd al-Saksakī, who was one of the Syrians who fought Shabīb, and Farwah b. Laqīṭ, who was one of the participants in his battles. I also have heard the following account from a man of Shabīb's own clan, the Banū Murrah b. Hammām: There were men from Shabīb's own tribe[469] fighting with him, but they did not fully share his zeal. He had killed many of their fellow tribesmen, and that had pained and angered them. Among Shabīb's associates was a man named Muqātil, from the Banū Taym b. Shaybān. When Shabīb killed some men from the Banū Taym b. Shaybān, this man set upon the Banū Murrah b. Hammām and inflicted a number of casualties among them. Shabīb asked him, "What impelled you to kill them without orders from me?" He replied, "May God cause you to prosper, you have killed the unbelievers among my people, and I have killed the unbelievers among your people." Shabīb said, "And do you have authority over me so you can make independent decisions without me?" He replied, "May God cause you to prosper, is it not part of our religion to kill those who do not subscribe to our opinions, whether they are our own kin or not?" Shabīb said, "Yes, it is." Muqātil said, "Then I have done nothing but what I ought. Besides, Commander of the Faithful, I have certainly not struck down from your clan a tenth of the number you have struck down from mine. In any case, Commander of the Faithful, you have no

---

466. *Faras unthā mādhiyānah.* See Ṭabarī, glossarium, s. v. Mādhiyānah.

467. Qur'ān 8:42, 44, in the context of God's predetermination of the Battle of Badr.

468. Qur'ān 6:96, 36:38, 41:12.

469. *'Ashīrah,* referring to other Shaybānid clans related to Shabīb's own clan (*rahṭ*), the Banū Murrah b. Hammām b. Murrah b. Dhuhl b. Shaybān; see note 153 above.

warrant to grieve over the killing of unbelievers." Shabīb said, "I do not grieve over that."

There were with him many men among whose kin he had inflicted casualties; according to their claim, when he stayed behind with the last of his forces, they said to one another, "What say you to cutting the bridge as he crosses and getting our revenge right now?" They cut the bridge, the boats rocked, the horse panicked and bolted, and Shabīb fell in the water and drowned. [976]

According to Abū Mikhnaf: That Murrī gave me this account, and some people from Shabīb's clan tell the same story. The standard account, however, is the one I gave first.

According to Abū Mikhnaf—Abū Yazīd al-Saksakī: We were preparing to go off when, by God, the bridgekeeper came and asked for our commander. We pointed him out to him, and he went up to him and said, "May God cause you to prosper, one of their men fell in the water, and they called to one another saying, 'The Commander of the Faithful has drowned!' Then they went off the way they had come, leaving not a soul behind in their camp."

Sufyān raised a cry of "God is great!" and we joined him in it. Then he set off for the bridge, and from there sent Muhāṣir b. Ṣayfī to cross over to their camp. He found not a whisper or a trace of them there; and when he dismounted, he found it to be the most well-appointed camp on God's earth! The next morning we searched for Shabīb until we found him and pulled him out, still wearing his cuirass. I have heard men say that they cut his chest open and took out his heart, and it turned out to be compact and hard as a rock; if one threw it to the ground, it would bounce as high as a man's stature. Sufyān said, "Praise God, Who has come to our aid!" We then took possession of their camp.[470]

According to Abū Zayd 'Umar b. Shabbah—Khallād b. Yazīd al-Arqaṭ: Shabīb's death was announced to his mother, but she re-

470. The first account given here, with the story of the mare, appears also in Mas'ūdī, *Murūj*, V, 322, and Ibn Khallikān, *Wafayāt*, II, 455, both of whom also give the story of Shabīb's heart. Ṭabarī's second account, implicating Shabīb's own followers in his death, is not found in other published early sources. According to Ibn A'tham al-Kūfī and Ya'qūbī (see note 461 above), it was Sufyān who cut the bridge. Ibn A'tham al-Kūfī also appends a long account of the captive Khārijite men and women led before al-Ḥajjāj, who pardoned some and had others executed.

fused to accept it when they said he had been killed; then, when she was told he had drowned, she accepted it and said, "When I gave birth to him I saw a flash of fire come out of me, and I knew that nothing but water would put it out."

[977] According to Hishām—Abū Mikhnaf—Farwah b. Laqīṭ al-Azdī al-Ghāmidī: Yazīd b. Nu'aym, Shabīb's father, was one of the men who joined the army of Salmān b. Rabī'ah when al-Walīd b. 'Uqbah sent him and those with him to the land of the Byzantines, on orders from 'Uthmān, as reinforcements to the Syrian forces.[471] When the Muslims returned from the campaign, the captives were put up for sale, and Shabīb's father, Yazīd b. Nu'aym, saw a tall, pretty, eye-catching girl, fair-skinned, but without a trace of gray or blue in her black eyes; and he bought her. Then he took her—this was at the beginning of the year 25 (645)—and brought her to al-Kūfah. There he asked her to convert to Islam, but she refused, and when he beat her, she only became more stubborn. Seeing this, he ordered her made ready, and then called for her, and she was brought in to him. When he had intercourse with her, she conceived Shabīb, who was born on Saturday, the Day of Sacrifice, in Dhū al-Ḥijjah of the year 25 (September 27, 646).[472] She loved her master dearly, and while she was in labor she said, "If you wish, I will convert to Islam as you asked me to." He said, "I do so wish." She then converted and was a Muslim when she bore Shabīb. She said, "I saw, in a dream, that a flash came forth from my vagina, which blazed forth to heaven and to the horizon on all sides, and then suddenly fell into a flood of running water, and went out. I gave birth to him on this day on which you shed blood, and I interpreted this vision of mine as meaning that I would see this son of mine, as he grew up, becoming a man of bloodshed, and that I
[978] would see him quickly rise and become great." His father used to take him and his mother often out to the desert, to his people's land at a watering hole called al-Laṣaf.[473]

According to Abū Mikhnaf—Mūsā b. Abī Suwayd b. Rādī: The Syrian forces that arrived brought with them a stone[474] and said,

471. In the year 24 (645); see text above, I, 2806ff.

472. The Day of Sacrifice is the tenth of Dhū al-Ḥijjah (see *EI²*, s.v. ḥadjdj). 10 Dhū al-Ḥijjah 25 (September 27, 646) was a Wednesday.

473. Another version of this story in Ibn Khallikān, *Wafayāt*, II, 457.

474. *Al-ḥajar*, literally, "the stone."

"We will not flee from Shabīb until this stone flees." Shabīb heard about this and decided to play a trick on them. He called for four horses and attached shields to their tails, two to the tail of each horse. Then he summoned eight of his companions to accompany him, as well as an attendant of his named Ḥayyān, and ordered Ḥayyān to bring along a waterskin. He then set out and came to one side of the camp. He ordered his companions to take up positions on the other sides of the camp, each two men with a horse, and then to touch the horses with their blades until they felt their keenness, and let them go into the camp. He arranged to meet his companions at a stream near the camp, saying, "Those of you who survive should meet at this stream." His companions were reluctant to carry out what he had ordered them to do, and when he saw this, he dismounted and himself did to the horses what he had ordered them to do. The horses rushed into the camp, and he went in behind them, crying, "Judgment is to God alone!" The men began to fight one another, but their commander, Ḥabīb b. ʿAbd al-Raḥmān al-Ḥakamī, called out, "Men! This is a trick! Stand where you are until you can see clearly what is going on!" and they did so. Shabīb was still in their camp and stood where he was when he saw them stop their commotion. He had been hit with a blow from a rod and was in a weakened condition. When the men quieted down and returned to their [979]
quarters, he managed to slip out amidst the crowd and reached the stream, where he found Ḥayyān. He said, "Ḥayyān, pour out some water on my head." When he stretched out his head for Ḥayyān to pour water over it, the latter was about to cut it off, saying to himself, "I will find no greater honor or celebrity than will come to me from killing this man, and it will be my safe-conduct with al-Ḥajjāj." But just as he had this thought, he felt a shudder of fear; and when he was slow opening the waterskin, Shabīb asked him, "Why are you so slow opening it?" and took his knife from his boot and cut it open and handed it back to him. He then poured out the water over his head. Ḥayyān explained, "It was cowardice, by God, and the shudder of fear that came over me, that kept me from cutting off his head after I intended to do so." Then Shabīb rejoined his companions in his camp.

According to Abū Jaʿfar: In this year, Muṭarrif b. al-Mughīrah b. Shuʿbah rebelled against al-Ḥajjāj, throwing off his allegiance to

ʿAbd al-Malik b. Marwān, and rode off to al-Jibāl, where he was killed.[475]

Account of Muṭarrif's Rebelling and Throwing Off His Allegiance to ʿAbd al-Malik b. Marwān

According to Hishām—Abū Mikhnaf—Yūsuf b. Bakr al-Azdī: The sons of al-Mughīrah b. Shuʿbah were excellent, noble men in their own right, aside from the nobility of their father and their status in their tribe. When al-Ḥajjāj came, and met and spoke with them, he learned that they were men of his own tribe and sons of his father,[476] and he made ʿUrwah b. al-Mughīrah governor of al-Kūfah,[477] Muṭarrif b. al-Mughīrah governor of al-
[980] Madā'in, and Ḥamzah b. al-Mughīrah governor of Hamadhān.

According to Abū Mikhnaf—al-Ḥuṣayn b. ʿAbdallāh b. Saʿd b. Nufayl al-Azdī: When Muṭarrif b. al-Mughīrah came to al-Madā'in as our governor, he ascended the pulpit, praised and glorified God, and said:

> Men! The amīr al-Ḥajjāj—may God cause him to prosper!—has appointed me governor over you and commanded me to rule with right and act with justice in all I do. If I do as he has commanded me, I will be the happiest of men; but if I do not, I will be the cause of my own perdition and the forfeiter of my own fortune. I shall sit to receive you morning and evening;[478] please come to me with your concerns, as

---

475. Ṭabarī's account from Abū Mikhnaf of Muṭarrif's rebellion is the most detailed we have; the version from Ibn al-Kalbī in Balādhurī's *Ansāb* (unpublished) differs little from it. See Dixon, *Umayyad Caliphate*, 191–95; Périer, *Vie d'al-Hadjdjâj*, 148–53. Ibn al-Athīr, *Kāmil*, IV, 433–37, summarizes Ṭabarī, adding only an anecdote to the effect that al-Ḥajjāj questioned Muṭarrif's parentage, because while many of the Rabīʿah became Khārijites, this was true of none of the Qays ʿAylān (to whom the Thaqīf, the tribe of al-Mughīrah and al-Ḥajjāj, were often, although not invariably, assigned); see note 92 above and Caskel, *Ǧamharat an-nasab*, I, 92.

476. Both al-Ḥajjāj and al-Mughīrah belonged to the tribe of Thaqīf. See Caskel, *Ǧamharat an-nasab*, II, 419f.

477. See text above, II, 873.

478. Muṭarrif here paraphrases a *ḥadīth* of ʿAlī: "Remind them of the days of God and sit to receive them morning and evening" (the first phrase of this being in turn a quotation of Qur'ān 14:5); see Ibn Manẓūr, *Lisān*, s. v. ʿaṣr, and Ibn Abī al-Ḥadīd, *Sharḥ Nahj al-balāghah* (Cairo, 1959–64), XVIII, 30f.

well as your advice on what will most benefit you and your land. I will work unceasingly for your good, to the extent I am able.

Then he came down. At that time there were in al-Madā'in men from the nobles of the garrison and the great families, as well as fighters too numerous for the town to hold, ready in case something should flare up in the Jūkhā region or the Anbār region. When Muṭarrif came down, he proceeded immediately to sit in the *īwān*[479] to receive people. He was approached by Ḥakīm b. al-Ḥārith al-Azdī, who was one of the prominent and noble men of the Azd—al Ḥajjāj later put him in charge of the treasury. He said, "May God cause you to prosper, I was some distance away when you spoke; I came forward to reply to you, but by then you were coming back down. We have understood what you told us, that you have been given authority—may God lead aright the giver and the receiver! You have encouraged us to hope for justice from you and you have asked for help in acting rightly. May God help [981] you in what you intend! You are like your father, whose actions always met with the approval of God and man." Muṭarrif said, "Come here to me," and he made room for him to sit beside him.

According to Abū Mikhnaf—al-Ḥuṣayn b. Yazīd: He was one of the best governors ever sent out to us, energetic in suppressing immorality and condemning injustice." Bishr b. al-Ajdaʿ al-Hamdānī al-Thawrī,[480] who was a poet, approached him and said:

I have fallen in love with a young woman of good character,
with sparkling teeth, languid limbs, and a fine neck.
She is like the sun coming out on a rainy day,
when she comes out to walk with her lithe and slender friends.
But turn your passions from her, and ride a great mannish she-camel
to that generous and beneficent source of favor,

---

479. Probably, if not quite certainly, the *īwān Kisrā*, the famous Sasanian palace in Ctesiphon, part of whose façade still stands. See *EI*², s. vv. īwān, al-Madā'in, and note 422 above.

480. Not a son of the known poet al-Ajdaʿ b. Mālik, as suggested by the editors; within the tribe of Hamdān, al-Ajdaʿ b. Mālik belonged to the Banū Wādiʿah, not the Banū Thawr. See Caskel, *Ǧamharat an-nasab*, I, 229, 230.

To that glorious young man, lavish in his gifts, whom we
recognize
among the people whenever there is an unpleasantness to
be got rid of.[481]
If you ask about lineage, his is a noble one;
he holds his head high with those who carry weight on the
day scores are settled.
May the All-Merciful be your refuge from a band of men
with red moustaches, like the black lions of the thicket—
[982] The horsemen of Shaybān! Never have we heard of their like,
sons of every lordly chief of noble descent.
They attacked Ibn Ḥuṣayn and his detachment,
and left him a corpse on the battlefield, on the night of the
feast.[482]
Ibn al-Mujālid fell victim to their spears,
as if he had slipped off a high, smooth rock.[483]
And every group assembled against them in Rūdhābār[484]
was broken up with spearthrusts, between the palms and
the desert.

Muṭarrif said to him, "Woe to you! You have only come to incite us!" Shabīb had advanced from Sātīdamā,[485] and Muṭarrif wrote to al-Ḥajjāj as follows:

> I hereby inform the amīr—may God cause him to prosper!—that Shabīb has advanced toward us. If the amīr should think it best to send me reinforcements with which to secure al-Madā'in, he will do so; for al-Madā'in is the gate and fortress of al-Kūfah.

Al-Ḥajjāj b. Yūsuf sent him Sabrah b. ʿAbd al-Raḥmān b. Mikhnaf with two hundred men and ʿAbdallāh b. Kannāz with

481. *Sā'ata yujlā kullu mardūdī.* Some manuscripts read *yaḥlā:* "whenever the unpleasant turns sweet."

482. On the defeat of ʿUthmān b. Qaṭan b. ʿAbdallāh b. al-Ḥuṣayn in Rādhān on the *ʿīd al-aḍḥā* of the previous year, see text above, II, 932–37.

483. On the defeat of Sa'īd b. al-Mujālid at either Qaṭīṭiyā or al-Dayr, see text above, II, 907–12.

484. So, *metrica causa,* for Rūdhabār = Rūdhbār. On the battle, see text above, II, 922–29.

485. See note 187 above. According to Abū Mikhnaf's earlier account, Shabīb's advance began from Māh Bihzādhān; see text above, II, 941, and note 371.

another two hundred. Shabīb advanced and halted at the bridges of Ḥudhayfah, then continued forward to Kalwādhā,[486] where he crossed the Tigris, and continued on to the city of Bahurasīr, where he halted. Muṭarrif b. al-Mughīrah was in the ancient city,[487] where Chosroes' residence and the White Palace are located. When Shabīb halted at Bahurasīr, Muṭarrif cut the bridge [983] between him and Shabīb and sent to Shabīb saying, "Send to me some of your worthy associates, together with whom I can study the Qur'ān and consider the stance that you advocate." Shabīb sent to him a number of men, including Suwayd b. Sulaym, Qaʿnab, and al-Muḥallil b. Wā'il; but when the ferry had been brought up and they were about to board it, Shabīb sent them a message, saying not to do so until his messenger had returned from Muṭarrif. He sent to Muṭarrif, saying, "Send to me a number of your companions, until you send my companions back to me." But Muṭarrif said to the messenger, "Go to him and say: Why should I trust you with my companions if I send them to you now when you do not trust me with your companions?" Shabīb sent back his reply, saying, "You know that in our religion we do not consider treachery permissible, while you do it and think nothing of it." Muṭarrif then sent to him al-Rabīʿ b. Yazīd al-Asadī, Sulaymān b. Ḥudhayfah b. Hilāl b. Mālik al-Muzanī, and Yazīd b. Abī Ziyād, the client of al-Mughīrah, who was in charge of Muṭarrif's guard. Once they were in Shabīb's custody, he sent his companions on to Muṭarrif.

According to Abū Mikhnaf—al Naḍr-b. Ṣāliḥ: I was with Muṭarrif b. al-Mughīrah b. Shuʿbah—I[488] do not know whether he[489] said, "I was among the troops that were with him" or "I was there in his presence"—when Shabīb's envoys came to him. Muṭarrif always treated me and my brother with affection and respect and was not in the habit of hiding anything from us. When the envoys entered, Muṭarrif was alone except for me and my brother Ḥullām [984] b. Ṣāliḥ. They were six and we were three, and they were fully armed, while we had only our swords. As they came forward,

486. From here this account closely parallels that given above, II, 946f.

487. *Al-madīnah al-ʿatīqah*, viz., Ctesiphon, on the east side of the river. On it and the White Palace, see *EI*², s. v. al-Madā'in.

488. Abū Mikhnaf.

489. Al-Naḍr.

Suwayd said, "Peace be to him who fears to stand before his Lord[490] and recognizes right guidance and its people." Muṭarrif replied, "Yes, indeed! May God bless them!" They then sat down, and Muṭarrif said to them, "Give me an account of your position[491] and inform me of what it is you seek and what it is you advocate." Suwayd b. Sulaym praised and glorified God, and said, "What we advocate is the Book of God and the *sunnah*[492] of Muḥammad, God bless him. What we object to for our people is the expropriation of the spoils, the failure to enforce the Qur'ānic punishments, and the autocratic nature of the regime."[493] Muṭarrif responded, "You summon only to right and object only to blatant injustice. I follow you in this; now follow me in what I summon you to, so that we may combine forces and our hands may work as one." They said, "Come, then, say what you want to say, and if what you summon us to is right, we will agree." He said, "I summon you to fight with me against these renegade tyrants over the innovation they have introduced and to summon them to the Book of God and the *sunnah* of His Prophet. Let this question of rule be decided by a council among the Muslims, choosing whomever they themselves approve as amīr over them, on the model of the situation in which ʿUmar b. al-Khaṭṭāb left them.[494] If the Arabs knew that all that is meant by 'council' is 'the approved one from Quraysh,'[495] they would approve and you would gain many followers from them and supporters against your enemy, and you would accomplish this purpose of yours."

At this, they jumped up to depart, saying, "This is something
[985] on which we will never agree with you." As they were leaving and just stepping out of the portico of the house, Suwayd b. Su-

490. Qur'ān 55:46, 79:40.

491. *Quṣṣū ʿalayya amrakum.* See the *qaṣaṣ* of Ṣāliḥ b. Musarriḥ, text above, II, 881–84, and note 139.

492. Way or custom; see *SEI*, s. v.

493. See the similar list of grievances in Ṣāliḥ b. Musarriḥ's *qaṣaṣ*, text above, II, 883, where they are directed specifically at ʿUthmān.

494. On the *shūrā*, the council of six appointed by the dying ʿUmar to appoint his successor, see text above, I, 2776ff.; and on its role in Khārijism, see text above, I, 3349, Qur'ān 42:38, and E. Salem, *Political Theory and Institutions of the Khawārij* (Baltimore, 1956), 52, 58.

495. *Al-riḍā min Quraysh.* The Khārijites were both unique and unanimous in rejecting the requirement that the leader of the community be from Quraysh; see *EI*², s. v. imāma.

laym turned to Muṭarrif and said, "Ibn al-Mughīrah, if our men had been hostile and treacherous, you would have been putting yourself at their mercy." Muṭarrif was shaken at this and said, "You speak truly, by the God of Moses and Jesus!"

The men returned to Shabīb and informed him of what Muṭarrif had to say. Shabīb had hopes of winning him over and told them, "In the morning, one of you is to go back to him." In the morning, then, he sent Suwayd to him, giving him his orders. Suwayd set forth and came to Muṭarrif's door. It was I who conveyed his request to enter, and when he had come in and sat down, I was about to leave; but Muṭarrif said to me, "Sit! I have no secrets from you." I sat. At the time I was a tender youth, and Suwayd asked Muṭarrif, "Who is this from whom you have no secrets?" He replied, "This noble man is the son of Mālik b. Zuhayr b. Jadhīmah."[496] Suwayd said, "Great! 'You have found a good horse, so keep him!'[497] If his religion is like his lineage, he is perfect."

Then he turned his attention to Muṭarrif and said, "We presented the Commander of the Faithful with what you said to us, and he said, 'Go to him and say, "Do you not know that for the Muslims to choose for themselves the one they consider the best among them is correct procedure, for that is how the *sunnah* proceeded after the death of the Messenger?" If he says yes, then say to him, "We, then, have chosen for ourselves that one among us whom we most approve and who has the greatest strength to bear the burden of responsibility; and so long as he makes no change or alteration, he is the one who wields authority over us."' Shabīb added to us, 'Tell him, "With regard to your comments on 'council,' when you said that if the Arabs knew that all [986]
we mean in this regard is simply Quraysh, many of them would follow us, we reply that the people of truth lose nothing with God for being few, and the oppressors gain no good for being many. Our abandoning our truth, for which we rebelled, and entering into this 'council' to which you summon us would be a sin and a defeat, giving aid and comfort to the oppressors and showing our

---

496. A chieftain of 'Abs in pre-Islamic times, whose murder initiated the celebrated war of Dāḥis and al-Ghabrā'; see *Aghānī*[1], XI, 155f., XVI, 23ff.

497. For the proverb, see Maydānī, *Amthāl*, II, 78.

weakness; for we are not of the opinion that Quraysh have any more rights in this matter than others among the Arabs."' Shabīb further instructed us, 'If he claims that they do have more rights in this matter than anyone else among the Arabs, ask him why; if he says it is because of their kinship to Muḥammad, then say to him, "If that were the case, then, by God, it would not have been fitting for our pious forefathers, the first Emigrants, to exercise authority over the family of Muḥammad—including even the children of Abū Lahab, if they had been the only surviving members.[498] Had they not known that the best of the people in God's eyes is the most pious of them[499] and that the one worthiest of this position is the most pious, the most excellent, and the one with the greatest strength to bear the burdens of their affairs, they would not have accepted authority over the people's affairs." We were the first to protest oppression, to work to undo tyranny,[500] and to fight against the factions. If Muṭarrif follows us, he will be treated as any one of us, both for good and bad, being one of the Muslims; if he does not, then he is as one of the polytheists whom we consider our enemy and whom we fight.'"

Muṭarrif replied, "I have understood what you say. Go back to your camp for this day, while we consider our position." Suwayd returned to his camp, and Muṭarrif summoned some of his most trusted advisers, including Sulaymān b. Ḥudhayfah al-Muzanī and al-Rabīʿ b. Yazīd al-Asadī.

[987] According to al-Naḍr b. Ṣāliḥ: I was standing with Yazīd b. Abī Ziyād, the client of al-Mughīrah b. Shuʿbah, next to Muṭarrif, each of us with his sword; Yazīd was in charge of his guard. Muṭarrif said to the men, "You are my advisers, my friends, and those in whose integrity and good judgment I trust. By God, I have abhorred the deeds of these oppressors all along, protesting against them in my heart and working to undo them as much as possible

498. The reference is probably specifically to the first two caliphs, whose authority was recognized by Muḥammad's family, including not only ʿAlī but also many other cousins, among them the sons of Muḥammad's old enemy ʿAbd al-ʿUzzā (Abū Lahab; see *EI*², s. v.). Abū Lahab's sons ʿUtbah and Muʿattib did become Muslims but played no prominent role in the government of the community; see Ibn Saʿd, *Ṭabaqāt*, IV, i, 41f., V, 336.

499. A paraphrase of Qurʾān 49:13.

500. *Ghayyara al-jawr*, literally "change tyranny." Compare Muṭarrif's statement below that he "worked to undo" the deeds of the oppressors.

with my own deeds and orders. Now that their sins have become so great, and I have encountered these people who strive against them,[501] I have decided I have no choice but to oppose and resist them, if I can find allies to support me against them. I summoned these people and said to them such-and-such, and they said to me such-and-such, and I have decided not to fight them; indeed, if they were willing to follow my opinion as I described it to them, I would cast off allegiance to ʿAbd al-Malik and al-Ḥajjāj and go off to strive against them." Al-Muzanī said to him, "These men will never follow you in your opinion, nor will you follow them. Keep this parley quiet and let no one know about it." Al-Asadī also said much the same thing. Then his client Ibn Abī Ziyād fell to his knees and said, "By God, not a single word of what was said between you and them will escape al-Ḥajjāj, and that with each word embellished with ten more just like it! By God, if you were to try to escape from al-Ḥajjāj over the clouds, he would still hunt you down to destroy you and those with you. Run for your life! Get out of this place! The people of al-Madā'in on this side, and on that side, and the people of Shabīb's camp, will talk about what went on between you and Shabīb, and before you go to bed tonight, the news will have reached al-Ḥajjāj. Find yourself a [988] home other than al-Madā'in!" The other two companions added, "Our view is just as he said." Muṭarrif asked them, "What is your decision, then?" They said, "To agree to what you summon us to, and to make common cause with you against al-Ḥajjāj or anyone else."

Then Muṭarrif looked at me and asked, "What is your decision?" I replied, "To kill your enemies, and to stand fast with you so long as you stand fast." He said, "That is what I expected of you."

He waited for three days. Then Qaʿnab came to him and said, "If you follow us, you are one of us; if you refuse, then any truce between us is over." Muṭarrif said, "Do not rush us today; we are still considering."

Then he sent to his men saying, "Ride out tonight, every last one of you, and come with me to al-Daskarah to deal with something that has happened there." He set out before dawn, with his

501. *Yujāhidūnahum.*

men, and went as far as Dayr Yazdajird, where he halted. There he was met by Qabīṣah b. ʿAbd al-Raḥmān al-Quḥāfī of Khathʿam.[502] He invited the latter to accompany him, and he did so; he outfitted him, gave him a mount, and ordered him given some money. Then he went on to al-Daskarah. After halting there, when he was ready to set out again, he had no choice but to inform his men of his intentions. He called together their leaders, and, after making appropriate mention of God and blessing His Messenger, he said to them:

> God has prescribed jihād for His creatures, and commanded them to act with justice and benevolence; He has said in the revelation He sent us, "Help one another to righteousness and piety, but help not one another to sin and injustice; fear God, God is harsh in punishment."[503] I make God my witness that I have cast off my allegiance to ʿAbd al-Malik and al-Ḥajjāj b. Yūsuf. Those of you who desire to accompany me, being of like mind with me, follow me, and you will have a good example and good company. As for those who refuse,
> [989] they may go wherever they wish; I have no desire for followers who are not committed to jihād against the tyrants. I summon you to the Book of God and the *sunnah* of His Prophet and to fight against the oppressors. If God determines affairs in our favor, this matter[504] will be decided by council among the Muslims, who will approve for themselves whomever they like.

His men responded with alacrity and gave him their oath of allegiance. Then he went into his quarters and sent for Sabrah b. ʿAbd al-Raḥmān b. Mikhnaf and ʿAbdallāh b. Kannāz al-Nahdī. Meeting with them in private, he summoned them as he had all of his men. They gave him their approval, but then, when he set out, they departed with those of his men who were with them and went to al-Ḥajjāj, whom they found had taken the field against Shabīb, and participated with him in the battle with Shabīb.

---

502. For the Banū Quḥāfah of Khathʿam, see Caskel, *Ğamharat an-nasab*, I, 226, II, 470. This man was Abū Mikhnaf's source for the *qaṣaṣ* of Ṣāliḥ b. Musarriḥ given above, II, 881f., where he is said to have been a sympathizer of the latter.

503. Qur'ān 5:2.

504. Determination of the legitimate leader of the community.

Muṭarrif set out with his men from al-Daskarah, heading toward Ḥulwān. Al-Ḥajjāj had this same year sent out Suwayd b. ʿAbd al-Raḥmān al-Saʿdī as governor of Ḥulwān and Māh Sabadhān.[505] When he heard that Muṭarrif b. al-Mughīrah was advancing toward his land, he realized that if he dealt with him gently or attempted to cajole him, al-Ḥajjāj would never put up with it; Suwayd accordingly mustered against him the townsmen and the Kurds, the latter holding the Ḥulwān pass against him. Suwayd marched out to him, hoping all the while to avoid fighting him and yet to be forgiven by al-Ḥajjāj; it was a poor excuse for a march.

According to Abū Mikhnaf—ʿAbdallāh b. ʿAlqamah al-Khathʿamī: When al-Ḥajjāj b. Jāriyah al-Khathʿamī[506] heard that Muṭarrif had set out from al-Madā'in toward al-Jabal, he followed after him with some thirty men, from his own tribe and others. I was one of them. We caught up with Muṭarrif at Ḥulwān and [990] participated with him in the battle against Suwayd b. ʿAbd al-Raḥmān.

According to Abū Mikhnaf—al-Naḍr: the same.

According to Abū Mikhnaf—ʿAbdallāh b. ʿAlqamah: As soon as we reached Muṭarrif b. al-Mughīrah, he showed great pleasure at our arrival and seated al-Ḥajjāj b. Jāriyah next to himself.

According to Abū Mikhnaf—al-Naḍr b. Ṣāliḥ and ʿAbdallāh b. ʿAlqamah: When Suwayd came out to meet them with his forces, he stayed with the infantry, not leading them out from their tents, while his son, al-Qaʿqāʿ, advanced with the cavalry; but his cavalry that day was not numerous.

According to Abū Mikhnaf—al-Naḍr b. Ṣāliḥ: I would say they were two hundred. According to Ibn ʿAlqamah: I would say they were less than three hundred.

Muṭarrif summoned al-Ḥajjāj b. Jāriyah and sent him out against them with about the same number. They advanced against al-Qaʿqāʿ, well-known horsemen determined to give him a good fight. When Suwayd saw them preparing to attack his son, he sent to them a boy of his named Rustam, who was later killed

505. This is a falsely etymologized form of Māsabadhān, a district south of Ḥulwān, in the front range of the Zagros. See Yāqūt, *Muʿjam*, IV, 393; Le Strange, *Lands*, 202; Morony, *Iraq after the Muslim Conquest*, 142.

506. A former partisan of Muṣʿab b. al-Zubayr; see text above, II, 773f.

with him at Dayr al-Jamājim[507] with the standard of the Banū Sa'd in his hand. This boy ran off quickly to al-Ḥajjāj b. Jāriyah and told him confidentially, "If you intend to leave this land of ours and go elsewhere, then leave us, for we do not wish to fight you. But if it is to us you have come by intent, then we must protect what is ours." When he delivered this message, al-Ḥajjāj b. Jāriyah told him, "Go to our amīr and tell him what you have told me." The boy then proceeded on to Muṭarrif and told him the same thing he had told al-Ḥajjāj b. Jāriyah. Muṭarrif said, "My aim is neither you nor your land." The boy said, "Then stay on this road until you have left our land. We have found ourselves
[991] obliged to arrange for people to see that we came out against you and for word of this to be passed on."

Muṭarrif sent for al-Ḥajjāj, and he joined him. They continued along the road until they reached the pass and found it held by the Kurds. Muṭarrif dismounted, as did all his men, and sent up al-Ḥajjāj b. Jāriyah with his right wing and Sulaymān b. Ḥudhayfah with his left wing to confront them. These two defeated and killed them, and Muṭarrif and his men continued safely on until they drew near Hamadhān. Muṭarrif avoided the latter, turning off to his left toward Māh Dīnār;[508] his brother Ḥamzah b. al-Mughīrah was governor of Hamadhān, and Muṭarrif preferred not to enter it and subject his brother to accusations from al-Ḥajjāj. But when Muṭarrif entered the land of Māh Dīnār, he wrote to his brother Ḥamzah, saying, "Our expenses have mounted and supplies have become a severe problem. Please help out your brother with what money and arms you can." He sent this message with Yazīd b. Abī Ziyād, the client of al-Mughīrah b. Shu'bah, who came to Ḥamzah with Muṭarrif's letter at night. When Ḥamzah saw him, he said to him, "May your mother be bereft of you! You have killed Muṭarrif!" Yazīd replied, "It is not I who has killed

507. Where al-Ḥajjāj b. Yūsuf defeated the rebel 'Abd al-Raḥmān b. al-Ash'ath, in 83 (702); see text below, II, 1070ff.

508. The district of Nihāwand, south of Hamadhān, according to an account in the text above (I, 2628, 2631) and in Dīnawarī, *al-Akhbār al-ṭiwāl* (Leiden), 145. Ḥamzah al-Iṣfahānī identified it rather with the district of Dīnawar, west of Hamadhān, according to Yāqūt, *Mu'jam*, IV, 406, which would agree better with a turn to the *left* here; but the statement below that Māh Dīnār bordered Iṣfahān must refer to the Nihāwand region. Dīnawar was officially named Māh al-Kūfah, and Nihāwand Māh al-Baṣrah; see *EI*², s. vv. Dīnawar, Māh al-Baṣra.

him, may I be your ransom, but Muṭarrif who has killed himself and me with him; I hope he does not kill you as well." Ḥamzah said, "Woe to you! Who seduced him into this business?" Yazīd said, "It was he who seduced himself into this"; then he sat with him and gave him a full acount of the whole affair, and handed him Muṭarrif's letter. Ḥamzah read it, then said, "Yes, I will send him money and arms. But tell me, do you think I can keep this secret?" Yazīd said that he thought it could not be kept secret, but [992]
Ḥamzah said to him, "By God, if I fail him in the more efficacious of the two kinds of support, that which is open, I will not forsake him in the lesser, that which is secret!"

He sent him money and arms with Yazīd b. Abī Ziyād, who brought them to Muṭarrif. We were camped in one of the rural districts of Māh Dīnār, called Sāmān,[509] on the borders of the Iṣfahān region; this was a district where some of the Ḥamrā' were settled.[510]

According to Abū Mikhnaf—al-Naḍr b. Ṣāliḥ: By God, no sooner had Yazīd b. Abī Ziyād set off than I heard the men of the camp spreading the word that the amīr was sending to his brother to ask him for money and arms. I went to Muṭarrif and informed him of this. He struck his brow with his hand and said, "Glory to God! One said, 'What can be kept secret?' The other replied, 'That which is not!'"

As soon as Yazīd b. Abī Ziyād arrived, Muṭarrif set off, halting at Qum, Qāshān,[511] and Iṣfahān.

According to Abū Mikhnaf—ʿAbdallāh b. ʿAlqamah: When Muṭarrif reached Qum and Qāshān and felt secure, he summoned al-Ḥajjāj b. Jāriyah and said to him, "Tell me about Shabīb's defeat the day at al-Sabakhah. Were you an eyewitness, or had you left before the battle?" Al-Ḥajjāj replied, "No, I was an eyewitness." Muṭarrif said, "Tell me, then, how things went with them." Al-Ḥajjāj told him, and he said, "I was hoping that Shabīb would win; even if he was in error, he would be killing another in error."

509. Mentioned, but without additional information, by Yāqūt, *Muʿjam*, III, 13f.

510. The Ḥamrā' ("red") were early Persian converts to Islam who participated in the conquest of Iran; some of them were settled near Ḥulwān after its conquest in 16 (637). See text above, I, 2473f.; Morony, *Iraq after the Muslim Conquest*, 197.

511. Modern Kāshān, between Qum and Iṣfahān; see *EI²*, s. v. Kāshān.

It seemed to me that this desire of his was actually because he was hoping to accomplish his own aims if al-Ḥajjāj perished. Then Muṭarrif sent out his officials.[512]

[993] According to Abū Mikhnaf—al-Naḍr b. Ṣāliḥ: Muṭarrif acted decisively, if only the fates had not been stronger. He sent the following message with al-Rabīʿ b. Yazīd to Suwayd b. Sirḥān al-Thaqafī and to Bukayr b. Hārūn al-Bajalī:[513]

> We summon you to the Book of God and the *sunnah* of His Prophet, and to jihād against him who has obstinately rejected the truth, expropriated the spoils, and abandoned the judgment of the Book.[514] When the truth appears and the false is overcome and the Word of God is rightfully exalted,[515] we will let this question be decided by council among the Community, the Muslims recognizing whom they please as the approved one. He who accepts this from us is our brother in religion and our comrade in life and death; but we will strive against[516] him who rejects this from us and ask God for His aid against him. It is sufficient to establish our claim against him, and sufficient to show his bad judgment in abandoning jihād in the way of God, and his weakness in conciliating the oppressors in the affairs of God, that God has prescribed fighting for the Muslims, calling it "hateful";[517] and no one can obtain God's good pleasure except by adhering steadfastly to God's command and waging jihād against God's enemies. Accept the truth, then, may God have mercy on you, and summon to it those for whose acceptance you hope, and let them know what they have not known. Let all who agree with our opinions, and accept our summons, and consider our enemy their own, come to me.

---

512. *ʿUmmāl,* usually tax officials, and probably so here as well, sent out to collect the *kharāj* of the surrounding districts for Muṭarrif.

513. On the Bajīlah tribe, of uncertain ancestry, see *EI²*, s. v. Badjīla. Both men were in al-Rayy, as emerges below.

514. *Taraka ḥukm al-kitāb.* It was ʿAlī's willingness to submit to the arbitration of man, rather than the judgment of the Qur'ān, that led to the original Khārijite revolt. The slogan "Judgment is to God alone" is a variant of this basic Khārijite tenet; see note 233 above.

515. *Kalimat Allāh hiya al-ʿulyā,* a paraphrase of Qur'ān 9:40.

516. *Jāhadnā.*

517. Qur'ān 2:216: *Kutiba ʿalaykum al-qitāl wa-huwa kurh lakum.*

May God lead you and us aright and be forgiving to you and us; He is the Forgiving, the Merciful. Peace.

When this letter reached the two men, they went among some of the men of al-Rayy and summoned those who would follow them. Then they departed secretly with some hundred from the men of al-Rayy, unremarked by anyone, and went to Muṭarrif. [994]

Then al-Barā' b. Qabīṣah, al-Ḥajjāj's governor of Iṣfahān, sent off a letter, saying, "If the amīr, may God cause him to prosper, has any care for Iṣfahān, or elsewhere, let him send out a massive army against Muṭarrif to annihilate him and those with him. He has just been joined by a band of men who came from some land or other to the place where he is staying now, and thus he has grown more powerful and his followers more numerous. Peace." Al-Ḥajjāj wrote back to him, saying, "When my messenger comes to you, muster those who are with you. Then, when ʿAdī b. Wattād comes to you, lead your forces forth with him, and heed and obey him. Peace." When al-Barā' read this letter, he went out and mustered his forces. Al-Ḥajjāj b. Yūsuf began sending out to al-Barā' b. Qabīṣah men on post horses, in groups of ten, fifteen, or twenty, until he had sent out to him some five hundred altogether. Al-Barā''s own forces numbered two thousand.

Meanwhile, al-Aswad b. Saʿd al-Hamdānī came out to al-Rayy, after[518] the victory God granted al-Ḥajjāj on the day he met Shabīb at al-Sabakhah. He passed through Hamadhān and al-Jibāl and stopped to see Ḥamzah, who excused himself to him.[519] According to al-Aswad: I informed al-Ḥajjāj about Ḥamzah, and he said, "I have already heard about that." He wanted to dismiss him, fearing that he would play him false if he held back,[520] and sent to Qays b. Saʿd al-ʿIjlī, who was at that time in charge of Ḥamzah b. al-Mughīrah's security force—there were a number of people from the Banū ʿIjl and Rabīʿah in Hamadhān.[521] He sent

518. *Kāna . . . atā al-Rayy fī fatḥ Allāh ʿalā al-Ḥajjāj.*

519. That is, he declined to supply troops for the fight against his brother. See Ibn al-Athīr, *Kāmil*, IV, 436.

520. *Fa-khashiya an yamkura bihi in yamtaniʿ minhu.* Some MSS read *wa-yamtaniʿ minhu* ("that he would play him false and elude him"), as was perhaps also read by Ibn al-Athīr, who paraphrases (*Kāmil*, IV, 436), "(al-Ḥajjāj) pretended to accept his excuse; he wanted to dismiss him but was afraid that he would elude him."

521. On the Banū ʿIjl, one of the Bakr b. Wā'il tribes and thus part of the Rabīʿah confederation, see *EI*², s. v. ʿIdjl.

Qays b. Sa'd a letter of appointment over Hamadhān and an order
[995] saying, "Put Ḥamzah b. al-Mughīrah in irons and keep him imprisoned there until further orders from me." When Qays received the letter and the order, he set out with a large number of his kinsmen. He entered the mosque just as the afternoon prayer was beginning and performed the prayer with Ḥamzah. When Ḥamzah went out, Qays b. Sa'd al-'Ijlī, the chief of his security force, went out with him, gave him al-Ḥajjāj's letter to read, and showed him the letter of appointment. Ḥamzah said, "Heed and obey." Qays put him in irons and held him in prison, and took over the governorship of Hamadhān. He sent out his officials over the district, choosing them all from his own people, and wrote to al-Ḥajjāj as follows: "I hereby inform the amīr—may God cause him to prosper!—that I have put Ḥamzah b. al-Mughīrah in irons and thrown him in prison. I have sent out my officials over the land revenue and have already begun to collect it.[522] Perhaps the amīr—may God prolong his life!—may give me permission to go out against Muṭarrif and strive against him with my people and those of my land who obey me; for I hope for a greater reward for jihād than for collecting the land revenue. Peace."

When al-Ḥajjāj read this letter, he laughed and said, "Here is the quarter where we are secure should all else fail!" Ḥamzah's position in Hamadhān had been the worst worry God could create for al-Ḥajjāj, who feared that he would support his brother with money or arms, or even, for all he knew, take it into his head to rebel himself. This is why he continued to scheme against him until he was able to dismiss him; once he felt secure there, he could go after Muṭarrif.

According to Abū Mikhnaf—Muṭarrif b. 'Āmir b. Wāthilah:[523] When al-Ḥajjāj read the letter of Qays b. Sa'd al-'Ijlī and his statement that "if the amīr would like, I will march out and strive

---

522. *Ba'athtu 'ummālī 'alā al-kharāj wa-waḍa'tu yadī fī al-jibāyah.*

523. His father, Abū al-Ṭufayl 'Āmir b. Wāthilah al-Kinānī, was a famous horseman and poet who had borne 'Alī's standard and supported al-Mukhtār; he was reputedly the last Companion to die, in 100 (718). See Sezgin, *GAS*, II, 412; Ziriklī, *A'lām*, IV, 26. Muṭarrif's brother al-Ṭufayl is mentioned below with the forces of al-Barā'.

against him with my people," he said, "How I hate to see the Arabs increasing in number in the *kharāj* land!"[524]

According to Ibn al-Ghariq:[525] The minute I heard this from al-Ḥajjāj, I realized that if he were free to do so, he would have dismissed him. [996]

According to al-Naḍr b. Ṣāliḥ: Al-Ḥajjāj wrote to ʿAdī b. Wattād al-Iyādī, the governor of al-Rayy, ordering him to march out against Muṭarrif b. al-Mughīrah, joining forces first with al-Barā' b. Qabīṣah; when they met, ʿAdī was to have command of the men.

According to Abū Mikhnaf—his father[526]—ʿAbdallāh b. Zuhayr[527]—ʿAbdallāh b. Sulaym al-Azdī:[528] I was sitting with ʿAdī b. Wattād in his council in al-Rayy when al-Ḥajjāj's letter arrived. He read it, then gave it to me, and I read it. It said: "When you read this letter, take three quarters of the men of al-Rayy there with you and advance to meet al-Barā' b. Qabīṣah in Jay,[529] then proceed on together. When you meet, you will be in command of the men until God kills Muṭarrif. Once God has rid the believers of him, return to your regular position, under God's protection, security, and shelter." When I had read it, ʿAdī said to me, "Go and prepare for war."

ʿAdī went out to muster the troops, summoning the secretaries, who called up[530] three quarters of the men. It was less than a week before we set out. We came to Jay, where we were met by Qabīṣah al-Quḥāfī[531] with nine[532] hundred Syrians, including

524. That is, land from whose non-Muslim (and non-Arab) owners the traditional land tax was collected; al-Ḥajjāj's policy was to preserve a strict segregation between a non-Arab taxpaying peasantry and an urban and military Arab aristocracy.

525. Presumably the 'Abd al-Raḥmān b. al-Ghariq mentioned above (II, 922, 945) as al-Ḥajjāj's messenger to the approaching Syrians.

526. Yaḥyā b. Sa'īd; see U. Sezgin, *Abū Mihnaf*, 224.

527. Probably a cousin of Abū Mikhnaf's grandfather, according to U. Sezgin, *Abū Mihnaf*, 225.

528. An uncle of Abū Mikhnaf's grandfather, and probably of 'Abdallāh b. Zuhayr, according to U. Sezgin, *Abū Mihnaf*, 225.

529. One of the twin cities comprising Iṣfahān; see Le Strange, *Lands*, 203ff.

530. *Ḍarabū al-ba'th 'alā*.

531. Last seen (II, 988) accompanying Muṭarrif. Is this a slip for al-Barā' b. Qabīṣah?

532. Perhaps to be emended to "seven" to match the number a few lines below (or vice versa).

ʿUmar b. Hubayrah. We remained at Jay only two days before ʿAdī b. Wattād set out with all the forces under his command. He had three thousand fighters from the men of al-Rayy; a thousand fighters with al-Barāʾ b. Qabīṣah, sent to him by al-Ḥajjāj from al-
[997] Kūfah; seven hundred Syrians; and some thousand men from the people of Iṣfahān and the Kurds. Altogether, they were nearly six thousand fighters. ʿAdī advanced until he came up against Muṭarrif b. al-Mughīrah.

According to Abū Mikhnaf—al-Naḍr b. Ṣāliḥ and[533] ʿAbdallāh b. ʿAlqamah: When Muṭarrif heard that they were marching against him, he had a trench dug around his forces; and they remained inside it until the government forces arrived.

According to Abū Mikhnaf—Yazīd, the client of ʿAbdallāh b. Zuhayr: I was with my master at that time. ʿAdī b. Wattād went out and put the men in battle array. He put ʿAbdallāh b. Zuhayr over his right wing, then sent word to[534] al-Barāʾ b. Qabīṣah to stand with the left. But al-Barāʾ was angry and said, "You order me to stand with the left, when I am a governor[535] like you! Those are my cavalry in the left, and I have put over them the horseman of Muḍar, al-Ṭufayl b. ʿĀmir b. Wāthilah."[536] This reply was conveyed to ʿAdī b. Wattād, and he said to Ibn Uqayṣir al-Khathʿamī, "You go out and take command of the cavalry. Go to al-Barāʾ b. Qabīṣah and tell him, 'You have been commanded to obey me. You have nothing to do with right and left and cavalry and infantry. Your duty is to obey your orders. Do not cross me in anything and lose my good will.' " Until then, he had treated him with full respect.

Then ʿAdī put ʿUmar b. Hubayrah over his left, sending with him a hundred Syrians; he went and took his position, with his standard. One of his men said to al-Ṭufayl b. ʿĀmir, "Take down your standard and go away; this position is ours." Al-Ṭufayl replied, "I will not quarrel with you. This standard was committed
[998] to me by al-Barāʾ b. Qabīṣah, and he is our commander. But we know that your man is in command of the assembled forces, and

533. Reading *wa-* for *ʿan*.
534. *Qāla li-*, "told," but apparently through a messenger; see below.
535. *Amīr*, also translated "commander" below.
536. See note 523 above, and Ziriklī, *Aʿlām*, III, 329.

if this has been committed to your master, then, may God bless him, we heed and obey immediately." Then ʿUmar b. Hubayrah said to his men, "Take it easy! Desist from your brother and cousin!" and to al-Ṭufayl, "Our standard is yours, and if you wish, we will gladly surrender it to you." We have never seen two men as coolheaded as those two in that situation.

Then ʿAdī b. Wattād dismounted and moved his forces against Muṭarrif.

According to Abū Mikhnaf—al-Naḍr b. Ṣāliḥ and ʿAbdallāh b. ʿAlqamah: Muṭarrif put al-Ḥajjāj b. Jāriyah in charge of his right wing, al-Rabīʿ b. Yazīd al-Asadī in charge of his left wing, and Sulaymān b. Ṣakhr al-Muzanī in charge of his rearguard. He himself dismounted and walked with the infantry. His standard was with Yazīd b. Abī Ziyād, the client of his father al-Mughīrah b. Shuʿbah.

As the two armies advanced and drew near each other, Muṭarrif said to Bukayr b. Hārūn al-Bajalī, "Go out to them and summon them to the Book of God and the *sunnah* of His Prophet and reproach them for their wicked deeds." Bukayr b. Hārūn went out to them on a black horse with a blaze and a fine tail, wearing a cuirass, a leather helmet, and armlets, and with a spear in his hand; he had fastened his cuirass with a red sash made from the fringes of woolen robes.[537] He called out in his loud, high voice: "Men of our *qiblah*,[538] men of our religion, men of our confession![539] We beseech you by God, than Whom there is no other god, Whose knowledge of what you hide is as His knowledge of what you display, to be fair and honest with us, to speak out of commitment to God, not to His creatures, and to be witnesses for God against His servants of what God knows of His servants. Tell me about ʿAbd al-Malik b. Marwān and al-Ḥajjāj b. Yūsuf: do you [999]
not recognize them as tyrants and despots, who follow their own vain opinions, seizing people on idle suspicions and killing them out of simple anger?"

The men called out from every side, "Enemy of God! You lie! It

537. *ʿIṣābah min ḥawāshī al-burūd.* See Dozy, *Dictionnaire détaillé des noms des vêtements chez les Arabes,* 59–64, 300–5.

538. The direction of prayer for Muslims, toward Mecca; see *EI*², s. v. ḳibla.

539. *Daʿwah.*

is not so!" He said to them, "'Woe to you! Do not forge a lie against God, lest He destroy you by some punishment; he who forges a lie fails.'[540] Woe to you! Will you teach God what He does not know?[541] We have called on you to testify, and God has said about testimony, 'He who hides it is sinful of heart.'"[542] Then Ṣārim, the client of ʿAdī b. Wattād and his standard-bearer, went out against him. He charged at Bukayr b. Hārūn al-Bajalī, and they fought with their swords. ʿAdī's client's blow had no effect; then Bukayr struck him with his sword and killed him. Then he went forward and said, "Horseman to horseman!" but no one would come out to meet him. He recited:

Ṣārim, you have encountered a cutting (*ṣārim*) sword,
And a powerful maned lion.

Then al-Ḥajjāj b. Jāriyah, who was in the right, attacked ʿUmar b. Hubayrah, who was in the left. With ʿUmar in the left was also al-Ṭufayl b. ʿĀmir b. Wāthilah, and al-Ḥajjāj encountered him. They were close friends, and recognized each other just as each was raising his sword against the other, and held back.

The two wings fought for a long time before ʿAdī b. Wattād's left gave a little ground, and al-Ḥajjāj b. Jāriyah moved to occupy the space. Then al-Rabīʿ b. Yazīd attacked ʿAbdallāh b. Zuhayr, and they also fought long, until the men made a concerted attack on al-Asadī and killed him; and Muṭarrif b. al-Mughīrah's left was
[1000] driven back as far as his own position. Then ʿUmar b. Hubayrah attacked al-Ḥajjāj b. Jāriyah and his forces and fought long with him. The latter finally decided to desist and went to join Muṭarrif. Ibn Uqayṣir al-Khathʿamī charged with the cavalry against Sulaymān b. Ṣakhr al-Muzanī, who was killed, and his cavalry driven back as far as Muṭarrif. This cavalry battle was the fiercest fighting the men had ever seen, but Ibn Uqayṣir finally reached Muṭarrif.

According to Abū Mikhnaf—al-Naḍr b. Ṣāliḥ: On that day Muṭarrif kept calling out to them, saying, "'People of the Book! Come to a word we may acknowledge equally: that we serve no

540. Qur'ān 20:61.
541. An echo of Qur'ān 49:16.
542: Qur'ān 2:283.

one but God, and associate nothing as partner to him, and we do not take one another as lords apart from him. If they turn their backs, say: We testify that we are Muslims.' "[543] He continued to fight until he was killed. ʿUmar b. Hubayrah cut off his head; it is said that it was he who killed him; although more than one had rushed at him, it was Ibn Hubayrah who cut off his head. ʿAdī b. Wattād dispatched him with the head, and this meant advancement for him.[544] ʿUmar b. Hubayrah fought bravely and well that day.

According to Abū Mikhnaf: Ḥakīm b. Abī Sufyān al-Azdī said he killed Yazīd b. Abī Ziyād, the client of al-Mughīrah b. Shuʿbah, who was Muṭarrif's standard-bearer.

They reached Muṭarrif's camp, which Muṭarrif had entrusted to ʿAbd al-Raḥmān b. ʿAbdallāh b. ʿAfīf al-Azdī. He was killed; he was a good, temperate, abstemious man.

According to Abū Mikhnaf—Zayd, their client:[545] I saw his head with Ibn Uqayṣir al-Khathʿamī and was unable to restrain myself from saying to him, "By God, you have killed a man who prayed and worshipped and thought much on God." He came [1001] toward me and asked who I was, and my master said to him, "This is my attendant. What is the matter?" Ibn Uqayṣir told him what I had said, and he said, "He is mentally deficient."

Then we went off to al-Rayy with ʿAdī b. Wattād. He sent some of the valiant men to al-Ḥajjāj, and he welcomed and honored them. When he returned to al-Rayy, the Bajīlah came to ʿAdī b. Wattād and asked for safe-conduct for Bukayr b. Hārūn, and he granted it. Then the Thaqīf asked for safe-conduct for Suwayd b. Sirḥān al-Thaqafī, and he granted it. Then the kin of every man who had been with Muṭarrif asked for and were granted safe-conduct for him, which was a good deed on his part. Some of Muṭarrif's men had been surrounded in Muṭarrif's camp; they called out, "Barā'! Get safe-conduct for us! Barā'! Intercede for us!" He interceded for them, and they were released. ʿAdī took many prisoners, and then he let them go.

---

543. Qur'ān 3:64.

544. *Awfadahu bihi ʿAdī b. Wattād wa-ḥaẓiya bihi*, presumably meaning that he took the head to al-Ḥajjāj, who was well pleased. See Ibn al-Athīr, *Kāmil*, IV, 436.

545. I.e., of the Azd.

According to Abū Mikhnaf—al-Naḍr b. Ṣāliḥ: He[546] set out and came to Suwayd b. ʿAbd al-Raḥmān at Ḥulwān, and was welcomed and honored by him; then he went on to al-Kūfah.

According to Abū Mikhnaf—ʿAbdallāh b. ʿAlqamah: Al-Ḥajjāj b. Jāriyah al-Khathʿamī came to al-Rayy, where he had formerly been stationed, and appeal was made to ʿAdī on his behalf. But ʿAdī said, "This is a notorious man, who won notoriety along with his companion; and here is a letter from al-Ḥajjāj to me about him."

According to Abū Mikhnaf—his father—ʿAbdallāh b. Zuhayr: I was among those who spoke to ʿAdī on al-Ḥajjāj b. Jāriyah's behalf. He took out and showed us this letter from al-Ḥajjāj b. Yūsuf: "If God has killed al-Ḥajjāj b. Jāriyah, good riddance! That is what I hope and desire. If he yet lives, seek him out from there,
[1002] put him in chains, and send him directly to me, God willing. Peace." ʿAdī said to us, "I have received specific orders about him, which I have no choice but to heed and obey. If I had not had these specific orders, I would have granted him safe-conduct for you and held back from him, not seeking him out." We then departed from him.

Al-Ḥajjāj b. Jāriyah remained in fear until ʿAdī b. Wattād was dismissed, and Khālid b. ʿAttāb b. Warqāʾ came in his place. I went to him and spoke to him on al-Ḥajjāj's behalf, and he granted him safe-conduct.

Verses by Ḥabīb b. Khidrah, a client of the Banū Hilāl b. ʿĀmir:[547]

Has Fāʾid ever heard of our speeding away[548]
    for fear of the sharp swords of an enemy,

---

546. It is not clear who is meant here, although al-Barāʾ seems the most likely. Already in the previous paragraph several pronouns are ambiguous, and the state of the text seems questionable.

547. Mentioned with Shabīb at al-Kūfah; see text above, II, 968, and note 455. Ṭabarī's placing these verses here, as a sort of coda to his account of Shabīb's revolt, implicitly includes Muṭarrif's rebellion as part of that movement. For a review of opinions on whether Muṭarrif was a "Khārijite," see Dixon, *Umayyad Caliphate,* 194.

548. *Hal atā Fāʾida ʿan īsādinā,* adopting a reading suggested by the editors for text *aysārinā.*

When fear came upon us from a quarter we thought secure,
  and we rode through the dark to another land?
Ask Hadyah whether she has ever seen
  men of nobler character than us.
Ask her whether they remain amicable with us,
  or are determined to hate us.
Many a sweetheart have I had before her,
  with whom I cut the knot, and let her go.
We have experienced life at its calmest,
  and we have experienced life at its most turbulent.
I have experienced Time—a Time of which
  I am eager for one part and shun another.
I have seen the horses packed closely together,
  only their eyes distinguishable,
Their riders passing, one to another, on the points of the spears,
  a cup overflowing with the black blood of death.
It is the charge of the horsemen that delights me,
  while diversion merely robs me of my delight
In the advancing helmets, as the horsemen leave
  creases from their Indian swords in them.[549]
Many a morning of battle has there been that suited me [1003]
  perfectly,
  Just like an old waterskin and its cover.[550]

According to Abū Ja'far: In this year, dissension arose among the Azraqites who followed Qaṭarī b. al-Fujā'ah.[551] Some of them dissented from him and withdrew from him, and gave allegiance to 'Abd Rabb al-Kabīr, while others maintained their allegiance to Qaṭarī.[552]

---

549. *Bi-mushīḥi l-bayḍi ḥattā yatrukū/ li-suyūfi l-Hindi fīhā ṭuraqā.*

550. Or: Just like Shann and Ṭabaqa(h). For the proverb and its interpretations, see Maydānī, *Amthāl*, II, 284f.

551. See text above, II, 944 and note 382, and *EI*[2], s. v. Ḳaṭarī.

552. Ṭabarī makes no mention of an 'Abd Rabb al-Ṣaghīr (the Younger, as opposed to al-Kabīr, the Greater or Elder), but other sources do. Both men are involved in the schism in the accounts in Ibn A'tham al-Kūfī (*Futūḥ*, VII, 55ff.) and Ya'qūbī (*Ta'rīkh*, II, 329ff.). Mubarrad (*Kāmil*, 678, 685ff.) has only 'Abd Rabb al-Ṣaghīr, whom he calls a client of the Banū Qays b. Tha'labah (of Bakr); Ibn Khayyāṭ (*Ta'rīkh*, 275) gives the same tribal affiliation for his 'Abd Rabb (unqualified). Like Ibn Khayyāṭ, Dīnawarī (*al-Akhbār al-ṭiwāl*, 286–88) mentions only one 'Abd

Account of the Dissension among the Azraqites and the Reason for Its Breaking Out, until They Came to Ruin

According to Hishām—Abū Mikhnaf—Yūsuf b. Yazīd: Al-Muhallab remained in Sābūr fighting Qaṭarī and his Azraqite supporters for about a year after al-Ḥajjāj recalled ʿAttāb b. Warqāʾ from his army.[553] Then he attacked them on the day of the Orchard,[554] fighting them fiercely. Kirmān was then in the hands of the Khārijites, and Fārs in the hands of al-Muhallab. The Khārijite forces found themselves straitened in the position they occupied, with no supplies coming to them from Fārs and themselves far from home; so they withdrew to Kirmān. Al-Muhallab came after them, halting at Jīruft—Jīruft is the capital of Kirmān.[555] He fought fiercely with them there for more than a year, keeping them out of Fārs altogether. Once all of Fārs was in the hands of al-Muhallab, al-Ḥajjāj sent out his officials to administer it, taking it over from al-Muhallab. Word of this reached ʿAbd al-Malik,
[1004] and he wrote as follows to al-Ḥajjāj: "Leave the land revenue of the mountains of Fārs in the hands of al-Muhallab; for it is imperative that the army be strong and the commander of the army adequately supported. Let him have the district of Fasā and Darābjird and the district of Iṣṭakhr."[556]

Al-Ḥajjāj left these to al-Muhallab, who sent out his officials to administer them; they served to give him strength against the

---

Rabb. Ibn al-Athīr (*Kāmil*, IV, 437ff.) combines the accounts of Ṭabarī and Mubarrad, but refers to the single rebel leader throughout as ʿAbd Rabb al-Kabīr.

553. See text above, II, 877f., 944.

554. *Yawm al-bustān.* Other independent published sources do not mention this battle under this name. Perhaps it is the same as the battle at Shiʿb Bawwān, mentioned by Ibn Aʿtham al-Kūfī (*Futūḥ*, VII, 34) and probably referred to in the verses by Kaʿb al-Ashqarī quoted below (II, 1012, and see note 575). Shiʿb Bawwān, fifty miles northwest of Shīrāz, was considered one of the world's beauty spots; see Thaʿālibī, *Laṭāʾif al-maʿārif* (Cairo, 1960), 157; Le Strange, *Lands*, 260.

555. Jīruft was some fifty miles southwest of Bam; see *EI*², s. v. Djīruft.

556. For these three cities (and here two districts) of central Fārs, see *EI*², s. vv. Fasā, Darābdjird, Iṣṭakhr.

enemy and his interests. In this regard, the poet of Azd has this to say, reproaching al-Muhallab:

We fight to defend the palaces of Darābjird
and collect taxes for al-Mughīrah and al-Ruqād.

Al-Ruqād b. Ziyād b. Hammām was a man of the ʿAtīk, held in high esteem by al-Muhallab.[557]

Al-Ḥajjāj sent al-Barāʾ b. Qabīṣah to al-Muhallab,[558] and wrote to him as follows: "By God, it seems to me that if you really wished to, you could have exterminated these renegade Khārijites by now; but you like their continuing presence, so you may consume the land around you. I have sent you al-Barāʾ b. Qabīṣah to rouse you to attack them; attack them, then, when he comes to you, with all the Muslims, and wage the fiercest jihād against them. Let me hear no excuses or petty lies, or other such things that, coming from you, are distasteful and unacceptable to me. Peace."

Al-Muhallab sent out his sons, each with a cavalry detachment, and his troops according to their standards, ranks, and fifths.[559]
05] Al-Barāʾ b. Qabīṣah came and was positioned by al-Muhallab on a hill near the troops, where he could see them. The detachments attacked the enemy detachments, and the infantry the infantry;

557. Al-Muhallab himself belonged to al-ʿAtīk b. al-Asd of the Azd ʿUmān; see Caskel, *Ǧamharat an-nasab*, I, 203, II, 421. The al-Mughīrah mentioned in the verses is al-Muhallab's son. Yāqūt, *Muʿjam*, II, 560, cites the verse and names its author as Abū al-Bahāʾ al-Iyādī (of Azd; see Caskel, *Ǧamharat an-nasab*, II, 220). Mubarrad (*Kāmil*, 684), in an account explicitly accusing al-Mughīrah and al-Ruqād of not passing the collected revenue on to the troops, quotes four other verses with the same meter and rhyme, and presumably from the same poem. See also Périer, *Vie d'al-Ḥadjdjâdj*, 98f.; Dixon, *Umayyad Caliphate*, 180.

558. This was presumably before al-Barāʾ's appointment as governor of Iṣfahān, but Ṭabarī gives no precise synchronisms. Mubarrad, *Kāmil*, 671f., recounts the following incident before ʿAttāb's arrival as co-commander.

559. *ʿAlā rāyātihim wa-maṣāffihim wa-akhmāsihim*. The first two terms probably refer to the cavalry and infantry respectively, while the "fifths" are those into which the Baṣran army was divided; see text above, II, 720, and Morony, *Iraq after the Muslim Conquest*, 250.

they fought as hard as the men ever had from the morning prayer to midday, then withdrew. Al-Barā' b. Qabīṣah came to al-Muhallab and said to him, "No, by God! Never have I seen horsemen like your sons, or Arab horsemen like your horsemen! Nor have I ever seen the like of these people who fight you, of such stamina and valor! By God, you have a good excuse!" Al-Muhallab withdrew with the men until afternoon prayer, then took them out again, with his sons over the cavalry detachments, and they fought as they had in the morning.

According to Abū Mikhnaf—Abū al-Mughallis al-Kinānī—his paternal uncle Abū Ṭalḥah: One of their detachments went against one of our detachments, and the battle between them grew fierce, neither side giving way to the other. They fought on until nightfall separated them. Then one side asked the other, "From what people are you?" They answered, "We are from the Banū Tamīm." Those on the other side then said, "We too are from the Banū Tamīm." They withdrew in the evening.

Al-Muhallab asked al-Barā', "What did you see?" He replied, "I saw a people, by God, against whom no help will avail you but God's!" Al-Muhallab rewarded al-Barā' b. Qabīṣah with generous treatment, giving him a mount and fine garments, and ordering ten thousand dirhams paid out to him. Al-Barā' then departed and returned to al-Ḥajjāj, conveying to him al-Muhallab's excuse and informing him of what he had seen. Al-Muhallab himself also wrote to al-Ḥajjāj as follows: "I have received the letter of the
[1006] amīr—may God cause him to prosper!—with his accusations against me concerning these renegade Khārijites. The amīr ordered me to attack them and let his messenger observe, and I have done so. Let him ask him about what he observed. As for me, by God, if I were able to exterminate them and eliminate them from this land, and desisted from doing so, I would be cheating the Muslims, betraying the Commander of the Faithful, and showing myself untrue to the amīr—may God cause him to prosper. God forbid that this should be my attitude and my way of serving God! Peace."[560]

---

560. Both Mubarrad (*Kāmil*, 667–77, 681f., 688f.) and Ibn Aʿtham al-Kūfī (*Futūḥ*,

Al-Muhallab continued to fight them there for eighteen months. He neither made a dent in them nor himself suffered, with the men of Iraq who were with him, an attack in any battle with sword and spear that would drive them off and cause them to desist. Then one of the rebels, a man from the Banū Ḍabbah named al-Muqaʿṭar, who was an official for Qaṭarī over one of the regions of Kirmān, set out with a detachment of them and killed a man who had been a valiant warrior for the Khārijites and entered into clientage with them. When al-Muqaʿṭar killed him, the Khārijites ran to Qaṭarī and told him, saying, "Permit us to kill the Ḍabbī as vengeance for our comrade." But he replied, "That is not my decision. A man interprets and errs in his interpretation:[561] it is not my judgment that you should kill him. He is, besides, one of the best and most preeminent among you." They said, "Yes, we should kill him!" He said, "No!" Thus conflict arose among them, and they gave authority to ʿAbd Rabb al-Kabīr, repudiating Qaṭarī; but a band of them maintained their alle- [1007] giance to Qaṭarī, perhaps a quarter or fifth of the whole. Qaṭarī fought these new opponents for nearly a month, morning and evening.

Al-Muhallab wrote as follows to al-Ḥajjāj to inform him of this: "God has cast the fierceness of the Khārijites in their own midst. Most of them have repudiated Qaṭarī and rendered allegiance to ʿAbd Rabb, while a band of them have remained with Qaṭarī. They now battle one another mornings and evenings, and I have hope that this may be the cause of their ruin, God willing. Peace."

Al-Ḥajjāj responded as follows: "I have received your letter in which you mention the internal conflict among the Khārijites. When this letter of mine reaches you, take the field against them, while they are in conflict and divided, before they can reunite and become a more formidable foe to you. Peace."

VII, 17–23) stress al-Ḥajjāj's persistent harassment of al-Muhallab. In Mubarrad, al-Barā' is the first of a series of envoys sent out to the latter, while Ibn Aʿtham al-Kūfī lacks al-Barā' but mentions two of Mubarrad's other envoys, as well as a third not reported elsewhere. (Although frequently divergent from other versions, Ibn Aʿtham al-Kūfī's account is in general the fullest we have for al-Muhallab's campaigns against the Azraqites.) See also Périer, *Vie d'al-Ḥadjdjādj*, 95–97; Dixon, *Umayyad Caliphate*, 179f.

561. *Ta'awwala fa-akhṭa'a fī al-ta'wīl.* The official was apparently carrying out judicial as well as fiscal responsibilities.

Al-Muhallab replied as follows: "I have received the amīr's letter and understood everything in it. I do not believe I should fight them now, when they are killing one another and reducing each other's numbers. If they keep at this, we will have what we want and they will perish; if they do reunite, they will be doing so only after having exhausted one another; and at that point I will immediately attack them, when they are at their weakest and most vulnerable, God willing. Peace."

Al-Ḥajjāj let him be, and al-Muhallab let them fight among themselves for a month without moving against them. Then Qaṭarī departed with his remaining followers for Ṭabaristān, while most of them rendered allegiance to ʿAbd Rabb al-Kabīr. Al-Muhallab attacked the latter, and they put up a good fight; but then God killed them, only a few of them surviving. Their camp and what was in it were seized, and the survivors taken captive, because they had been taking Muslims captive.[562]

Kaʿb al-Ashqarī—al-Ashqar is a clan of Azd—recited these verses on the battle day of Rāmhurmuz and the days of Sābūr and the days of Jīruft:[563]

562. The word used here, *saby*, refers to taking captives, usually noncombatants, after a battle, to be sold into slavery, as opposed to *asr*, taking captives on the battlefield, who were often killed; see Fries, *Heereswesen*, 90. Both measures should apply only to non-Muslims; but the Khārijites considered non-Khārijites non-Muslims, which is the point here.

Mubarrad (*Kāmil*, 677–79, 684–96) gives a much more detailed account of the schism among the Azraqites, referring to seven separate incidents that created tensions before the final split over Qaṭarī's refusal to remove the unpopular al-Muqaʿṭar al-ʿAbdī (of ʿAbd al-Qays, not Ḍabbah), and labeling the struggle one between *mawālī* and Persians (under ʿAbd Rabb al-Ṣaghīr) and Arabs (under Qaṭarī). Ibn Aʿtham al-Kūfī (*Futūḥ*, VII, 55–69) makes the split a three-way one, with separate parties under Qaṭarī, ʿAbd Rabb al-Kabīr, and ʿAbd Rabb al-Ṣaghīr, but gives no indication of the origin of the dispute; his very detailed account of the ensuing four-way struggle has al-Muhallab defeating the temporarily reallied forces of Qaṭarī and al-Ṣaghīr, the latter dying in battle and the former fleeing to al-Rayy, then taking the city of Jīruft from al-Kabīr, whose forces were scattered. Dīnawarī, *al-Akhbār al-ṭiwāl*, 286–88, is hopelessly muddled; Yaʿqūbī, *Taʾrīkh*, 329f., and Ibn Khayyāṭ, *Taʾrīkh*, 275, give only brief summaries; Ibn al-Athīr, *Kāmil*, IV, 437–39, combines information found in Ṭabarī and in Mubarrad. See also Périer, *Vie d'al-Ḥadjdjādj*, 99–103; Dixon, *Umayyad Caliphate*, 180f.

563. On the poet Abū Mālik Kaʿb b. Maʿdān (d. c. 95 [714]), see Sezgin, *GAS*, II, 377f., and *Aghānī*[1], X, 54–61; on al-Ashqar (Saʿd b. ʿĀʾidh) of Azd, see Caskel, *Ǧamharat an-nasab*, I, 212, II, 492. According to Mubarrad (*Kāmil*, 694), Kaʿb was one of two envoys sent by al-Muhallab to al-Ḥajjāj to announce the victory and

Ḥafṣ! Traveling has taken me far from you, [1008]
and I have been sleepless, my eyes sore from wakeful nights.
Despite your gray hairs, Ka'b, you have been hooked by a girl;
gray hairs usually keep idle fancies at bay.
Do you still retain the commitment she made,
or, now that she is far away, is the tie severed?
I have been hooked by a girl who lives at the top of al-Ṭaff,[564]
in an upper chamber, beyond many doors and rooms,
Fleshy in the shoulders, and so full in the hips
that when she gets up to walk away, they almost stay behind.
I have left behind, on the banks of the two Zābīs,[565]
a home of hers where nomad and settled alike find good fortune;
And I have chosen an abode with a clan that pleases me,
among whom there are still select men if you choose them.[566]
When my land became disagreeable to me, I set out to seek favors
(and he who seeks good is full of desire and expectation)
From Abū Sa'īd[567]—for I came seeking favors, [1009]
hoping for your generosity, when I was touched by want.
Had it not been for al-Muhallab, we would never have visited their land,
so long as trees and water remain on the earth;
But there is no clan I know of among the people
among whom there is no visible sign of your beneficence.

---

recited this ode before the latter; the *Aghānī* has the same account and quotes seventeen lines from the poem. Ibn A'tham al-Kūfī (*Futūḥ*, VII, 69) gives only one line of the poem in his account of al-Muhallab's occupation of Jīruft after the defeat and death of 'Abd Rabb al-Kabīr.

564. The transition zone between the southern Euphrates valley and the desert to the west; see Yāqūt, *Mu'jam*, III, 539f.; Musil, *Northern Neǧd*, 198–200.

565. Probably a district south of al-Madā'in, named for the Zābī canal or canals, rather than the two Zāb or Zābī Rivers of northern Iraq; see Yāqūt, *Mu'jam*, II, 905f. Qudāmah, *Kharāj* (*BGA*, VI), 236, and other geographers refer to the former in the plural as al-Zawābī, with upper, middle, and lower subdistricts.

566. *Mā zāla fīhim li-man nakhtāruhum khiyaru* (in some MSS *yakhtāruhum*).

567. Al-Muhallab.

You have revived them with your munificent gifts
just as the land revives when touched by rain.
If I should fall into indigence, I would hope
to find it forestalled by favor from God through your hands.
Restore a brother whose strength has been sapped by poverty,
and perhaps the strength sapped from his bones will be restored.
My relations shun me, and my expectations have betrayed me;
God bless me, what can I do on my own?
You who have bestowed a slave girl with a face radiant in beauty
like the sun, fine of figure, with languor in her glance—
From you continue to come forth full moons of evening,
as well as others with blazes from your munificence gleaming like the dawn—
You were brought up for glory by kings whose heir you are,
proud-seeming men, yet of gentle character,
[1010] Who took vengeance for their dead, by acts they recount with glory,
at a time when no casualty of war was avenged.
When the enemy came upon them, the men resigned themselves,
and were at a loss what to do;
Not one of them would go beyond the gate of the bridge—
war had bitten the men of the garrison, and they had run to hide in their hole.[568]
Fear was brought into the interiors of the houses,
and fell on womanish men, men one would pay no bloodwit for.
But then the war intensified, and we were sorely tested,
and faced with something for which one must tuck up one's robe;
We kept at them without letup,

568. Here begins the poet's account of the Azraqite wars. The next few verses are too allusive to tie closely to the chronology but apparently refer to the period just before al-Muhallab's reappointment to the command directly by ʿAbd al-Malik; see text above, II, 855. The bridge here is probably that over the Dujayl at al-Ahwāz; see the account in Ibn Aʿtham al-Kūfī, *Futūḥ*, VI, 298–309.

and when the danger grew great, the shaykh tucked up his robe.[569]
Before that day, we had belittled the threat they posed,
but then the insignificant became critical.
When we were worn out, and they had occupied our territory,
and the men had been called up repeatedly but not responded,
A call went forth from a man preeminent among his people,[570]
a man in no way unequal to the situation.
He distributed among them what had been there since they took refuge,[571] [1011]
benefits that had been stored up for them.
They dressed themselves in battle gear,
and the next morning had crossed the bridge and were beyond it.
They marched with standards of glory raised high,
above lions steady in the fray.
They had already left al-Ahwāz behind them,
and assembled at Rāmhurmuz when they heard the news—
The death of Bishr. Then the men broke up and scattered,
except for a few who remained, recalled to their sense of duty.[572]
Then there came to us one satisfied with his appointment,
a man of sincere loyalty; and we did not betray him as the others did.[573]
Then we assembled at Sābūr of the Armies,[574] and a fire
that threw sparks was kindled between us and them.
The bold warriors we encountered were mad dogs,
as if it were jinn we were fighting, nothing recognizably human.

---

569. *Fa-shammara l-shaykhu lammā aʿẓama l-khaṭaru.* If this is not simply proverbial, it is unclear to whom it refers.

570. *Nādā mru'un lā khilāfa fī ʿashīratihi/ ʿanhu.* This is al-Muhallab's reappointment by ʿAbd al-Malik.

571. *Afshā hunālika mimmā kāna mudh ʿaṣarū/ fīhim (ṣanā'iʿa mimmā kāna yuddakharū).*

572. See text above, II, 857–59.

573. Probably a reference to al-Ḥajjāj and the rebellion of Ibn al-Jārūd; see text above, II, 873f.

574. *Sābūr al-junūd,* an epithet also given above, I, 2810, in some MSS, but undocumented by geographical writers.

In furious fighting we exchanged poisonous potions with them,
from nightfall until the break of dawn.
[1012] The dead there had no blood price and no vengeance;
our blood and theirs flowed unrequited.
Finally they began to withdraw before us from the place,
driven back by our lions boldly advancing.
That morning on the hill, among the spears, all their cunning
and all the tricks they could devise availed them nothing—
Our detachments ran on at will
around al-Muhallab, until the moon shone forth.
There the foe turned away, cheerless after their joy,
and put fences and rivers between them and us.
They mustered their forces below the mountains, when they halted
at Kāzarūn, but they neither overcame nor conquered.
They found us earnest fighters, in an encounter
where they thought they would win, but did not,
At Dasht Bārīn, on the day of the pass,[575] when those lions
who roared as they shed human blood were overtaken—
[1013] They encountered detachments that left them no gap to exploit,
disdainful of those who had the misfortune to fight them,
Advancing when challenged by the enemy cavalry,
and attacking again as they exposed their rear.
And at Jubayrayn,[576] when they advance in lines,
they turned back humiliated, having been defeated and routed.
By God, there was not a day they engaged us in combat
that they were not overcome by yet another of our victories,

575. *Yawm al-shi'b.* Dasht Bārīn was a *rustāq* of the district of Sābūr, whose capital was al-Nawbandajān; see Ibn Khurradādhbih, *Masālik*, 45; Yāqūt, *Mu'jam*, II, 576. The "day of the pass" probably refers to the battle described by Ibn A'tham al-Kūfī (*Futūḥ*, VII, 34) at Shi'b Bawwān, just east of al-Nawbandajān; see Ibn Khurradādhbih, *Masālik*, 43, and note 554 above.

576. Considerable variation in pointing and even ductus in various manuscripts; the reading adopted is from Iṣṭakhrī, *Masālik* (*BGA*, I), 105, 136, where this place is mentioned immediately after Dasht Bārīn. See also Ibn Ḥawqal, *Masālik* (*BGA*, II), 204, reading Jīnzīr.

Driven back from every position by our lances,
beset morning and night by our mad dogs.
They prudently retreated, having had enough of our spears,
toward al-Ḥarūb;[577] but their prudence could not save them.
A fair countenance, a generous hand, a man thoughtful,
generous, lacking neither strength nor experience,
Tested in battle, a man who achieves what he sets out to do,
not to be taken lightly, with opinions not to be ignored—
For three years he kept us at it, [1014]
engaged alternately in battle and planning,
Saying, "Tomorrow will come to him who waits for it,[578]
and there are lessons to be learned from the days and the nights;
Leave off running after them, and watch and wait;
a good warrior knows how to be patient,[579]
Until the situation changes, bringing hope of success,
and it becomes clear what he should and should not do."
Then he drove them back to Kirmān, and they broke up,
and their fate was sealed.
We marched against them, moving like a wave, and they came to meet us;
we already had plenty of reasons to hate each other.
Our abhorrence was only the greater when we called to mind our dead,
from whose memory our eyes would never dry.
When we remember al-Jazūr[580] and the dead there
who lay two years unburied,
We feel the pain in our breasts, and spare them nothing, [1015]
just as they spare us nothing if they can.
They allow us no slips in battle,
nor do we ever let their slips go by.

---

577. Unidentified, unless this is a corruption of al-Jazūr, mentioned below.

578. *Inna ghadan mubdin li-nāẓirihī;* see Maydānī, *Amthāl,* I, 63f., for the proverb *inna ghadan li-nāẓirihi qarīb.*

579. Ibn Aʿtham al-Kūfī, *Futūḥ,* VII, 57, cites this line in his account of the initial split between Qaṭarī and the two ʿAbd Rabbs.

580. Site of the defeat by Qaṭarī of ʿAbd al-ʿAzīz b. ʿAbdallāh b. Khālid b. Asīd; see Yāqūt, *Muʿjam,* II, 66, and text above, II, 821ff.

They will accept no excuse from us but death,
just as no excuse they may offer is acceptable to us.
Two lines of men across the plain, like two mountains,
with flashes of lightning between them that rivet the eye
On a zeal that none will give up,
each side fighting to the recitation of Qur'ānic chapters.
As they advance, they walk in their helmets and cuirasses
like pack animals led in file by small bands of men.
Our chief has a crowd of us around him,
a clan from Azd, steadfast in adversity,
In a battle the very sight of which undoes valiant heroes,
and in which men are cut down at the first engagement.
But we still had men there smiting them
with Mashrafī swords, as the fire of battle blazed;
[1016] No blade one relied on could survive that vortex of death,
except the keenest and most deadly.
We trample them with our swift armored steeds,
with fragments of hardwood spears scattered among us,
Covering dead men and the still-dying wounded,
who look as if they have been sprinkled with saffron.
Dead men for dead men, retaliation taken in kind,
easing the breasts of men who have long awaited its fulfillment,
Lie there next to slaughtered steeds,
their bodies, like the horses, prey for scavengers,
In a battle where the dead on the field
look like palm trunks uprooted[581] by the driving wind.
So it was in previous battles, before this day,
in which the Azd won praise and victory,
In every battle in which the Azd faced a hideous foe,
the terror of whom would turn hair white in an hour.
The Azd, my people, are the best people ever known,
when their chieftains stride forth on the day of battle,
[1017] Citadels of might, where refuge can be sought
on the day war streaming with blood tucks up its robe—
A clan who seek their glory with their swords;
hateful war brings out noble actions quickly.

581. *A'jāzu nakhlin . . . yanqa'iru*, an echo of Qur'ān 54:20.

Had al-Muhallab not been over the army that came
to the rivers of Kirmān, under God, they would never have come back.
We held fast to the cord of God, while they denied
the clear pronouncements of revelation;[582] nor did we disbelieve as they disbelieved.
They strayed from the straight path and from Islam,
and followed a religion opposed to that brought by the Warners.

Verses by al-Ṭufayl b. ʿĀmir b. Wāthilah, describing the death of ʿAbd Rabb al-Kabīr and his comrades and Qaṭarī's wanderings, how they pursued him, and how he eluded them:

At our hands, ʿAbd Rabb and his troops have felt the touch of punishment,[583]
and their captives have become part of the booty.
He marched against them with his army, and in Kirmān
he swept them off a level plain of land.
The Qaṭarī of unbelief was then nothing but an ostrich[584]
tracked across the desert, running through the night without sleep.
When he ran from us in flight, he headed down a way
other than the true well-marked path;
Flight will not save him—not even were he to be carried
by an Ark over the still expanse of the sea.

According to Abū Jaʿfar: In this year, Qaṭarī, ʿAbīdah b. Hilāl,[585] [1018] ʿAbd Rabb al-Kabīr, and the Azraquites with them were destroyed.

---

582. *Al-muḥkamāt*, as opposed to the obscure or ambiguous passages, *al-mutashābihāt*, both terms from Qur'ān 3:7; for various interpretations, see Ṭabarī, *Jāmiʿ al-bayān ʿan ta'wīl āy al-Qur'ān* (Cairo, 1955–60), VI, 169–83.

583. *ʿIqāb*. If the next line in the text followed this one in the original poem, perhaps a better reading would be *ʿuqāb*, "eagle," referring to al-Muhallab.

584. *Naʿāmah*. Qaṭarī's *kunyah* in war was Abū Naʿāmah; see Jāḥiẓ, *Bayān*, I, 34f., III, 264. Ibn Manẓūr, *Lisān*, s. v. qṭr, cites a verse mentioning *naʿā'im qaṭariyyah*, "ostriches from Qaṭar."

585. ʿAbīdah b. Hilāl al-Yashkurī, of the Banū Yashkur of Bakr b. Wā'il, known for his oratory and poetry. See text above, II, 515; Mubarrad, *Kāmil*, 652, 682ff.; Ziriklī, *Aʿlām*, IV, 357f.

Destruction of the Azraqites

The circumstances of this were as follows: When those Azraqites of whom we have given an account split up because of the internal dissension that arose among them in Kirmān, and some followed ʿAbd Rabb al-Kabīr while others followed Qaṭarī, the latter, finding his strength much reduced, set out for Ṭabaristān.

According to Hishām—Abū Mikhnaf—Yūnus b. Yazīd: When word of this reached al-Ḥajjāj, he sent Sufyān b. al-Abrad with a large army of Syrians in pursuit of Qaṭarī. Advancing first to al-Rayy, Sufyān set out after him. Meanwhile, al-Ḥajjāj wrote to Isḥāq b. Muḥammad b. al-Ashʿath, who was in command of an army of Kūfans in Ṭabaristān, ordering him to heed and obey Sufyān. Isḥāq advanced to join Sufyān and accompanied him in pursuit of Qaṭarī until they caught up with him in one of the defiles of Ṭabaristān and engaged him in battle. Qaṭarī's forces were scattered, and he fell off his mount down into the defile and rolled down until he lay prostrate at the bottom.

According to Muʿāwiyah b. Miḥṣan al-Kindī: I saw him fall but did not know who he was. Then I saw fifteen Arab women, all of them as comely and pleasing to the eye as your Lord willed, except for one old woman among them. I charged at them and drove them off toward Sufyān b. al-Abrad; but when I had brought them up close to him, the old woman lunged at me with her
[1019] sword and struck my neck with it, cutting through my under-helmet and nicking a piece from my neck. I brandished my sword and struck at her face; the blow broke through her skull and she fell dead. Then I turned to the young women and pushed them back to Sufyān. He laughed about the old woman and said, "What did you kill her for, may God shame her?" I replied, "Did you not see how she struck me, may God cause you to prosper? By God, she almost killed me!" He said, "I did see, and, by God, I do not blame you for what you did, may God curse her."

Then one of the local inhabitants went to Qaṭarī where he had tumbled down the defile. Qaṭarī, who was very thirsty, said, "Bring me some water to drink." The man replied, "Give me something for bringing you drink." Qaṭarī said, "Woe to you! By God, I have nothing with me but my weapon, as you see; I will give it to you if you bring me water." The man replied, "No, give it to me now!" Qaṭarī said, "No, bring me the water first." The man went around until he reached a point above Qaṭarī, and he sent a large stone rolling down on him from above, which struck him in the hip and prostrated him. This person then cried out to the men, and they came running to him—he did not know at the time that this man was Qaṭarī, although he assumed he must be one of their nobles, from his good appearance and the quality of his weapon. A group of Kūfans ran and got to him first and killed him; in this group were Sawrah b. Abjar al-Tamīmī; Jaʿfar b. ʿAbd al-Raḥmān b. Mikhnaf; al-Ṣabāḥ b. Muḥammad b. al-Ashʿath; Bādām, a client of the Banū al-Ashʿath; and ʿUmar b. Abī al-Ṣalt b. Kanārā, a client of the Banū Naṣr b. Muʿāwiyah,[586] who was one [1020] of the *dihqān*s. All of these claimed to be his killer. Then Abū al-Jahm b. Kinānah al-Kalbī came up to them, and each claimed that it was he who killed Qaṭarī. Abū al-Jahm then said, "Give it[587] up to me until you can settle this among yourselves." They gave it up to Abū al-Jahm, and he took it to Isḥāq b. Muḥammad, who was in command of the Kūfans. Jaʿfar did not join Isḥāq, because of something that had arisen between them, so that Jaʿfar was not speaking to Isḥāq, and was with Sufyān b. al-Abrad rather than with him—Jaʿfar was in command of the quarter of the Medinese in al-Rayy, but when Sufyān met the forces from al-Rayy, he had selected their best horsemen to accompany him and marched them out with him. When, then, the men came to him[588] with Qaṭarī's head, arguing over it, and he saw the head in the possession of Abū al-Jahm b. Kinānah al-Kalbī, he said to him, "You go with it and leave these quarrelers here." Abū al-Jahm set out with Qaṭarī's head and brought it to al-Ḥajjāj; then he took it on to ʿAbd al-Malik b. Marwān. He was granted a bonus of two thousand dirhams and given a *fuṭm*—which means to assign to the younger soldiers a place in the military roll.[589]

Jaʿfar came to Sufyān and said to him, "May God cause you to prosper, Qaṭarī had cut down my father, and this was my only concern in the matter. Bring me together with those who claim

586. The vocalization Kanārā is uncertain. The Banū Naṣr b. Muʿāwiyah were a clan of the Qays ʿAylān; see Caskel, *Ǧamharat an-nasab,* II, 446.

587. Qaṭarī's head.

588. Sufyān, according to the paraphrase in Ibn al-Athīr, *Kāmil,* IV, 442.

589. *Fa-ulḥiqa fī alfayn wa-uʿṭiya fuṭman yaʿnī annahu yufraḍa lil-ṣighār fī al-dīwān.* See Ṭabarī, glossarium, s. v. fuṭm, and note 168 above.

that they killed him, and ask them whether I was not ahead of them and got to him before them and struck him a blow that felled him, after which they came up to me and began to strike him with their swords. If they confirm this account of mine, they will be telling the truth; if they deny it, I swear by God that I am the one who did it; and if I did not, then let them swear by God that it is they who killed him and that they know nothing of what I say and that I have no claim to him." Sufyān replied, "You come to me now, after we have sent off the head!" When he had gone away, he said to his comrades, "By God, you[590] have the best claim among the men to him."

Then Sufyān b. al-Abrad set off for the camp of ʿAbīdah b. Hilāl,
[1021] who had fortified himself in a castle in Qūmis,[591] besieged him, and fought him for some days. Then Sufyān b. al-Abrad marched out with us against them, surrounded them, and ordered his herald to proclaim to them, "Any man who kills his master and then comes out to us will be granted safe-conduct." To this ʿAbīdah b. Hilāl said:[592]

By my life! The deaf one[593] has given the doubter a speech
that fills our breasts with outrage!
By my life! If I were to give Sufyān my allegiance,
and forsake my religion, I would indeed be a fool!
I raise my complaint to God for the state in which you see our horses,
emaciated and stumbling, their marrow almost exhausted,
Beset by slingers from all sides,
in Qūmis, until the most spirited are beaten down.
If this siege is now their end,
yet many a dead man has lain at their feet, soaked in his own blood.

---

590. Singular, probably referring to Jaʿfar; the speaker is probably Sufyān.

591. A province southeast of Ṭabaristān and west of Khurāsān; see *EI²*, s. v. Ḳūmis; Le Strange, *Lands*, 264–68. Yāqūt, *Muʿjam*, III, 62, V, 65, quotes a verse (also in Ibn Aʿtham al-Kūfī, *Futūḥ*, VII, 83) identifying the castle as Sadhawwar.

592. Ibn Aʿtham al-Kūfī, *Futūḥ*, VII, 82–83, gives a partly overlapping selection of verses from the same poem, with many variants. For other citations, see ʿAbbās, *Shiʿr al-Khawārij*, 52f., 166.

593. *Al-Aṣamm*, Sufyān's sobriquet, probably meaning "undeterrable"; see Caskel, *Ǧamharat an-nasab*, II, 515; Lane, *Lexicon*, s. v. aṣamm.

These were formerly steeds that, if led out on sore hooves,
would neigh at the doors of the tents.[594]

Sufyān maintained his siege of them until they were reduced to misery and ate their riding animals; then they came out and fought him, and he killed them and sent their heads to al-Ḥajjāj. He then proceeded on to Dunbāwand[595] and Ṭabaristān, and remained there until al-Ḥajjāj dismissed him, before the battle of al-Jamājim.[596]

According to Abū Ja'far: In this year, Umayyah b. 'Abdallāh b. Khālid b. Asīd killed Bukayr b. Wishāḥ al-Sa'dī. [1022]

Umayyah b. 'Abdallāh Kills Bukayr b. Wishāḥ in Khurāsān

According to 'Alī b. Muḥammad[597]—al-Mufaḍḍal b. Muḥammad: Umayyah b. 'Abdallāh, 'Abd al-Malik's governor over Khurāsān, put Bukayr in charge of the campaign in Transoxania. He had earlier put him in charge of Tukhāristān, and Bukayr had made his preparations for setting out for it and spent a great deal of money; but then Baḥīr b. Warqā' al-Ṣuraymī slandered him to Umayyah, as I have already recounted, and Umayyah ordered him to remain where he was.[598] Now, when he put him in charge of the campaign in Transoxania, he again made his preparations,

594. *Wa-qad kunna mimmā in yuqadna 'alā l-wajā/ lahunna bi-abwābi l-qibābi ṣahīlū.*

595. Modern Damāwand, the highest peak in the Elburz, south and west of Ṭabaristān; see *EI*², s. v. Damāwand.

596. On the final defeats of Qaṭarī and 'Abīdah, see Ibn Khayyāṭ, *Ta'rīkh*, 275 (Qaṭarī only, killed by Sawrah and Bādhān, year 78 [697–698]); Jāḥiẓ, *Bayān*, III, 264 (Qaṭarī killed by Sawrah); Dīnawarī, *al-Akhbār al-ṭiwāl*, 289 (Sufyān takes Qaṭarī's head to al-Ḥajjāj). Ya'qūbī, *Ta'rīkh*, II, 329f., asserts that Qaṭarī was received hospitably by the *ispahbadh* of Ṭabaristān until he demanded that the latter convert to Islam; the *ispahbadh* then fetched the governor of al-Rayy, Sufyān b. al-Abrad, and defeated and killed Qaṭarī, in the year 79 (698–699). According to Ibn A'tham al-Kūfī, *Futūḥ*, VII, 79–84, Qaṭarī was killed by Bādhām after being pinned by his fallen horse; Ibn A'tham al-Kūfī adds an account of a parley at the siege in Qūmis, in which 'Abīdah offered Sufyān's men the choice of Qur'ānic recitation or his own poetry but then reproached them for requesting the latter. See also Périer, *Vie d'al-Ḥadjdjādj*, 105f.; Dixon, *Umayyad Caliphate*, 182.

597. Al-Madā'inī.

598. See text above, II, 859–62.

spending a great deal of money on horses and weapons, and going into debt with the Soghdians and their merchants. But Baḥīr said to Umayyah, "Once the river is between him and you and he encounters the kings there, he will cast off allegiance to the caliph and summon to his own authority." Umayyah then sent to Bukayr, saying, "Stay where you are; perhaps I will go on campaign myself, and you will accompany me." Bukayr was angry and said, "He seems to be doing me a deliberate injury." 'Attāb al-Liqwah al-Ghudānī[599] had gone into debt in order to accompany
[1023] Bukayr, and when he did not go, his creditors took him and had him put in prison; Bukayr paid off his debts and he was released. Then Umayyah made up his mind to go on campaign.

He ordered preparations made for a campaign against Bukhārā, to be followed by a march against Mūsā b. 'Abdallāh b. Khāzim in al-Tirmidh.[600] The men made preparations and readied themselves. Umayyah left his son Ziyād as his deputy over Khurāsān, and Bukayr marched out with him. He camped at Kushmāhan,[601] and remained there a few days; then he ordered the army to move on. Then Baḥīr said to him, "I am afraid the men may lag behind; tell Bukayr to ride in the rear guard and keep the men together."

Umayyah gave Bukayr this order, and he took charge of the rear guard until they reached the river. Then Umayyah said, "Cross, Bukayr!" But 'Attāb al-Liqwah al-Ghudānī said, "May God cause the amīr to prosper, you cross, then let the troops cross after you." Umayyah crossed, and then the troops crossed. Then Umayyah said to Bukayr, "I am afraid my son will not be able to carry out his duties properly; he is, after all, little more than a boy. Return to Marw and see to its affairs for me; I put you in charge of it. Help my son in this way and see to his affairs." Bukayr selected horsemen from the cavalry of Khurāsān, men he knew and trusted, and

---

599. In Ibn al-Athīr (*Kāmil*, IV, 444), 'Uqāb ("eagle") Dhū al-Liqwah ("the one of the swift eagle"); perhaps a better reading would be "al-Luqwah," "palsy of the mouth." Ghudānah b. Yarbū' was a clan of Tamīm; see Caskel, *Ǧamharat an-nasab*, I, 59, 71, II, 275.

600. Mūsā's band had taken al-Tirmidh, after various adventures in Transoxania, and held it since before the death of Mūsā's father; see text below, II, 1145–49. On al-Tirmidh, on the Oxus some two hundred miles southeast of Bukhārā, see Le Strange, *Lands*, 440f.

601. The first stage northeast of Marw, at the edge of the cultivation on the Bukhārā road; see Le Strange, *Lands*, 400.

crossed back over. Umayyah went on to Bukhārā, with Abū Khālid Thābit, a client of Khuzāʿah, over his vanguard. As Bukayr crossed back, after Umayyah had left, ʿAttāb al-Liqwah said to him, "We killed ourselves and our kin gaining control of Khurāsān. Then we asked for a governor from Quraysh who would bring us together, and we were sent a governor who plays with us and transfers us from one prison to another." Bukayr asked, "What are you suggesting?" He replied, "Burn these boats, [1024] go back to Marw, throw off your allegiance to Umayyah, and stay in Marw for a while, exploiting its revenues."

ʿAttāb's opinion was seconded by al-Aḥnaf b. ʿAbdallāh al-ʿAnbarī;[602] but Bukayr said, "I fear lest these horsemen who are with me may perish." Al-Aḥnaf said, "Are you afraid that you will lack men? I will bring you as many as you like from the people of Marw if these who are with you perish." Bukayr said, "I fear the Muslims may perish." He said, "All you have to do is have a herald proclaim that anyone who converts to Islam will be exempted from the land tax, and fifty thousand will come praying to you, men who will heed and obey better than these."[603] Bukayr said, "I fear Umayyah and those with him will perish." He said, "Why should they perish, when they have the equipment, numbers, courage, weapons, and everything they need to defend themselves as far as China?"

Bukayr burned the boats, returned to Marw, seized and imprisoned Umayyah's son, and summoned the people to renounce their allegiance to Umayyah, which they did. When Umayyah heard of this, he made peace with the Bukhārans for a small payment and headed back. He ordered boats constructed, and they were made for him and assembled. Then he said to the notables of Tamīm who were with him, "Does not Bukayr amaze you? When I came to Khurāsān, I was warned about him, and received all sorts of complaints and accusations about him and about various ill-gotten gains; but I turned a deaf ear to all of that and launched no investigation of him or of a single one of his

602. The Banū al-ʿAnbar b. ʿAmr were a clan of the Tamīm; see Caskel, *Ǧamharat an-nasab*, II, 189.

603. Umayyah's imposition on Muslim landowners of the *kharāj*, which was collected by non-Muslim *dihqāns*, is cited below, II, 1029, as a source of dissatisfaction with Umayyah exploited by Bukayr.

officials. Then I offered him command of my security force, but he refused it, and I let it pass. Then I gave him a governorship, but I was warned against him and ordered him to stay where he was; I only did so out of consideration for him. Then I sent him back to Marw and give him authority there. But he showed no gratitude for any of this and now repays me in the way you see!" But some of the men replied, "O amīr, this was not his idea; the suggestion
[1025] to burn the boats came to him from ʿAttāb al-Liqwah." Umayyah said, "And what is ʿAttāb? Is ʿAttāb anything but a hen sitting on her eggs?" When ʿAttāb heard about this comment, he recited the following verses:

When you encounter these brooders, you will find them
armored, thick-necked, mounted on noble steeds.
You left off what you were about, out of cowardice and weakness,
and foolishly came to us, O basest of the Arabs;
When you saw how forbidding were the mountains of Soghdia,
you turned tail on Mūsā and Nūḥ,[604]
And came running to us, like a bold hyena, without a word;[605]
but you flew from the palms of al-Baḥrayn like a cowardly bustard.[606]
Make all the threats you like! You will find me
under the fluttering standards before a dark and rumbling cloud of men,
Advancing slowly on a fine horse with sleek cheekbones,
which alternately ambles and runs as it goes to meet the detachment.

When the boats were ready, Umayyah crossed over and headed for Marw, leaving Mūsā b. ʿAbdallāh unmolested. Umayyah said, "O God, I was good to Bukayr, but he was ungrateful for my good treatment and did what he did. O God, take care of him for me!"
[1026] Shammās b. Dithār,[607] who had returned from Sijistān after the

604. Sons of ʿAbdallāh b. Khāzim; on Nūḥ, who accompanied his brother Mūsā in Transoxania, see text below, II, 1155–60.

605. *Wa-ji'ta dhīkhan mughidhdhan mā tukallimunā.*

606. A reference to Umayyah's defeat in battle with Abū Fudayk; see text above, II, 829, 860f.

607. Al-ʿUṭāridī, one of the leaders of the revolt of Tamīm against Ibn Khāzim,

death of Ibn Khāzim and gone on campaign with Umayyah, said, "O amīr, I will take care of him for you, God willing!" Umayyah sent him ahead with eight hundred men; he advanced as far as Bāsān,[608] which belongs to the Banū Naṣr,[609] and halted there. Bukayr marched out against him, having with him Mudrik b. Unayf, whose father was with Shammās. Bukayr sent a message to Shammās, saying, "Could Tamīm find no one to fight me but you?" and blaming him. Shammās sent back to him, saying, "You are more blameworthy and have behaved more badly than I. You broke faith with Umayyah and showed him no gratitude for his favor to you when he came and honored you, not laying a finger on you or any of your agents."

Bukayr launched a surprise night attack against Shammās and scattered his forces; but he told his men, "Do not kill any of them, but take their weapons." Accordingly, when they took a man, they stripped him of his equipment and left him. The troops were scattered, Shammās himself going to a village of Ṭayyi' named Būyanah.[610] Umayyah, meanwhile, advanced as far as Kushmāhan, and Shammās b. Dithār returned to him there. Then Umayyah sent out Thābit b. Quṭbah, a client of Khuzāʿah. Bukayr offered battle, took Thābit captive, and scattered his forces; but then Bukayr let Thābit go because of a favor he owed him.

Thābit returned to Umayyah, and Umayyah advanced with his forces. Bukayr engaged him in combat. Bukayr's security force was under the command of Abū Rustam al-Khalīl b. Aws al-ʿAbshamī; he fought valiantly that day, but Umayyah's men called out to him, "O commander of the security force of ʿĀrimah!" ʿĀrimah was Bukayr's concubine. Abū Rustam drew back, but Bukayr said to him, "Damn it, pay no mind to what

---

and a personal enemy of Bukayr; see text above, II, 495f., 593–96. On ʿUṭārid b. Ḥājib of Tamīm, see Caskel, *Ǧamharat an-nasab*, I, 60, II, 580.

608. Yāqūt, *Muʿjam*, I, 468, 766f., mentions Bāshān or Fāshān as a village of Marw. It was northwest of the city; see Le Strange, *Lands*, 399.

609. Probably the Banū Naṣr b. Muʿāwiyah, of Qays ʿAylān, mentioned above, II, 1019f. On the mass migration that brought fifty thousand Kūfan and Baṣran fighters with their families to the Marw oasis in 51 (671), see text above, II, 81, 155f., and Balādhurī, *Futūḥ*, 410. Ṣ. al-ʿAlī, "Istīṭān al-ʿarab fī Khurāsān," *Majallat Kulliyyat al-ādāb—Baghdād*, 1958, 37f., 67f., suggests that villages were residences for "their" Arab clans rather than sources of revenue.

610. Two *farsakhs* from Marw, according to Yāqūt, *Muʿjam*, I, 766f.

these people call out! This ʿĀrimah has a stallion to protect her! Advance your standard!" They fought until Bukayr was forced back. He withdrew inside the wall and quartered in the old market, while Umayyah quartered in Bāsān. Then followed a series of encounters in the Field of Yazīd.[611] One day Bukayr's forces were driven back, but Bukayr protected them. Another day, there was another encounter in the Field, in which one of the men of the
[1027] Banū Tamīm was hit in the foot and began to hobble away, while Huraym[612] gave him protection. The man said, "O God, help us and strengthen us with angels!" Huraym said to him, "Fight for yourself, man! The angels have better things to do!" The man restrained himself for a time, but then again called out, "O God, strengthen us with angels!" Huraym said, "Either you spare me this or I leave you to the angels!" But he continued to protect him until he brought him back to the men.

One of the men of the Banū Tamīm called out, "Umayyah! Scandal of Quraysh!" Umayyah swore an oath that if he got the better of this man, he would slit his throat. He did get the better of him, and did slit his throat, between two of the battlements of the city. Another day, in yet another encounter, Bukayr b. Wishāḥ struck Thābit b. Quṭbah on the head, calling out his ancestry and saying, "I am Ibn Wishāḥ!" Thābit's brother Ḥurayyith b. Quṭbah then attacked Bukayr, and Bukayr was thrown back and his forces driven off. Ḥurayyith pursued Bukayr until he reached the bridge, and called to him, "Where are you going, Bukayr?" Bukayr turned back to attack him, and Ḥurayyith gave him a sword blow on the head that cut through the underhelmet and penetrated to his head, and he fell. His comrades took him and brought him into the city.

That is the way they fought them. But otherwise, Bukayr's men would go around garbed in brightly dyed garments, with red and yellow mantles and wrappers,[613] and sit talking in the outskirts

---

611. *Maydān Yazīd,* mentioned below (II, 1477) as a place of assembly. Perhaps it was named (subsequently) for Yazīd b. al-Muhallab b. Abī Ṣufrah, governor of Khurāsān 82–85 (701–704); see text below, II, 1083, 1138ff.

612. Huraym b. Abī Ṭaḥmah al-Mujāshiʿī, later noted as commander of the cavalry of Tamīm; see text below, II, 1202, and Caskel, *Ǧamharat an-nasab,* II, 287.

613. *Mutafaḍḍilīn fī thiyāb muṣabbaghah wa-malāḥif wa-uzur ṣufr wa-ḥumr.* See Dozy, *Dictionnaire détaillé des noms des vêtements chez les Arabes,* 24–46,

of the city, while a herald proclaimed, "He who shoots an arrow will be shot at by us with the head of one of his children or his kin." No one took any shots at them.

But Bukayr was worried, and feared that if the siege was prolonged, the men would desert him; so he asked for a truce. Umayyah's forces also favored a truce, because of their families inside the city, and asked Umayyah to make a truce with Bukayr. Umayyah was a peace-loving man, and made the truce, on the following terms: Umayyah was to pay Bukayr 400,000 dirhams, as well as gifts to his comrades, to appoint Bukayr to any of the districts of Khurāsān he wished, and not to listen to what Baḥīr [1028] said about him; if Umayyah found any reason to be suspicious of him, he would have forty days safe-conduct to get out of Marw. Umayyah got safe-conduct for Bukayr from ʿAbd al-Malik and wrote the document up for him at the Sanjān Gate.[614] Then Umayyah entered the city.

Some people say that Bukayr did not go out on campaign with Umayyah, but rather that when Umayyah went out on campaign, he left Bukayr as his deputy over Marw. Then Bukayr rebelled, and Umayyah returned and fought him, then made a truce with him and entered Marw. Umayyah kept faith with Bukayr and treated him with the same honor and complaisance as formerly. He also sent for ʿAttāb al-Liqwah and said to him, "You were the mastermind of the plot." ʿAttāb said, "Yes, may God cause the amīr to prosper." Umayyah asked, "Why?" ʿAttāb replied, "I had little money and many debts, so I turned against my creditors." Umayyah said, "Woe to you! So you stirred up strife among the Muslims, and burned the boats, with the Muslims in the middle of enemy territory, with no fear of God?" ʿAttāb said, "That is the way it was, and I ask God for forgiveness." Umayyah asked, "How large are your debts?" ʿAttāb answered, "Twenty thousand." Umayyah said, "If you will refrain from stirring up trouble among the Muslims, I will pay off your debts." ʿAttāb said, "I will, may God make me your ransom!" Umayyah laughed and said, "I have little faith in what you say, but I will nevertheless pay off

---

401–3. Bright colors apparently indicated non-bellicose intentions, as with the red sash of Muṭarrif's summoner, mentioned above, II, 998.

614. On the southeast side of the city; see Le Strange, *Lands*, 399.

your debts." He paid the twenty thousand. Umayyah was a gentle, easygoing, and generous man; no one among the governors of Khurāsān gave out such generous gifts there as he.[615]

He was nevertheless at the same time oppressive to them. He was extremely pompous and used to say, "Khurāsān and Sijistān hardly suffice me for my kitchen!"[616] Umayyah dismissed Baḥīr from the command of his security force and gave it to ʿAṭā' b. Abī
[1029] al-Sā'ib. He wrote to ʿAbd al-Malik explaining the affair with Bukayr and his pardoning him, and ʿAbd al-Malik responded by selecting an expeditionary force to send to Umayyah in Khurāsān; the men made their arrangements for who would pay and who would go, and Shaqīq b. al-Sulayk al-Asadī transferred his stipend to a man of Jarm.[617] Umayyah levied the land tax on the people[618] and pressed them hard. One day Bukayr was sitting in the mosque with some people from the Banū Tamīm, and they spoke of Umayyah's harshness to the people, blaming him and saying, "He has made the *dihqāns* masters over us in collecting taxes." Also present in the mosque were Baḥīr, Ḍirār b. Ḥuṣayn,[619] and ʿAbd al-ʿAzīz b. Jāriyah b. Qudāmah.[620] Baḥīr brought

---

615. Bukayr's rebellion is mentioned very briefly in Balādhurī, *Futūḥ*, 416f., Yaʿqūbī, *Ta'rīkh*, II, 324, and Ibn Ḥabīb, *Asmā' al-mughtālīn min al-ashrāf fī al-jāhiliyyah wa-al-Islām* (in A. S. Hārūn, ed., *Nawādir al-makhṭūṭāt* [Cairo, 1951–54], II), 176f. According to the slightly fuller account in Ibn Aʿtham al-Kūfī, *Futūḥ*, VI, 290f., the siege of Marw lasted four months, and Umayyah's payoff to Bukayr was 200,000 dirhams in addition to whatever wealth Bukayr had already laid his hands on. See also Ibn al-Athīr, *Kāmil*, IV, 443–46; Dixon, *Umayyad Caliphate*, 111.

616. According to *Aghānī*[1], XIII, 54, Umayyah wrote back to ʿAbd al-Malik that "the revenue of Khurāsān is insufficient to cover the expenses of my kitchen" but was dismissed after ʿAbd al-Malik read a confidential note (of undisclosed contents) slipped by the poet Thābit Quṭnah into the same delivery.

617. On the process of *juʿālah*, or paying for substitutes on expeditions, see Lane, *Lexicon*, s. v. juʿālah; Ṣ. al-ʿAlī, *al-Tanẓīmāt al-ijtimāʿiyyah wa-al-iqtiṣādiyyah fī al-Baṣrah fī al-qarn al-awwal al-hijrī* (Baghdad, 1953), 139–40. The point of the specific reference to the Asadī and the Jarmī is unclear.

618. *Akhadha Umayyah al-nās bi-al-kharāj.* The "people" here and in the following sentence are the Arab emigrés, who were acquiring land and paying *kharāj* on it; since in Marw collection was in the hands of the *dihqāns*, non-Arabs and non-Muslims were now collecting taxes from Arab Muslims. See Shaban, *Islamic History*, I, 173f.

619. Last mentioned as an intermediary between Baḥīr and Bukayr, text above, II, 860.

620. Son of Jāriyah b. Qudāmah al-Tamīmī, a prominent supporter of ʿAlī against Muʿāwiyah; see Ibn Saʿd, *Ṭabaqāt*, VII, i, 38f.

word of this incident to Umayyah, but Umayyah refused to believe him. Baḥīr appealed to the witness of these men, as well as to the witness of Muzāḥim b. Abī al-Mujashshir al-Sulamī.[621] Umayyah summoned Muzāḥim and asked him, but he said, "He was only joking." Umayyah then left Bukayr alone. But Baḥīr came to him and said, "May God cause the amīr to prosper, Bukayr—I swear to God—has summoned me to cast off my allegiance to you; he said, 'Were it not for your position, I would kill this Qurayshite and enjoy the fruits of Khurāsān.'" But Umayyah said, "I cannot believe this, after he has done what he has done and I have granted him safe-conduct and given him gifts."

Then Baḥīr brought him Ḍirār b. Ḥuṣayn and ʿAbd al-ʿAzīz b. Jāriyah, and they bore witness that Bukayr said to them, "If you would obey me, I would kill that effeminate Qurayshite," and thus summoned them to assassinate Umayyah. Umayyah said, "You know best what you saw. I would not suspect this of him; but to let him be, after the witness you have borne, would show weakness." Then he told his chamberlain,[622] ʿUbaydah, and the captain of his guard,[623] ʿAṭāʾ b. Abī al-Sāʾib, "When Bukayr comes in with his brother's sons Badal and Shamardal, and I stand up, seize them." When Umayyah sat in public audience, Bukayr and his brother's sons came; when they sat down, Umayyah stood up from his dais and withdrew. The people left, and as Bukayr was [1030]
leaving, they arrested him and his brother's sons. Umayyah summoned Bukayr and said, "You are the one who said thus-and-so?" Bukayr replied, "Be not rash, may God cause you to prosper, and do not listen to the words of that son of a bitch."[624] But Umayyah threw him in prison, and took his concubine al-ʿĀrimah and imprisoned her; he also imprisoned al-Aḥnaf b. ʿAbdallāh al-ʿAnbarī, saying, "You are one of those who counseled Bukayr to rebel."

The next day, Umayyah brought out Bukayr; and Baḥīr, Ḍirār,

---

621. Probably of the Banū Sulaym b. Manṣūr, a tribe of Qays; see Caskel, *Ǧamharat an-nasab*, II, 516.

622. *Ḥājib*, perhaps "chief bodyguard;" see *EI*², s. v. ḥādjib.

623. *Ṣāḥib ḥarasihi*. This man has been identified above as the head of the *shurṭah*, which suggests that, at least in Khurāsān, the two terms may refer to the same body of men.

624. *Ibn al-maḥlūqah*. For various interpretations of the meaning of this mild imprecation, see Lane, *Lexicon*, s. v. ḥalaqa.

and ʿAbd al-ʿAzīz b. Jāriyah bore witness against him that he had summoned them to rebel against Umayyah and assassinate him. Bukayr said, "May God cause you to prosper, be not hasty; for these are my enemies." Then Umayyah asked Ziyād b. ʿUqbah, the chief of the Ahl al-ʿĀliyah,[625] Ibn Wālān al-ʿAdawī, at that time one of the chiefs of the Banū Tamīm,[626] and Yaʿqūb b. Khālid al-Dhuhlī,[627] "Will you kill him?"—but they declined. Then he asked Baḥīr, "Will you kill him?" and he answered, "Yes." Umayyah handed Bukayr over to Baḥīr; but then Yaʿqūb b. al-Qaʿqāʿ al-Aʿlam al-Azdī,[628] who was a friend of Bukayr's, got up from his place and embraced Umayyah, saying, "I appeal to you to think of God, O amīr, in Bukayr's case—after you have been so generous to him." Umayyah said, "Yaʿqūb, no one will kill him but his own people, who have borne witness against him."[629] Then ʿAṭāʾ b. Abī al-Sāʾib al-Laythī, who was the captain of Umayyah's guard, said, "Leave the amīr alone!" Yaʿqūb said, "No!" and ʿAṭāʾ struck him with the hilt of his sword and bloodied his nose, and then withdrew. Then Yaʿqūb said to Baḥīr, "O Baḥīr, the men pledged Bukayr their word when they made peace with him, and you were one of them. Do not break your pledge!" Baḥīr replied, "O Yaʿqūb, I gave him no pledge!" Then Baḥīr took Bukayr's extended[630] sword, which he had taken from Uswār al-Turjumān, Ibn Khāzim's interpreter. Bukayr said, "O Baḥīr, you will break up the Banū Saʿd if you kill me; let this Qurayshite
[1031] himself do with me as he will." But Baḥīr said, "No, by God, O son of an Iṣfahānī mother! The Banū Saʿd will not be at peace so

625. Tribes from the upper Ḥijāz, mostly Qays ʿAylān, constituting one of the "fifths" of the Baṣran army, operative also in Khurāsān; see Morony, *Iraq after the Muslim Conquest*, 246; al-ʿAlī, "Istīṭān al-ʿarab fī Khurāsān," 40ff.

626. ʿAbdallāh b. Wālān al-ʿAdawī is mentioned below (II, 1188) as a confidant of Qutaybah b. Muslim and identified as one of the Banū Milkān. The latter were a branch of the Thawr b. ʿAbd Manāt, who were joined with the related clans of Taym, ʿAdī, ʿUkl, and Ḍabbah in a confederation called al-Ribāb, itself related to and allied with Tamīm. See Caskel, *Ǧamharat an-nasab*, I, 59, 85, II, 486.

627. Probably of the Banū Dhuhl b. Taym b. ʿAbd Manāt of al-Ribāb; see Caskel, *Ǧamharat an-nasab*, I, 85.

628. Called Ibn al-Aʿlam and *qāḍī Khurāsān* below, II, 1485. See Ibn Saʿd, *Ṭabaqāt*, VII, ii, 103.

629. That is, the Tamīm and their allies of al-Ribāb, or specifically the Banū Saʿd b. Zayd Manāt b. Tamīm, to which both Baḥīr and Bukayr belonged.

630. *Mawṣūl*, fitted with an extension called a *ṣilah*; see Ṭabarī, glossarium, s. v. waṣala.

long as we are both alive!" Bukayr said, "Get on with it, then, you son of a bitch!" Baḥīr killed Bukayr. It was a Friday. Umayyah killed Bukayr's brother's two sons and gave Bukayr's concubine, al-ʿĀrimah, to Baḥīr. Umayyah also heard accusations against al-Aḥnaf b. ʿAbdallāh al-ʿAnbarī; he summoned him from prison and said, "You too are one of those who gave Bukayr this counsel," and reviled him, then said, "I hereby hand you over to these men."

Then Umayyah sent out a man from Khuzāʿah against Mūsā b. ʿAbdallāh b. Khāzim, but he was treacherously murdered by ʿAmr b. Khālid b. Ḥuṣayn al-Kilābī, and his army scattered. One group of them asked Mūsā for safe-conduct, and joined him; others returned to Umayyah.[631]

In this year, Umayyah crossed the river of Balkh to campaign. He and his forces were surrounded and reduced to misery, and were on the point of perishing before they escaped. Umayyah and the troops with him then returned to Marw. ʿAbd al-Raḥmān b. Khālid b. al-ʿĀṣ b. Hishām b. al-Mughīrah[632] satirized Umayyah in the following verses:

Tell Umayyah that he will get his reward for bad actions—
and these do have their reward.
Whoever may consider reproaching you or desire to do so,
I myself have no such intention with you.[633]
Any good you have done is wiped out by your bad qualities,
whose evil fruits have been parceled out to you.
Whoever named you Umayyah,[634] when passing out names
at the time of your birth, got it right.

According to Abū Jaʿfar: In this year, the leader of the pilgrimage was Abān b. ʿUthmān, who was the governor of Medina.[635] The governor of al-Kūfah and al-Baṣrah was al-Ḥajjāj b.

---

631. A fuller account of this appears below, II, 1149–51.

632. A Makhzūmī of Quraysh, and brother of the well-known poet al-Ḥārith b. Khālid al-Makhzūmī, whom ʿAbd al-Malik appointed governor of Mecca in 80 (699–700); see *Aghānī¹*, III, 97; Caskel, *Ǧamharat an-nasab*, II, 307; Sezgin, *GAS*, II, 417.

633. *Wa-man yanẓur ʿitābaka aw yuridhū/fa-lastu bi-nāẓirin minka l-ʿitābā.*

634. Diminutive of *amah*, "slave woman."

635. Ibn Khayyāṭ, *Taʾrīkh*, 275, 301; Yaʿqūbī, *Taʾrīkh*, II, 336.

[1032] Yūsuf, and the governor of Khurāsān was Umayyah b. ʿAbdallāh b. Khālid b. Asīd.

According to Aḥmad b. Thābit—anonymous—Isḥāq b. ʿĪsā—Abū Maʿshar: Abān b. ʿUthmān was leader of the pilgrimage twice while he was governor of Medina, in the years 76 (695–696) and 77 (696–697).[636] According to some, Shabīb perished in the year 78 (697–698);[637] some say the same for the deaths of Qaṭarī, ʿAbīdah b. Hilāl, and ʿAbd Rabb al-Kabīr.[638] In this year, al-Walīd conducted a summer expedition.[639]

---

636. See text above, II, 940, and note 369.

637. So Yaʿqūbī, *Taʾrīkh*, II, 328; see text above, II, 972, and note 461.

638. Ibn Khayyāṭ, *Taʾrīkh*, 275, dates Qaṭarī's death to 78, and Yaʿqūbī, *Taʾrīkh*, II, 330, dates it to 79.

639. Ibn Khayyāṭ, *Taʾrīkh*, 275, reports that al-Walīd campaigned in the region between Malaṭyah and al-Miṣṣīṣah. According to Yaʿqūbī, *Taʾrīkh*, II, 337, Yaḥyā b. al-Ḥakam had done this the previous summer, and in 78 al-Walīd raided Aṭmār (?) from the direction of Malaṭyah. See F. ʿUthmān, *al-Ḥudūd al-islāmiyyah al-bīzanṭiyyah bayn al-iḥtikāk al-ḥarbī wa-al-ittiṣāl al-ḥiḍārī* (Cairo, 1966), II, 74, and note 655 below.

The Events of the Year 78

(March 30, 697—March 19, 698)

The Important Events Occurring in This Year

ʿAbd al-Malik b. Marwān dismissed Umayyah b. ʿAbdallāh from the governorship of Khurāsān and included Khurāsān and Sijistān under the jurisdiction of al-Ḥajjāj b. Yūsuf. When they were included in his jurisdiction, al-Ḥajjāj dispersed his officials throughout them.

The Officials Whom al-Ḥajjāj Appointed in Khurāsān and Sijistān, and Why He Appointed Whom He Did, with Further Details

It is reported: When al-Ḥajjāj had finished with Shabīb and Muṭarrif, he transferred from al-Kūfah to al-Baṣrah, leaving as his deputy over al-Kūfah al-Mughīrah b. ʿAbdallāh b. Abī ʿAqīl.[640] According to some reports, he first deputized ʿAbd al-Raḥmān b. ʿAbdallāh b. ʿĀmir al-Ḥaḍramī, but then dismissed him and replaced

640. Al-Thaqafī, according to text below, II, 1381. He was probably a cousin of al-Ḥajjāj b. Yūsuf (b. al-Ḥakam b. Abī ʿAqīl).

[1033] him with al-Mughīrah b. ʿAbdallāh.[641] Al-Muhallab came to him in al-Baṣrah, having finished with the Azraqites.

According to Hishām—Abū Mikhnaf—Abū al-Mukhāriq al-Rāsibī: When al-Muhallab b. Abī Ṣufrah had finished with the Azraqites, he came to al-Ḥajjāj; this was in the year 78. Al-Ḥajjāj seated him beside him and called for the distinguished fighters among his forces. Whomever al-Muhallab mentioned as a man who showed valor among his forces, al-Ḥajjāj took his word for it. Al-Ḥajjāj gave them mounts and good bonuses and increased their stipends; he said, "These are men of action and have the best claim to the wealth; these are the defenders of the frontiers and the bane of the enemy."[642]

According to Hishām—Abū Mikhnaf—Yūnus b. Abī Isḥāq: Al-Ḥajjāj assigned al-Muhallab Sijistān as well as Khurāsān. But al-Muhallab said to him, "Let me refer you to a man who is better acquainted with Sijistān than I; he was formerly governor of Kābul and Zābul,[643] and collected taxes, waged war, and made peace with the people there." Al-Ḥajjāj replied, "Indeed! Who is that?" Al-Muhallab said, "ʿUbaydallāh b. Abī Bakrah."[644]

Then al-Ḥajjāj sent out al-Muhallab over Khurāsān and ʿUbaydallāh b. Abī Bakrah over Sijistān. The governor over these provinces had been Umayyah b. ʿAbdallāh b. Khālid b. Asīd b. Abī al-ʿĪṣ b. Umayyah; he was ʿAbd al-Malik b. Marwān's governor, al-Ḥajjāj having nothing to do with him, from the time he was sent out to Iraq until this year, when ʿAbd al-Malik dismissed Umayyah and added the area of his authority to that of al-Ḥajjāj. Al-

---

641. Ibn Khayyāṭ, *Ta'rīkh*, 296, mentions only ʿAbd al-Raḥmān as al-Ḥajjāj's deputy over al-Kūfah at this time. This man is called ʿAbd al-Raḥmān b. ʿAbd al-Raḥmān b. ʿAbdallāh b. ʿĀmir below, II, 1069f.

642. A parallel account in Balādhurī, *Ansāb*, XI, 310; more briefly in Ibn Aʿtham al-Kūfī, *Futūḥ*, VII, 78 (620 fighters honored), and Dīnawarī, *al-Akhbār al-ṭiwāl*, 289.

643. The regions around Kābul and to its southwest, toward Ghaznah and Qandahār; see Yāqūt, *Muʿjam*, II, 904f., IV, 220f.; Le Strange, *Lands*, 334, 349f.; *EI*², s. vv. Kābul, Kābulistān.

644. On him, see C. E. Bosworth, "'Ubaidallāh b. Abī Bakra and the 'Army of Destruction' in Zābulistān," *Der Islam* 50 (1973), 268–83; Ziriklī, *Aʿlām*, IV, 345. His father Abū Bakrah was a slave of Thaqīf who became a client of the Prophet, but ʿUbaydallāh later tried to pass himself off as a real Thaqafī; see *Aghānī*¹, XVII, 9; Goldziher, *Muhammedanische Studien*, I, 137f., 141. ʿUbaydallāh was governor of Kābul under Ziyād b. Abīhi, 51–53 (671–673); see Balādhurī, *Futūḥ*, 397.

Muhallab went out to Khurāsān and ʿUbaydallāh b. Abī Bakrah to Sijistān; ʿUbaydallāh b. Abī Bakrah remained inactive the rest of this year.[645] This is the account of Abū Mikhnaf from Abū al-Mukhāriq.

The account of ʿAlī b. Muḥammad—al-Mufaḍḍal b. Muḥammad: Khurāsān and Sijistān were joined with Iraq under al-Ḥajjāj's authority at the beginning of the year 78, after the Khārijites had been killed. He appointed ʿUbaydallāh b. Abī Bakrah over Khurāsān and al-Muhallab b. Abī Ṣufrah over Sijistān. But al-Muhallab disliked Sijistān. He met ʿAbd al-Raḥmān b. ʿUbayd b. Ṭāriq al-ʿAbshamī,[646] who was the head of al-Ḥajjāj's security force, and said, "The amīr has appointed me to Sijistān and Ibn Abī Bakrah to Khurāsān, even though I know Khurāsān better than he does, since I got to know it in the time of al-Ḥakam b. ʿAmr al-Ghifārī,[647] and Ibn Abī Bakrah is better able to deal with Sijistān than I. Speak to the amīr and get him to switch me to Khurāsān and Ibn Abī Bakrah to Sijistān." ʿAbd al-Raḥmān replied, "I will; you speak also to Zādhān Farrūkh[648] and get him to help me." Al-Muhallab spoke to him, and he agreed to help. Then ʿAbd al-Raḥmān b. ʿUbayd said to al-Ḥajjāj, "You have appointed al-Muhallab to Sijistān, but Ibn Abī Bakrah is better able to deal with it than he." Zādhān Farrūkh added, "That is true!" Al-Ḥajjāj said, "But we have already written up his letter of appointment." Zādhān Farrūkh said, "His letter of appointment could be changed without difficulty." Al-Ḥajjāj then reassigned Ibn Abī Bakrah to Sijistān, and al-Muhallab to Khurāsān. [1034]

Al-Muhallab was, however, required to pay up 1,000,000 dirhams from the revenue of al-Ahwāz, where he had been governor under Khālid b. ʿAbdallāh. Al-Muhallab said to his son al-Mughīrah, "Khālid made me governor of al-Ahwāz, and made you

---

645. That is, before launching an expedition against Zunbīl; see the continuation of this account below, II, 1036. The following year, 79, began in late March.

646. Of the Banū ʿAbd Shams b. Saʿd of Tamīm; see Caskel, *Ǧamharat an-nasab*, I, 78, II, 130.

647. See text above, II, 109.

648. Zādhān Farrūkh b. Payrōazh, head of the *dīwān al-kharāj* and the last to keep the accounts in Persian; according to Jahshiyārī, *Wuzarāʾ* (Cairo, 1980), 38, his assistant, Ṣāliḥ b. ʿAbd al-Raḥmān, converted them to Arabic in this same year (78). See also Balādhurī, *Futūḥ*, 300f.; Morony, *Iraq after the Muslim Conquest*, 53f.

governor of Iṣṭakhr.[649] Now al-Ḥajjāj has demanded that I pay up 1,000,000 dirhams. I will pay half of it, and you pay the other half." Al-Muhallab had no money when he was dismissed, and had had to borrow. He spoke to Abū Māwiyyah, the client of ʿAbdallāh b. ʿĀmir, who had been in charge of ʿAbdallāh b. ʿĀmir's treasury,[650] and he lent al-Muhallab 300,000 dirhams. But
[1035] Khayrah al-Qushayriyyah, al-Muhallab's wife, said, "This will not cover your obligation," and she sold some jewelry and other things, bringing the total up to 500,000. Then al-Mughīrah brought 500,000 to his father, and he took the money to al-Ḥajjāj. Al-Muhallab then sent out his son Ḥabīb with his vanguard.[651] The latter came to al-Ḥajjāj to bid him farewell, and al-Ḥajjāj ordered him given 10,000 dirhams and a gray mule. Ḥabīb set out on this mule for Khurāsān, traveling with his men, who rode the post. He traveled for twenty days, and then as they entered the city, they were met by a beast carrying a load of firewood, and the mule shied; they marveled at her shying after all that traveling and fatigue. Ḥabīb did not interfere with Umayyah or his officials. He stayed there ten months, until al-Muhallab came out to him in the year 79 (698–699).[652]

The leader of the pilgrimage in this year was al-Walīd b. ʿAbd al-Malik;[653] so I was informed by Aḥmad b. Thābit—anonymous—

649. See text above, II, 822–26.

650. It is unclear whether ʿAbdallāh b. ʿĀmir is here in both instances ʿAbdallāh b. ʿĀmir b. Kurayz, governor of al-Baṣrah under Muʿāwiyah (see *EI*², s. v. ʿAbdallāh b. ʿĀmir), or, in one or both instances, ʿAbdallāh b. ʿĀmir b. Misma', later head of the *shurṭah* in al-Baṣrah (see text below, II, 1062).

651. *Muqaddimah*, here apparently more an advance party.

652. According to Balādhurī, *Ansāb*, XI, 266, 310f., and Ibn Aʿtham al-Kūfī, *Futūḥ*, VI, 293, Umayyah was dismissed because of his avoidance of raiding and the corresponding decrease in plunder; but Balādhurī also reports (*Futūḥ*, 399) that Umayyah's son ʿAbdallāh, who deputized for his father in Sijistān, made a disgraceful truce with Zunbīl there, and Ibn Aʿtham al-Kūfī (*Futūḥ*, VII, 111f.) has a distorted version of the same incident, attributing it to Umayyah himself. Balādhurī further states (*Ansāb*, XI, 266, 310f.) that al-Ḥajjāj sent ʿUbaydallāh b. Abī Bakrah to ʿAbd al-Malik to ask for the governorship of Khurāsān (for al-Ḥajjāj) and that it was only after the caliph had offered it to ʿUbaydallāh himself, who declined it, that he granted it to al-Ḥajjāj. Al-Muhallab's being preceded to Khurāsān by his son Ḥabīb is mentioned in neither the above sources nor the short notices in Ibn Khayyāṭ, *Ta'rīkh*, 275, 297; Yaʿqūbī, *Ta'rīkh*, II, 330; Ibn Aʿtham al-Kūfī, *Futūḥ*, VII, 78. See also Périer, *Vie d'al-Ḥadjdjādj*, 154f.; Bosworth, *Sīstān under the Arabs*, 52f., and the article cited in note 644; M. A. Shaban, *The ʿAbbāsid Revolution* (Cambridge, 1970), 54f.

653. So also Ibn Khayyāṭ, *Ta'rīkh*, 276, 301. Yaʿqūbī, *Ta'rīkh*, II, 336, has Abān b. ʿUthmān, but the text is questionable.

Isḥāq b. ʿĪsā—Abū Maʿshar. The governor of Medina in this year was Abān b. ʿUthmān. The governor of al-Kūfah, al-Baṣrah, Khurāsān, Sijistān, and Kirmān was al-Ḥajjāj b. Yūsuf; his deputy in Khurāsān was al-Muhallab, and in Sijistān ʿUbaydallāh b. Abī Bakrah. Shurayḥ was in charge of the judiciary in al-Kūfah, and it is reported that Mūsā b. Anas was in charge of the judiciary in al-Baṣrah.[654] In this year ʿAbd al-Malik sent out Yaḥyā b. al-Ḥakam on campaign.[655]

---

654. Son of Anas b. Mālik; see Ibn Saʿd, *Ṭabaqāt*, VII, i, 140.

655. Against the Byzantines. Ibn Khayyāṭ, *Taʾrīkh*, 275–78, dates a campaign by Yaḥyā against Marj al-Shaḥm to the following year, 79, as well as a campaign by al-Walīd "from the direction of Malaṭyah," and, for 78, reports rather a campaign by Muḥriz b. Abī Muḥriz, who conquered Azqalah (? Ibn Kathīr, *Bidāyah*, IX,21, reads Irqīliyyah), but whose army was devastated by a storm on its way back. The plague that prevented campaigning in 79, according to Ṭabarī, however, is dated by Ibn Khayyāṭ to 80. See also note 639 above.

The Events of the Year 79

(March 20, 698–March 8, 699)

The Important Events of This Year

In this year the people of Syria were visited by a plague so severe
[1036] that they were all but annihilated. No one launched any campaigns in this year, it is reported, because of the plague there and the large number of deaths.[656]

In this year, it is reported, the Byzantines attacked the people of Antioch.[657]

656. The same information in Elias of Nisibis, *Opus chronologicum* (Baethgen), year 79. Theophanes, *Chronographia,* A. M. 6192, mentions a great plague, without specifying its location, in the same year in which al-Ḥajjāj defeated Ibn al-Ash'ath (dated 82 or 83 [701–702] by Ṭabarī, text below, II, 1070); Michael the Syrian, *Chronique* (Paris, 1899–1910), II, 474f., dates the beginning of a great seven-year plague to the year 75 (694–695). This plague is not included in what became the (rather Iraqi-oriented) standard list; see M. Dols, "Plague in Early Islamic History," *Journal of the American Oriental Society* 94 (1974), 378.

657. Theophanes, *Chronographia,* A. M. 6192, records a major Byzantine raid on Syria, as far as Samosata (not Antioch), for the year of the "great plague" (see previous note). See also 'Uthmān, *al-Ḥudūd al-islāmiyyah al-bīzanṭiyyah,* II, 74.

In this year, ʿUbaydallāh b. Abī Bakrah campaigned against Zunbīl.[658]

The Campaign by ʿUbaydallāh b. Abī Bakrah in Sijistān

According to Hishām—Abū Mikhnaf—Abū al-Mukhāriq al-Rāsibī: When al-Ḥajjāj appointed al-Muhallab to Khurāsān and ʿUbaydallāh b. Abī Bakrah to Sijistān, al-Muhallab went out to Khurāsān and ʿUbaydallāh b. Abī Bakrah to Sijistān; this was in the year 78 (697–698). ʿUbaydallāh b. Abī Bakrah remained inactive the rest of this year, then attacked Zunbīl.[659] Zunbīl had been under a truce, with the Arabs collecting land taxes from him; but he had several times held back and refused to pay.[660] Al-Ḥajjāj then wrote to ʿUbaydallāh b. Abī Bakrah saying, "Take the field against him with the Muslims you have with you and do not return until you have plundered his land, razed his fortresses, killed his fighting men, and taken his women captive." ʿUbaydallāh set out with the Muslims he had with him, Kūfans and Baṣrans. In command of the Kūfans was Shurayḥ b. Hāniʾ al-Ḥārithī al-Ḍabābī,[661] who had been a companion of ʿAlī; in command of the Baṣrans was ʿUbaydallāh, who also commanded the entire army. He advanced and penetrated into the lands of Zunbīl, seizing cattle, sheep, and other property as he wished, and razing fortresses and castles. He conquered a great deal of their territory, [1037] as Zunbīl's Turkish[662] forces fell back from one land after an-

658. For a full analysis of this episode, with a review of the sources, see Bosworth, "ʿUbaidallāh b. Abī Bakra and the 'Army of Destruction' in Zābulistān (79/698)." For the reading Zunbīl, emended from text Rutbīl (and representing a local title, not a personal name), see Bosworth, *Sīstān under the Arabs,* 34–36.

659. Ṭabarī here resumes the account interrupted above, II, 1033.

660. According to Balādhurī and Ibn Aʿtham al-Kūfī, Umayyah b. ʿAbdallāh (or his son ʿAbdallāh) had exempted Zunbīl from tribute for the duration of his governorship, as part of a disgraceful treaty that led to his replacement; see note 652 above.

661. Of Madhḥij; see Caskel, *Ǧamharat an-nasab,* I, 261, II, 533. For his long and eventful career, and his fervent support of ʿAlī, see text above, I, 3259–62, 3354–60, II, 134–37, and Bosworth, "ʿUbaidallāh b. Abī Bakra," 275. According to Ibn Aʿtham al-Kūfī, *Futūḥ,* VII, 113, he was at this time nearly a hundred years old.

662. On the vagueness of this term in early sources, see Bosworth, "ʿUbaidallāh b. Abī Bakra," 271.

other, until they were in the heart of their territory and drew near their city.[663] But when they were within eighteen *farsakh*s of the city, Zunbīl's forces occupied the passes and defiles against the Muslims, leaving them in the country districts.[664]

The Muslims were in a predicament and feared they were doomed. Ibn Abī Bakrah sent to Shurayḥ b. Hāni', saying, "I am going to offer the enemy a truce, giving them money in exchange for safe passage out of here"; he then sent them this message, offering them 700,000 dirhams for a truce.[665] But Shurayḥ came to him and said, "Any amount you pay out for a truce will be credited by the government against your stipends." Ibn Abī Bakrah replied, "Even if the government should withhold our stipends for the rest of our lives, that would not be as bad as perishing!" But Shurayḥ said, "By God, I have reached an age where my pleasures are at an end, and there is not an hour, day or night, that I do not expect to die before it elapses. I have been seeking martyrdom for a long time, and if I miss it today, I do not think I will find it before dying a natural death." Then he said to the men, "People of Islam! Help one another against your enemy!" Ibn Abī Bakrah said to him, "You are an old man and have gone senile." Shurayḥ retorted, "Your only claim to nobility is that people say 'the Orchard of Ibn Abī Bakrah' and 'the Bath of Ibn Abī Bakrah!'[666] People of Islam! Those of you who wish for martyrdom, come to me!" A few of the volunteers followed him, and some of the horsemen in the army and some of the more dedicated. They fought until all but a few were cut down.[667]

---

663. The summer capital, in Zābulistān (probably in the Ghaznah region), according to Bosworth, *ibid.*, 276.

664. *Wa-khallawhum wa-al-rasātīq*; see note 213 above.

665. According to Balādhurī, *Ansāb*, XI, 312, the terms were either 500,000 or 700,000 dirhams, plus a number of hostages, including Ibn Abī Bakrah's three sons, and a pledge not to raid Zunbīl's territory while Ibn Abī Bakrah remained governor; Ibn A'tham al-Kūfī, *Futūḥ*, VII, 112, has one million dirhams, half the invaders' arms, and ten years' exemption from *kharāj*, as well as the hostages.

666. 'Ubaydallāh b. Abī Bakrah, whose origins were extremely lowly (see note 644 above), had built a bath in al-Baṣrah after his brother Muslim had reaped great profit from his bath and a third brother, 'Abd al-Raḥmān, had followed suit; see Balādhurī, *Futūḥ*, 353–54, and Morony, *Iraq after the Muslim Conquest*, 270. Ibn A'tham al-Kūfī, *Futūḥ*, VII, 113, also has Shurayḥ refer to 'Ubaydallāh's bath and orchard (*bustān*) in al-Baṣrah.

667. Balādhurī, *Ansāb*, XI, 313, states that Shurayḥ had previously attempted to

On that day Shurayḥ recited the following *rajaz* verses:[668]

I have become a man of sorrow, suffering from old age. [1038]
Long did I live among the polytheists;
Then I lived to see the Prophet, the Warner,
and after him his Ṣiddīq and 'Umar;
And the Day of Mihrān,[669] and the Day of Tustar,[670]
and the assemblies at Ṣiffīn and al-Naharā,[671]
And at Bājumayrāt[672] as well as al-Mushaqqar[673]—
Fie! How long this life is!

He fought until he was killed, along with many of his comrades, although some escaped.

They then withdrew from the territory of Zunbīl and were met by Muslims with food. But when one of them ate his fill of the food, he would die. When the people saw that, they were afraid to feed them, but then began to feed them ghee, little by little, until they were able to eat properly.[674] Word of all this came to al-

---

persuade Ibn Abī Bakrah to retreat, having acquired sufficient booty, without attempting to capture towns; but at this juncture Shurayḥ offered an eloquent speech in favor of martyrdom and persuaded some volunteers of Madhḥij and Hamdān to join him; the ensuing casualties included members of the Baṣran and Kūfan contingents, as well as some Syrians. Ibn A'tham al-Kūfī, *Futūḥ*, VII, 113, also refers to Madhḥij and Hamdān but makes the conflict essentially one between Shurayḥ and the Kūfans and Ibn Abī Bakrah and the Baṣrans; ten thousand Kūfans entered the battle and were killed.

668. Also in Balādhurī, *Ansāb*, XI, 313f., and, with variants, Ibn A'tham al-Kūfī, *Futūḥ*, VII, 113f.

669. A victory by the Muslims, under al-Muthannā b. Ḥārithah, over the Persians, under Mihrān b. Mihribandādh al-Hamadhānī, in 13–14 (634–635), a little over a year before the great victory at al-Qādisiyyah; also known as *yawm al-nakhīlah* or the Battle of al-Buwayb. See text above, I, 2184–2201; Balādhurī, *Futūḥ*, 253f.; Donner, *The Early Islamic Conquests*, 197–200.

670. On the siege and conquest of Tustar (modern Shushtar) by the Muslims under Abū Mūsā al-Ash'arī in the year 17 (638), see text above, I, 2551f.; Balādhurī, *Futūḥ*, 380; Donner, *The Early Islamic Conquests*, 215f.

671. On Shurayḥ's participation at the confrontation between 'Alī and Mu'āwiyah at Ṣiffīn in 37 (657), see text above, I, 3354–60. Al-Naharā is for al-Nahrawān, where 'Alī's forces massacred the Khārijites in 38 (658); see text above, I, 3360–89.

672. For Bājumayrā, near Takrīt, where Muṣ'ab b. al-Zubayr encamped before his final defeat by 'Abd al-Malik in 72 (691), see text above, II, 797, 805; Yāqūt, *Mu'jam*, I, 454f.

673. In al-Baḥrayn, site of the defeat of the Khārijite Abū Fudayk by 'Umar b. 'Ubaydallāh b. Ma'mar in 73 (693); see text above, II, 853; Yāqūt, *Mu'jam*, IV, 541f.

674. Balādhurī, *Ansāb*, XI, 314–17, reports that only five thousand men made it

Ḥajjāj, whose dismay at the entire story from start to finish knew no bounds. He wrote as follows to ʿAbd al-Malik:

> The troops of the Commander of the Faithful that are in Sijistān have met disaster, and only a few of them escaped. The enemy has been emboldened by this success against the people of Islam and has entered their lands and conquered all their fortresses and castles. Now I want to send out against them a massive force of men from the two garrisons and would like to consult the opinion of the Commander of the Faithful on that. If it is his opinion that I should dispatch this force, I will do so. If that is not his opinion, the Commander of the Faithful remains the supreme authority over his own
> [1039] forces; but I fear that if Zunbīl and the polytheists with him are not met quickly by a massive force, they will overrun that entire frontier.

In this year, al-Muhallab arrived in Khurāsān as governor, and Umayyah b. ʿAbdallāh quit the province.[675] It is reported that the judge Shurayḥ asked to be relieved of his position in this year and suggested Abū Burdah b. Abī Mūsā al-Ashʿarī as his replacement. Al-Ḥajjāj relieved him and appointed Abū Burdah.[676]

The leader of the pilgrimage in this year was Abān b. ʿUthmān, according to Aḥmad b. Thābit—anonymous—Isḥāq b. ʿĪsā—Abū Maʿshar; the same is reported by al-Wāqidī and other historians.[677] Abān was in this year governor over Medina for ʿAbd al-Malik b. Marwān. Governor over Iraq and the entire East was al-Ḥajjāj b. Yūsuf. Al-Muhallab was governor over Khurāsān for al-Ḥajjāj; according to some, al-Muhallab was the military governor and his son al-Mughīrah the tax governor. In charge of the judiciary in al-Kūfah was Abū Burdah b. Abī Mūsā, and in charge of the judiciary in al-Baṣrah was Mūsā b. Anas.

---

back to Bust and quotes verses by Aʿshā Hamdān attacking Ibn Abī Bakrah for attempting to profit from their misery; see Bosworth, "ʿUbaidallāh b. Abī Bakra," 278–83.

675. Ibn Khayyāṭ, *Ta'rīkh*, 297, and see note 652 above.

676. Ibn Khayyāṭ, *Ta'rīkh*, 298, and see notes 49 and 322 above.

677. *Ahl al-siyar.* The same information in Ibn Khayyāṭ, *Ta'rīkh*, 277, 301; Yaʿqūbī, *Ta'rīkh*, II, 336.

The Events of the Year 80

(March 9, 699–February 25, 700)

The Important Events of This Year

In this year, according to Ibn Sa'd[678]—Muḥammad b. 'Umar al-Wāqidī, there was a flash flood in Mecca that swept away the pilgrims and inundated the buildings. That year was named the [1040] Year of Sweeping Away[679] because that flash flood swept away everything in its path.

According to Muḥammad b. 'Umar—Muḥammad b. Rifā'ah b. Tha'labah—his father—his grandfather: The flash flood came down and swept away the pilgrims in the valley of Mecca; that is why it was called the Year of Sweeping Away. I saw loaded camels, men, and women caught in the flood and unable to resist it. While I was watching the water, it reached the Rukn[680] and rose above it.

---

678. Muḥammad b. Sa'd, d. 230 (845), the author of the *K. al-Ṭabaqāt al-kabīr*; see *EI*², s. v. Ibn Sa'd.

679. *'Ām al-Juḥāf*. A fuller account in Azraqī, *Akhbār Makkah*, 395f. See also Balādhurī, *Futūḥ*, 54; Elias of Nisibis, *Opus chronologicum* (Baethgen), year 80; Ibn Qutaybah, *Ma'ārif*, 357.

680. The "corner," that is, the eastern corner of the Ka'bah, where the Black

In this year the Sweeping Plague struck al-Baṣrah, according to the statement of al-Wāqidī.[681]

In this year al-Muhallab crossed the river of Balkh and attacked Kish.[682]

Al-Muhallab Attacks Kish

According to ʿAlī b. Muḥammad—al-Mufaḍḍal b. Muḥammad and others: When al-Muhallab attacked Kish, his vanguard was under the command of Abū al-Adham Ziyād b. ʿAmr al-Zimmānī, with three thousand, which really counted as five thousand[683] because Abū al-Adham by himself was worth two thousand in valor, leadership, and strategy.

While al-Muhallab was attacking Kish, there came to him the paternal cousin of the king of al-Khuttal,[684] urging him to attack that province. Al-Muhallab sent off with him his son Yazīd. Yazīd camped with his forces and the king's cousin camped apart. The king, whose name was al-Sabal,[685] was at that time encamped at
[1041] some distance. But then al-Sabal surprised his cousin by night, raising the call "God is great!" in his camp. Al-Sabal's cousin thought that the Arabs had betrayed him out of fear lest he betray them after he encamped apart from them. Al-Sabal took him captive and had him brought to his fortress and killed.

Yazīd b. al-Muhallab surrounded al-Sabal's fortress, and the latter's forces made peace with him on the basis of a ransom that they brought him. Yazīd then returned to al-Muhallab. The mother of the one whom al-Sabal killed sent to al-Sabal's mother,

---

Stone is mounted; see *EI²*, s. v. Kaʿba. Balādhurī, *Futūḥ*, 54, and Azraqī, *Akhbār Makkah*, 395, state that the water surrounded the Kaʿbah.

681. *Ṭāʿūn al-Jārif*, usually dated to 69 (688–689), as observed by Ibn Kathīr, *Bidāyah*, IX, 31, quoting Ṭabarī here; see Dols, "Plague in Early Islamic History," 379.

682. Modern Shahrisabz, about fifty miles south of Samarqand; see *EI²*, s. v. Kishsh.

683. *Abū al-Adham . . . fī thalāthat ālāf wa-hum khamsat ālāf illā ann Abā al-Adham kāna yughnī ghanāʾ alfayn . . . .* Ibn al-Athīr, *Kāmil*, IV, 45, understands this as meaning that Abū al-Adham had three thousand men and al-Muhallab himself five thousand.

684. A princedom of the Upper Oxus, east of modern Dushanbe; see *EI²*, s. v. Khuttalān.

685. Possibly a title; see J. Marquart, *Ērānšahr* (Berlin, 1901), 302f.

saying, "What hope have you for al-Sabal's survival after killing his cousin? He has seven brothers whose vengeance al-Sabal has drawn on himself, and you are the mother of only one." Al-Sabal's mother sent back to her saying, "Lions have few offspring, but pigs have many."

Then al-Muhallab sent his son Ḥabīb out to Rabinjan,[686] where he encountered the lord of Bukhārā with forty thousand men. One of the polytheists called out a challenge for single combat, and Ḥabīb's personal retainer[687] Jabalah came forward to engage him. He killed the polytheist, then attacked the rest of them, and killed three of them before he withdrew. The entire army then withdrew, as did the enemy to their territory. When a group of enemy forces halted at a village, Ḥabīb marched against them with four thousand men, fought and defeated them, burned the village, and then returned to his father. This village was subsequently called "the Burned";[688] according to some, it was Ḥabīb's retainer Jabalah who burned it.

Al-Muhallab remained at Kish for two years. It was suggested to him that he advance to al-Sughd[689] and beyond, but he said, "All I ask from fortune in this campaign is the well-being of these troops until they get back to Marw safe and sound."

One day a man from the enemy came out with a challenge to single combat. Huraym b. ʿAdī, the father of Khālid b. Huraym,[690] went out to meet him, wearing a turban wound around his [1042] helmet. He came to a brook, where the polytheist circled about him for some time until Huraym killed and despoiled him. But al-Muhallab reproached him and said, "If you had been cut down, and then I received reinforcements of a thousand horsemen, they would not have offset my loss."

While he was at Kish, al-Muhallab became suspicious of a

686. Or Arbinjan, halfway between Bukhārā and Samarqand. See Le Strange, *Lands*, 468; Yāqūt, *Muʿjam*, I, 189f.; Barthold, *Turkestan*, 99.

687. *Ghulām*; see note 421 above.

688. *Al-Muḥtariqah*, between Kish and Samarqand. According to the text below, II, 1229, the village, formerly known as Faryāb (or Qaryāt), was burned by the forces of Qutaybah b. Muslim in 91 (710). See Barthold, *Turkestan*, 137f.

689. Soghdia, the Zarafshan valley, north of Kish; see Le Strange, *Lands*, 460.

690. According to Ibn al-Kalbī, Huraym b. ʿAdī belonged to the Banū Mujāshiʿ of Tamīm (Caskel, *Ǧamharat an-nasab*, I, 61, II, 287); but the text below (II, 1569) identifies his son Khālid as one of the Banū Thaʿlabah b. Yarbūʿ, also of Tamīm.

group of Muḍarites, and held them confined there; but when he withdrew, after a truce had been arranged, he let them go. Al-Ḥajjāj wrote to him saying, "If you were right to confine them, you were wrong to let them go; and if you were right to let them go, you wronged them by confining them." Al-Muhallab replied, "I feared them, so I confined them. Once I felt secure, I let them go." Among those he confined was ʿAbd al-Malik b. Abī Shaykh al-Qushayrī.[691]

Then al-Muhallab agreed on a truce with the people of Kish on the basis of a ransom. While he was waiting to collect it, he received a letter from Ibn al-Ashʿath informing him of his rebellion against al-Ḥajjāj and summoning him to support him in his rebellion. Al-Muhallab sent Ibn al-Ashʿath's letter on to al-Ḥajjāj.[692]

ʿAbd al-Raḥmān b. al-Ashʿath Campaigns in Sijistān

In this year, al-Ḥajjāj sent out ʿAbd al-Raḥmān b. Muḥammad b. al-Ashʿath to Sijistān to do battle with Zunbīl, the lord of the Turks. There is disagreement among the historians on the reason why al-Ḥajjāj sent him out there and on where ʿAbd al-Raḥmān was when al-Ḥajjāj appointed him to Sijistān and to do battle with Zunbīl.

According to Hishām—Abū Mikhnaf—Yūnus b. Abī Isḥāq: When ʿAbd al-Malik received the letter of al-Ḥajjāj b. Yūsuf informing him of the army that had been with ʿUbaydallāh b. Abī Bakrah in the territory of Zunbīl and their fate there, he wrote to him as follows:

> I have received your letter reporting the blow suffered by
> [1043] the Muslims in Sijistān. These are people whom God had

---

691. Probably of the Banū Qushayr b. Kaʿb, a clan of ʿĀmir b. Ṣaʿṣaʿah (of Qays ʿAylān of Muḍar); see Caskel, *Ǧamharat an-nasab*, I, 105. Al-Muhallab presumably feared a return of the Muḍarite leader ʿAbdallāh b. Khāzim. On conflict between Azd and Qays under al-Muhallab, see also *Aghānī*[1], XIII, 56f.; Dixon, *Umayyad Caliphate*, 112.

692. Reported also by Balādhurī, *Ansāb*, XI, 329, 335–36, where al-Muhallab expresses his indignation at this proposal from someone younger than some of his sons. Ṭabarī (text below, II, 1058f.) and Ibn Aʿtham al-Kūfī, (*Futūḥ*, VII, 118f.) give two versions of al-Muhallab's reply to Ibn al-Ashʿath, attempting to dissuade him from his rebellion.

decreed would be killed; they came out to where they were to lie, and their reward is with God.[693] As for your request for my opinion—whether to lead out the troops and direct them to that frontier where the Muslims suffered this blow or to keep them there—my opinion in this matter is that you should carry on according to your own opinion, proceeding rightly; and I wish you all success.

There was no one in all of Iraq whom al-Ḥajjāj hated more than ʿAbd al-Raḥmān b. Muḥammad b. al-Ashʿath; he used to say, "I never see him without wanting to kill him!"

According to Abū Mikhnaf—Numayr b. Waʿlah al-Hamdānī al-Yanāʿī[694]—al Shaʿbī:[695] I was sitting with al-Ḥajjāj when ʿAbd al-Raḥmān b. Muḥammad b. al-Ashʿath was admitted. When al-Ḥajjāj saw him, he said, "Look at the way he walks! By God, I would like to cut off his head!" When ʿAbd al-Raḥmān withdrew, I also withdrew, and got ahead of him and awaited him at the door of Saʿīd b. Qays al-Sabīʿī.[696] When he came up, I said, "Let us go in the door here. I want to speak to you about something, but I adjure you by God never to mention it so long as al-Ḥajjāj is alive." He agreed, and I told him what al-Ḥajjāj had said about him. He said, "May I fare as al-Ḥajjāj said if I do not expend every effort to strip him of his power! We have coexisted for too long!"[697]

Then al-Ḥajjāj set to fitting out twenty thousand Kūfans and twenty thousand Baṣrans, devoting himself to this task with great zeal. He paid the men their stipends in full, ordering them to equip themselves with excellent horses and full arms. Then he began to [1044] review the troops, and whenever he saw a man who had been cited

693. A paraphrase of Qur'ān 3:154, revealed after the defeat at Uḥud.

694. On the Yanāʿ b. Dawmān of Hamdān, see Caskel, *Ǧamharat an-nasab*, I, 230, II, 590.

695. Abū ʿAmr ʿĀmir b. Sharāḥīl al-Shaʿbī, d. 103 (721), the famous traditionist; see Sezgin, *GAS*, I, 277.

696. Of the Banū al-Sabīʿ b. Sabʿ of Hamdān, an important clan in al-Kūfah; see Caskel, *Ǧamharat an-nasab*, II, 492.

697. Variants of this account in Balādhurī, *Ansāb*, XI, 318f., and Dīnawarī, *al-Akhbār al-ṭiwāl*, 322. Ibn Aʿtham al-Kūfī, *Futūḥ*, VII, 108–10, records from al-Shaʿbī Ibn al-Ashʿath's earlier rejection of an offer to head al-Ḥajjāj's *shurṭah*, as well as other illustrations of his arrogance. On the former amity between the two men and the marriage of al-Ḥajjāj's son to ʿAbd al-Raḥmān's sister, see Périer, *Vie d'al-Ḥadjdjādj*, 159f.; *EI²*, s. v. Ibn al-Ashʿath.

for bravery, he gave him a generous bonus.[698] ʿUbaydallāh b. Abī Miḥjan al-Thaqafī came upon ʿAbbād b. al-Ḥuṣayn al-Ḥabiṭī,[699] who was with al-Ḥajjāj, as he was going to meet ʿAbd al-Raḥmān b. Umm al-Ḥakam al-Thaqafī,[700] who was reviewing the troops. ʿAbbād said, "I have never seen a finer or more beautiful horse than this. A horse provides both strength and a weapon.[701] This is also a powerful mule." Al-Ḥajjāj thereupon gave ʿUbaydallāh a bonus of 550 dirhams. Then ʿAṭiyyah al-ʿAnbarī[702] came upon him, and al-Ḥajjāj said, "ʿAbd al-Raḥmān, be generous to this one."

When al-Ḥajjāj had these two forces in good order, he sent out ʿUṭārid b. ʿUmayr al-Tamīmī, who encamped at al-Ahwāz. Then he sent out ʿUbaydallāh b. Ḥujr b. Dhī al-Jawshan al-ʿĀmirī of the Banū Kilāb,[703] but then changed his mind and sent out to command them ʿAbd al-Raḥmān b. Muḥammad b. al-Ashʿath, dismissing ʿUbaydallāh b. Ḥujr. ʿAbd al-Raḥmān's paternal uncle, Ismāʿīl b. al-Ashʿath, came to al-Ḥajjāj and said, "Do not send him out! I fear that he may disobey your orders. By God, he has never crossed the Euphrates bridge and continued to recognize the authority or claim to obedience of any governor." Al-Ḥajjāj replied, "Not in this case. He both fears and respects me too much to disobey my orders or throw off his obedience to me." He then sent him out in command of that army, and he led them forth and came to Sijistān in the year 80 (699–700).[704] Upon arrival, he assembled the men already there.

---

698. *Aḥsana maʿūnatahu.*

699. A descendant of al-Ḥārith b. ʿAmr b. Tamīm, known as al-Ḥabiṭ, and formerly a commander for Muṣʿab b. al-Zubayr in al-Baṣrah. See text above, II, 720ff; Caskel, *Ǧamharat an-nasab,* II, 102; Ziriklī, *Aʿlām,* IV, 28. According to Balādhurī, *Futūḥ,* 368f., the city of ʿAbbādān was named for this ʿAbbād.

700. Governor of al-Kūfah under Muʿāwiyah in 58 (678); see text above, II, 181. Umm al-Ḥakam was Muʿāwiyah's sister.

701. *Wa-inn al-faras quwwah wa-silāḥ.*

702. ʿAṭiyyah b. ʿAmr of al-ʿAnbar b. ʿAmr b. Tamīm; see Caskel, *Ǧamharat an-nasab,* I, 81, II, 205.

703. On Dhū al-Jawshan Shuraḥbīl b. al-Aʿwar b. ʿAmr b. Muʿāwiyah al-Ḍibāb b. Kilāb b. Rabīʿah b. ʿĀmir b. Ṣaʿṣaʿah, see Caskel, *Ǧamharat an-nasab,* I, 98, II, 532.

704. Balādhurī, *Ansāb,* XI, 319f., has either twelve thousand or ten thousand men from al-Kūfah, put initially under the command of either ʿUṭārid or a descendant of Dhū al-Jawshan; these marched to al-Baṣrah, where a like number of men were chosen and commanded by ʿAṭiyyah. Balādhurī agrees with Ṭabarī on the transferral to ʿAbd al-Raḥmān, despite the warning by the latter's uncle, but dates this to the end of 79 (699). The account in Ibn Aʿtham al-Kūfī, *Futūḥ,* VII, 114ff.,

According to Abū Mikhnaf—Abū al-Zubayr al-Arḥabī, a man of Hamdān who was with ʿAbd al-Raḥmān: He ascended the pulpit, praised and glorified God, and said:

> Men, the amīr al-Ḥajjāj has appointed me to your frontier district and charged me with jihād against your enemy, who [1045] has plundered your land and destroyed your property. Let no man of you shirk his duty and bring punishment down on himself. Go out to your camp and muster there with the troops.

The men all mustered in their camp. Markets were set up for them, and the men began to ready themselves and prepare their equipment for battle. When word of this reached Zunbīl, he wrote to ʿAbd al-Raḥmān b. Muḥammad, apologizing to him for the blow inflicted on the Muslims and informing him that he had acted only reluctantly and that they had forced him to fight them; and he asked for peace if ʿAbd al-Raḥmān would accept payment of the land tax from him. ʿAbd al-Raḥmān neither accepted nor replied but immediately set out against him with his forces and came to the borders of his territory.[705] Zunbīl began to call in his forces, leaving the land to ʿAbd al-Raḥmān, district by district and fortress by fortress. Ibn al-Ashʿath, as he took control of an area, would send out a tax official over it, accompanied by armed attendants.[706] He also set up a post between the various areas, positioned lookouts in the passes and ravines, and stationed advance parties[707] in every potentially dangerous spot. Then, when he had taken possession of a large part of Zunbīl's territory and filled his hands with cattle, sheep, and great amounts of plunder, he held the men back from further penetration into Zunbīl's lands, saying, "We will content ourselves with the territory we have conquered from them this year until we can collect the taxes and get to know it and the Muslims may boldly travel its roads. Next year we will advance farther, and so we will continue year by year to [1046]

---

which parallels Ṭabarī's second version below, has Ibn al-Ashʿath's four half-brothers warning al-Ḥajjāj against him.

705. Ibn Aʿtham al-Kūfī, *Futūḥ*, VII, 116, records a threatening letter sent by Ibn al-Ashʿath to Zunbīl, and the latter's conciliatory reply.

706. *Aʿwān.*

707. *Masāliḥ.*

deprive them of more pieces of their territory, until, in the end, we will fight them for their treasures and their women, in their most remote districts and in their most impregnable fortresses; and we will not leave their land until God destroys them." Then he wrote to al-Ḥajjāj, informing him of the conquests God had given him in the land of the enemy and His gracious favor to the Muslims, and explaining the strategy he was pursuing.[708]

The other account, beside that of Yūnus b. Abī Isḥāq and the others that I have given in the matter of Ibn al-Ash'ath, explains his appointment to Sijistān and his march against the territory of Zunbīl differently from what is reported on the authority of Abū Mikhnaf. According to this account, the reason for that was as follows: Al-Ḥajjāj sent out Himyān b. 'Adī al-Sadūsī[709] to Kirmān with an advance party to provide reinforcements to the administrator over Sijistān and Sind if such reinforcements were needed. But Himyān and his comrades rebelled, and al-Ḥajjāj sent out Ibn al-Ash'ath to fight him, and he defeated him and took his place. Then 'Ubaydallāh b. Abī Bakrah, who was the administrator over Sijistān, died, and al-Ḥajjāj wrote out a letter of appointment for Ibn al-Ash'ath to administer it. Al-Ḥajjāj also mustered an army, on which he expended two million dirhams, in addition to the stipends. It was called the Peacock Army, and al-Ḥajjāj ordered Ibn al-Ash'ath to march out with it against Zunbīl.[710]

The leader of the pilgrimage in this year was Abān b. 'Uthmān, according to Aḥmad b. Thābit—anonymous—Isḥāq b. 'Īsā—Abū
[1047] Ma'shar, and also according to Muḥammad b. 'Umar al-Wāqidī.

---

708. Balādhurī, *Ansāb*, XI, 321–23, reports that Ibn al-Ash'ath was based in Bust and posted his brother in al-Rukhkhaj; according to his account, Zunbīl was advised by a renegade Tamīmī Khārijite named 'Ubayd b. Suba'. The summary account in Ya'qūbī, *Ta'rīkh*, II, 331, which gives Ibn al-Ash'ath ten thousand picked troops, also places Ibn al-Ash'ath in Bust, from which he led a preliminary campaign which frightened him enough to put off further campaigning for a year; his letter to al-Ḥajjāj explaining this was answered with threats, which led him to revolt.

709. Formerly head of the *shurṭah* in al-Baṣrah; see text above, II, 445–47, 464.

710. The term "Peacock Army" is also mentioned by Balādhurī, *Ansāb*, XI, 319ff., and many other sources. Balādhurī has versions of both of Ṭabarī's accounts, as well as a third stating that Ibn al-Ash'ath was fighting the Khārijites when appointed by al-Ḥajjāj. Ibn A'tham al-Kūfī, *Futūḥ*, VII, 115f., has Ibn al-Ash'ath defeat Himyān on his way to Sijistān, after his appointment there. See Dixon, *Umayyad Caliphate*, 152ff.; Bosworth, *Sīstān under the Arabs*, 58ff.

According to others, the leader of the pilgrimage in this year was Sulaymān b. ʿAbd al-Malik.[711] The governor of Medina in this year was Abān b. ʿUthmān. The governor of Iraq and the entire East was al-Ḥajjāj b. Yūsuf. The governor of Khurāsān under al-Ḥajjāj was al-Muhallab b. Abī Ṣufrah. Abū Burdah b. Abī Mūsā was in charge of the judiciary in al-Kūfah, and Mūsā b. Anas was in charge of the judiciary in al-Baṣrah. In this year ʿAbd al-Malik sent out his son al-Walīd on campiagn.

---

711. Ibn Khayyāṭ, *Ta'rīkh*, 278, 301, and Yaʿqūbī, *Ta'rīkh*, II, 336, agree that Abān led the pilgrimage.

The Events of the Year 81
(February 26, 700–February 14, 701)

The Events of This Year

In this year occurred the conquest of Qālīqalā.

According to ʿUmar b. Shabbah—ʿAlī b. Muḥammad: ʿAbd al-Malik sent out his son ʿUbaydallāh b. ʿAbd al-Malik in the year 81, and he conquered Qālīqalā.[712]

In this year, Baḥīr b. Warqāʾ al-Ṣuraymī was killed in Khurāsān.

Account of Baḥīr b. Warqāʾ's Death in Khurāsān

The circumstances of his being killed: It was Baḥīr who undertook to kill Bukayr b. Wishāḥ when Umayyah b. ʿAbdallāh ordered him to do so.[713] Then ʿUthmān b. Rajāʾ b. Jābir b. Shaddād, one of the Banū ʿAwf b. Saʿd, of the Abnāʾ, incited a man from the Abnāʾ, one of Bukayr's clan, to vengeance with these verses:[714]

---

712. Modern Erzurum; see Le Strange, *Lands*, 116f., and *EI*², s. v. Erzurum.

713. See text above, II, 1022–31.

714. On the Abnāʾ and the Banū ʿAwf b. Saʿd (possibly to be understood as ʿAwf b. Kaʿb b. Saʿd), see text above, II, 860, and note 38.

By my life! How patiently you bear this mote in your eye! [1048]
You sleep well at night with a bellyful of the best wine.
You have left a killing unavenged, preferring gentle sleep;
but he who drinks the ruby liquor is in debt for a slaying![715]
If you were a true noble of the ʿAwf b. Saʿd,
you would have left Baḥīr in a pool of blood.
Tell Baḥīr: Sleep well and fear no avenger from ʿAwf!
for ʿAwf are simple herders of little lambs.
Forget the mutton for one day! You are all in debt for a slaying!
And you have become a subject for wagging tongues east and west.
Rouse yourselves! If Bukayr were here tonight, as he used to be,
well and healthy, he would meet them tomorrow in a dusky detachment.[716]

He also said:

If Bakr had gone out in his armor, to challenge him,
by the Lord of the Throne, Baḥīr would not have come out to fight him.
I seek something of Time, if Time should let me live,
as one fully qualified, before God, for such a quest.

Baḥīr heard that the Abnāʾ were threatening him, and said:

The Abnāʾ threaten me in ignorance, as if
they see my halls empty of the Banū Kaʿb!
I raise against them my hand with a sharpened blade, [1049]
a sword the color of salt, keen and glittering.

According to ʿAlī b. Muḥammad—al-Mufaḍḍal b. Muḥammad: Seventeen men of the Banū ʿAwf b. Kaʿb b. Saʿd made a compact to take blood vengeance for Bukayr. One of them, a young man named al-Shamardal, came out of the desert to Khurāsān, found Baḥīr standing, and assaulted and stabbed him. Baḥīr fell to the ground, and he thought that he had killed him. The men cried

715. *Wa-man shariba l-ṣahbāʾa bi-l-witri yusbaqī.*
716. *La-ghādāhum bi-jaʾwāʾa faylaqī.* The usual phrase is *katībah jaʾwāʾ*; see Zamakhsharī, *Asās*, s. v. jaʾwāʾ.

out, "A Khārijite!" Al-Shamardal raced to get away from them, but his horse stumbled and threw him, and he was killed.

Then Ṣaʿṣaʿah b. Ḥarb al-ʿAwfī, one of the Banū Jundab,[717] came out of the desert, having sold some of his booty and bought an ass. He went to Sijistān and took up residence near some of Baḥīr's relatives there. He befriended them and told them he was a man from the Banū Ḥanīfah, from the people of al-Yamāmah.[718] He continued to come and sit with them often until they became friends with him; then he said to them. "I have a legacy in Khurāsān that I have been cheated out of. I hear that Baḥīr is a very powerful man in Khurāsān. Please write to him on my behalf and ask him to help me obtain my rights." They wrote to him, and Ṣaʿṣaʿah set out, arriving at Marw while al-Muhallab was on campaign.

He met some people from the Banū ʿAwf and told them what he was about. A client of Bukayr's, an armorer, came up and kissed his head. Ṣaʿṣaʿah said to him, "Make me a dagger." He made him a dagger, heating it and plunging it into ass's milk repeatedly. Then Ṣaʿṣaʿah set out from Marw, crossed the river, and came to al-Muhallab's camp, which was at that time at Akharūn.[719] He met Baḥīr, gave him the letter, and said, "I am a man from the
[1050] Banū Ḥanīfah. I was a companion of Ibn Abī Bakrah. I lost my money in Sijistān, but I have a legacy in Marw. I have come to sell it and then return to al-Yamāmah."

Baḥīr ordered him given expense money, had him stay with him, and told him to ask him for whatever he wished. Ṣaʿṣaʿah replied, "I will stay with you until the troops withdraw." He stayed a month or so, accompanying him to al-Muhallab's public and private audiences until he became known.

Baḥīr was afraid of attempts on his life and trusted no one. But when Ṣaʿṣaʿah turned up with a letter from his relatives, he said, "This is a man from Bakr b. Wā'il," and trusted him. Ṣaʿṣaʿah came one day when Baḥīr was sitting in al-Muhallab's private

---

717. Neither Ibn al-Kalbī (*apud* Caskel) nor Ibn Ḥazm mentions a Jundab of the ʿAwf b. Kaʿb b. Saʿd.

718. The Ḥanīfah b. Lujaym of the oases of al-Yamāmah in central Arabia were a tribe of Bakr b. Wā'il; see *EI²*, s. v. Ḥanīfa b. Ludjaym.

719. Or Kharūn, a district north of the Oxus, near modern Dushanbe; see Barthold, *Turkestan*, 76; *Ḥudūd al-ʿĀlam* (trans. Minorsky), 337, 353.

audience, wearing a shirt, a robe, and sandals.[720] He sat down behind him, then drew up close to him and leaned over him as if he were going to say something to him, and stabbed him in the flank with his dagger, burying it deep inside him. The people cried out, "A Khārijite!" He cried, "O slayers of Bukayr! I have taken vengeance for Bukayr!" He was seized by Abū al-ʿAjfāʾ b. Abī al-Kharqāʾ, who was then head of al-Muhallab's security force, and brought to al-Muhallab. Al-Muhallab said, "Woe to you! You have not achieved your vengeance, and have killed yourself, while Baḥīr does well!" Ṣaʿṣaʿah said, "I stabbed him with a thrust that, if divided up among the army, would have killed them all! I also felt the wind from his belly on my hand." Al-Muhallab imprisoned him; some of the Abnāʾ came to the prison to visit him and kissed his head.

Baḥīr died the next day around midday. Ṣaʿṣaʿah was told of his death and said, "Do with me now as you like and however seems best to you. Have not the vows of the women of the Banū ʿAwf been fulfilled, and have I not achieved my vengeance? I am indifferent to my fate. By God, he gave me more than one chance to do the deed while he was alone, but I was unwilling to kill him in private." Al-Muhallab said, "Never have I seen a man more generously willing to give up his life while in bonds than this one!" [1051]
Then he ordered Abū Suwayqah, a paternal cousin of Baḥīr's, to kill him. Anas b. Ṭalq said, "Woe to you! Baḥīr has already been killed; do not kill this one as well!" But Abū Suwayqah refused to heed him, and killed Ṣaʿṣaʿah. Anas reviled him.

According to others, al-Muhallab sent Ṣaʿṣaʿah to Baḥīr before the latter died. Anas b. Ṭalq al-ʿAbshamī said to him, "Baḥīr, you killed Bukayr; now let this one live." But Baḥīr said, "Bring him nearer me! No, by God, I will not die while you still live!" They brought him nearer him, and he put his head between his legs and said, "Kill ʿIfāq in cold blood—he is an abiding evil!"[721] Ibn Ṭalq

---

720. *Qamīṣ wa-ridāʾ wa-naʿlān.* See Dozy, *Dictionnaire détaillé des noms des vêtements chez les Arabes,* 59n., 371–75, 421–24.

721. *Iṣbir ʿIfāq innahu sharr bāqin.* This line, which must have been proverbial, occurs in a variant form in an anecdote recorded by Ibn Abī al-Ḥadīd, *Sharḥ Nahj al-balāghah,* IV, 85, according to which a man known for his eloquence in rhymed prose was asked by the Shīʿites of al-Kūfah to silence the militantly anti-Shīʿite ʿIfāq b. Shuraḥbīl al-Taymī (so read for text al-Tamīmī; see Caskel, *Ǧamharat an-*

said to Baḥīr, "God curse you! I speak to you on his behalf, and you kill him right in front of me!" Baḥīr stabbed him with his sword until he was dead; then Baḥīr himself died. Al-Muhallab said, " 'We are God's, and to God we return'—so I say of a campaign in which Baḥīr has been cut down."[722]

ʿAwf b. Kaʿb and the Abnā' were angry and said, "Why was our comrade killed, when he was only seeking his vengeance?" They were opposed by Muqāʿis and the Buṭūn, until people feared the situation would get out of hand. But the more temperate men said,[723] "Take responsibility for the blood of Ṣaʿṣaʿah and accept the blood of Baḥīr as retribution for Bukayr." So they paid the bloodwit[724] for Ṣaʿṣaʿah.

One of the men of the Abnā' praised Ṣaʿṣaʿah with these verses:

God be praised for a young man whose ambition
    went beyond Iraq, across deserts and seas;
He kept pressing and driving himself
    until he caught up with Baḥīr at Kharūn.

ʿAbd Rabbih al-Kabīr Abū Wakīʿ, who was one of Ṣaʿṣaʿah's kin, went out into the desert and told Bukayr's kin, "Ṣaʿṣaʿah has been killed seeking vengeance for the death of your comrade. Pay his bloodwit!" Thus he received two bloodwits for Ṣaʿṣaʿah.[725]

---

nasab, I, 150, II, 353); he said to ʿIfāq, "O God, kill ʿIfāq! He is a hypocrite within and a troublemaker without, an unabashed schismatic with an unstable character!" (*Allāhumma qtul ʿIfāq fa-innahu asarra nifāqā, wa-aẓhara shiqāqā, wa-bayyana firāqā, wa-talawwana akhlaqā*).

722. The quotation is from Qur'ān 2:156, where it is introduced by the phrase "Those who say, when afflicted by a disaster . . ."

723. To Muqāʿis and the Buṭūn.

724. Reading *waddaw* for text *waddū*.

725. A garbled version of this in Ibn Ḥabīb, *Asmā' al-mughtālīn*, 176f.; see also Ibn Kathīr, *Bidāyah*, IX, 34f.

Bibliography of Cited Works

ʿAbbās, I. *Shiʿr al-Khawārij.* Beirut, 1963.

Aghānī[1]*:* Abū al-Faraj al-Iṣfahānī. *K. al-Aghānī.* 20 vols. Būlāq, 1285 [1868].

Ahlwardt, W. *The Divans of the Six Ancient Arabic Poets.* London, 1870.

al-ʿAlī, Ṣ. "Istīṭān al-ʿarab fī Khurāsān." *Majallat Kulliyyat al-ādāb—Baghdād,* 1958, 36–83.

———. "Al-Madā'in and Its Surrounding Area in Arabic Literary Sources." *Mesopotamia* 3–4 (1968–69):417–39.

———. "Minṭaqat al-Kūfah." *Sumer* 21 (1965):229–53.

———. *al-Tanẓīmāt al-ijtimāʿiyyah wa-al-iqtiṣādiyyah fī al-Baṣrah fī al-qarn al-awwal al-hijrī.* Baghdad, 1953.

al-Aʿshā, Maymūn b. Qays. *The Diwan of al-Aʿṣhā.* Edited by R. Geyer. E. J. W. Gibb Memorial Series, N. S., VI. London, 1928.

al-Ashʿarī, Abū al-Ḥasan ʿAlī b. Ismāʿīl. *Maqālāt al-islāmiyyīn wa-ikhtilāf al-muṣallīn.* Edited by H. Ritter. 2nd edition. Wiesbaden, 1963.

al-Aṣmaʿī, Abū Saʿīd ʿAbd al-Malik b. Qurayb. *al-Aṣmaʿiyyāt.* Edited by A. M. Shākir and A. S. Hārūn. Cairo, 1964.

al-Azraqī, Abū al-Walīd Muḥammad b. ʿAbdallāh. *Akhbār Makkah.* Edited by F. Wüstenfeld. Leipzig, 1858.

al-Baghdādī, ʿAbd al-Qāhir b. Ṭāhir. *al-Farq bayn al-firaq.* Edited by M. Badr. Cairo, 1910.

al-Balādhurī, Abū al-Ḥasan Aḥmad b. Yaḥyā. *Ansāb al-ashrāf.* Vol. IVA edited by M. Schloessinger and M. J. Kister, Jerusalem, 1971; vol. IVB edited by M. Schloessinger, Jerusalem, 1938; vol. V edited by D. F.

Goitein, Jerusalem, 1938; vol. XI edited by W. Ahlwardt, *Anonyme arabische Chronik*, Greifswold, 1883.
———. *Futūḥ al-buldān*. Edited by M. J. de Goeje. Leiden, 1866.
Barthold, W. *Turkestan Down to the Mongol Invasion*. London, 1928.
Bates, M. "History, Geography and Numismatics in the First Century of Islamic Coinage." *Schweizerische Numismatische Rundschau* 65 (1986):231–63.
Bosworth, C. E. *Sīstān under the Arabs*. Rome, 1968.
———. "'Ubaidallāh b. Abī Bakra and the 'Army of Destruction' in Zābulistān (79/698)." *Der Islam* 50 (1973):268–83.
Brünnow, R. *Die Charidschiten unter den ersten Omayyaden*. Leiden, 1884.
Caskel, W. *Ǧamharat an-nasab: Das genealogische Werk des Hišām ibn Muḥammad al-Kalbī*. 2 vols. Leiden, 1966.
———. "al-Ukhaiḍir." *Der Islam* 39 (1964):28–37.
Creswell, K. A. C. *Early Muslim Architecture*. Oxford, 1969.
al-Dīnawarī, Abū Ḥanīfah Aḥmad b. Dā'ūd. *al-Akhbār al-ṭiwāl*. 2 vols. Edited by W. Guirgass and I. Kratchkovsky. Leiden, 1888–1912.
Dixon, A. A. *The Umayyad Caliphate 65–86/684–705*. London, 1971.
Dols, M. "Plague in Early Islamic History." *Journal of the American Oriental Society* 94 (1974):371–83.
Donner, F. M. *The Early Islamic Conquests*. Princeton, 1981.
Dozy, R. *Dictionnaire détaillé des noms des vêtements chez les Arabes*. Amsterdam, 1845.
———. *Supplément aux dictionnaires arabes*. 2 vols. Leiden, 1881.
EI¹: Encyclopaedia of Islam. 1st edition. Leiden, 1913–38.
EI²: Encyclopaedia of Islam. 2nd edition. Leiden, 1960–.
EI² Suppl.: Encyclopaedia of Islam, 2nd edition, *Supplement*. Leiden, 1982–.
Elias of Nisibis. *Opus chronologicum*. Edited by F. Baethgen, *Fragmente syrischer und arabischer Historiker*. Abhandlungen für die Kunde des Morgenlandes, VIII.3. Leipzig, 1884.
Fahmī, A. *Fajr al-sikkah al-ʿarabiyyah*. Cairo, 1965.
Fiey, J. M. *Assyrie chrétienne*. 3 vols. Beirut, 1965–68.
———. "The Topography of al-Madā'in." *Sumer* 23 (1967):3–38.
Forand, P. G. "Notes on *ʿUshr* and *Maks*." *Arabica* 8 (1961):137–41.
Freytag, G. W. *Lexicon Arabico-Latinum*. Halle, 1830–37.
Fries, N. *Das Heereswesen der Araber zur Zeit der Omaijaden nach Ṭabarī*. Tübingen, 1921.
GAL: C. Brockelmann. *Geschichte der arabischen Litteratur*. 2nd edition. 2 vols. Leiden, 1945–49.
Gardīzī, Abū Saʿīd ʿAbd al-Ḥayy b. al-Ḍaḥḥāk. *Zayn al-akhbār*. Tehran, 1374 solar.

Gaube, H. "Numismatik," in *Grundriss der arabischen Philologie,* I, Wiesbaden, 1982, 226–50.

Goldziher, I. *Muhammedanische Studien.* 2 vols. Halle, 1888–90.

Grierson, P. "The Monetary Reform of 'Abd al-Malik." *Journal of the Economic and Social History of the Orient* 3 (1960):241–64.

Ḥassān b. Thābit. *The Diwan of Ḥassān b. Thābit.* Edited by W. N. 'Arafat. E. J. W. Gibb Memorial Series, N. S., XXV. London, 1971.

Hawting, G. R. "The Significance of the Slogan *Lā ḥukm^a illā lillāh* and the References to the *Ḥudūd* in the Traditions about the Fitna and the Murder of 'Uthmān." *Bulletin of the School of Oriental and African Studies* 41 (1978):453–63.

Hinz, W. *Islamische Masse und Gewichte.* Leiden, 1970.

Ḥudūd al-'Alam. Translated by V. Minorsky. 2nd edition. London, 1970.

Ibn 'Abd Rabbih, Aḥmad b. Muḥammad. *al-'Iqd al-farīd.* 8 vols. Cairo, 1940.

Ibn Abī al-Ḥadīd. *Sharḥ Nahj al-balāghah.* Edited by M. A. Ibrāhīm. 20 vols. Cairo, 1959–64.

Ibn Abī Uṣaybi'ah, Muwaffaq al-Dīn Aḥmad b. al-Qāsim. *'Uyūn al-anbā'.* Edited by A. Müller. Königsberg, 1884.

Ibn A'tham al-Kūfī, Abū Muḥammad Aḥmad. *K. al-Futūḥ.* 8 vols. Edited by M. A. Khan et al. Hyderabad, 1968–75.

Ibn al-Athīr, 'Izz al-Dīn Abū al-Ḥasan 'Alī b. Muḥammad. *al-Kāmil fī al-ta'rīkh.* Edited by C. J. Tornberg. 12 vols. Leiden, 1851–76.

Ibn Durayd, Abū Bakr Muḥammad b. al-Ḥasan. *K. al-Ishtiqāq.* Cairo, 1958.

Ibn al-Faqīh. *Mukhtaṣar K. al-Buldān.* Edited by M. J. de Goeje. *BGA* V. Leiden, 1855.

Ibn Ḥabīb, Abū Ja'far Muḥammad. *Asmā' al-mughtālīn min al-ashrāf fī al-jāhiliyyah wa-al-Islām.* Edited by A. S. Hārūn, *Nawādir al-makhṭūṭāt,* Cairo, 1951–54, II, 112–275.

Ibn Ḥajar al-'Asqalānī, Aḥmad b. 'Alī. *al-Iṣābah fī tamyīz al-ṣaḥābah.* 4 vols. Cairo, 1328 [1910].

———. *Tabṣīr al-muntabih bi-taḥrīr al-mushtabih.* Edited by A. M. al-Bajāwī and M. A. al-Najjār. 4 vols. Cairo, 1964–67.

———. *Tahdhīb al-tahdhīb.* 12 vols. Hyderabad, 1329–31 [1911–13].

Ibn Ḥawqal, Abū al-Qāsim b. 'Alī. *K. al-masālik wa-al-mamālik.* Edited by M. J. de Goeje. *BGA* II. Leiden, 1897.

Ibn Ḥazm, Abū Muḥammad 'Alī b. Aḥmad. *Jamharat ansāb al-'arab.* Cairo, 1948.

Ibn Juljul, Abū Dā'ūd Sulaymān b. Ḥassān. *Ṭabaqāt al-aṭibbā' wa-al-ḥukamā'.* Edited by F. Sayyid. Cairo, 1955.

Ibn Kathīr, 'Imād al-Dīn Ismā'īl b. 'Umar. *al-Bidāyah wa-al-nihāyah.* 14 vols. Cairo, 1932.

Ibn Khallikān, Abū al-ʿAbbās Aḥmad b. Muḥammad. *Wafayāt al-aʿyān.* Edited by I. ʿAbbās. 8 vols. Beirut, 1968–72.
Ibn Khayyāṭ, Khalīfah. *Taʾrīkh.* Edited by A. D. al-ʿUmarī. Najaf, 1967.
Ibn Khurradādhbih, Abū al-Qāsim ʿUbaydallāh. *K. al-Masālik wa-al-mamālik.* Edited by M. J. de Goeje. *BGA* VI. Leiden, 1889.
Ibn Manẓūr, Jamāl al-Dīn Abū al-Faḍl Muḥammad b. Mukarram. *Lisān al-ʿarab.* 6 vols. Cairo, 1980.
Ibn Qutaybah, Abū Muḥammad ʿAbdallāh b. Muslim. *K. al-Maʿārif.* Edited by Th. ʿUkkāshah. Cairo, 1969.
———. *ʿUyūn al-akhbār.* 4 vols. Cairo, 1925.
Ibn Rustah, Abū ʿAlī Aḥmad b. ʿUmar. *al-Aʿlāq al-nafīsah.* Edited by M. J. de Goeje. *BGA* VII. Leiden, 1892.
Ibn Saʿd, Abū ʿAbdallāh Muḥammad. *K. al-Ṭabaqāt al-kabīr.* Edited by E. Sachau et al. 9 vols. Leiden, 1905–40.
Ibn al-Sikkīt, Abū Yūsuf Yaʿqūb b. Isḥāq. *Iṣlāḥ al-manṭiq.* Edited by A. M. Shākir and A. S. Hārūn. Cairo, 1949.
al-Iṣṭakhrī, Abū Isḥāq Ibrāhīm b. Muḥammad. *K. al-Masālik wa-al-mamālik.* Edited by M. J. de Goeje. *BGA* I. Leiden, 1870.
al-Jāḥiẓ, Abū ʿUthmān ʿAmr b. Baḥr. *al-Bayān wa-al-tabyīn.* Edited by A. S. Hārūn. 4 vols. in two. Cairo, 1956.
———. *K. al-Qawl fī al-bighāl.* Edited by Ch. Pellat. Cairo, 1955.
al-Jahshiyārī, Abū ʿAbdallāh Muḥammad b. ʿAbdūs. *K. al-Wuzarāʾ.* Cairo, 1980.
Kaḥḥālah, ʿU. *Muʿjam qabāʾil al-ʿarab.* 3 vols. Damascus, 1949.
al-Kumayt, Abū Ayyūb b. Maʿrūf. *Die Hāšimijjāt des Kumait.* Edited and translated by J. Horovitz. Leiden, 1904.
Lane, E. W. *An Arabic-English Lexicon.* 8 vols. London, 1863–93.
Le Strange, G. *The Lands of the Eastern Caliphate.* Cambridge, 1930.
Løkkegaard, F. *Islamic Taxation in the Classic Period.* Copenhagen, 1950.
Markwart, J. *Südarmenien und die Tigrisquellen.* Wien, 1930.
Marquart, J. *Ērānšahr.* Berlin, 1901.
Massignon, L. "Explication du plan de Kufa." *Mélanges Maspéro,* III, 1935–40, 337–60.
al-Masʿūdī, Abū al-Ḥasan ʿAlī b. al-Ḥusayn. *Murūj al-dhahab.* Edited by C. Barbier de Maynard. 9 vols. Paris, 1861–77.
———. *al-Tanbīh wa-al-ishrāf.* Edited by M. S. de Goeje. *BGA* VIII. Leiden, 1894.
al-Maydānī, Abū al-Faḍl Aḥmad b. Muḥammad. *Majmaʿ al-amthāl.* 2 vols. Cairo, 1342 [1926].
Michael the Syrian. *Chronique.* 4 vols. Edited and translated by J.-B. Chabot. Paris, 1899–1910.

Morony, M. *Iraq after the Muslim Conquest.* Princeton, 1984.
al-Mubarrad, Abū al-ʿAbbās Muḥammad b. Yazīd. *al-Kāmil fī al-lughah.* Edited by W. Wright. 3 vols. Leipzig, 1874.
al-Muqaddasī, Abū ʿAbdallāh Muḥammad b. Aḥmad. *Aḥsan al-taqāsīm fī maʿrifat al-aqālīm.* Edited by M. J. de Goeje. *BGA* III. Leiden, 1877.
Musil, A. *The Middle Euphrates.* New York, 1927.
———. *Northern Neğd.* New York, 1928.
Noth, A. *Quellenkritische Studien zur Themen, Formen und Tendenzen frühislamischer Geschichtsüberlieferung.* Bonn, 1973.
Pedersen, J. "The Islamic Preacher: wāʿiẓ, mudhakkir, qāṣṣ." *Ignace Goldziher Memorial Volume* I, Budapest, 1948, 226–51.
Périer, J. *La vie d'al-Ḥajjāj ibn Yousof.* Paris, 1904.
Qudāmah b. Jaʿfar. *K. al-Kharāj.* Edited by M. J. de Goeje. *BGA* VI. Leiden, 1889.
Ṣafwat, A. *Jamharat rasā'il al-ʿarab.* 4 vols. Cairo, 1937.
Salem, E. *Political Theory and Institutions of the Khawārij.* Baltimore, 1956.
al-Samʿānī, Abū Saʿd ʿAbd al-Karīm b. Muḥammad. *K. al-Ansāb.* Edited in facsimile by D. S. Margoliouth. London, 1912.
Sayed, R. *Die Revolte des Ibn al-Ašʿaṯ und die Koranleser.* Freiburg, 1977.
Schmucker, W. *Untersuchungen zu einigen wichtigen bodensrechtlichen Konsequenzen der islamischen Eroberungsbewegung.* Bonn, 1972.
Schwarz, P. *Iran im Mittelalter.* 9 parts. Leipzig, 1896–1936.
SEI: Shorter Encyclopaedia of Islam. Leiden, 1953.
Sezgin, F. *Geschichte des arabischen Schrifttums.* Leiden, 1967–.
Sezgin, U. *Abū Miḫnaf: ein Beitrag zur Historiographie der Umaiyadischen Zeit.* Leiden, 1971.
Shaban, M. A. *The ʿAbbāsid Revolution.* Cambridge, 1970.
———. *Islamic History: A New Interpretation,* I. Cambridge, 1971.
Spuler, B. *Iran in frühislamischer Zeit.* Wiesbaden, 1952.
al-Ṭabarī, Abū Jaʿfar Muḥammad b. Jarīr. *Jāmiʿ al-bayān ʿan ta'wīl āy al-Qur'ān.* 30 vols. Cairo, 1955–60.
al-Thaʿālibī, Abū Manṣūr ʿAbd al-Malik b. Muḥammad. *Laṭā'if al-maʿārif.* Edited by I. al-Abyārī and Ḥ. K. al-Ṣayrafī. Cairo, 1960.
———. *Thimār al-qulūb fī al-muḍāf wa-al-mansūb.* Cairo, 1908.
Theophanes. *Chronographia.* Edited by C. de Boor. Leipzig, 1883.
Trimingham, J. S. *Christianity among the Arabs in Pre-Islamic Times.* London, 1979.
ʿUthmān, F. *al-Ḥudūd al-islāmiyyah al-bīzanṭiyyah bayn al-iḥtikāk al-ḥarbī wa-al-ittiṣāl al-ḥiḍārī.* 3 vols. Cairo, 1966.

Watt, W. M. *The Formative Period of Islamic Thought.* Edinburgh, 1973.
WKAS: A. Fischer et al. *Wörterbuch der klassischen arabischen Sprache.* Wiesbaden, 1970–.
al-Ya'qūbī, Abū al-'Abbās Aḥmad b. Isḥāq, Ibn Wāḍiḥ. *K. al-Buldān.* Edited by M. J. de Goeje. *BGA* VII. Leiden, 1892.
———. *Ta'rīkh.* Edited by M. Th. Houtsma. 2 vols. Leiden, 1883.
Yāqūt, Abū 'Abdallāh al-Ḥamawī al-Rūmī. *Mu'jam al-Buldān.* Edited by F. Wüstenfeld. 6 vols. Leipzig, 1866–73.
Yarshater, E., editor. *The Cambridge History of Iran,* III. Cambridge, 1983.
al-Zabīdī, Abū al-Fayḍ Muḥammad Murtaḍā b. Muḥammad. *Tāj al-'arūs.* 10 vols. Cairo, 1888–90.
al-Zamakhsharī, Abū al-Qāsim Maḥmūd b. 'Umar. *Asās al-balāghah.* Beirut, 1979.
Ziriklī, Kh. *al-A'lām.* 11 vols. Cairo, 1954–59.

Index

The index contains all proper names of persons, places, tribal and other groups, as well as topographical data, occurring in the text and the footnotes. However, as far as the footnotes are concerned, only those names that belong to the medieval or earlier periods are listed.

The definite article, the abbreviation b. (for ibn, "son") and bt. (for bint, "daughter"), and everything in parentheses are disregarded for the purposes of alphabetization. Where a name occurs in both the text and the footnotes on the same page, only the page number is given.

A

'abā'ah 117
Abān b. Dārim (Banū) 48
Abān b. Nawfal 92 n. 367
Abān b. 'Uthmān 22, 92, 175–76, 180 n. 653, 181, 186, 194–95
Abarshahr 10
'Abbād b. al-Ḥuṣayn al-Ḥabiṭī 192
'Abbādān 192 n. 699
'Abd al-A'lā b. 'Abdallāh b. 'Āmir b. Kurayz al-Qurashī 72, 75
'Abdallāh b. Abī 'Ubaydah (b. Muḥammad b. 'Ammār b. Yāsir) 13, 18, 20
'Abdallāh b. Abī 'Uṣayfīr 51–52, 54, 65, 81
'Abdallāh b. 'Alqamah al-Khath'amī 32–33, 35, 44, 48, 53, 137, 139, 144–45, 148
'Abdallāh b. 'Āmir 180
'Abdallāh b. 'Āmir b. Kurayz 180 n. 650
'Abdallāh b. 'Āmir b. Misma' 180 n. 650
'Abdallāh b. 'Ayyāsh al-Mantūf 87
'Abdallāh b. al-Jārūd al-'Abdī 23–24, 157 n. 573
'Abdallāh b. Kannāz (?) al-Nahdī 73, 130, 136
'Abdallāh b. Khāzim, see Ibn Khāzim
'Abdallāh b. Mas'ūd 26
'Abdallāh b. al-Mughīrah b. 'Aṭiyyah 112
'Abdallāh b. Qays b. Makhramah 11
'Abdallāh b. Sa'īd b. Ḥayyān b. Abjar 65 n. 255
'Abdallāh b. Sulaym al-Azdī 143
'Abdallāh b. Umayyah b. 'Abdallāh 180 n. 652, 183 n. 660
'Abdallāh b. Wālān al-'Adawī, see Ibn Wālān al-'Adawī

'Abdallāh b. al-Zabīr 21
'Abdallāh b. al-Zubayr, see Ibn al-Zubayr
'Abdallāh b. Zuhayr 143–44, 146, 148
'Abd al-'Azīz b. 'Abdallāh b. Khālid b. Asīd 159 n. 580
'Abd al-'Azīz b. Jāriyah b. Qudāmah 172–74
'Abd al-Malik b. Abī Shaykh al-Qushayrī 190
'Abd al-Malik b. Abjar (?) 65 n. 255
'Abd al-Malik b. Marwān 1–4, 6–9, 11–14, 20, 22, 24, 27, 31, 32 n. 134, 44 n. 178, 45, 71, 78–79, 90–92, 95–96, 107 n. 417, 108, 113–15, 128, 135–36, 145, 150, 152, 156 n. 568, 157 n. 570, 163–65, 171–72, 175 n. 632, 177–78, 180 n. 652, 181, 185 n. 672, 186, 190, 195–96
'Abd al-Malik b. Sa'īd b. Ḥayyān b. Abjar 65 n. 255
'Abd al-Malik b. Shaybān b. 'Abd al-Malik b. Misma' 20
'Abd al-Qays (Banū) 24 n. 110, 154 n. 562
'Abd Rabb 149 n. 552, 159 n. 579
'Abd Rabb al-Kabīr 149, 153–54, 161–62, 176
'Abd Rabb al-Ṣaghīr 149 n. 552, 154 n. 562
'Abd Rabbih al-Kabīr Abū Wakī' 200
'Abd al-Raḥmān b. 'Abdallāh b. Abī al-Zinād, see Ibn Abī al-Zinād
'Abd al-Raḥmān b. 'Abdallāh b. 'Afīf al-Azdī 147
'Abd al-Raḥmān b. 'Abdallāh b. 'Āmir al-Ḥaḍramī 177, 178 n. 641
'Abd al-Raḥmān b. 'Abd al-Raḥmān b. 'Abdallāh b. 'Āmir (?) 178 n. 641
'Abd al-Raḥmān b. Abī Bakrah 184 n. 666
'Abd al-Raḥmān b. al-Ash'ath, see 'Abd al-Raḥmān b. Muḥammad b. al-Ash'ath
'Abd al-Raḥmān b. 'Awf Abū Ḥāmid al-Ru'āsī 59
'Abd al-Raḥmān b. al-Ghariq 74, 97, 143
'Abd al-Raḥmān b. al-Ḥakam 10 n. 41
'Abd al-Raḥmān b. Jarīr al-Laythī 91
'Abd al-Raḥmān b. Jundab 74, 76–77, 80, 83, 93, 100
'Abd al-Raḥmān b. Khālid b. al-'Aṣ b. Hishām b. al-Mughīrah 175
'Abd al-Raḥmān b. Mikhnaf (Abū Ḥakīm) 4–5, 25–27, 29–30, 96
'Abd al-Raḥmān b. Muḥammad b. al-Ash'ath (Ma'dīkarib) 81–85, 88–90, 93, 94 n. 372, 102, 104, 106, 138 n. 507, 182 n. 656, 190–94
'Abd al-Raḥmān b. 'Ubayd b. Ṭāriq al-'Abshamī 179
'Abd al-Raḥmān b. Umm al-Ḥakam al-Thaqafī 192
'Abd Shams b. Sa'd (Banū) 179 n. 646
'Abīdah b. Hilāl al-Yashkurī 161, 164, 165 n. 596, 176
al-Abnā' (division of Banū Tamīm) 8, 196–97, 199–200
al-Abrad b. Rabī'ah al-Kindī 88
'Abs (Banū) 26 n. 119, 133 n. 496
Abū al-Adham Ziyād b. 'Amr al-Zimmānī 188
Abū al-Aḥwaṣ 26
Abū al-'Ajfā' b. Abī al-Kharqā' 199
Abū 'Amr al-Shaybānī 17
Abū 'Amr al-'Udhrī 112, 119
Abū 'Aqīl 117 n. 447
Abū 'Aqīl (? Ibn Abī 'Aqīl?) 74 n. 305, 97
Abū 'Awn 2
Abū al-Bahā' al-Iyādī 151 n. 557
Abū Bakr (al-Ṣiddīq) 34, 134 n. 498, 185
Abū Bakr b. 'Ayyāsh 70
Abū Bakr b. Muḥammad b. Abī Jahm al-'Adawī 102
Abū Bakrah 178 n. 644
Abū Burdah b. Abī Mūsā al-Ash'arī 80, 186, 195
Abū Du'ād al-Ru'āsī 16 n. 72
Abū al-Ḍurays 71, 76–77, 80
Abū al-Faraj al-Iṣfahānī, see al-Aghānī

Abū Fudayk 4 n. 17, 9–10, 79, 168 n. 606, 185 n. 673
Abū Ḥakīm, see ʿAbd al-Raḥmān b. Mikhnaf
Abū al-Ḥasan, see al-Madāʾinī
Abū Idrīs al-Khawlānī 2
Abū Isḥāq 3
Abū Jaʿfar, see al-Ṭabarī
Abū al-Jahm b. Kinānah al-Kalbī 163
Abū Kaʿb 117
Abū Khālid Thābit 167
Abū Khaythamah b. ʿAbdallāh 105
Abū Lahab 134
Abū Layth b. Abī Sulaym 69
Abū Maʿshar 22, 92, 176, 181, 186, 194
Abū Māwiyyah 180
Abū Mikhnaf 3–4, 23, 25, 27, 28 n. 125, 29 n. 126, 32–33, 35, 37–38, 41, 44, 46, 48, 53–54, 56–58, 61 n. 239, 63, 66, 74–76, 78, 80, 83, 87, 89, 93, 94 n. 372, 98 n. 387, 99–101, 105–7, 110, 112, 119–26, 128–29, 130 n. 485, 131, 136 n. 502, 137, 139–40, 142–48, 150, 152, 162, 178–79, 183, 190–91, 193–94
Abū Mudallah, see Shabīb b. Yazīd
Abū al-Mughallis al-Kinānī 152
Abū al-Mukhāriq al-Rāsibī 178–79, 183
Abū al-Mundhir 68
Abū Mūsā al-Ashʿarī 80, 185 n. 670
Abū Naʿāmah, see Qaṭarī b. al-Fujāʾah
Abū al-Najm al-ʿIjlī 18
Abū Rabīʿah b. Dhuhl (Banū) 117
Abū al-Rawwāgh (?) al-Shākirī 42
Abū Rustam al-Khalīl b. Aws al-ʿAbshamī 169
Abū al-Ruwāʿ (?) al-Shākirī 42 n. 173
Abū al-Ṣaḥārā (? al-Ṣaḥārī?), see Shabīb b. Yazīd
Abū Saʿīd, see al-Muhallab b. Abī Ṣufrah
Abū al-Ṣuqayr al-Muḥallimī al-Shaybānī, see Ibrāhīm b. Ḥujr
Abū Suwayqah 199
Abū Ṭalḥah (al-Kinānī) 152
Abū al-Ṭufayl ʿĀmir b. Wāthilah al-Kinānī 142 n. 523
Abū ʿUbaydah (Maʿmar b. al-Muthannā) 79
Abū al-Ward 109, 112 n. 432, 117
Abū Yaʿfūr, see ʿUrwah b. al-Mughīrah b. Shuʿbah
Abū Yazīd al-Saksakī 120, 122, 124–25
Abū Zayd, see ʿUmar b. Shabbah
Abū Zayd al-Anṣārī 16 n. 72
Abū Zayd al-Aṣmaʿī (?) 16
Abū al-Zinād (ʿAbdallāh b. Dhakhwān al-Qurashī) 91
Abū al-Zubayr al-Arḥabī 193
Abū Zughbah al-Khazrajī 14 n. 59
Abū Zuhayr al-ʿAbsī, see al-Naḍr b. Ṣāliḥ
al-ʿAdhāb (? al-ʿAdhdhāb?), see Maymūn
Ādharbayjān 45 n. 181, 48, 67
ʿAdī (Banū) 174 n. 626
ʿAdī b. ʿAdī b. ʿUmayrah al-Kindī al-Shaybānī 39–40, 48–49, 51, 73
ʿAdī b. ʿAmr al-Thaqafī 69
ʿAdī b. Kaʿb (Banū) 102 n. 402
ʿAdī b. ʿUmayrah al-Shaybānī, see ʿAdī b. ʿAdī b. ʿUmayrah
ʿAdī b. Wattād al-Iyādī 141, 143–48
al-Aghānī 10 n. 41, 13 nn. 56 and 57, 14 n. 59, 19 n. 87, 21 nn. 92 and 94, 133 n. 496, 154 n. 563, 172 n. 616, 175 n. 632, 178 n. 644, 190 n. 691
Ahl al-ʿĀliyah 174
Aḥmad b. Thābit 22, 92, 176, 180, 186, 194
al-Aḥnaf b. ʿAbdallāh al-ʿAnbarī 167, 173, 175
al-Ahwāz 3 n. 13, 5, 24 n. 107, 80 n. 321, 122, 156 n. 568, 157, 179, 192
ʿĀʾishah bt. Mūsā b. Ṭalḥah b. ʿUbaydallāh 79 n. 318
al-Ajdaʿ b. Mālik 129 n. 480
Akharūn (Kharūn) 198, 200

Aleppo 78 n. 313
ʿAlī b. Abī Ṭālib 13 n. 55, 35, 51, 80 n. 323, 128 n. 478, 134 n. 498, 140 n. 514, 142 n. 523, 172 n. 620, 183, 185 n. 671
ʿAlī b. Muḥammad, see al-Madāʾinī
ʿAlqamah b. ʿAbd al-Raḥmān al-Ḥakamī 119 n. 457
ʿAlwān (Khārijite) 118
al-Aʿmāq (? al-ʿAmq?) 12 n. 51
Āmid 40
ʿĀmir b. ʿAmr b. ʿAbd ʿAmr 104
ʿĀmir b. Luʾayy (Banū) 92
ʿĀmir b. Ṣaʿṣaʿah (Banū) 40 n. 164, 59 n. 229, 190 n. 691
ʿĀmir b. Wāthilah, see Abū al-Ṭufayl ʿĀmir b. Wāthilah al-Kinānī
ʿAmmār b. Yazīd al-Kalbī 104, 105
al-ʿAmq (? al-Aʿmāq?) 12 n. 51
ʿAmr b. Ḥurayyith 5, 7
ʿAmr b. Khālid b. Ḥuṣayn al-Kilābī 175
ʿAmr b. Muʿāwiyah (Banū) 53
ʿAmr b. Saʿd (Banū) 9 n. 38
ʿAmr b. Saʿīd 20–21
ʿAmr b. Shahrān (Banū) 48
Anas b. Mālik 2, 181 n. 654
Anas b. Ṭalq al-ʿAbshamī 199
ʿAnazah (Banū) 44–45
al-Anbār 67, 81 n. 327, 97, 119, 129
al-ʿAnbar b. ʿAmr (Banū) 167 n. 602, 192 n. 702
ʿAnbasah b. Abī Sufyān 69
ʿAnbasah b. Saʿīd 19, 21, 113, 117
ʿAntarah (b. Shaddād) 102
Antioch 182
ʿAqarqūf (ʿAqraqūfā) 68
ʿAqīl b. Shaddād b. Ḥubshī al-Salūlī 85–87
al-ʿAqr 61 n. 241
ʿAqr al-Malik 61
ʿAqraqūfā (ʿAqarqūf) 68 n. 274
Arab, Arabs 78 n. 314, 132–34, 143, 154 n. 562, 162, 168, 169 n. 609, 172 n. 618, 183, 188
Arabic (language) 179 n. 648
al-Aʿraj (Banū) (al-Ḥārith b. Kaʿb b. Saʿd b. Zayd Manāt) 95 n. 378, 97
Arbinjan (Rabinjan) 189 n. 686
ʿāriḍ 23 n. 104
ʿarīf (pl. ʿurafāʾ), see marshals
ʿĀrimah (al-ʿĀrimah) 169–70, 173, 175
Arrajān 27 n. 121
Asad (Banū) 5, 21, 71 n. 289, 86
al-Asadī, see al-Rabīʿ b. Yazīd
al-Aṣamm, see Sufyān b. al-Abrad
Aṣghar (Khārijite) 112
al-Aʿshā (Maymūn) 17
Aʿshā Hamdān 186 n. 674
al-Ashʿarī (Abū Burdah), see Abū Burdah b. Abī Mūsā
al-Ashʿarī (Abū al-Ḥasan) 30 n. 131
al-Ashʿarī (Abū Mūsā), see Abū Mūsā al-Ashʿarī
al-Ashʿath (Banū) 7, 163
al-Ashʿath b. Qays 81 n. 328
ʿashīrah 124 n. 469, 157 n. 570
al-Ashqar (Banū) 154
ʿĀṣim b. Ḥujr 56
ʿaskar 53 n. 208
ʿAskar Mukram 23 n. 105. See also Rustaqubādh
al-Aṣmaʿī (Abū Saʿīd) 13 n. 57, 16 n. 72, 18
al-Aṣmaʿī, Abū Zayd (?), see Abū Zayd al-Asmaʿī
asr 154 n. 562
astān 50 n. 198, 74 n. 304, 81 n. 327, 83 n. 334
al-Aswad b. Saʿd al-Hamdānī 141
ʿaṭāʾ, see stipend
ʿAṭāʾ b. Abī al-Sāʾib al-Laythī 172–74
ʿAṭāʾ b. ʿArfajah b. Ziyād b. ʿAbdallāh al-Wirthī 66
al-ʿAtīk b. al-Asd (Banū) 72 n. 292, 151
ʿAṭiyyah al-ʿAnbarī (b. ʿĀmr) 192
Aṭmār (?) 176 n. 639
ʿAttāb al-Liqwah al-Ghudānī 166–68, 171
ʿAttāb b. Warqāʾ al-Riyāḥī 27–28, 93,

96–104, 106–8, 112 n. 432, 116, 119, 150, 151 n. 558
a'wān 193 n. 706
'Awf b. Ka'b b. Sa'd (Banū) 8, 196–200
'Awf b. Sa'd (Banū), see 'Awf b. Ka'b b. Sa'd (Banū)
A'yan 71, 76–77, 80, 109 n. 424, 114, 117
'Ayn al-Tamr 74, 97, 99
'Ayyāsh b. 'Abdallāh b. 'Ayyāsh (?) 87 n. 352
Azd (Banū) 4 n. 19, 28 n. 125, 29–30, 57 n. 223, 72 n. 292, 76, 94 n. 372, 106 n. 413, 129, 147 n. 545, 151, 154, 160, 190 n. 691
Azd Shanū'ah (Banū) 30
Azd 'Umān (Banū) 30, 151 n. 557
Azhar b. 'Abdallāh al-'Āmirī 69
Azqalah (? Irqīliyyah?) 181 n. 655
al-Azraqī 2 n. 4, 187 n. 679, 188 n. 680
Azraqites 3, 25, 27 n. 123, 30 n. 131, 79 n. 316, 81 n. 328, 96 n. 382, 149–50, 153 n. 560, 154 n. 562, 156 n. 568, 161–62, 178

B

Bāb al-Fīl (in mosque of al-Kūfah) 114
Bābil (Bābil al-Kūfah, Babylon) 50 n. 198, 61 n. 241, 106 n. 414
Bābil Mahrūdh 50–51, 67, 94
Badal 173
Bādām (? Bādhām? Bādhān?) 163, 165 n. 596
Badr, Battle of 124 n. 467
Badr b. 'Amr (Banū) 56 n. 220
Badr b. Fazārah (Banū) 56
Baghdad 52 n. 204, 61, 65, 67 nn. 269–270 and 272, 68 n. 274, 80, 84 nn. 335 and 337, 122 n. 463
al-Baghdādī ('Abd al-Qāhir) 32 n. 134, 43 n. 176, 44 n. 178, 70 n. 283, 90 n. 357, 114 n. 439
Baḥīr b. Warqā' al-Ṣuraymī 8, 10–11, 165–66, 171–75, 196–200
al-Baḥrayn 168, 185 n. 673
Bahurasīr 98, 100 n. 396, 103 n. 404, 131. See also al-Madā'in
Bajīlah (Banū) 140 n. 513, 147
Bājumayrāt (Bājumayrā) 185
Bakr b. Wā'il 10, 28 n. 125, 37 n. 153, 39 n. 160, 47, 69 n. 282, 70 nn. 284 and 285, 71 n. 290, 102 n. 403, 105, 117, 141 n. 521, 149 n. 552, 161 n. 585, 198
al-Balādhurī 1 n. 2, 2 nn. 4 and 6, 3 n. 12, 7 n. 29, 8 n. 34, 9 n. 39, 11 n. 48, 12 nn. 51–53, 13 n. 56, 19 nn. 87 and 88, 21 n. 94, 22 nn. 95 and 96, 23 nn. 100 and 103, 24 n. 111, 39 n. 158, 42 n. 168, 61 n. 242, 62 n. 248, 71 n. 290, 91 nn. 358 and 360–61, 92 n. 365, 94 n. 376, 99 n. 395, 109 n. 426, 114 n. 436, 128 n. 475, 169 n. 609, 172 n. 615, 178 nn. 642 and 644, 179 n. 648, 180 n. 652, 183 n. 660, 184 nn. 665–67, 185 nn. 668–70 and 674, 187 n. 679, 188 n. 680, 190 n. 692, 191 n. 697, 192 nn. 699 and 704, 194 nn. 708 and 710
Balkh, river of 175, 188. See also Oxus
Bam 150 n. 555
Bandanījān 93 n. 371
Bāniqiyā 45
Ba'qūbā 84 n. 335
al-Barā' b. Qabīṣah 28 n. 125, 141, 142 n. 523, 143–44, 147, 148 n. 546, 151–52
barā'āt 16 n. 69
Barājim (clan) 19 n. 86
Barāz al-Rūz 57, 58 n. 225, 59, 61
barīd, see post
Bāsān (Bāshān, Fāshān) 169–70
Bashīr b. Ḥassān al-Nahdī 122
al-Baṣrah 2 n. 9, 3, 5, 11, 13 n. 56, 20 n. 89, 22–24, 28 n. 125, 30 n. 128, 67, 72, 74 n. 304, 84 n. 336, 92,

al-Başrah (*cont'd*)
122, 175, 177–78, 180 n. 650, 181, 184 n. 666, 186, 188, 192 nn. 699 and 704, 194 n. 709, 195
Başrans, Başran forces 5, 23–25, 27 n. 121, 28 n. 125, 96 n. 383, 151 n. 559, 169 n. 609, 174 n. 625, 183, 185 n. 667, 191
ba'th 54 n. 212, 143 n. 530
Bath of Ibn Abī Bakrah 184
al-Baṭīn (Khārijite) 31 78, 106, 116, 118
al-Batt 84–85
Bayt Qurrah 105
Bayṭarā 107
Bihqubādh al-Asfal (Lower Bihqubādh) 73 n. 299, 74
Bishāpūr, see Sābūr
Bishr b. al-Ajda' al-Hamdānī al-Thawrī 129
Bishr b. Ghālib al-Asadī 71, 74, 76
Bishr b. Jarīr 5
Bishr b. Marwān 3–5, 7, 11, 13, 23, 32 n. 134, 71, 81 n. 328, 96, 157
Bisṭām b. Maşqalah b. Hubayrah 27–28
Black Stone (of Ka'bah) 187 n. 680
Bukayr b. Hārūn al-Bajalī 140, 145–47
Bukayr b. Wishāḥ al-Sa'dī 7–8, 10–11, 165–75, 196–200
Bukhārā 166–67, 189
Burmah b. Mālik (Banū) 58 n. 226
Bust 186 n. 674, 194 n. 708
Bustān Zā'idah 111. See also Orchard
al-Buṭūn (clans of Tamīm) 8, 200
al-Buwayb, Battle of 185 n. 669
Būyanah 169
Byzantines 2 n. 6, 12, 90 n. 358, 91 nn. 360 and 361, 126, 181 n. 655, 182

C

China 167
Christian, Christians 74 n. 302, 91 n. 360, 102 n. 403, 105
council (shūrā) 132–33, 136, 140
Ctesiphon 37 n. 156, 98 n. 388, 108 n. 422, 129 n. 479, 131 n. 487. See also al-Madā'in, al-madīnah al-'atīqah

D

Ḍabbah (Banū) 153, 154 n. 562, 174 n. 626
Dāḥis and al-Ghabrā', war of 133 n. 496
Damascus 2 n. 11, 13 n. 53, 44 n. 178, 78 n. 313, 92
Damāwand see Dunbāwand
Daqūqā' 67, 83
dār al-imārah (al-Kūfah) 108 n. 422
dār al-rizq (al-Kūfah), see provision depot
Dār al-Siqāyah Road (al-Kūfah) 114
Dārā 33, 37–38
Darābjird 150–51
Darqīṭ Canal, see Durqīṭ Canal
Dasht Bārīn 158
al-Daskarah 41–42, 48, 50 n. 198, 54 n. 214, 55 n. 216, 57 n. 221, 99 n. 394, 107, 135–37
Daskarat al-Malik (al-Daskarah) 107
Dastawā 24
da'wah 145 n. 539
Dawghān 39–40
al-Dayr (Dayr Abī Maryam?) 62–63, 130 n. 483
Dayr 'Abd al-Raḥmān 53, 81
Dayr Abī Maryam 58, 61, 62 n. 252, 88, 90. See also al-Dayr
Dayr Bayrimmā 54, 56
Dayr al-Jamājim 138. See also al-Jamājim, battle of
Dayr al-Kharārah (? al-Ḥarārah? al-Jarādah? al-Jarārah?) 55–56
Dayr Qurrah 105 n. 411
Dayr al-Ya'ār (? al-B.qār? al-N.'ār?) 89
Dayr Yazdajird 55–56, 136

dhimma, dhimmīs 2 n. 6. See also Christians, Jews
Dhū al-Jawshan Shuraḥbīl b. al-Aʿwar al-ʿĀmirī 192 nn. 703 and 704
Dhū Murrān al-Hamdānī 60 n. 237
Dhū Qār, Battle of 70 n. 285
Dhuhl, mosque of Banū 69
Dhuhl b. al-Ḥārith 69
Dhuhl b. Muʿāwiyah (Banū) 60, 69 n. 282
Dhuhl b. Shaybān (Banū) 37, 39 n. 163, 44 n. 178, 69 n. 282, 70 n. 285, 102 n. 403
Dhuhl b. Taym b. ʿAbd Manāt (Banū) 174 n. 627
Dhuhl b. Thaʿlabah (Banū) 69 n. 282, 70 n. 284, 118 n. 452
dihqān 59, 62–63, 67, 94, 163, 167 n. 603, 172
Dīnawar 138 n. 508
al-Dīnawarī 2 n. 4, 138 n. 508, 149 n. 552, 154 n. 562, 165 n. 596, 178 n. 642, 191 n. 697
Ḍirār b. Ḥuṣayn al-Ḍabbī 8, 172–73
dīwān 4, 163 n. 589
dīwān al-kharāj 179 n. 648
Diyālā River 41 n. 166, 45 n. 181, 46 n. 184, 83 n. 334
Diyarbakr, see Āmid
Dujayl (canal) 68 n. 274, 122 n. 463
Dujayl al-Ahwāz (river) 122 n. 463, 156 n. 568
Dujayl Bridge (at al-Ahwāz) 122, 156 n. 568
Dunbāwand (Damāwand) 165
Dur Kurigalzu 68 n. 274
Durqīṭ (? Darqīṭ?) Canal 94

E

Egypt, Egyptian 91 n. 360, 92
Elephant Door, see Bāb al-Fīl
Elias of Nisibis 182 n. 656, 187 n. 679
Emigrants (Muhājirūn) 134
Erzurum, see Qālīqalā
Euphrates 45 n. 182, 62, 66, 67 n. 269, 71, n. 290, 72, 74, 80 n. 325, 97, 105 n. 411, 106 n. 414, 107, 108 n. 420, 116, 155 n. 564, 192

F

Faḍālah (b. Sayyār al-Taymī) 44–45
al-Faḍl b. ʿĀmir al-Shaybānī 37, 76, 104
Fā'id 148
farḍ 41 n. 168, 44 n. 178, 45 n. 183
Fārs 3 n. 13, 25 n. 113, 79 n. 316, 122, 150
farsakh 5 n. 22, 24
Farwah b. al-Daffān (? al-D.qān? al-D.fār?) al-Kalbī 111
Farwah b. Laqīṭ al-Azdī al-Ghāmidī 37, 54, 75–77, 93, 94 n. 372, 99–100, 105–6, 110, 112, 121, 123–24, 126
Faryāb (? Qaryāt?) 189 n. 688
Fasā 150
Fāshān, see Bāsān
fāsiq 24 n. 109, 106 n. 416
fay', see spoil
Fazārah (Banū) 56 n. 220
fi'ah 9 n. 40
Field of Yazīd (Marw), see Maydān Yazīd
Firās (Banū) 65
al-Fizr b. al-Aswad 66
Fuḍayl b. Khadīj al-Kindī 53
al-Fusayfisā' (horse) 83
fuṭm 163

G

Gardīzī 7 n. 29
al-Gel 45 n. 181. See also al-Jāl
Ghāḍirah 57
Ghāḍirah (Banū) 21
Ghaṭafān (Banū) 26 n. 119
Ghazālah (wife of Shabīb) 44, 111–12, 114, 117–19
Ghaznah 178 n. 643, 184 n. 663

Ghazwān 49
al-Ghilẓah (? al-'Ulṭah?) 66
Ghudānah b. Yarbū' (Banū) 166 n. 599
ghulām (pl. ghilmān) 88, 108 n. 421, 189 n. 687

H

ḥabbah 91–92
Ḥabīb b. 'Abd al-Raḥmān al-Ḥakamī 96, 105, 119–20, 122, 127
Ḥabīb b. Khidrah (? Khudrah? Jadarah? Judrah?) 118, 148
Ḥabīb b. al-Muhallab b. Abī Ṣufrah 28, 180, 189
al-Ḥabiṭ, see al-Ḥārith b. 'Amr b. Tamīm
ḥadd (pl. ḥudūd) (Qur'ānic punishment) 34, 35 n. 147, 132
Ḥaḍramawt 72, 81
Hadyah 149
Ḥafṣ 155
Hagar 2 n. 4
ḥājib 173 n. 622
al-Ḥajjāj b. Jāriyah al-Khath'amī 137–39, 145–46, 148
al-Ḥajjāj b. Qutaybah (b. Muslim) 114–15
al-Ḥajjāj b. Yūsuf (b. al-Ḥakam b. Abī 'Aqīl) 1, 2, 7, 11–13, 15, 18–28, 31, 41, 44, 48, 50–51, 53–54, 57–58, 61–64, 66–68, 70–74, 78–79, 81–85, 90, 92–100, 102 n. 401, 105–19, 121 n. 460, 122, 125 n. 470, 127–30, 135–38, 140–45, 147–48, 150–54, 157 n. 573, 162–63, 165, 175, 177–81, 182 n. 656, 183, 185–86, 190–95
al-Ḥakam b. 'Amr al-Ghifārī 179
al-Ḥakam b. Ayyūb b. al-Ḥakam b. Abī 'Aqīl al-Thaqafī 22, 122
al-Ḥakam b. Sa'd al-'Ashīrah (Banū) 96 n. 381
Ḥakamah (market) 99–100
Ḥakīm b. Abī Sufyān al-Azdī 147
Ḥakīm b. al-Ḥārith al-Azdī 129
Hamadhān 99 n. 392, 128, 138, 141–42
Hamdān (Banū) 5, 41 n. 167, 42 n. 173, 58 n. 226, 60 n. 237, 63, 86, 87 n. 352, 101 n. 397, 103, 106 n. 413, 129 n. 480, 185 n. 667, 191 nn. 694 and 696, 193
Ḥammām A'yan 71, 98, 108, 109 n. 424, 114, 117
Ḥammām Ibn Abī Bakrah, see Bath of Ibn Abī Bakrah
Ḥammām Ibn 'Umar, see Ḥammām 'Umar b. Sa'd
Ḥammām 'Umar b. Sa'd (b. Abī Waqqāṣ) 61, 107
al-Ḥamrā' 139
Ḥamrīn, Jabal, see Sātīdamā
Ḥamzah al-Iṣfahānī 138 n. 508
Ḥamzah b. al-Mughīrah (b. Shu'bah) 128, 138–39, 141–42
Hāni' b. Qabīṣah al-Shaybānī 70 n. 285
Ḥanīfah (Banū) 198
Ḥanẓalah (Banū) 19 n. 86
Ḥanẓalah b. al-Ḥārith al-Yarbū'ī 101
Ḥanẓalah b. Mālik (al-Wirthī) 66
ḥaras 173 n. 623
Ḥarbā (Ḥarbā') 67, 68 n. 274
ḥarbah 11 n. 46
al-Ḥārith (Banū, of Madhḥij) 71 n. 288
al-Ḥārith b. 'Amr b. Tamīm (al-Ḥabiṭ) 192 n. 699
al-Ḥārith b. Ja'wanah al-'Āmirī 40
al-Ḥārith b. Ka'b b. Sa'd b. Zayd Manāt (Banū), see al-A'raj (Banū)
al-Ḥārith b. Khālid al-Makhzūmī 175 n. 632
al-Ḥārith b. Mu'āwiyah b. Abī Zur'ah b. Mas'ūd al-Thaqafī 108, 116
al-Ḥārith b. Mu'āwiyah b. Thawr (Banū) 39
al-Ḥārith b. 'Umayrah b. Dhī al-Mish'ar al-Hamdānī 41–43, 48
Ḥarrān 39
al-Ḥarūb 159

Ḥarūrā' 13 n. 55
al-Ḥarūriyyah 13, 57. See also Khārijism, Khārijites
al-Ḥasan al-Baṣrī 21 n. 92, 24 n. 109
Ḥaṣīrah b. 'Abdallāh 101
Ḥassān b. Thābit 18, 68 n. 278
al-Ḥaṣṣāṣah 67
Hawāzin (tribe) 85 n. 341
Ḥawlāyā (river) 46 n. 186, 84–86
Ḥawlāyā (village) 46
Ḥawshab b. Ruwaym, see Ḥawshab b. Yazīd al-Shaybānī
Ḥawshab b. Yazīd (b. al-Ḥārith b. Ruwaym al-Shaybānī) 23 n. 102, 69, 116
Ḥawṭ (? Khūṭ?) b. 'Umayr al-Sadūsī 118
Ḥawtharah b. Asad 46
Ḥayyān 127
Ḥayyān b. Abjar al-Kinānī 65
Ḥāzim b. Qudāmah al-Khath'amī 52
Herat 113
al-Ḥijāz 174 n. 625
al-Ḥijr 1
Hilāl 91
Hilāl b. 'Āmir (Banū) 118 n. 455, 148
Hilāl b. Usāmah 91
al-Ḥillah 61 n. 242
Himyān b. 'Adī al-Sadūsī 194
al-Ḥīrah 21, 45 n. 182, 66, 71 n. 290, 73 n. 299, 74 n. 304, 105
Hishām b. Hubayrah 11
Hishām b. Muḥammad (al-Kalbī) 3, 23, 25, 32, 44, 61 n. 239, 62, 70, 76, 93, 107, 112, 122, 126, 128, 150, 162, 178, 183, 190
Hīt 97
Ḥubshī b. Junādah 85 n. 341
Ḥudhayfah b. al-Yamān, bridges of 94
Ḥullām b. Sāliḥ 131
Ḥulwān 55–56, 83 nn. 333 and 334, 137, 139 n. 510, 148
Ḥulwān pass 137
Ḥumayd b. Muslim 29
Ḥumrān b. Mālik (al-Wirthī) 66
Huraym (b. Abī Ṭaḥmah al-Mujāshi'ī) 170
Huraym b. 'Adī 189
Ḥurayyith b. Quṭbah 170
al-Ḥurr b. 'Abdallāh b. 'Awf 94
al-Ḥuṣayn b. 'Abdallāh b. Sa'd b. Nufayl al-Azdī 128
al-Ḥuṣayn b. Yazīd 129
al-Ḥuṣayn b. Yazīd Dhū al-Ghuṣṣah 71 n. 288
Ḥusayn b. Zafar 56
al-Ḥuṭam al-Qaysī 14 n. 59

I

'Ibādīs 71 n. 290
Ibāḍites 31 n. 131
Ibn 'Abd Rabbih 2 n. 9, 13 n. 56
Ibn Abī al-'Āliyah, see Sufyān b. Abī al-'Āliyah
Ibn Abī 'Aqīl (? Abū 'Aqīl?) 74, 97 n. 385
Ibn Abī 'Aqīl, see al-Ḥajjāj b. Yūsuf
Ibn Abī Bakrah, see 'Ubaydallāh b. Abī Bakrah
Ibn Abī Dhi'b 2
Ibn Abī al-Ḥadīd 128 n. 478, 199 n. 721
Ibn Abī Sabrah al-Ju'fī, see Muḥammad b. 'Abd al-Raḥmān b. Abī Sabrah
Ibn Abī 'Ubaydah, see 'Abdallāh b. Abī 'Ubaydah
Ibn Abī Uṣaybi'ah 65 n. 255
Ibn Abī 'Uṣayfir, see 'Abdallāh b. Abī Uṣayfir
Ibn Abī al-Zinād ('Abd al-Raḥmān b. 'Abdallāh) 91
Ibn Abī Ziyād, see Yazīd b. Abī Ziyād
Ibn al-A'lam, see Ya'qūb b. al-Qa'qā' al-A'lam al-Azdī
Ibn 'Alqamah, see 'Abdallāh b. 'Alqamah
Ibn al-Aṣamm 82

Ibn al-Ash'ath, see 'Abd al-Raḥmān b. Muḥammad b. al-Ash'ath
Ibn A'tham al-Kūfī 3 nn. 12 and 13, 7 n. 29, 8 n. 37, 12 n. 53, 13 nn. 56 and 57, 19 n. 87, 21 n. 94, 27 n. 121, 29 n. 125, 30 n. 129, 44 n. 178, 47 n. 190, 70 n. 283, 80 n. 321, 90 n. 357, 109 nn. 423 and 424, 112 n. 432, 114 n. 439, 119 n. 457, 122 n. 461, 125 n. 470, 149 n. 552, 150 n. 554, 152 n. 560, 154 n. 562, 155 n. 563, 156 n. 568, 158 n. 575, 159 n. 579, 164 nn. 591 and 592, 165 n. 596, 172 n. 615, 178 n. 642, 180 n. 652, 183 nn. 660 and 661, 184 nn. 665 and 666, 185 nn. 667 and 668, 190 n. 692, 191 n. 697, 192 n. 704, 193 n. 705, 194 n. 710
Ibn al-Athīr 2 nn. 4 and 9, 3 n. 13, 7 n. 29, 8 nn. 33 and 38, 12 nn. 51 and 53, 16 n. 70, 19 n. 87, 21 n. 94, 22 n. 96, 23 nn. 102 and 103, 25 n. 111, 27 n. 121, 32 n. 134, 44 n. 178, 46 n. 189, 66 n. 265, 70 n. 286, 80 n. 321, 81 n. 327, 89 n. 356, 90 n. 357, 99 n. 394, 111 n. 430, 128 n. 475, 141 nn. 519 and 520, 147 n. 544, 150 n. 552, 154 n. 562, 163 n. 588, 166 n. 599, 172 n. 615, 188 n. 683
Ibn Ḍābi', see 'Umayr b. Ḍābi'
Ibn Dhī Murrān, see Sa'īd b. Mujālid
Ibn Durayd 76 n. 307
Ibn al-Faqīh 109 n. 426
Ibn al-Ghariq, see 'Abd al-Raḥmān b. al-Ghariq
Ibn Ḥabīb (Muḥammad) 172 n. 615, 200 n. 725
Ibn Ḥajar al-'Askalānī 2 n. 10, 37 n. 152, 42 n. 173, 65 n. 255, 103 n. 407
Ibn Ḥawqal 158 n. 576
Ibn Ḥazm 5 n. 24, 9 n. 38, 19 n. 86, 37 n. 153, 71 n. 291, 79 n. 318, 117 n. 444, 198 n. 717
Ibn Hilāl 91
Ibn Hubayrah, see 'Umar b. Hubayrah al-Fazārī
Ibn al-Jārūd, see 'Abdallāh b. al-Jārūd al-'Abdī
Ibn Juljul 65 n. 255
Ibn al-Kalbī see Hishām b. Muḥammad
Ibn Kathīr 2 nn. 4 and 8, 3 n. 13, 7 n. 29, 11 n. 49, 12 nn. 51–53, 19 n. 87, 22 nn. 96 and 99, 25 n. 111, 181 n. 655, 188 n. 681, 200 n. 725
Ibn Khallikān 11 n. 49, 37 n. 153, 44 n. 178, 47 n. 190, 79 n. 316, 125 n. 470, 126 n. 473
Ibn Khayyāṭ 1 n. 2, 2 n. 4, 3 n. 12, 7 n. 29, 11 nn. 47 and 48, 12 nn. 51–53, 22 nn. 95–96 and 99–100, 23 n. 102, 24 n. 111, 32 n. 134, 43 nn. 176 and 177, 44 n. 178, 53 n. 209, 70 n. 283, 80 n. 321, 90 n. 357, 92 n. 369, 309 nn. 423 and 424, 112 n. 432, 119 n. 457, 149 n. 552, 154 n. 562, 165 n. 596, 175 n. 635, 176 nn. 638 and 639, 178 n. 641, 180 nn. 652 and 653, 181 n. 655, 186 nn. 675–77, 195 n. 711
Ibn Khāzim ('Abdallāh) 8, 166 n. 600, 168 nn. 604 and 607, 169, 174, 190 n. 691
Ibn Khurradādhbih 55 n. 214, 73 n. 299, 74 n. 304, 84 nn. 334 and 338, 94 n. 373, 158 n. 575
Ibn Manẓūr 14 nn. 59 and 60, 15 n. 66, 16 n. 72, 33 n. 136, 70 n. 287, 117 n. 448, 128 n. 478, 161 n. 584
Ibn Mas'ūd 26 n. 118
Ibn Mikhnaf, see 'Abd al-Raḥmān b. Mikhnaf
Ibn al-Mughīrah, see Muṭarrif b. al-Mughīrah b. Shu'bah
Ibn al-Mujālid, see Sa'īd b. Mujālid
Ibn Nihyah 20
Ibn Qutaybah 13 n. 56, 25 n. 111, 32

n. 134, 39 n. 163, 43 nn. 176 and 177, 44 n. 178, 65 n. 255, 70 n. 283, 71 n. 291, 80 n. 321, 187 n. 679
Ibn Rustah 54 n. 214, 109 n. 427
Ibn Sa'd (Muḥammad) 11 nn. 49 and 50, 23 n. 101, 26 n. 117, 91 n. 360, 92 nn. 366 and 367, 103 n. 407, 134 n. 498, 172 n. 620, 174 n. 628, 181 n. 654, 187
Ibn al-Sikkīt 44 n. 178
Ibn Ṭalq, see Anas b. Ṭalq al-'Abshamī
Ibn 'Umar, see al-Wāqidī
Ibn Uqayṣir al-Khath'amī 120, 144, 146–47
Ibn 'Uwaymir (Khārijite) 118
Ibn Wālān al-'Adawī ('Abdallāh) 174
Ibn Wishāḥ, see Bukayr b. Wishāḥ al-Sa'dī
Ibn al-Zabīr, see 'Abdallāh b. al-Zabīr
Ibn al-Zubayr ('Abdallāh) 1
Ibn al-Zubayr (Muṣ'ab), see Muṣ'ab b. al-Zubayr
Ibrāhīm b. 'Āmir 21
Ibrāhīm b. Ḥujr al-Muḥallimī al-Shaybānī Abū al-Ṣuqayr 37, 41, 47, 76, 89
'Ifāq (b. Shuraḥbīl al-Taymī) 199
'Ijl (Banū) 141
'ilj (pl. 'ulūj) 85 n. 343
Imru' al-Qays (Banū) 30–31
Imru' al-Qays b. Ḥujr 17 n. 77
Iraq 12–14, 18, 20, 55 n. 216, 84 nn. 336 and 337, 94 n. 376, 95 n. 378, 96–97, 114, 122 n. 464, 153, 155 n. 565, 178–79, 182 n. 656, 186, 191, 195, 200
Irqīliyyah (?), see Azqalah
'Īsā (Khārijite) 118
iṣbahbadh (ispahbadh) 48 n. 193, 165 n. 596
Iṣfahān 27 n. 123, 138 n. 508, 139, 141, 143 n. 529, 144, 151 n. 558, 174
Isḥāq b. 'Īsā 22, 92, 176, 181, 186, 194
Isḥāq b. Muḥammad b. al-Ash'ath 5, 7, 162–63
Isḥāq b. Yazīd 2
Ishmael 2 n. 4
Ismā'īl b. al-Ash'ath 192
Ismā'īl b. Nu'aym al-Hamdānī al-Namirī (? al-Bursumī? al-Burmī?) 58
ispahbadh see iṣbahbadh
Iṣṭakhr 150, 180
al-Iṣṭakhrī 158 n. 576
isti'rāḍ 30 n. 131, 37 n. 157
īwān 108, 129
īwān Kisrā 108 n. 422, 129 n. 479
'Iyāḍ b. Abī Līnah al-Kindī 54–55, 59–60, 63
Iyād b. Nizār 68 n. 278
'iyāfah 67 n. 273

J

al-Jabal (al-Jibāl) 55 n. 216, 99, 107, 128, 137, 141
Jabalah (ghulām of Ḥabīb b. al-Muhallib) 189
Jābir b. 'Abdallāh 2
Ja'far b. 'Abd al-Raḥmān b. Mikhnaf 5, 27, 163–64
al-Jaḥḥāf b. Nubayṭ al-Shaybānī 69
al-Jāḥiẓ 13 n. 56, 70 n. 287, 109 n. 425, 118 n. 455, 161 n. 584, 165 n. 596
Jahīzah (al-Jahīzah) (mother of Shabīb) 47 n. 190, 114 n. 439, 125–26 (unnamed)
al-Jahshiyārī 179 n. 648
al-Jāl 45–47
al-Jalḥā' 22
Jalūlā' 42, 50 n. 198, 83
al-Jamājim, Battle of 165. See also Dayr al-Jamājim
jār 78 n. 312
jarīdah 72 n. 298
al-Jārif, ṭā'ūn (Sweeping Plague) 188
Jarīr b. al-Ḥusayn al-Kindī 56

Jāriyah b. Qudāmah al-Tamīmī 172 n. 620
Jarjarāyā 57
Jarm (Banū) 172
al-Jarrāḥ b. 'Abdallāh 29 n. 125
Jay 143
al-Jazīraḥ 33, 39, 41
al-Jazl ('Uthmān) b. Sa'īd (b. Shuraḥbīl b. 'Amr al-Kindī) 53–61, 62 n. 251, 63, 65 n. 257, 81–83, 88
al-Jazūr 159
Jesus 133
Jews 105
al-Jibāl, see al-Jabal
jibāyah 142 n. 522
jihād, jāhada (strive) 34–36, 135–36, 140, 142, 151, 193
Jīnzīr (?), see Jubayrayn
Jīruft 150, 154
jiwār 78 n. 312
jizyah 85
ju'ālah 172 n. 617
Jubayrayn (? Jīnzīr?) 158
Juday' b. Sa'īd b. Qabīṣah b. Sarrāq al-Azdī 4
Ju'fī b. Sa'd al-'Ashīrah (Banū) 88 n. 355
al-Juḥāf, 'Ām (Year of Sweeping Away) 187 n. 679
Jūkhā 42, 46 n. 186, 48, 51, 53–54, 57, 81, 84, 121, 129
jund 53 n. 208
Jundab (Banū) 198

K

Ka'b (b. Sa'd, Banū) 9 n. 38, 197
Ka'b al-Ashqarī 150 n. 554, 154–55
Ka'bah 1, 187 n. 680
kabkabah 73 n. 301
Kābul 178
Kalb (Banū) 96 n. 380
al-Kalbī, see Hishām b. Muḥammad
Kalwādhā 52, 53, 61 n. 240, 98, 131
Karbalā' 67 n. 268
al-Karkh 61, 65
Karun (river), see Dujayl al-Ahwāz
Kāshān, see Qāshān
katībah 26 n. 115, 42 n. 174
Kāzarūn (Kāzirūn, Kāzir) 25, 30, 158
Khaffān 66
Khālid (Banū) 39
Khālid b. 'Abdallāh (b. Khālid b. Asīd) 3 nn. 12 and 13, 5–6, 9, 22, 179
Khālid b. Abī Rabī'ah 91
Khālid b. 'Attāb b. Warqā' al-Riyāḥī 111, 115–19, 148
Khālid b. Huraym (b. 'Adī) 189
Khālid b. Jaz' al-Sulamī 40–41
Khālid b. Nahīk (b. Qays al-Kindī) 60, 63, 86–87
al-Khalīl b. Aws, see Abū Rustam al-Khalīl b. Aws
Khallād b. Yazīd al-Arqaṭ 114–15, 125
Khandaq (village) 103 n. 404
Khānījār 67, 80
Khāniqīn 42, 48, 50, 83
kharāj, see land revenue
Khārijism, Khārijites 3 n. 13, 4 n. 17, 5, 9 n. 39, 13, 15 n. 66, 24–27, 30, 33 nn. 139 and 140, 35 nn. 147 and 149, 39–40, 42 n. 173, 43, 47, 51 n. 200, 53, 58, 60 n. 233, 71, 79 n. 314, 80 n. 323, 85 n. 345, 102 n. 403, 110, 114, 116, 118 n. 455, 119–20, 125 n. 470, 128 n. 475, 132 nn. 494 and 495, 140 n. 514, 150–53, 154 n. 562, 179, 185 nn. 671 and 673, 194 nn. 708 and 710, 198–99
Kharūn, see Akharūn
Khath'am (Banū) 48 n. 195, 136
al-Khawarnaq 73 n. 299
al-Khawlānī, see Abū Idrīs al-Khawlānī
Khayrah al-Qushayrīyah 180
Khāzim b. Sufyān al-Khath'amī 48
Khazraj (Banū) 2 n. 5
khums (pl. akhmās) 151 n. 559
Khurāsān 7–12, 22–23, 92, 113 n.

433, 165–67, 170 n. 611, 171–73, 174 nn. 625 and 628, 176–81, 183, 186, 195–98
Khurāsān highway 51 n. 200, 54 n. 214, 55 nn. 215 and 216, 57 n. 221
Khurrazād (? Kh.r.dāb?) 46
Khurrazād Ardashīr 46 n. 185
Khūṭ (?) b. 'Umayr, see Ḥawṭ b. 'Umayr
al-Khuttal 188
Khuzā'ah (Banū) 167, 169, 175
Khuzaymah b. Naṣr (al-'Absī) 26
Khūzistān 42 n. 172
Kilāb (Banū) 192
Kinānah (Banū) 65 n. 255
Kindah (Banū) 5, 39 n. 159, 48 n. 196, 53 n. 210, 56 n. 219, 60 n. 238, 69 n. 282, 81, 82 n. 331, 86–87, 89, 106 n. 413, 120 n. 459
Kirmān 80 n. 321, 122, 150, 153, 159, 161–62, 181, 194
Kish 188–90
al-Kūfah 3, 5, 7, 11–13, 15 n. 64, 20–23, 26, 28, 31, 33 n. 135, 37 n. 156, 44, 45 n. 182, 47 n. 190, 48, 53, 55, 57–58, 60–63, 65 nn. 255 and 257–258, 66–68, 70, 71 nn. 288 and 290, 72–74, 78–81, 84, 90, 92, 96–97, 99–100, 105–8, 112, 114, 116–17, 118 n. 454, 119, 126, 128, 144, 148, 175, 177, 178 n. 641, 181, 186, 191 n. 696, 192 nn. 700 and 704, 195, 199 n. 721
Kūfans, Kūfan forces 3–5, 23, 26–27, 28 n. 125, 41, 56, 58–59, 62, 85, 89, 96–97, 99, 105, 107–8, 111, 116, 162–63, 169 n. 609, 183, 185 n. 667, 191
al-Kumayt 17
kūrah 50 n. 198
Kurds 137–38, 144
kurdūs 42 n. 174
Kushmāhan 166, 169
Kūthā Canal 94 n. 373

L

Laḥḥām Jarīr Road 110
land revenue, land tax (kharāj) 57–58, 81, 84–85, 94, 106, 140 n. 512, 142–43, 150, 151 n. 557, 167, 172, 179, 183, 184 n. 665, 186, 193
al-Laṣaf 66, 126
Lower Bihqubādh, see Bihqubādh al-Asfal

M

al-Madā'in 37, 41 n. 166, 43, 45 n. 181, 48, 50–54, 57 n. 222, 60, 63–65, 80 n. 325, 81–82, 85, 93 n. 371, 94–95, 98 n. 388, 99–101, 107, 108 n. 422, 109 n. 426, 119, 121 n. 460, 128–29, 135, 137, 155 n. 565. See also Ctesiphon, al-madīnah al-'atīqah, Bahurasīr
al-Madā'inī, Abū al-Ḥasan 'Alī b. Muḥammad 7–8, 20, 165, 179, 188, 196–97
Mādharwāsb 67, 94
Madhḥij (Banū) 5, 20, 71 n. 288, 86, 88 n. 355, 96, 105, 183 n. 661, 185 n. 667
madīnah 59 n. 232
al-madīnah al-'atīqah 131 n. 487. See also Ctesiphon, al-Madā'in
maghāzī 44 n. 179
Māh al-Baṣrah 138 n. 508
Māh Bihzādhān 93–94, 130 n. 485
Māh Dīnār 138–39
Māh al-Kūfah 138 n. 508
Māh Sabadhān (Māsabadhān) 137
Mahrūdh 50 n. 198. See also Bābil Mahrūdh
maktab 6 n. 27
Malaṭyah 176 n. 639, 181 n. 655
Mālik b. 'Abdallāh al-Hamdānī al-Murhibī 87
Malik Canal 100 n. 396

Mālik b. Ḥanẓalah (al-Wirthī) 66
Mālik b. Zuhayr b. Jadhīmah (al-ʿAbsī) 133
manāẓir 48 n. 194
maqṣūrah 113
Marʿash 12
al-Mardamah 70, 72
Mardin 33 n. 137
Marj al-Shaḥm 181 n. 655
Marrār b. ʿAbd al-Raḥmān b. Abī Bakrah 9
marshals (ʿurafāʾ, sg. ʿarīf) 16, 20, 54, 89
Marw 10, 166–68, 169 nn. 608–10, 171, 172 nn. 615 and 618, 175, 189, 198
Marwān b. Muḥammad b. Marwān 92
Māsabadhān, see Māh Sabadhān
Maṣād (?) b. Yazīd, see Muṣād b. Yazīd
maṣaffah 151 n. 559
maslaḥah 55 n. 218, 193 n. 707
Maṣqalah b. Muhalhil al-Ḍabbī 117
maṣṭabah 68
al-Masʿūdī 12 n. 53, 13 n. 56, 19 n. 87, 20 n. 89, 21 nn. 93 and 94, 25 n. 111, 61 n. 241, 70 n. 283, 114 n. 439, 125 n. 470
Maṭar b. Nājiyah al-Riyāḥī 117–18
maʿūnah 81, 192 n. 698
mawṣūl 174 n. 630
Maydān Yazīd (Marw) 170 n. 611
al-Maydānī 4 n. 20, 8 n. 36, 13 nn. 57 and 58, 14 nn. 62 and 63, 18 nn. 82 and 83, 43 n. 175, 52 n. 202, 60 n. 236, 79 n. 320, 82 nn. 329 and 330, 97 n. 384, 118 n. 453, 133 n. 497, 149 n. 550, 159 n. 578
Maymūn (al-ʿAdhāb) 69
Mecca 1 nn. 1–3, 11, 27 n. 122, 85 n. 340, 145 n. 538, 175 n. 632, 187
Medina 1–2, 11–13, 22, 92, 175–76, 181, 186, 195
Medinese 5, 86, 104, 163
Michael the Syrian 182 n. 656
Mihrān (b. Mihribandādh al-Hamadhānī) 185
Mikhnaf 30
mīl 5
Milkān (Banū) 174 n. 626
Minā 27
al-Miṣṣīṣah 176 n. 639
mithqāl 91–92
Moses 133
Mosul 33, 41–42, 44, 46 n. 185, 48, 53 n. 205, 83–84
Muʿattib (b. Abī Lahab) 134 n. 498
Muʿāwiyah (b. Abī Sufyān) 10 n. 41, 35 n. 148, 80 n. 323, 172 n. 620, 180 n. 650, 185 n. 671, 192 n. 700
Muʿāwiyah b. Miḥṣan al-Kindī 162
Muʿayṭ, Āl Banī 109 n. 424
al-Mubarrad 3 n. 13, 4 n. 17, 5 n. 21, 13 nn. 55–57, 14 n. 59, 15 n. 64, 16 nn. 70–71 and 73, 17 n. 74, 19 n. 87, 20 n. 89, 21 nn. 92 and 94, 23 n. 103, 27 n. 121, 28 n. 125, 30 n. 129, 47 n. 191, 79 n. 314, 118 n. 455, 149 n. 552, 151 nn. 557 and 558, 152 n. 560, 154 nn. 562 and 563, 161 n. 585
al-Mudabbaj (? al-Mudabbij?) 42, 44
Muḍar (Banū), Muḍarites 21, 40 n. 164, 71 n. 289, 144, 190
Mudrik b. Unayf 169
al-Mufaḍḍal b. Bakr 46
al-Mufaḍḍal b. Muḥammad (al-Ḍabbī) 8, 165, 179, 188, 197
al-Mughīrah b. ʿAbdallāh b. Abī ʿAqīl (al-Thaqafī) 177–78
al-Mughīrah b. ʿAṭiyyah 112
al-Mughīrah b. al-Muhallab b. Abī Ṣufrah 28, 151, 179–80, 186
al-Mughīrah b. Shuʿbah 128, 131, 134, 138, 145, 147
al-Muhadhdhab (Khārijite) 118
Muhājirūn, see Emigrants
al-Muhallab b. Abī Ṣufrah 3–5, 13–14, 16, 20–21, 23–28, 30, 96, 150–55, 156 n. 568, 157 n. 570, 158, 161, 178–81, 183, 186, 188–90, 195, 198–200
al-Muḥallil b. Wāʾil al-Yashkurī 36–37, 55, 98, 102, 110, 123, 131

Muḥallim (Banū) 37–38
al-Muḥallimī, see Ibrāhīm b. Ḥujr
Muḥammad (the Prophet) 2, 33–35, 103, 132–34, 136, 140, 145, 178 n. 644, 185
Muḥammad b. 'Abd al-Raḥmān b. Abī Sabrah al-Ju'fī 88–90
Muḥammad b. 'Abd al-Raḥmān b. Sa'īd b. Qays al-Hamdānī 5, 7, 101, 103, 106
Muḥammad b. Abī Sabrah, see Muḥammad b. 'Abd al-Raḥmān b. Abī Sabrah
Muḥammad b. Ḥabīb, see Ibn Ḥabīb
Muḥammad b. Ḥafṣ b. Mūsā b. 'Ubaydallāh b. Ma'mar b. 'Uthmān al-Taymī 115
Muḥammad b. Marwān 12, 38–40
Muḥammad b. Mūsā b. Ṭalḥah b. 'Ubaydallāh 71, 76–79, 80 n. 321
Muḥammad b. Rifā'ah b. Tha'labah 187
Muḥammad b. Sa'd, see Ibn Sa'd
Muḥammad b. 'Umar, see al-Wāqidī
Muḥammad b. 'Umayr (b. 'Uṭārid al-Tamīmī?) 15
Muḥammad b. Yaḥyā Abū Ghassān 13, 18
Muhāṣir b. Ṣayfī al-'Udhrī 122, 125
muḥkamāt 161 n. 582
Muḥriz b. Abī Muḥriz 181 n. 655
al-Muḥtariqah 189 n. 688
Mujālid b. Sa'īd 58 n. 227
Mujāshi' (Banū) 189 n. 690
al-Mukhtār 15 n. 64, 26 n. 119, 61 n. 244, 81 n. 328, 142 n. 523
munāfiq 24 n. 109
al-Muqaddasī 55 n. 214
muqaddimah 180 n. 651
muqā'is (Banū) 8, 200
al-Muqa'ṭar al-Ḍabbī (? al-'Abdī?) 153, 154 n. 562
Muqātil (Khārijite) 124
Murhibah b. Du'ām (Banū) 87 n. 352
Murrah b. Hammām (Banū) 124–25
Murrah b. Ṣa'ṣa'ah 85 n. 341
Mūsā b. 'Abdallāh b. Khāzim 166, 168, 175
Mūsā b. Abī Suwayd b. Rādī 126
Mūsā b. Anas (b. Mālik) 181, 186, 195
Mūsā b. Suwār 106–7
Muṣ'ab b. al-Zubayr 2 n. 9, 3 n. 13, 24, 79 n. 316, 81 n. 328, 137 n. 506, 185 n. 672, 192 n. 699
Muṣād (?Maṣād?) b. Yazīd b. Nu'aym 37, 47, 49, 55, 57, 63, 74, 76, 87–88, 99, 111, 118
muṣallā 22
al-Mushaqqar 185
Muslim b. Abī Bakrah 184 n. 666
Muṭarrif b. 'Āmir b. Wāthilah 142
Muṭarrif b. al-Mughīrah b. Shu'bah 85, 94, 98–99, 107, 127–35, 137–47, 148 n. 547, 171 n. 613, 177
mutashābihāt 161 n. 582
al-Muthannā b. Ḥārithah 185 n. 669
Muzāḥim b. Abī al-Mujashshir al-Sulamī 173
Muzāḥim b. Zufar b. Jassās al-Taymī 112
al-Muzanī, see Sulaymān b. Ḥudhayfah
Muzaynah (Banū) 65

N

al-Nābighah al-Dhubyānī 16 n. 73
al-Naḍr b. al-Qa'qā' b. Shawr al-Dhuhlī 70, 72, 118 n. 454
al-Naḍr b. Ṣāliḥ al-'Absī (Abū Zuhayr) 23, 25, 53, 87, 131, 134, 137, 139–40, 143–46, 148
Nāfi' b. Azraq 3 n. 13
al-Naharā, see al-Nahrawān (town)
Nahd b. Zayd (Banū) 73 n. 300
al-Nahrawān (canal) 46 n. 186, 51 n. 200, 84 n. 334
al-Nahrawān (town) 51–52, 54 n. 214, 57 n. 221, 58, 185
Najdah b. 'Āmir 35 n. 147
Najdites 31 n. 131

Nājiyah bt. Hānī' b. Qabīṣah b. Hānī' al-Shaybānī 70
Nājiyah b. Marthad (?Mazyad? Murayd?) al-Ḥaḍramī 72
Najrān (al-Kūfah) 74
Najrān (Yemen) 74 n. 302
Namirah b. Aslam (Banū) 58 n. 226
Naṣr (Banū) 45, 109 n. 423, 169
Naṣr b. Khuzaymah al-'Absī 26
Naṣr b. Mu'āwiyah (Banū) 163, 169 n. 609
al-Nawbandajān 158 n. 575
Nawfal b. Musāḥiq b. 'Amr b. Khudāsh 92
Niffar 80–81
Nihāwand 138 n. 508
Nippur, see Niffar
Nishapur 10
Nisibis 33 n. 137, 38, 39 n. 162
Nu'aym b. 'Ulaym (al-Taghlibī) 101, 103
Nūḥ (b. 'Abdallāh b. Khāzim) 168
al-Nu'mān b. Sa'd al-Ḥimyarī 120
Numayr b. Wa'lah al-Hamdānī al-Yanā'ī 191

O

Orchard of Ibn Abī Bakrah 184. See also Bustān
Oxus 166 n. 600, 188 n. 684, 198 n. 719. See also Balkh, river of

P

Peacock Army 194
Persian, Persians 10, 139 n. 510, 154 n. 562, 179 n. 648, 185 n. 669. See also Sasanians
post (barīd) 109, 180, 193
post road (sikkat al-barīd) 109
provision depot (dār al-rizq, al-Kūfah) 62, 116–18

Q

qabā' harawī 113 n. 435
Qabīṣah b. 'Abd al-Raḥmān al-Quḥāfī al-Khath'amī 33, 44, 136, 143
Qabīṣah b. Wāliq al-Taghlibī 97, 101, 103
al-Qādisiyyah 72, 73 n. 299, 95 n. 378, 185 n. 669
Qālīqalā 196
qamīṣ 199 n. 720
Qa'nab al-Muḥallimī (Khārijite) 49, 78, 98, 106, 117–18, 123, 131, 135
Qandahār 178 n. 643
al-Qa'qā' b. Shawr al-Dhuhlī 70 n. 284
al-Qa'qā' b. Suwayd b. 'Abd al-Raḥmān al-Sa'dī 137
Qaryāt (?), see Faryāb
qaṣaṣ (sermon) 33 n. 139, 101–2, 132 nn. 491 and 493, 136 n. 502
Qāshān 139
Qaṣr Ibn Hubayrah 61, 67 n. 268
Qaṣr Muqātil 67
Qaṭan b. 'Abdallāh b. al-Ḥuṣayn Dhī al-Ghuṣṣah 71 n. 288
Qaṭar 161 n. 584
Qaṭarī b. al-Fujā'ah 3 n. 13, 96, 149–50, 153–54, 159 nn. 579 and 580, 161–63, 165 n. 596, 176
Qaṭīṭiyā (?) 59, 130 n. 483
Qaṭrāthā (?) 51, 58
Qays 'Aylān (Banū) 26 n. 119, 40 n. 164, 56 n. 220, 85 n. 341, 122 n. 464, 128 n. 475, 164 n. 586, 169 n. 609, 173 n. 621, 174 n. 625, 190 n. 691
Qays b. Sa'd al-'Ijlī 141–42
Qays b. Tha'labah (Banū) 149 n. 552
Qayṣar 57
qiblah 145
qīrāṭ 91–92
Qubbīn 61
Quḍā'ah (Banū) 73 n. 300
Qudāmah b. Ḥāzim b. Sufyān al-Khath'amī 89
Qudāmah b. Ja'far 155 n. 565

Quḥāfah (Banū) 136 n. 502
Qum 139
Qūmis 164, 165 n. 596
Quraysh 9, 71 n. 291, 79 n. 316, 92 n. 367, 100, 102 n. 402, 132–34, 167, 170, 173–74, 175 n. 632
qurrā' 26 n. 116
Qushayr b. Ka'b (Banū) 190 n. 691
Qutaybah (b. Muslim) 112 n. 432, 113–16, 174 n. 626, 189 n. 688
al-Quṭquṭānah 67

R

al-Rabī' b. Yazīd al-Asadī 98, 131, 134–35, 140, 145–46
Rabī'ah (Banū) 5, 24 n. 110, 39, 40 n. 164, 44 n. 180, 86–87, 102–3, 128 n. 475, 141
Rabī'ah b. 'Āmir b. Ṣa'ṣa'ah (Banū) 40
Rabinjan (Arbinjan) 189
Rādhān 46, 84, 86, 130 n. 482
Rādhān al-A'lā (Upper Rādhān) 46 n. 186, 84
raḥabah (raḥbah) (al-Kūfah) 117–18
raḥt 46 n. 189, 124 n. 469
Rāmhurmuz 5, 20, 23–25, 27 n. 121, 101 n. 397, 154, 157
Ra's al-'Ayn 39 n. 162
raṭl 78, 117
Rawḥ b. Zinbā' 44 n. 178
rāyah 151 n. 559
al-Rayy 141, 143–44, 147–48, 154 n. 562, 162–63, 165 n. 596
Razīn 10
al-Ribāb (confederation) 174 nn. 626–27 and 629
riḍā (approved one) 132, 140
ridā' 199 n. 720
riddah, riddī 78 n. 314
Rifā'ah b. Tha'labah 187
Riyāḥ b. Yarbū' b. Ḥanẓalah (Banū) 27 n. 123
Ru'ās b. al-Ḥārith (Banū) 59 n. 229
Rūdhbār (Rūdhabār, Rūdhābār) 74, 87, 130
Rūdhmastān 74 n. 304
al-Rukhkhaj 194 n. 708
Rukn (of Ka'bah) 187
al-Ruqād b. Ziyād b. Hammām 151
Rustam 137
rustāq (pl. rasātīq) 54, 158 n. 575, 184 n. 664
Rustaqubādh 23–24
Rutbīl, see Zunbīl
Ruwayshid b. Rumayḍ al-'Anazī 14 n. 59

S

al-Ṣabāḥ b. Muḥammad b. al-Ash'ath 163
al-Sabakhah (al-Kūfah) 61–62, 68, 94, 102 n. 401, 108–9, 111 n. 429, 114, 116, 139, 141
al-Sabal 188–89
Sābāṭ 100
al-Sabī' b. Sab' (Banū) 191 n. 696
Sabrah b. 'Abd al-Raḥmān b. Mikhnaf 107–9, 130, 136
Sābūr (Shāpūr, Bishāpūr) 25, 27 n. 121, 28 n. 125, 30, 150, 154, 157, 158 n. 575
Sābūr al-Junūd (Sābūr of the Armies) 157
saby 154 n. 562
Sa'd b. Abī Waqqās 61 n. 242, 71 n. 290
Sa'd b. Bajal al-'Āmirī 120
Sa'd b. Rāshid 90
Sa'd b. Zayd Manāt b. Tamīm (Banū) 61 n. 244, 138, 174
Sadhawwar (castle) 164 n. 591
Sadūs b. Shaybān (Banū) 118 n. 452
ṣāḥib ḥaras 173 n. 623
Sahl b. Sa'd 2
Sa'īd b. 'Amr al-Kindī (?) 53 n. 209

Sa'īd b. Mujālid (al-Mujālid), Ibn Dhī Murrān 58–60, 62 n. 251, 63–64, 65 n. 257, 130
Sa'īd b. al-Musayyab 91–92
Sa'īd b. Qays al-Sabī'ī 191
Sakāsik (clans of Kindah) 120 n. 459
Sakūn (Banū) 56 n. 219
Salāmah b. Sayyār b. al-Maḍā' al-Taymī 44–45
Ṣāliḥ b. 'Abd al-Raḥmān 179 n. 648
Ṣāliḥ b. Kaysān 90
Ṣāliḥ b. Musarriḥ al-Tamīmī 30–33, 36–45, 48, 53 n. 209, 117, 132 nn. 491 and 493, 136 n. 502
Salimah (b. Sa'd, Banū) 2
Sallām b. Ḥayyān 47
Sallām b. Sayyār al-Shaybānī 101
Salmān b. Rabī'ah 126
al-Ṣalt (Banū), see al-Ṣulb (Banū)
Salūl (Banū) 85 n. 341
Salūl bt. Dhuhl b. Shaybān 85 n. 341, 87
Sāmān 139
al-Sam'ānī 120 n. 459
samarajjah 106 n. 415
Samarqand 188 n. 682, 189 nn. 686 and 688
Samosata 182 n. 657
Sanjān Gate (Marw) 171
al-Ṣaqr b. Ḥātim 37
Sarakhs 10
al-Ṣarāt 80, 99
Ṣarāt Canal 80 n. 325, 106–7
Ṣārim 146
Ṣa'ṣa'ah b. Ḥarb al-'Awfī 198–200
Sasanians 2 n. 6, 37 n. 156, 54 n. 213, 59 n. 231, 91 n. 361, 106 n. 414, 108 n. 422, 129 n. 479. See also Persian, Persians
Sātīdamā 46, 130
Sawād 84 n. 336
Sawād al-Kūfah 84
Sawrah b. Abjar al-Tamīmī 48, 50–53, 163, 165 n. 596
Sayf b. Hāni' 116
al-Saylaḥīn (Saylaḥūn) 73
security force (shurṭah, pl. shuraṭ) 10–11, 20 n. 89, 23 n. 102, 69, 81 n. 326, 108, 141–42, 168–69, 172, 173 n. 623, 179, 180 n. 650, 191 n. 697, 194 n. 709, 199
Shabath (?), mosque of (al-Kūfah) 111
al-Sha'bī (Abū 'Amr 'Āmir b. Sharāḥīl) 191
Shabīb (?), mosque of (al-Kūfah) 111 n. 430
Shabīb b. Yazīd 28, 31, 32 n. 134, 36–37, 40–49, 51–63, 65–69, 70 nn. 283 and 285, 71–81, 83–90, 93–112, 114–27, 130–31, 133–36, 139, 141, 148 n. 547, 176–77
Shāhī 107
Shahrān (Banū) 48 n. 195
Shahrazūr 83
Shahrisabz, see Kish
al-Shajarah 45
Shākir b. Rabī'ah (Banū) 42 n. 173
shākiriyyah 115 n. 442
Shamardal 173
al-Shamardal 197
Shammās b. Dithār (al-'Uṭāridī) 168–69
Shāpūr, see Sābūr
Shaqīq b. al-Sulayk al-Asadī 172
Sharīk b. 'Amr Dhū al-Kursufah 23 n. 103
Shaybān (Banū, of Kindah?) 48 n. 196
Shaybān b. Tha'labah (Banū) 28 n. 125, 37 n. 153, 40, 117 n. 444, 124 n. 469, 130
al-Shaybānī, see Abū 'Amr al-Shaybānī
Shi'b Bawwān 150 n. 554, 158 n. 575
Shī'ites 199 n. 721
Shīrāz 25 n. 113, 150 n. 554
shūrā, see council
Shurāh (Khārijites) 35 n. 149
Shuraḥbīl b. Abī 'Awn 2
shuraṭ, see security force
Shurayḥ b. Hāni' al-Ḥārithī al-Ḍabābī 183–85

Shurayḥ b. al-Ḥārith 11, 23, 92, 181, 186
shurṭah, see security force
Shushtar, see Tustar
Ṣiffīn 35 n. 148, 80 n. 323, 185
Sijistān 7 n. 29, 12, 71, 78–79, 168, 172, 177–79, 180 n. 652, 181, 183, 186, 190, 192, 194, 198
sikkat al-barīd, see post road
ṣilah 174 n. 630
Sinān (Khārijite) 118
Sind 194
al-Sinj 10
Sinjar 38
Soghdia (al-Sughd), Soghdians 166, 168, 189
spoil (fay') 15, 34–35, 75, 87, 95, 96 n. 379, 132, 140
stipend ('aṭā') 6, 23–24, 178, 184, 191, 194
Ṣufriyyah 30, 33 n. 136
Sufyān b. Abī al-'Āliyah al-Khath'amī 48–50
Sufyān b. al-Abrad al-Kalbī 96, 105, 107–8, 122–23, 125, 162–65
al-Sughd, see Soghdia
Suḥaym b. Wathīl al-Riyāḥī 13 n. 57
Sulaym (Banū) 40 n. 164, 65, 173 n. 621
Sulaymān b. 'Abd al-Malik 195
Sulaymān b. Ḥudhayfah b. Hilāl b. Mālik al-Muzanī 98, 131, 134–35, 138
Sulaymān b. Ṣakhr al-Muzanī 145–46
al-Ṣulb (Banū) 66
sunnah 34 nn. 145 and 146, 37 n. 154, 132–33, 136, 140, 145
Sūrā 106
Surāqah b. Mirdās al-Bāriqī 29–30
Ṣuraym b. Muqā'is b. 'Amr b. Ka'b b. Sa'd (Banū) 8 n. 38
Suwayd b. 'Abd al-Raḥmān al-Sa'dī 61–62, 65–66, 137, 148
Suwayd b. Sirḥān al-Thaqafī 140, 147
Suwayd b. Sulaym al-Hindī al-Shaybānī 31, 40, 42, 49, 55, 68–70, 74–75, 78, 86–88, 98, 102–3, 106, 110–11, 121, 123, 131–34
Sweeping Away, Year of, see al-Juḥāf, 'Ām
Sweeping Plague, see al-Jārif, ṭā'ūn
Syria 78 n. 313, 92, 120 n. 459, 182
Syrians, Syrian forces 96–97, 99, 105, 107–11, 112 n. 432, 114, 119–20, 121 n. 460, 124, 126, 143–44, 162, 185 n. 667

T

al-Ṭabarī (Abū Ja'far) 18, 127, 149, 161, 165, 175 and passim in the notes
Ṭabaristān 48, 154, 162, 164 n. 591, 165
al-Ṭaff 155
Taghlib (Banū) 101, 102 n. 403, 103–4
Ṭahmān 109, 112 n. 432
takbīr 18
Takrīt 46 n. 187, 53, 185 n. 672
Ṭalḥah b. 'Ubaydallāh 71 n. 291
Tāmarrā 83
Tamīm (Banū) 5, 8, 9, 19 n. 86, 21 n. 91, 27 n. 123, 28, 30 n. 130, 61 n. 244, 71, 76, 86, 95 n. 378, 101 n. 397, 103–4, 152, 166 n. 599, 167, 168 n. 607, 169–70, 172, 174, 179 n. 646, 189 n. 690, 194 n. 708
Tamīm b. al-Ḥārith al-Azdī 101
Ṭāriq b. 'Amr 1
taslīm 77
ṭassūj 50 n. 198, 54, 73 n. 299, 74 n. 304, 83 n. 334, 103 n. 404
Taym (Banū) (Quraysh) 71 n. 291, 79 n. 316
Taym (Banū) (al-Ribāb) 174 n. 626
Taym b. Shaybān (Banū) 37, 44, 46–47, 124
Ṭayyi' (Banū) 169
al-Tha'ālibī 4 n. 20, 8 n. 36, 150 n. 554
Thābit (client of Zuhayr) 63

Thābit b. Quṭbah 169–70
Thābit Quṭnah 172 n. 616
Tha'labah b. Yarbū' (Banū) 189 n. 690
Thamūd (Banū) 21, 68
Thaqīf 21 n. 92, 68 n. 278, 128 nn. 475 and 476, 147, 178 n. 644
Thawr (Banū) (Hamdān) 129 n. 480
Thawr (Banū) (Kindah) 39 n. 159
Thawr b. 'Abd Manāt (Banū) 174 n. 626
Theophanes 2 n. 4, 182 nn. 656 and 657
Tigris 37 n. 156, 42 n. 172, 46 nn. 184 and 187, 51 n. 200, 53 n. 205, 57 n. 222, 61, 65, 67, 80 n. 325, 84 n. 337, 98, 119, 121, 131
ṭinfisah (carpet) 102 n. 401, 103
al-Tirmidh 166
Transoxania 113 n. 433, 165, 166 n. 600, 168 n. 604
al-Ṭufayl b. 'Āmir b. Wāthilah 142 n. 523, 144–46, 161
Tukhāristān 11, 165
al-Ṭuqṭuqānah 67 nn. 266 and 267
Turks 183, 190
Tustar 185

U

'Ubayd b. al-Ḥulays, see 'Ubaydallāh b. al-Ḥulays
'Ubayd b. Suba' al-Tamīmī 194 n. 708
'Ubaydah 173
'Ubaydah b. Mikhrāq al-Qaynī 44 n. 178
'Ubaydallāh b. 'Abd al-Malik b. Marwān 196
'Ubaydallāh b. Abī Bakrah 178–79, 180 n. 652, 181, 183–84, 185 n. 667, 186 n. 674, 190, 194, 198
'Ubaydallāh b. Abī Miḥjan al-Thaqafī 192
'Ubaydallāh b. Ḥujr b. Dhī al-Jawshan al-'Āmirī 192
'Ubaydallāh ('Ubayd) b. al-Ḥulays 101, 103
'Ubaydallāh b. Ziyād b. Abīhi 5 n. 25
al-'Udhaym River 84 nn. 335 and 337
Uḥud, Battle of 191 n. 693
al-Ukhayḍir 67 n. 267
'Ukl (Banū) 174 n. 626
al-'Ulṭah (?), see al-Ghilẓah
'ulūj, see 'ilj
'Umar b. 'Abd al-'Azīz 65 n. 255
'Umar b. Abī al-Ṣalt b. Kanārā (?) 163
'Umar b. Bashīr 62
'Umar b. Hubayrah al-Fazārī 122, 144–47
'Umar b. al-Khaṭṭāb 34, 132, 134 n. 498, 185
'Umar b. Sa'd b. Abī Waqqāṣ 61 n. 242. See also Ḥammām 'Umar b. Sa'd
'Umar b. Shabbah, Abū Zayd 13, 18, 20, 79, 112, 114–15, 125, 196
'Umar b. 'Ubaydallāh b. Ma'mar 4 n. 17, 79, 185 n. 673
'Umayr b. Ḍābi' al-Tamīmī al-Ḥanẓalī al-Burjumī 15 n. 64, 19–21, 23
'Umayr b. al-Qa'qā' 118
Umayyads 1 n. 2, 5 n. 24, 13 n. 56, 71 n. 288, 78 n. 313, 120 n. 459
Umayyah b. 'Abdallāh b. Khālid b. Asīd b. Abī al-'Īṣ b. Umayyah 7–11, 23, 92, 165–78, 180, 183 n. 660, 186, 196
Umm al-Fawāris 16
Umm al-Ḥakam bt. Abī Sufyān 192 n. 700
Umm 'Uthmān bt. 'Umar b. 'Ubaydallāh b. Ma'mar 79
'umrah 1
Upper Rādhān, see Rādhān al-A'lā
'Uqāb Dhū al-Liqwah (?) 166 n. 599. See also 'Attāb al-Liqwah al-Ghudānī
'Uqayl b. Muṣ'ab al-Wādi'ī 69
Uqaysh (Banū) 16
'urafā', see marshals
'Urwah b. al-Mughīrah b. Shu'bah, Abū Ya'fūr 23, 67–68, 110, 128
'Urwah b. Zuhayr b. Nājidh al-Azdī 76
'ushūr 72 n. 293

Uswār al-Turjumān 174
'Uṭārid b. Ḥājib al-Tamīmī 169 n. 607
'Uṭārid b. 'Umayr al-Tamīmī 192
'Utbah (b. Abī Lahab) 134 n. 498
'Uthmān b. 'Affān 2, 19–21, 22 n. 100, 34, 35 n. 147, 109 n. 424, 126, 132 n. 493
'Uthmān b. Qaṭan b. 'Abdallāh b. al-Ḥuṣayn Dhī al-Ghuṣṣah 62, 71, 81–82, 84–88, 90 n. 357, 93, 130
'Uthmān b. Rajā' b. Jābir b. Shaddād 196
'Uthmān b. Sa'īd, see al-Jazl b. Sa'īd
'Uthmān b. Sa'īd al-'Udhrī 120

V

Veh-Ardashir, see Bahurasīr

W

Wabarah b. 'Āṣim 47
Wādi'ah (Banū) 129 n. 480
Wā'il (Banū) 102 n. 403
Wālibah (Banū) 71
al-Walīd b. 'Abd al-Malik 176, 180, 181 n. 655, 195
al-Walīd b. 'Uqbah 126
al-Wāqidī (Muḥammad b. 'Umar) 2, 5 n. 23, 11, 90, 91 n. 360, 92, 186–88, 194
Wāṣil b. 'Aṭā' 47 n. 191
Wāṣil b. al-Ḥārith al-Sakūnī 56, 88–89
Wāsiṭ 121
White Palace (al-Madā'in) 131
al-Wirthah (Banū) 39, 66

Y

Yaḥyā b. al-Ḥakam b. Abī al-'Aṣ 12, 22, 92, 176 n. 639, 181
Yaḥyā b. Sa'īd (father of Abū Mikhnaf) 143, 148
al-Yamāmah 198
Yanā' b. Dawmān (Banū) 191 n. 694
Yaqdum 68
Ya'qūb b. Khālid al-Dhuhlī 174
Ya'qūb b. al-Qa'qā' al-A'lam al-Azdī 174
al-Ya'qūbī 2 n. 4, 7 n. 29, 10 n. 44, 11 n. 47, 12 nn. 51 and 53, 13 n. 56, 22 n. 99, 44 n. 178, 48 n. 193, 68 nn. 276 and 278, 69 n. 281, 70 n. 283, 92 n. 369, 100 n. 396, 119 n. 457, 122 n. 461, 125 n. 470, 149 n. 552, 154 n. 562, 165 n. 596, 172 n. 615, 175 n. 635, 176 nn. 638 and 639, 180 nn. 652 and 653, 186 n. 677, 194 n. 708, 195 n. 711
Yāqūt 10 n. 42, 24 n. 107, 39 n. 162, 42 nn. 171 and 172, 45 n. 181, 46 nn. 185 and 186, 61 n. 243, 62 n. 248, 66 n. 263, 67 nn. 268 and 271, 68 n. 274, 73 n. 299, 84 n. 335, 93 n. 371, 94 nn. 373 and 376, 99 n. 395, 137 n. 505, 138 n. 508, 139 n. 509, 151 n. 557, 155 nn. 564 and 565, 158 n. 575, 159 n. 580, 164 n. 591, 169 nn. 608 and 610, 178 n. 643, 185 nn. 672 and 673, 189 n. 686
Yashkur (Banū) 23, 37 n. 153, 161 n. 585
Yazīd (client of 'Abdallāh b. Zuhayr) 144
Yazīd b. Abī Ziyād 98, 131, 134–35, 138–39, 145, 147
Yazīd b. Hubayrah al-Muḥāribī 44 n. 178
Yazīd b. al-Muhallab b. Abī Ṣufrah 4, 170 n. 611, 188
Yazīd b. Nu'aym (father of Shabīb) 126
Yūnus b. Abī Isḥāq 3, 178, 190, 194
Yūnus b. Yazīd 162
Yūsuf b. Bakr al-Azdī 128
Yūsuf b. Yazīd 27–28, 150

Z

Zāb (Zābī) (rivers) 155 n. 565
Zābī (canals) 155
al-Zabīdī 69 n. 281
Zābul (Zābulistān) 178, 183 n. 658, 184 n. 663
Zādhān Farrūkh b. Payrōazh 179
Zaḥr b. Qays 5–7, 72–73, 80 n. 321
Zā'idah b. Qudāmah al-Thaqafī 71, 74–77, 80 n. 321, 90 n. 357, 104 n. 410
al-Zamakhsharī 118 n. 451, 197 n. 716
Zārah 76
Zārah (Banū) 76 n. 307
Zarīr 10
al-Zawābī (canals) 155 n. 565
Zayd (client of Azd) 147
Zayd b. 'Alī (b. Abī Ṭālib) 26
Zayd Allāh (Zayd Allāt) b. 'Amr 104 n. 409
Zayd b. 'Amr (Banū) 104
Ziyād b. 'Abdallāh (al-Wirthī) 39
Ziyād b. Abīhi 5 n. 25, 178 n. 644
Ziyād b. 'Amr al-'Atakī 72, 74–76, 122
Ziyād b. 'Amr al-Zimmānī, see Abū al-Adham Ziyād b. 'Amr al-Zimmānī
Ziyād b. Umayyah b. 'Abdallāh 166–67
Ziyād b. 'Uqbah 174
al-Zubayr b. al-Arwaḥ al-Tamīmī 42
Zuhayr 63
Zuhayr b. Rabī'ah b. Nājid b. al-Akram 76 n. 307
Zuhrah b. Ḥawiyyah al-Sa'dī 93, 95, 97, 102–4
Zunbīl 179 n. 645, 180 n. 652, 183–86, 190, 193–94
Zurārah (?), see Zārah
Zurārah (village) 62, 108, 116
Zurārah b. Awfā (al-Ḥarashī) 23, 92

www.ingramcontent.com/pod-product-compliance
Lightning Source LLC
Chambersburg PA
CBHW020650230426
43665CB00008B/375
9780887069765